STATA PROGRAMMING REFERENCE MANUAL

RELEASE 11

A Stata Press Publication
StataCorp LP
College Station, Texas

Published by Stata Press, 4905 Lakeway Drive, College Station, Texas 77845
Typeset in TEX
Printed in the United States of America

10 9 8 7 6 5 4 3 2 1

ISBN-10: 1-59718-060-2
ISBN-13: 978-1-59718-060-3

The suggested citation for this software is

StataCorp. 2009. *Stata: Release 11*. Statistical Software. College Station, TX: StataCorp LP.

Table of contents

intro . . . . Introduction to programming manual   1

automation . . . . Automation   6

break . . . . Suppress Break key   7
byable . . . . Make programs byable   9

capture . . . . Capture return code   16
char . . . . Characteristics   20
class . . . . Class programming   24
class exit . . . . Exit class-member program and return result   59
classutil . . . . Class programming utility   61
comments . . . . Add comments to programs   66
confirm . . . . Argument verification   68
continue . . . . Break out of loops   73
creturn . . . . Return c-class values   75

_datasignature . . . . Determine whether data have changed   86
#delimit . . . . Change delimiter   89
dialog programming . . . . Dialog programming   91
discard . . . . Drop automatically loaded programs   92
display . . . . Display strings and values of scalar expressions   93

ereturn . . . . Post the estimation results   103
error . . . . Display generic error message and exit   118
estat programming . . . . Controlling estat after user-written commands   132
_estimates . . . . Manage estimation results   136
exit . . . . Exit from a program or do-file   140

file . . . . Read and write ASCII text and binary files   143
file formats .dta . . . . Description of .dta file format   161
findfile . . . . Find file in path   162
foreach . . . . Loop over items   164
forvalues . . . . Loop over consecutive values   172
fvexpand . . . . Expand factor varlists   176

gettoken . . . . Low-level parsing   177

if . . . . if programming command   181
include . . . . Include commands from file   184

levelsof . . . . Levels of variable   187

macro . . . . Macro definition and manipulation   190
macro lists . . . . Manipulate lists   210
makecns . . . . Constrained estimation   214
mark . . . . Mark observations for inclusion   220
matlist . . . . Display a matrix and control its format   226
matrix . . . . Introduction to matrix commands   238
matrix accum . . . . Form cross-product matrices   242
matrix define . . . . Matrix definition, operators, and functions   251
matrix dissimilarity . . . . Compute similarity or dissimilarity measures   269
matrix eigenvalues . . . . Eigenvalues of nonsymmetric matrices   274
matrix get . . . . Access system matrices   277

matrix mkmat .... Convert variables to matrix and vice versa 280
matrix rownames .... Name rows and columns 286
matrix score .... Score data from coefficient vectors 291
matrix svd .... Singular value decomposition 294
matrix symeigen .... Eigenvalues and eigenvectors of symmetric matrices 297
matrix utility .... List, rename, and drop matrices 300
more .... Pause until key is pressed 303

nopreserve option .... nopreserve option 304
numlist .... Parse numeric lists 305

pause .... Program debugging command 308
plugin .... Load a plugin 311
postfile .... Save results in Stata dataset 312
_predict ...... Obtain predictions, residuals, etc., after estimation programming command 316
preserve .... Preserve and restore data 318
program .... Define and manipulate programs 321
program properties .... Properties of user-defined programs 325

quietly .... Quietly and noisily perform Stata command 330

_return .... Preserve saved results 334
return .... Return saved results 337
_rmcoll .... Remove collinear variables 345
rmsg .... Return messages 349
_robust .... Robust variance estimates 350

scalar .... Scalar variables 374
serset .... Create and manipulate sersets 381
signestimationsample .... Determine whether the estimation sample has changed 389
sleep .... Pause for a specified time 392
smcl .... Stata Markup and Control Language 393
sortpreserve .... Sort within programs 417
syntax .... Parse Stata syntax 420
sysdir .... Query and set system directories 436

tabdisp .... Display tables 441
timer .... Time sections of code by recording and reporting time spent 449
tokenize .... Divide strings into tokens 451
trace .... Debug Stata programs 453

unab .... Unabbreviate variable list 459
unabcmd .... Unabbreviate command name 462

varabbrev .... Control variable abbreviation 463
version .... Version control 464
viewsource .... View source code 466

while .... Looping 467
window programming .... Programming menus and windows 470

Subject and author index 471

Combined subject table of contents

This is the complete contents for this manual. References to inserts from other Stata manuals that we feel would be of interest to programmers are also included.

Data manipulation and management

Functions and expressions

[U]	Chapter 13	Functions and expressions
[D]	dates and times	Date and time (%t) values and variables
[D]	egen	Extensions to generate
[D]	functions	Functions

Utilities

Basic utilities

[U]	Chapter 4	Stata's help and search facilities
[U]	Chapter 15	Saving and printing output—log files
[U]	Chapter 16	Do-files
[R]	about	Display information about your Stata
[D]	by	Repeat Stata command on subsets of the data
[R]	copyright	Display copyright information
[R]	do	Execute commands from a file
[R]	doedit	Edit do-files and other text files
[R]	exit	Exit Stata
[R]	help	Display online help
[R]	hsearch	Search help files
[R]	level	Set default confidence level
[R]	log	Echo copy of session to file
[D]	obs	Increase the number of observations in a dataset
[R]	#review	Review previous commands
[R]	search	Search Stata documentation
[R]	translate	Print and translate logs
[R]	view	View files and logs
[D]	zipfile	Compress and uncompress files and directories in zip archive format

Error messages

[U]	Chapter 8	Error messages and return codes
[P]	error	Display generic error message and exit
[R]	error messages	Error messages and return codes
[P]	rmsg	Return messages

Saved results

[U]	Section 13.5	Accessing coefficients and standard errors
[U]	Section 18.8	Accessing results calculated by other programs
[U]	Section 18.9	Accessing results calculated by estimation commands
[U]	Section 18.10	Saving results
[P]	creturn	Return c-class values

[P] ereturn .... Post the estimation results
[R] estimates .... Save and manipulate estimation results
[R] estimates describe .... Describe estimation results
[R] estimates for .... Repeat postestimation command across models
[R] estimates notes .... Add notes to estimation results
[R] estimates replay .... Redisplay estimation results
[R] estimates save .... Save and use estimation results
[R] estimates stats .... Model statistics
[R] estimates store .... Store and restore estimation results
[R] estimates table .... Compare estimation results
[R] estimates title .... Set title for estimation results
[P] _return .... Preserve saved results
[P] return .... Return saved results
[R] saved results .... Saved results

Internet

[U] Chapter 28 .... Using the Internet to keep up to date
[R] adoupdate .... Update user-written ado-files
[D] checksum .... Calculate checksum of file
[D] copy .... Copy file from disk or URL
[P] file .... Read and write ASCII text and binary files
[R] net .... Install and manage user-written additions from the Internet
[R] net search .... Search the Internet for installable packages
[R] netio .... Control Internet connections
[R] news .... Report Stata news
[R] sj .... Stata Journal and STB installation instructions
[R] ssc .... Install and uninstall packages from SSC
[R] update .... Update Stata
[D] use .... Use Stata dataset

Data types and memory

[U] Chapter 6 .... Setting the size of memory
[U] Section 12.2.2 .... Numeric storage types
[U] Section 12.4.4 .... String storage types
[U] Section 13.11 .... Precision and problems therein
[U] Chapter 23 .... Working with strings
[D] compress .... Compress data in memory
[D] data types .... Quick reference for data types
[R] matsize .... Set the maximum number of variables in a model
[D] memory .... Memory size considerations
[D] missing values .... Quick reference for missing values
[D] recast .... Change storage type of variable

Advanced utilities

[D] assert .... Verify truth of claim
[D] cd .... Change directory
[D] changeeol .... Convert end-of-line characters of text file
[D] checksum .... Calculate checksum of file
[D] copy .... Copy file from disk or URL
[P] _datasignature .... Determine whether data have changed
[D] datasignature .... Determine whether data have changed

[R]	db	Launch dialog
[P]	dialog programming	Dialog programming
[D]	dir	Display filenames
[P]	discard	Drop automatically loaded programs
[D]	erase	Erase a disk file
[D]	filefilter	Convert ASCII text or binary patterns in a file
[D]	hexdump	Display hexadecimal report on file
[D]	mkdir	Create directory
[R]	more	The —more— message
[R]	query	Display system parameters
[P]	quietly	Quietly and noisily perform Stata command
[D]	rmdir	Remove directory
[R]	set	Overview of system parameters
[R]	set seed	Specify initial value of random-number seed
[R]	set_defaults	Reset system parameters to original Stata defaults
[D]	shell	Temporarily invoke operating system
[P]	signestimationsample	Determine whether the estimation sample has changed
[P]	smcl	Stata Markup and Control Language
[P]	sysdir	Query and set system directories
[D]	type	Display contents of a file
[R]	which	Display location and version for an ado-file

Matrix commands

Basics

[U]	Chapter 14	Matrix expressions
[P]	matlist	Display a matrix and control its format
[P]	matrix	Introduction to matrix commands
[P]	matrix define	Matrix definition, operators, and functions
[P]	matrix utility	List, rename, and drop matrices

Programming

[P]	ereturn	Post the estimation results
[P]	matrix accum	Form cross-product matrices
[P]	matrix rownames	Name rows and columns
[P]	matrix score	Score data from coefficient vectors
[R]	ml	Maximum likelihood estimation

Other

[P]	makecns	Constrained estimation
[P]	matrix dissimilarity	Compute similarity or dissimilarity measures
[P]	matrix eigenvalues	Eigenvalues of nonsymmetric matrices
[P]	matrix get	Access system matrices
[P]	matrix mkmat	Convert variables to matrix and vice versa
[P]	matrix svd	Singular value decomposition
[P]	matrix symeigen	Eigenvalues and eigenvectors of symmetric matrices

Mata

[M]	*Mata Reference Manual*	

Programming

Basics

[U]	Chapter 18	Programming Stata
[U]	Section 18.3	Macros
[U]	Section 18.11	Ado-files
[P]	comments	Add comments to programs
[P]	fvexpand	Expand factor varlists
[P]	macro	Macro definition and manipulation
[P]	program	Define and manipulate programs
[P]	return	Return saved results

Program control

[U]	Section 18.11.1	Version
[P]	capture	Capture return code
[P]	continue	Break out of loops
[P]	error	Display generic error message and exit
[P]	foreach	Loop over items
[P]	forvalues	Loop over consecutive values
[P]	if	if programming command
[P]	version	Version control
[P]	while	Looping

Parsing and program arguments

[U]	Section 18.4	Program arguments
[P]	confirm	Argument verification
[P]	gettoken	Low-level parsing
[P]	levelsof	Levels of variable
[P]	numlist	Parse numeric lists
[P]	syntax	Parse Stata syntax
[P]	tokenize	Divide strings into tokens

Console output

[P]	dialog programming	Dialog programming
[P]	display	Display strings and values of scalar expressions
[P]	smcl	Stata Markup and Control Language
[P]	tabdisp	Display tables

Commonly used programming commands

[P]	byable	Make programs byable
[P]	#delimit	Change delimiter
[P]	exit	Exit from a program or do-file
[P]	mark	Mark observations for inclusion
[P]	matrix	Introduction to matrix commands
[P]	more	Pause until key is pressed
[P]	nopreserve option	nopreserve option
[P]	preserve	Preserve and restore data
[P]	quietly	Quietly and noisily perform Stata command
[P]	scalar	Scalar variables
[P]	smcl	Stata Markup and Control Language

[P]   sortpreserve . . . . Sort within programs

[P]   timer . . . . Time sections of code by recording and reporting time spent

[TS]   tsrevar . . . . Time-series operator programming command

Debugging

[P]   pause . . . . Program debugging command

[P]   timer . . . . Time sections of code by recording and reporting time spent

[P]   trace . . . . Debug Stata programs

Advanced programming commands

[P]   automation . . . . Automation

[P]   break . . . . Suppress Break key

[P]   char . . . . Characteristics

[M-2]   class . . . . Object-oriented programming (classes)

[P]   class . . . . Class programming

[P]   class exit . . . . Exit class-member program and return result

[P]   classutil . . . . Class programming utility

[P]   estat programming . . . . Controlling estat after user-written commands

[P]   _estimates . . . . Manage estimation results

[P]   file . . . . Read and write ASCII text and binary files

[P]   findfile . . . . Find file in path

[P]   include . . . . Include commands from file

[P]   macro . . . . Macro definition and manipulation

[P]   macro lists . . . . Manipulate lists

[R]   ml . . . . Maximum likelihood estimation

[M-5]   moptimize( ) . . . . Model optimization

[M-5]   optimize( ) . . . . Function optimization

[P]   plugin . . . . Load a plugin

[P]   postfile . . . . Save results in Stata dataset

[P]   _predict . . Obtain predictions, residuals, etc., after estimation programming command

[P]   program properties . . . . Properties of user-defined programs

[P]   _return . . . . Preserve saved results

[P]   _rmcoll . . . . Remove collinear variables

[P]   _robust . . . . Robust variance estimates

[P]   serset . . . . Create and manipulate sersets

[D]   snapshot . . . . Save and restore data snapshots

[P]   unab . . . . Unabbreviate variable list

[P]   unabcmd . . . . Unabbreviate command name

[P]   varabbrev . . . . Control variable abbreviation

[P]   viewsource . . . . View source code

Special interest programming commands

[R]   bstat . . . . Report bootstrap results

[MV]   cluster programming subroutines . . . . Add cluster-analysis routines

[MV]   cluster programming utilities . . . . Cluster-analysis programming utilities

[P]   matrix dissimilarity . . . . Compute similarity or dissimilarity measures

[ST]   st_is . . . . Survival analysis subroutines for programmers

[SVY]   svymarkout . . . Mark observations for exclusion on the basis of survey characteristics

[TS]   tsrevar . . . . Time-series operator programming command

File formats

[P]   file formats .dta . . . . Description of .dta file format

Mata

[M]   *Mata Reference Manual* . . . .

Interface features

[P]   dialog programming . . . . Dialog programming

[R]   doedit . . . . Edit do-files and other text files

[D]   edit . . . . Browse or edit data with Data Editor

[P]   sleep . . . . Pause for a specified time

[P]   smcl . . . . Stata Markup and Control Language

[D]   varmanage . . . . Manage variable labels, formats, and other properties

[P]   viewsource . . . . View source code

[P]   window programming . . . . Programming menus and windows

Cross-referencing the documentation

When reading this manual, you will find references to other Stata manuals. For example,

[U] **26 Overview of Stata estimation commands**
[R] **regress**
[D] **reshape**

The first example is a reference to chapter 26, *Overview of Stata estimation commands*, in the *User's Guide*; the second is a reference to the regress entry in the *Base Reference Manual*; and the third is a reference to the reshape entry in the *Data-Management Reference Manual*.

All the manuals in the Stata Documentation have a shorthand notation:

[GSM]	*Getting Started with Stata for Mac*
[GSU]	*Getting Started with Stata for Unix*
[GSW]	*Getting Started with Stata for Windows*
[U]	*Stata User's Guide*
[R]	*Stata Base Reference Manual*
[D]	*Stata Data-Management Reference Manual*
[G]	*Stata Graphics Reference Manual*
[XT]	*Stata Longitudinal-Data/Panel-Data Reference Manual*
[MI]	*Stata Multiple-Imputation Reference Manual*
[MV]	*Stata Multivariate Statistics Reference Manual*
[P]	*Stata Programming Reference Manual*
[SVY]	*Stata Survey Data Reference Manual*
[ST]	*Stata Survival Analysis and Epidemiological Tables Reference Manual*
[TS]	*Stata Time-Series Reference Manual*
[I]	*Stata Quick Reference and Index*
[M]	*Mata Reference Manual*

Detailed information about each of these manuals may be found online at

http://www.stata-press.com/manuals/

Title

> **intro** — Introduction to programming manual

Description

This entry describes this manual and what has changed since Stata 10.

Remarks

In this manual, you will find

- matrix-manipulation commands, which are available from the Stata command line and for ado-programming (for advanced matrix functions and a complete matrix programming language, see the *Mata Reference Manual*)

- commands for programming Stata, and

- commands and discussions of interest to programmers.

This manual is referred to as [P] in cross-references and is organized alphabetically.

If you are new to Stata's programming commands, we recommend that you first read the chapter about programming Stata in the *User's Guide*; see [U] **18 Programming Stata**. After you read that chapter, we recommend that you read the following sections from this manual:

[P] **program**	Define and manipulate programs
[P] **sortpreserve**	Sorting within programs
[P] **byable**	Making programs byable
[P] **macro**	Macro definition and manipulation

You may also find the subject table of contents helpful; it immediately follows the table of contents.

We also recommend the Stata NetCourses^{TM}. At the time this introduction was written, our current offerings of Stata programming NetCourses included

NC-151 Introduction to Stata programming
NC-152 Advanced Stata programming

You can learn more about NetCourses and view the current offerings of NetCourses by visiting http://www.stata.com/netcourse/.

Stata also offers public training courses. Visit http://www.stata.com/training/public.html for details.

To learn about writing your own maximum-likelihood estimation commands, read the book *Maximum Likelihood Estimation with Stata*; see http://www.stata-press.com/books/ml.html. To view other Stata Press titles, see http://www.stata-press.com.

What's new

1. The big news concerning programming has to do with the new factor variables: the parsing of varlists having factor variables, dealing with factor variables, and processing matrices whose row or column names contain factor variables.

   a. `syntax` will allow varlists to contain factor variables if new specifier `fv` is among the specifiers in the description of the varlist, for instance,

1

syntax varlist(fv) [if] [in] [, Detail]

Similarly, syntax will allow a varlist option to include factor variables if fv is included among its specifiers:

syntax varlist(fv) [if] [in] [, Detail] EQ(varlist fv)

See [P] **syntax**.

b. You can use resulting macro 'varlist' as the varlist for any Stata command that allows factor varlists.

c. Factor varlists come in two flavors, general and specific. An example of a general factor varlist is mpg i.foreign. The corresponding specific factor varlist might be

mpg i(0 1)b0.foreign

A specific factor varlist is specific with respect to a given problem, which is to say, a given dataset and subsample. The specific varlist identifies the values taken on by factor variables and the base.

Users usually specify general factor varlists, although they can specify specific ones. In the process of your program, a factor varlist, if it is general, will become specific. This is usually automatic.

Existing commands _rmcoll and _rmdcoll now accept a general or specific factor varlist and return a specific varlist in r(varlist). See [P] **_rmcoll**.

Existing command ml accepts a general or specific factor varlist and returns a specific varlist, in this case in the row and column names of the vectors and matrices it produces; see [R] **ml**. The same applies to Mata's new moptimize() function, which is equivalent to ml; see [M-5] **moptimize( )**.

Similarly, all Stata estimation commands that allow factor varlists return the specific varlist in the row and column names of e(b) and e(V).

Factor varlist mpg i(0 1)b0.foreign is specific. The same varlist could be written mpg i0b.foreign i1.foreign, so that is specific, too. The first is specific and unexpanded. The second is specific and expanded. New command fvexpand takes a general or specific (expanded or unexpanded) factor varlist, if or in, and returns a fully expanded, specific varlist. See [P] **fvexpand**.

New command fvunab takes a general or specific factor varlist and returns it in the same form, but with variable names unabbreviated. See [P] **unab**.

d. Matrix row and column names are now generalized to include factor variables. The row or column names contain the elements from a fully expanded, specific factor varlist. Because a fully expanded, specific factor varlist is a factor varlist, the contents of the row or column names can be used with other Stata commands as a varlist. Unrelatedly, the equation portion of the row or column name now has a maximum length of 127 rather than the previous 32.

e. The treatment of variables that are omitted because of collinearity has changed. Previously, such variables were dropped from e(b) and e(V) except by regress, which included the variables but set the corresponding element of e(b) to zero and similarly set the corresponding row and column of e(V) to zero. Now all Stata estimators that allow factor variables work like regress.

Also, if you want to know why the variable was dropped, you can look at the corresponding element of the row or column name. The syntax of an expanded, specific varlist allows operators o and b. Operator o indicates omitted either because the user specified omitted or because of collinearity; b indicates omitted due to being a base category. For instance, o.mpg would indicate that mpg was omitted, whereas i0b.foreign would indicate that foreign==0 was omitted because it was the base category. Either way, the corresponding element of e(b) will be zero, as will the corresponding rows and columns of e(V).

This new treatment of omitted variables—previously called dropped variables—can cause old user-written programs to break. This is especially true of old postestimation commands not designed to work with regress. If you set version to 10 or earlier before estimation, however, then estimation results will be stored in the old way and the old postestimation commands will work. The solution is

```
. version 10
. estimation_command ...
. old_postestimation_command ...
. version 11
```

When running under version 10 or earlier, you may not use factor variables with the estimation command.

f. Because omitted variables are now part of estimation results, constraints play a larger role in the implementation of estimators. Omitted variables have coefficients constrained to be zero. ml now handles such constraints automatically and posts in e(k_autoCns) the number of such constraints, which can be due to the variable being used as the base, being empty, or being omitted. makecns similarly saves in r(k_autoCns) the number of such constraints, and in r(clist), the constraints used. The matrix of constraints is now posted with ereturn post and saved, as usual, in e(Cns). ereturn matrix no longer posts constraints. Old behavior is preserved under version control. See [R] **ml**, [P] **makecns**, and [P] **ereturn**.

g. There are additional commands to assist in using and manipulating factor varlists that are documented only online; type help undocumented in Stata.

2. Factor variables also allow interactions. Up to eight-way interactions are allowed.

a. Consider the interaction a#b. If each took on two levels, the unexpanded, specific varlist would be i(1 2)b1.a#i(1 2)b1.b. The expanded, specific varlist would be 1b.a#1b.b 1b.a#2.b 2.a#1b.b 2.a#2.b.

b. Consider the interaction c.x#c.x, where x is continuous. The unexpanded and expanded, specific varlists are the same as the general varlist: c.x#c.x.

c. Consider the interaction a#c.x. The unexpanded, specific varlist is i(1 2).a#c.x, and the expanded, specific varlist is 1.a#c.x 2.a#c.x.

d. All these varlists are handled in the same way factor variables are handled, as outlined in item 1) above.

3. Existing command ml has been rewritten. It is now implemented in terms of new Mata function and optimization engine moptimize(). The new ml handles automatic or implied constraints, posts some additional information to e(), and allows evaluators written in Mata as well as ado. See [R] **maximize** for an overview and see [R] **ml** and [M-5] **moptimize( )**.

4. Existing command estimates save now has option append that allows storing more than one set of estimation results in the same file; see [R] **estimates save**.

5. Existing commands ereturn post and ereturn repost now work with more commands, including logit, mlogit, ologit, oprobit, probit, qreg, _qreg, regress, stcox, and tobit. Also, ereturn post and ereturn repost now allow weights to be specified and save them in e(wtype) and e(wexp). See [P] **ereturn**.

6. Existing command `markout` has new option `sysmissok` that excludes observations with variables equal to system missing (`.`) but not to extended missing (`.a`, `.b`, ..., `.z`); see [P] **mark**. This has to do with new emphasis on imputation of missing values; see [MI] **mi**.

7. New commands `varabbrev` and `unabbrev` make it easy to temporarily reset whether Stata allows variable-name abbreviations; see [P] **varabbrev**.

8. New programming function `smallestdouble()` returns the smallest double-precision number greater than zero; see [D] **functions**.

9. `creturn` has new returned values:

   a. `c(noisily)` returns 0 when output is being suppressed and 1 otherwise. Thus programmers can avoid executing code whose only purpose is to display output.

   b. `c(smallestdouble)` returns the smallest double-precision value that is greater than 0.

   c. `c(tmpdir)` returns the temporary directory being used by Stata.

   d. `c(eqlen)` returns the maximum length that Stata allows for equation names.

10. Existing extended macro function `:dir` has new option `respectcase` that causes `:dir` to respect uppercase and lowercase when performing filename matches. This option is relevant only for Windows.

11. Stata has new string functions `strtoname()`, `soundex()`, and `soundex_nara()`; see [D] **functions**.

12. Stata has 17 new numerical functions: `sinh()`, `cosh()`, `asinh()`, and `acosh()`; `hypergeometric()` and `hypergeometricp()`; `nbinomial()`, `nbinomialp()`, and `nbinomialtail()`; `invnbinomial()` and `invnbinomialtail()`; `poisson()`, `poissonp()`, and `poissontail()`; `invpoisson()` and `invpoissontail()`; and `binomialp()`; see [D] **functions**.

13. Stata has nine new random-variate functions for beta, binomial, chi-squared, gamma, hypergeometric, negative binomial, normal, Poisson, and Student's t: `rbeta()`, `rbinomial()`, `rchi2()`, `rgamma()`, `rhypergeometric()`, `rnbinomial()`, `rnormal()`, `rpoisson()`, and `rt()`. Also, old function `uniform()` is renamed to `runiform()`. All random-variate functions start with `r`. See [D] **functions**.

14. Existing function `clear` has new syntax `clear matrix`, which clears (drops) all Stata matrices, as distinguished from `clear mata`, which drops all Mata matrices and functions. See [D] **clear**.

15. These days, commands intended for use by end-users are often being used as subroutines by other end-user commands. Some of these commands preserve the data simply so that, should something go wrong or the user press *Break*, the original data can be restored. Sometimes, when such commands are used as subroutines, the caller has already preserved the data. Therefore, all programmers are requested to include option `nopreserve` on commands that preserve the data for no other reason than error recovery, and thus speed execution when commands are used as subroutines. See [P] **nopreserve option**.

16. Mata now supports object-oriented programming. See [M-2] **class**.

There are other new additions to Stata that will be of interest to programmers, but because they are also of interest to others, they are documented in [U] **1.3 What's new**.

References

Baum, C. F. 2009. *An Introduction to Stata Programming.* College Station, TX: Stata Press.

Gould, W. W., J. Pitblado, and W. M. Sribney. 2006. *Maximum Likelihood Estimation with Stata.* 3rd ed. College Station, TX: Stata Press.

Also see

[U] **18 Programming Stata**

[U] **1.3 What's new**

Maximum Likelihood Estimation with Stata

An Introduction to Stata Programming

[R] **intro** — Introduction to base reference manual

Title

automation — Automation

Description

Automation (formerly known as OLE Automation) is a communication mechanism between Microsoft Windows applications. It provides an infrastructure whereby Windows applications (automation clients) can access and manipulate functions and properties implemented in another application (automation server). A Stata Automation object exposes internal Stata methods and properties so that Windows programmers can write automation clients to directly use the services provided by Stata.

Remarks

A Stata Automation object is most useful for situations that require the greatest flexibility to interact with Stata from user-written applications. A Stata Automation object enables users to directly access Stata macros, scalars, saved results, and dataset information in ways besides the usual log files.

For documentation on using a Stata Automation object, see http://www.stata.com/automation/.

Note that the standard Stata end-user license agreement (EULA) does not permit Stata to be used as an embedded engine in a production setting. If you wish to use Stata in such a manner, please contact StataCorp at service@stata.com.

Also see

[P] **plugin** — Load a plugin

Title

> **break** — Suppress Break key

Syntax

> nobreak *stata_command*
>
> break   *stata_command*

Typical usage is

> nobreak {
>
>   ...
>
>   capture noisily break ...
>
>   ...
>
> }

Description

nobreak temporarily turns off recognition of the *Break* key. It is seldom used. break temporarily reestablishes recognition of the *Break* key within a nobreak block. It is even more seldom used.

Remarks

Stata commands honor the *Break* key. This honoring is automatic and, for the most part, requires no special code, as long as you follow these guidelines:

1. Obtain names for new variables from tempvar; see [U] **18.7.1 Temporary variables**.

2. Obtain names for other memory aggregates, such as scalars and matrices, from tempname; see [U] **18.7.2 Temporary scalars and matrices**.

3. If you need to temporarily change the user's data, use preserve to save it first; see [U] **18.6 Temporarily destroying the data in memory**.

4. Obtain names for temporary files from tempfile; see [U] **18.7.3 Temporary files**.

If you follow these guidelines, your program will be robust to the user pressing *Break* because Stata itself will be able to put things back as they were.

Still, sometimes a program must commit to executing a group of commands that, if *Break* were honored in the midst of the group, would leave the user's data in an intermediate, undefined state. nobreak is for those instances.

▷ Example 1

You are writing a program and following all the guidelines listed above. In particular, you are using temporary variables. At a point in your program, however, you wish to list the first five values of the temporary variable. You would like, temporarily, to give the variable a pretty name, so you temporarily rename it. If the user were to press *Break* during the period, the variable would be renamed; however, Stata would not know to drop it, and it would be left behind in the user's data. You wish to avoid this. In the code fragment below, 'myv' is the temporary variable:

```
nobreak {
        rename 'myv' Result
        list Result in 1/5
        rename Result 'myv'
}
```

It would not be appropriate to code the fragment as

```
nobreak rename 'myv' Result
nobreak list Result in 1/5
nobreak rename Result 'myv'
```

because the user might press *Break* during the periods between the commands.

◁

Also see

[P] **capture** — Capture return code

[P] **continue** — Break out of loops

[P] **quietly** — Quietly and noisily perform Stata command

[P] **varabbrev** — Control variable abbreviation

[U] **9 The Break key**

Title

byable — Make programs byable

Description

This entry describes the writing of programs so that they will allow the use of Stata's by *varlist*: prefix. If you take no special actions and write the program myprog, then by *varlist*: cannot be used with it:

```
. by foreign:  myprog
myprog may not be combined with by
r(190);
```

By reading this section, you will learn how to modify your program so that by does work with it:

```
. by foreign:  myprog
```

```
-> foreign = Domestic
```
   (*output for first by-group appears*)

```
-> foreign = Foreign
```
   (*output for first by-group appears*)

```
. _
```

Remarks

Remarks are presented under the following headings:

> *byable(recall) programs*
> *Using sort in byable(recall) programs*
> *Byable estimation commands*
> *byable(onecall) programs*
> *Using sort in byable(onecall) programs*
> *Combining byable(onecall) with byable(recall)*
> *The by-group header*

If you have not read [P] **sortpreserve**, please do so.

Programs that are written to be used with by *varlist*: are said to be "byable". Byable programs do not require the use of by *varlist*:; they merely allow it. There are two ways that programs can be made byable, known as byable(recall) and byable(onecall).

byable(recall) is easy to use and is sufficient for programs that report the results of calculation (class-1 programs as defined in [P] **sortpreserve**). byable(recall) is the method most commonly used to make programs byable.

byable(onecall) is more work to program and is intended for use in all other cases (class-2 and class-3 programs as defined in [P] **sortpreserve**).

byable(recall) programs

Say that you already have written a program (ado-file) and that it works; it merely does not allow by. If your program reports the results of calculations (such as summarize, regress, and most of the other statistical commands), then probably all you have to do to make your program byable is add the byable(recall) option to its program statement. For instance, if your program statement currently reads

```
program myprog, rclass sortpreserve
        ...
end
```

change it to read

```
program myprog, rclass sortpreserve byable(recall)
        ...
end
```

The only change you should need to make is to add byable(recall) to the program statement. Adding byable(recall) will be the only change required if

- Your program leaves behind no newly created variables. Your program might create temporary variables in the midst of calculation, but it must not leave behind new variables for the user. If your program has a generate() option, for instance, some extra effort will be required.

- Your program uses marksample or mark to restrict itself to the relevant subsample of the data. If your program does not use marksample or mark, some extra effort will be required.

Here is how byable(recall) works: if your program is invoked with a by *varlist*: prefix, your program will be executed K times, where K is the number of by-groups formed by the by-variables. Each time your program is executed, marksample will know to mark out the observations that are not being used in the current by-group.

Therein is the reason for the two guidelines on when you need to include only byable(recall) to make by *varlist*: work:

- If your program creates permanent, new variables, then it will create those variables when it is executed for the first by-group, meaning that those variables will already exist when it is executed for the second by-group, causing your program to issue an error message.

- If your program does not use marksample to identify the relevant subsample of the data, then each time it is executed, it will use too many observations—it will not honor the by-group—and will produce incorrect results.

There are ways around both problems, and here is more than you need:

function _by()	takes no arguments; returns 0 when program is not being by'd; returns 1 when program is being by'd.
function _byindex()	takes no arguments; returns 1 when program is not being by'd; returns 1, 2, ... when by'd and 1st call, 2nd call, ...
function _bylastcall()	takes no arguments; returns 1 when program is not being by'd and is being called with the last by-group; returns 0 otherwise.
function _byn1()	takes no arguments; returns the beginning observation number of the by-group currently being executed; returns 1 if _by()==0. The value returned by _byn1() is valid only if the data have not been re-sorted since the original call to the by program.
function _byn2()	takes no arguments; returns the ending observation number of the by-group currently being executed; returns 1 if _by()==0. The value returned by _byn2() is valid only if the data have not been re-sorted since the original call to by program.
macro '_byindex'	contains nothing when program is not being by'd; contains name of temporary variable when program is being by'd: variable contains 1, 2, ... for each observation in data and recorded value indicates to which by-group each observation belongs.
macro '_byvars'	contains nothing when program is not being by'd; contains names of the actual by-variables otherwise.
macro '_byrc0'	contains ", rc0" if the rc0 option is specified; contains nothing otherwise.

So let's consider the problems one at a time, beginning with the second problem. Your program does not use marksample, and we will assume that your program has good reason for not doing so, because the easy fix would be to use marksample. Still, your program must somehow be determining which observations to use, and we will assume that you are creating a 'touse' temporary variable containing 0 if the observation is to be omitted from the analysis and 1 if it is to be used. Somewhere, early in your program, you are setting the 'touse' variable. Right after that, make the following addition (shown in bold):

```
program ..., ... byable(recall)
        ...
        if _by() {
                quietly replace 'touse' = 0 if '_byindex' != _byindex()
        }
        ...
end
```

The fix is easy: you ask if you are being by'd and, if so, you set 'touse' to 0 in all observations for which the value of 'byindex' is not equal to the by-group you are currently considering, namely, _byindex().

The first problem is also easy to fix. Say that your program has a generate(*newvar*) option. Your code must therefore contain

```
program ..., ...
        ...
        if "'generate'" != "" {
                ...
        }
        ...
end
```

Change the program to read

```
program ..., ... byable(recall)
        ...
        if "'generate'" != "" & _bylastcall() {
                ...
        }
        ...
end
```

_bylastcall() will be 1 (meaning true) whenever your program is not being by'd and, when it is being by'd, whenever the program is being executed for the last by-group. The result is that the new variable will be created containing only the values for the last by-group, but with a few exceptions, that is how all of Stata works. Alternatives are discussed under byable(onecall).

All the other macros and functions that are available are for creating special effects and are rarely used in byable(recall) programs.

Using sort in byable(recall) programs

You may use sort freely within byable(recall) programs, and in fact, you can use any other Stata command you wish; there are simply no issues. You may even use sortpreserve to restore the sort order at the conclusion of your program; see [P] **sortpreserve**.

We will discuss the issue of sort in depth just to convince you that there is nothing with which you must be concerned.

When a byable(recall) program receives control and is being by'd, the data are guaranteed to be sorted by '_byvars' only when _byindex() = 1—only on the first call. If the program re-sorts the data, the data will remain re-sorted on the second and subsequent calls, even if sortpreserve is specified. This may sound like a problem, but it is not. sortpreserve is not being ignored; the data will be restored to their original order after the final call to your program. Let's go through the two cases: either your program uses sort or it does not.

1. If your program needs to use sort, it will probably need a different sort order for each by-group. For instance, a typical program that uses sort will include lines such as

   sort 'touse' 'id' ...

   and so move the relevant sample to the top of the dataset. This byable(recall) program makes no reference to the '_byvars' themselves, nor does it do anything differently when the by prefix is specified and when it is not. That is typical; byable(recall) programs rarely find it necessary to refer to the '_byvars' directly.

   In any case, because this program is sorting the data explicitly every time it is called (and we know it must be because byable(recall) programs are executed once for each by-group), there is no reason for Stata to waste its time restoring a sort order that will just be undone anyway. The original sort order needs to be reestablished only after the final call.

2. The other alternative is that the program does not use sort. Then it is free to exploit that the data are sorted on '_byvars'. Because the data will be sorted on the first call, the program does no sorts, so the data will be sorted on the second call, and so on. byable(recall) programs rarely exploit the sort order, but the program is free to do so.

Byable estimation commands

Estimation commands are natural candidates for the byable(recall) approach. There is, however, one issue that requires special attention. Estimation commands really have two syntaxes: one at the time of estimation,

[*prefix_command* :] *estcmd varlist* . . . [, *estimation_options replay_options*]

and another for redisplaying results:

estcmd [, *replay_options*]

With estimation commands, by is not allowed when results are redisplayed. We must arrange for this in our program, and that is easy enough. The general outline for an estimation command is

```
program estcmd, ...
        if replay() {
                if "`e(cmd)'"!="estcmd"  error 301
                syntax [, replay_options]
        }
        else {
                syntax ... [, estimation_options replay_options]
                ...estimation logic...
        }
        ...display logic...
```

and to this, we make the changes shown in bold:

```
program estcmd, ... byable(recall)
        if replay() {
                if "`e(cmd)'"!="estcmd" error 301
                if _by() error 190
                syntax [, replay_options]
        }
        else {
                syntax ... [, estimation_options replay_options]
                ...estimation logic...
        }
        ...display logic...
```

In addition to adding byable(recall), we add the line

```
                if _by() error 190
```

in the case where we have been asked to redisplay results. If we are being by'd (if _by() is true), then we issue error 190 (request may not be combined with by).

byable(onecall) programs

byable(onecall) requires more work to use. We strongly recommend using byable(recall) whenever possible.

The main use of byable(onecall) is to create programs such as generate and egen, which allow the by prefix but operate on all the data and create a new variable containing results for all the different by-groups.

byable(onecall) programs are, as the name implies, executed only once. The byable(onecall) program is responsible for handling all the issues concerning the by, and it is expected to do that by using

function ⎽by()	takes no arguments
	returns 0 when program is not being by'd
	returns 1 when program is being by'd
macro '⎽byvars'	contains nothing when program is not being by'd
	contains names of the actual by-variables otherwise
macro '⎽byrc0'	contains nothing or "rc0"
	contains ", rc0" if by's rc0 option was specified

In byable(onecall) programs, you are responsible for everything, including the output of by-group headers if you want them.

The typical candidates for byable(onecall) are programs that do something special and odd with the by-variables. We offer the following guidelines:

1. Ignore that you are going to make your program byable when you first write it. Instead, include a by() option in your program. Because your program cannot be coded using byable(recall), you already know that the by-variables are entangled with the logic of your routine. Make your program work before worrying about making it byable.

2. Now go back and modify your program. Include byable(onecall) on the program statement line. Remove by(varlist) from your syntax statement, and immediately after the syntax statement, add the line

   local by "'⎽byvars'"

3. Test your program. If it worked before, it will still work now. To use the by() option, you put the by *varlist*: prefix out front.

4. Ignore the macro '⎽byrc0'. Byable programs rarely do anything different when the user specifies by's rc0 option.

Using sort in byable(onecall) programs

You may use sort freely within byable(onecall) programs. You may even use sortpreserve to restore the sort order at the conclusion of your program.

When a byable(onecall) program receives control and is being by'd, the data are guaranteed to be sorted by '⎽byvars'.

Combining byable(onecall) with byable(recall)

byable(onecall) can be used as an interface to other byable programs. Let's pretend that you are writing a command—we will call it switcher—that calls one of two other commands based perhaps on some aspect of what the user typed or, perhaps, based on what was previously estimated. The rule by which switcher decides to call one or the other does not matter for this discussion; what is important is that switcher switches between what we will call prog1 and prog2. prog1 and prog2 might be actual Stata commands, Stata commands that you have written, or even subroutines of switcher.

We will further imagine that prog1 and prog2 have been implemented using the byable(recall) method and that we now want switcher to allow the by prefix, too. The easy way to do that is

```
program switcher, byable(onecall)
        if _by() {
                local by "by '_byvars' '_byrc0':"
        }
        if (whatever makes us decide in favor of prog1) {
                'by' prog1 '0'
        }
        else    'by' prog2 '0'
end
```

switcher works by re-creating the by *varlist*: prefix in front of prog1 or prog2 if by was specified. switcher will be executed only once, even if by was specified. prog1 and prog2 will be executed repeatedly.

In the above outline, it is not important that prog1 and prog2 were implemented using the byable(recall) method. They could just as well be implemented using byable(onecall), and switcher would change not at all.

The by-group header

Usually, when you use a command with by, a header is produced above each by-group:

```
. by foreign:  summarize mpg weight
```

```
-> foreign = Domestic
   (output for first by-group appears )
```

```
-> foreign = Foreign
   (output for first by-group appears )
 . _
```

The by-group header does not always appear:

```
. by foreign:  generate new = sum(mpg)
 . _
```

When you write your own programs, the header will appear by default if you use byable(recall) and will not appear if you use byable(onecall).

If you want the header and use byable(onecall), you will have to write the code to output it.

If you do not want the header and use byable(recall), you can specify byable(recall, noheader):

```
program ..., ... byable(recall, noheader)
        ...
end
```

Also see

[P] **program** — Define and manipulate programs

[P] **sortpreserve** — Sort within programs

[D] **by** — Repeat Stata command on subsets of the data

Title

capture — Capture return code

Syntax

<u>cap</u>ture [:] *command*

<u>cap</u>ture {
        stata_commands
}

Description

    capture executes *command*, suppressing all its output (including error messages, if any) and issuing a return code of zero. The actual return code generated by *command* is stored in the built-in scalar _rc.

    capture can be combined with {} to produce capture blocks, which suppress output for the block of commands. See the technical note following example 6 for more information.

Remarks

    capture is useful in do-files and programs because their execution terminates when a command issues a nonzero return code. Preceding sensitive commands with the word capture allows the do-file or program to continue despite errors. Also do-files and programs can be made to respond appropriately to any situation by conditioning their remaining actions on the contents of the scalar _rc.

▷ Example 1

    You will never have cause to use capture interactively, but an interactive experiment will demonstrate what capture does:

```
. drop _all
. list myvar
no variables defined
r(111);
. capture list myvar
. display _rc
111
```

When we said list myvar, we were told that we had no variables defined and got a return code of 111. When we said capture list myvar, we got no output and a zero return code. First, you should wonder what happened to the message "no variables defined". capture suppressed that message. It suppresses all output produced by the command it is capturing. Next we see no return code message, so the return code was zero. We already know that typing list myvar generates a return code of 111, so capture suppressed that, too.

16

capture places the return code in the built-in scalar _rc. When we display the value of this scalar, we see that it is 111.

◁

▷ Example 2

Now that we know what capture does, let's put it to use. capture is used in programs and do-files. Sometimes you will write programs that do not care about the outcome of a Stata command. You may want to ensure, for instance, that some variable does not exist in the dataset. You could do so by including capture drop result.

If result exists, it is now gone. If it did not exist, drop did nothing, and its nonzero return code and the error message have been intercepted. The program (or do-file) continues in any case. If you have written a program that creates a variable named result, it would be good practice to begin such a program with capture drop result. This way, you could use the program repeatedly without having to worry whether the result variable already exists.

◁

❑ Technical note

When combining capture and drop, never say something like capture drop var1 var2 var3. Remember that Stata commands do either exactly what you say or nothing at all. We might think that our command would be guaranteed to eliminate var1, var2, and var3 from the data if they exist. It is not. Imagine that var3 did not exist in the data. drop would then do nothing. It would *not* drop var1 and var2. To achieve the desired result, we must give three commands:

```
capture drop var1
capture drop var2
capture drop var3
```

❑

▷ Example 3

Here is another example of using capture to dispose of nonzero return codes: When using do-files to define programs, it is common to begin the definition with capture program drop *progname* and then put program *progname*. This way, you can rerun the do-file to load or reload the program.

◁

▷ Example 4

Let's consider programs whose behavior is contingent upon the outcome of some command. You write a program and want to ensure that the first argument (the macro '1') is interpreted as a new variable. If it is not, you want to issue an error message:

```
capture confirm new variable `1'
if _rc!=0 {
        display "`1' already exists"
        exit _rc
}
(program continues. . .)
```

You use the `confirm` command to determine if the variable already exists and then condition your error message on whether `confirm` thinks '1' can be a new variable. We did not have to go to the trouble here. `confirm` would have automatically issued the appropriate error message, and its nonzero return code would have stopped the program anyway.

◁

▷ Example 5

As before, you write a program and want to ensure that the first argument is interpreted as a new variable. This time, however, if it is not, you want to use the name _answer in place of the name specified by the user:

```
capture confirm new variable '1'
if _rc!=0 {
        local 1 _answer
        confirm new variable '1'
}
(program continues. . .)
```

◁

▷ Example 6

There may be instances where you want to capture the return code but not the output. You do that by combining `capture` with `noisily`. For instance, we might change our program to read

```
capture noisily confirm new variable '1'
if _rc!=0 {
        local 1 _answer
        display "I'll use _answer"
}
(program continues. . .)
```

`confirm` will generate some message such as "...already exists", and then we will follow that message with "I'll use _answer".

◁

❏ Technical note

`capture` can be combined with {} to produce *capture blocks*. Consider the following:

```
capture {
        confirm var '1'
        confirm integer number '2'
        confirm number '3'
}
if _rc!=0 {
        display "Syntax is variable integer number"
        exit 198
}
(program continues. . .)
```

If any of the commands in the capture block fail, the subsequent commands in the block are aborted, but the program continues with the `if` statement.

Capture blocks can be used to intercept the *Break* key, as in

```
capture {
        stata_commands
}
if _rc==1 {
        Break key cleanup code
        exit 1
}
(program continues. . .)
```

Remember that *Break* always generates a return code of 1. There is no reason, however, to restrict the execution of the cleanup code to *Break* only. Our program might fail for some other reason, such as insufficient room to add a new variable, and we would still want to engage in the cleanup operations. A better version would read

```
capture {
        stata_commands
}
if _rc!=0 {
        local oldrc = _rc
        Break key and error cleanup code
        exit 'oldrc'
}
(program continues. . .)
```

❏

❏ Technical note

If, in our program above, the *stata_commands* included an exit or an exit 0, the program would terminate and return 0. Neither the *cleanup* nor the *program continues* code would be executed. If *stata_commands* included an exit 198, or any other exit that sets a nonzero return code, however, the program would not exit. capture would catch the nonzero return code, and execution would continue with the *cleanup code*.

❏

Also see

[P] **break** — Suppress Break key

[P] **confirm** — Argument verification

[P] **quietly** — Quietly and noisily perform Stata command

[U] **18.2 Relationship between a program and a do-file**

Title

| char — Characteristics |

Syntax

Define characteristics

char [define] *evarname*[*charname*] [["] *text* ["]]

List characteristics

char <u>l</u>ist [*evarname*[[*charname*]]]

Rename characteristics

char <u>ren</u>ame *oldvar newvar* [, replace]

where *evarname* is a variable name or _dta and *charname* is a characteristic name. In the syntax diagrams, distinguish carefully between [ ], which you type, and [ ], which indicates that the element is optional.

Description

See [U] **12.8 Characteristics** for a description of characteristics. These commands allow manipulating characteristics.

Option

replace (for use only with char rename) specifies that if characteristics of the same name already exist, they are to be replaced. replace is a seldom-used, low-level, programmer's option.

char rename *oldvar newvar* moves all characteristics of *oldvar* to *newvar*, leaving *oldvar* with none and *newvar* with all the characteristics *oldvar* previously had. char rename *oldvar newvar* moves the characteristics, but only if *newvar* has no characteristics with the same name. Otherwise, char rename produces the error message that *newvar*[*whatever*] already exists.

Remarks

We begin by showing how the commands work mechanically and then continue to demonstrate the commands in more realistic situations.

char define sets and clears characteristics, although there is no reason to type define:

```
. char _dta[one] this is char named one of _dta
. char _dta[two] this is char named two of _dta
. char mpg[one]  this is char named   one    of mpg
. char mpg[two] "this is char named   two    of mpg"
. char mpg[three] "this is char named three of mpg"
```

20

Whether we include the double quotes does not matter. You clear a characteristic by defining it to be nothing:

```
. char mpg[three]
```

char list is used to list existing characteristics; it is typically used for debugging:

```
. char list
    _dta[two]       :   this is char named two of _dta
    _dta[one]       :   this is char named one of _dta
    mpg[two]        :   this is char named   two   of mpg
    mpg[one]        :   this is char named   one   of mpg
. char list _dta[]
    _dta[two]       :   this is char named two of _dta
    _dta[one]       :   this is char named one of _dta
. char list mpg[]
    mpg[two]        :   this is char named   two   of mpg
    mpg[one]        :   this is char named   one   of mpg
. char list mpg[one]
    mpg[one]        :   this is char named   one   of mpg
```

The order may surprise you—it is the way it is because of how Stata's memory-management routines work—but it does not matter.

char rename moves all the characteristics associated with *oldvar* to *newvar*:

```
. char rename mpg weight
. char list
    _dta[two]       :   this is char named two of _dta
    _dta[one]       :   this is char named one of _dta
    weight[two]     :   this is char named   two   of mpg
    weight[one]     :   this is char named   one   of mpg
. char rename weight mpg                    // put it back
```

The contents of specific characteristics may be obtained in the same way as local macros by referring to the characteristic name between left and right single quotes; see [U] **12.8 Characteristics**.

```
. display "`mpg[one]'"
this is char named   one     of mpg
. display "`_dta[]'"
two one
```

Referring to a nonexisting characteristic returns a null string:

```
. display "the value is |`mpg[three]'|"
the value is ||
```

How to program with characteristics

> Example 1

You are writing a program that requires the value of the variable recording "instance" (first time, second time, etc.). You want your command to have an option ins(*varname*), but after the user has specified the variable once, you want your program to remember it in the future, even across sessions. An outline of your program is

```
program ...
        version 11
        syntax ... [, ... ins(varname) ... ]
        ...
        if "'ins'"=="" {
                local ins "'_dta[Instance]'"
        }
        confirm variable 'ins'
        char _dta[Instance] : 'ins'
        ...
end
```

◁

▷ Example 2

You write a program, and among other things, it changes the contents of one of the variables in the user's data. You worry about the user pressing *Break* while the program is in the midst of the change, so you correctly decide to construct the replaced values in a temporary variable and, only at the conclusion, drop the user's original variable and replace it with the new one. In this example, macro 'uservar' contains the name of the user's original variable. Macro 'newvar' contains the name of the temporary variable that will ultimately replace it.

The following issues arise when you duplicate the original variable: you want the new variable to have the same variable label, the same value label, the same format, and the same characteristics.

```
program ...
        version 11
        ...
        tempvar newvar
        ...
        ( code creating 'newvar')
        ...
        local varlab : variable label 'uservar'
        local vallab : value label 'uservar'
        local format : format 'uservar'
        label var 'newvar' "'varlab'"
        label values 'newvar' 'vallab'
        format 'newvar' 'format'
        char rename 'uservar' 'newvar'
        drop 'uservar'
        rename 'newvar' 'uservar'
end
```

You are supposed to notice the char rename command included to move the characteristics originally attached to 'uservar' to 'newvar'. See [P] **macro**, [D] **label**, and [D] **format** for information on the commands preceding the char rename command.

This code is almost perfect, but if you are really concerned about the user pressing *Break*, there is a potential problem. What happens if the user presses *Break* between the char rename and the final rename? The last three lines would be better written as

```
nobreak {
        char rename 'uservar' 'newvar'
        drop 'uservar'
        rename 'newvar' 'uservar'
}
```

Now even if the user presses *Break* during these last three lines, it will be ignored; see [P] **break**.

◁

Also see

[P] **macro** — Macro definition and manipulation

[D] **notes** — Place notes in data

[U] **12.8 Characteristics**

[U] **18.3.6 Extended macro functions**

[U] **18.3.13 Referring to characteristics**

Title

class — Class programming

Description

Stata's two programming languages, ado and Mata, each support object-oriented programming. This manual entry explains object-oriented programming in ado. Most users interested in object-oriented programming will wish to do so in Mata. See [M-2] **class** to learn about object-oriented programming in Mata.

Ado *classes* are a programming feature of Stata that are especially useful for dealing with graphics and GUI problems, although their use need not be restricted to those topics. Ado class programming is an advanced programming topic and will not be useful to most programmers.

Remarks

Remarks are presented under the following headings:

1. Introduction
2. Definitions
    2.1 Class definition
    2.2 Class instance
    2.3 Class context
3. Version control
4. Member variables
    4.1 Types
    4.2 Default initialization
    4.3 Specifying initialization
    4.4 Specifying initialization 2, .new
    4.5 Another way of declaring
    4.6 Scope
    4.7 Adding dynamically
    4.8 Advanced initialization, .oncopy
    4.9 Advanced cleanup, destructors
5. Inheritance
6. Member programs' return values
7. Assignment
    7.1 Type matching
    7.2 Arrays and array elements
    7.3 lvalues and rvalues
    7.4 Assignment of reference
8. Built-ins
    8.1 Built-in functions
    8.2 Built-in modifiers
9. Prefix operators
10. Using object values
11. Object destruction
12. Advanced topics
    12.1 Keys
    12.2 Unames
    12.3 Arrays of member variables
Appendix A. Finding, loading, and clearing class definitions
Appendix B. Jargon
Appendix C. Syntax diagrams
    Appendix C.1 Class declaration
    Appendix C.2 Assignment
    Appendix C.3 Macro substitution
    Appendix C.4 Quick summary of built-ins

1. Introduction

A *class* is a collection of member variables and member programs. The member programs of a class manipulate or make calculations based on the member variables. Classes are defined in .class files. For instance, we might define the class coordinate in the file coordinate.class:

── begin coordinate.class ────────

```
version 11
class coordinate {
            double  x
            double  y
}
program .set
            args x y
            .x = 'x'
            .y = 'y'
end
```

── end coordinate.class ────────

The above file does not create anything. It merely defines the concept of a "coordinate". Now that the file exists, however, you could create a "scalar" variable of type coordinate by typing

```
.coord = .coordinate.new
```

.coord is called an *instance of* coordinate; it contains .coord.x (a particular x coordinate) and .coord.y (a particular y coordinate). Because we did not specify otherwise, .coord.x and .coord.y contain missing values, but we could reset .coord to contain (1,2) by typing

```
.coord.x = 1
.coord.y = 2
```

Here we can do that more conveniently by typing

```
.coord.set 1 2
```

because coordinate.class provides a member program called .set that allows us to set the member variables. There is nothing especially useful about .set; we wrote it mainly to emphasize that classes could, in fact, contain member programs. Our coordinate.class definition would be nearly as good if we deleted the .set program. Classes are not required to have member programs, but they may.

If we typed

```
.coord2 = .coordinate.new
.coord2.set 2 4
```

we would now have a second instance of a coordinate, this one named .coord2, which would contain (2,4).

Now consider another class, line.class:

(Continued on next page)

─────────────────────────────────────── begin line.class ───────────

```
version 11
class line {
              coordinate c0
              coordinate c1
}
program .set
              args x0 y0 x1 y1
              .c0.set 'x0' 'y0'
              .c1.set 'x1' 'y1'
end
program .length
              class exit sqrt(('.c0.y'-'.c1.y')^2 + ('.c0.x'-'.c1.x')^2)
end
program .midpoint
              local cx = ('.c0.x' + '.c1.x')/2
              local cy = ('.c0.y' + '.c1.y')/2
              tempname b
              .'b'=.coordinate.new
              .'b'.set 'cx' 'cy'
              class exit .'b'
end
```

─────────────────────────────────────── end line.class ───────────

Like `coordinate.class`, `line.class` has two member variables—named `.c0` and `.c1`—but rather than being numbers, `.c0` and `.c1` are coordinates as we have previously defined the term. Thus the full list of the member variables for `line.class` is

.c0	first coordinate
.c0.x	x value (a double)
.c0.y	y value (a double)
.c1	second coordinate
.c1.x	x value (a double)
.c1.y	y value (a double)

If we typed

    .li = .line.new

we would have a line named `.li` in which

.li.c0	first coordinate of line .li
.li.c0.x	x value (a double)
.li.c0.y	y value (a double)
.li.c1	second coordinate of line .li
.li.c1.x	x value (a double)
.li.c1.y	y value (a double)

What are the values of these variables? Because we did not specify otherwise, `.li.c0` and `.li.c1` will receive default values for their type, `coordinate`. That default is (.,.) because we did not specify otherwise when we defined lines or coordinates. Therefore, the default values are (.,.) and (.,.), and we have a missing line.

As with `coordinate`, we included the member function `.set` to make setting the line easier. We can type

    .li.set 1 2 2 4

and we will have a line going from (1,2) to (2,4).

`line.class` contains the following member programs:

.set	program to set .c0 and .c1
.c0.set	program to set .c0
.c1.set	program to set .c1
.length	program to return length of line
.midpoint	program to return coordinate of midpoint of line

.set, .length, and .midpoint came from line.class. .c0.set and .c1.set came from coordinate.class.

Member program .length returns the length of the line.

```
.len = .li.length
```

would create .len containing the result of .li.length. The result of running the program .length on the object .li. .length returns a double, and therefore, .len will be a double.

.midpoint returns the midpoint of a line.

```
.mid = .li.midpoint
```

would create .mid containing the result of .li.midpoint, the result of running the program .midpoint on the object .li. .midpoint returns a coordinate, and therefore, .mid will be a coordinate.

2. Definitions

2.1 Class definition

Class *classname* is defined in file *classname*.class. The definition does not create any instances of the class.

The *classname*.class file has three parts:

────────────────────────────────────── begin *classname*.class ──────────

```
version ...            // Part 1: version statement
class  classname {     // Part 2: declaration of member variables
          ...
}
program ...            // Part 3: code for member programs
          ...
end
program ...
          ...
end
...
```

────────────────────────────────────── end *classname*.class ──────────

2.2 Class instance

To create a "variable" *name* of type *classname*, you type

```
.name = .classname.new
```

After that, *.name* is variously called an identifier, class variable, class instance, object, object instance, or sometimes just an instance. Call it what you will, the above creates new *.name*—or replaces existing *.name*—to contain the result of an application of the definition of *classname*. And, just as with any variable, you can have many different variables with many different names all the same type.

.name is called a first-level or top-level identifier. *.name1.name2* is called a second-level identifier, and so on. Assignment into top-level identifiers is allowed if the identifier does not already exist or if the identifier exists and is of type *classname*. If the top-level identifier already exists and is of a different type, you must drop the identifier first and then re-create it; see *11. Object destruction*.

Consider the assignment

> *.name1.name2* = *.classname*.new

The above statement is allowed if *.name1* already exists and if *.name2* is declared, in *.name1*'s class definition, to be of type *classname*. In that case, *.name1.name2* previously contained a *classname* instance and now contains a *classname* instance, the difference being that the old contents were discarded and replaced with the new ones. The same rule applies to third-level and higher identifiers.

Classes, and class instances, may also contain member programs. Member programs are identified in the same way as class variables. *.name1.name2* might refer to a member variable or to a member program.

2.3 Class context

When a class program executes, it executes in the context of the current instance. For example, consider the instance creation

> .mycoord = .coordinate.new

and recall that coordinate.class provides member program .set, which reads

```
program .set
                args x y
                .x = 'x'
                .y = 'y'
        end
```

Assume that we type ".mycoord.set 2 4". When .set executes, it executes in the *context* of .mycoord. In the program, the references to .x and .y are assumed to be to .mycoord.x and .mycoord.y. If we typed ".other.set", the references would be to .other.x and .other.y.

Look at the statement ".x = 'x'" in .set. Pretend that 'x' is 2 so that, after macro substitution, the statement reads ".x = 2". Is this a statement that the first-level identifier .x is to be set to 2? No, it is a statement that *.impliedcontext*.x is to be set to 2. The same would be true whether .x appeared to the right of the equal sign or anywhere else in the program.

The rules for resolving things like .x and .y are actually more complicated. They are resolved to the implied context if they exist in the implied context, and otherwise they are interpreted to be in the global context. Hence, in the above examples, .x and .y were interpreted as being references to *.impliedcontext*.x and *.impliedcontext*.y because .x and .y existed in *.impliedcontext*. If, however, our program made a reference to .c, that would be assumed to be in the global context (i.e., to be just .c), because there is no .c in the implied context. This is discussed at length in *9. Prefix operators*.

If a member program calls a regular program—a regular ado-file—that program will also run in the same class context; for example, if .set included the lines

```
move_to_right
.x = r(x)
.y = r(y)
```

and program `move_to_right.ado` had lines in it referring to `.x` and `.y`, they would be interpreted as *.impliedcontext*`.x` and *.impliedcontext*`.y`.

In all programs—member programs or ado-files—we can explicitly control whether we want identifiers in the implied context or globally with the `.Local` and `.Global` prefixes; see *9. Prefix operators*.

3. Version control

The first thing that should appear in a `.class` file is a `version` statement; see [P] **version**. For example, `coordinate.class` reads

———————————————————————— begin coordinate.class ————————

```
version 11
[ class statement defining member variables omitted ]
program .set
                args x y
                .x = 'x'
                .y = 'y'
end
```

———————————————————————— end coordinate.class ————————

The `version 11` at the top of the file specifies not only that, when the class definition is read, it be interpreted according to version 11 syntax, but also that when each of the member programs runs, it be interpreted according to version 11. Thus you do not need to include a `version` statement inside the definition of each member program, although you may if you want that one program to run according to the syntax of a different version of Stata.

Including the `version` statement at the top, however, is of vital importance. Stata is under continual development, and so is the class subsystem. Syntax and features can change. Including the `version` command ensures that your class will continue to work as you intended.

4. Member variables

4.1 Types

The second thing that appears in a `.class` file is the definition of the member variables. We have seen two examples:

———————————————————————— begin coordinate.class ————————

```
version 11
class coordinate {
                double  x
                double  y
}
[ member programs omitted ]
```

———————————————————————— end coordinate.class ————————

and

```
───────────────────────────────────────── begin line.class ─────────

    version 11
    class line {
                coordinate c0
                coordinate c1
    }
```
[*member programs omitted*]
```
───────────────────────────────────────── end line.class ─────────
```

In the first example, the member variables are `.x` and `.y`, and in the second, `.c0` and `.c1`. In the first example, the member variables are of type `double`, and in the second, of type `coordinate`, another class.

The member variables may be of *type*

`double`	double-precision scalar numeric value, which includes missing values `.`, `.a`, . . . , and `.z`
`string`	scalar string value, with minimum length 0 (`""`) and maximum length the same as for macros, in other words, long
classname	other classes, excluding the class being defined
`array`	array containing any of the *types*, including other `arrays`

A class definition might read

```
──────────────────────────────────────── begin todolist.class ─────────

    version 11
    class todolist {
                double  n        // number of elements in list
                string  name     // who the list is for
                array   list     // the list itself
                actions x        // things that have been done
    }
──────────────────────────────────────── end todolist.class ─────────
```

In the above, `actions` is a class, not a primitive type. Somewhere else, we have written `actions.class`, which defines what we mean by `actions`.

`arrays` are not typed when they are declared. An `array` is not an array of `doubles` or an array of `strings` or an array of `coordinates`; rather, each array element is separately typed at run time, so an array may turn out to be an array of `doubles` or an array of `strings` or an array of `coordinates`, or it may turn out that its first element is a `double`, its second element is a `string`, its third element is a `coordinate`, its fourth element is something else, and so on.

Similarly, `arrays` are not declared to be of a predetermined size. The size is automatically determined at run time according to how the array is used. Also arrays can be sparse. The first element of an array might be a `double`, its fourth element a `coordinate`, and its second and third elements left undefined. There is no inefficiency associated with this. Later, a value might be assigned to the fifth element of the array, thus extending it, or a value might be assigned to the second and third elements, thus filling in the gaps.

4.2 Default initialization

When an instance of a class is created, the member variables are filled in as follows:

double	. (missing value)
string	""
classname	as specified by class definition
array	empty, an array with no elements yet defined

4.3 Specifying initialization

You may specify in *classname*.class the initial values for member variables. To do this, you type an equal sign after the identifier, and then you type the initial value. For example,

─────────────────────────────────── begin todolist.class ───────────

```
version 11
class todolist {
              double  n    = 0
              string  name = "nobody"
              array   list = {"show second syntax", "mark as done"}
              actions x    = .actions.new arguments
}
```

─────────────────────────────────── end todolist.class ───────────

The initialization rules are as follows:

double *membervarname* = ...

> After the equal sign, you may type any number or expression. To initialize the member variable with a missing value (., .a, .b, ..., .z), you must enclose the missing value in parentheses. Examples include

```
double n = 0
double a = (.)
double b = (.b)
double z = (2+3)/sqrt(5)
```

> Alternatively, after the equal sign, you may specify the identifier of a member variable to be copied or program to be run as long as the member variable is a double or the program returns a double. If a member program is specified that requires arguments, they must be specified following the identifier. Examples include

```
double n = .clearcount
double a = .gammavalue 4 5 2
double b = .color.cvalue, color(green)
```

> The identifiers are interpreted in terms of the global context, not the class context being defined. Thus .clearcount, .gammavalue, and .color.cvalue must exist in the global context.

string *membervarname* = ...

> After the equal sign, you type the initial value for the member variable enclosed in quotes, which may be either simple (" and ") or compound (`" and "'). Examples include

```
string name = "nobody"
string s = '"quotes "inside" strings"'
string a = ""
```

You may also specify a string expression, but you must enclose it in parentheses. For example,

```
string name = ("no" + "body")
string b    = (char(11))
```

Or you may specify the identifier of a member variable to be copied or a member program to be run, as long as the member variable is a `string` or the program returns a `string`. If a member program is specified that requires arguments, they must be specified following the identifier. Examples include

```
string n = .defaultname
string a = .recapitalize "john smith"
string b = .names.defaults, category(null)
```

The identifiers are interpreted in terms of the global context, not the class context being defined. Thus `.defaultname`, `.recapitalize`, and `.names.defaults` must exist in the global context.

array *membervarname* = {...}

After the equal sign, you type the set of elements in braces ({ and }), with each element separated from the next by a comma.

If an element is enclosed in quotes (simple or compound), the corresponding array element is defined to be `string` with the contents specified.

If an element is a literal number excluding `.`, `.a`, `...`, and `.z`, the corresponding array element is defined to be `double` and filled in with the number specified.

If an element is enclosed in parentheses, what appears inside the parentheses is evaluated as an expression. If the expression evaluates to a string, the corresponding array element is defined to be `string` and the result is filled in. If the expression evaluates to a number, the corresponding array element is defined to be `double` and the result is filled in. Missing values may be assigned to array elements by being enclosed in parentheses.

An element that begins with a period is interpreted as an object identifier in the global context. That object may be a member variable or a member program. The corresponding array element is defined to be of the same type as the specified member variable or of the same type as the member program returns. If a member program is specified that requires arguments, the arguments must be specified following the identifier, but the entire syntactical elements must be enclosed in square brackets ([and]).

If the element is nothing, the corresponding array element is left undefined.

Examples include

```
array mixed = {1, 2, "three", 4}
array els   = {.box.new, , .table.new}
array rad   = {[.box.new 2 3], , .table.new}
```

Note the double commas in the last two initializations. The second element is left undefined. Some programmers would code

```
array els   = {.box.new, /*nothing*/, .table.new}
array rad   = {[.box.new 2 3], /*nothing*/, .table.new}
```

to emphasize the null initialization.

classname membervarname = . . .

After the equal sign, you specify the identifier of a member variable to be copied or a member program to be run, as long as the member variable is of type *classname* or the member program returns something of type *classname*. If a member program is specified that requires arguments, they must be specified following the identifier. In either case, the identifier will be interpreted in the global context. Examples include

```
box mybox1 = .box.new
box mybox2 = .box.new 2 4 7 8, tilted
```

All the types can be initialized by copying other member variables or by running other member programs. These other member variables and member programs must be defined in the global context and not the class context. In such cases, each initialization value or program is, in fact, copied or run only once—at the time the class definition is read—and the values are recorded for future use. This makes initialization fast. This also means, however, that

- If, in a class definition called, say, `border.class`, you defined a member variable that was initialized by `.box.new`, and if `.box.new` counted how many times it is run, then even if you were to create 1,000 instances of `border`, you would discover that `.box.new` was run only once. If `.box.new` changed what it returned over time (perhaps because of a change in some state of the system being implemented), the initial values would not change when a new border object was created.

- If, in `border.class`, you were to define a member variable that is initialized as `.system.curvals.no_of_widgets`, which we will assume is another member variable, then even if `.system.curvals.no_of_widgets` were changed, the new instances of `border.class` would always have the same value—the value of `.system.curvals.no_of_widgets` current at the time `border.class` was read.

In both of the above examples, the method just described—the prerecorded assignment method of specifying initial values—would be inadequate. The method just described is suitable for specifying constant initial values only.

4.4 Specifying initialization 2, .new

Another way to specify how member variables are to be initialized is to define a `.new` program within the class.

To create a new instance of a class, you type

. *name* =. *classname*.new

`.new` is, in fact, a member program of *classname*; it is just one that is built in, and you do not have to define it to use it. The built-in `.new` allocates the memory for the instance and fills in the default or specified initial values for the member variables. If you define a `.new`, your `.new` will be run after the built-in `.new` finishes its work.

For example, our example `coordinate.class` could be improved by adding a `.new` member program:

```
                                            begin coordinate.class
   version 11
   class coordinate {
                   double  x
                   double  y
   }
   program .new
                   if "'0'" != "" {
                           .set '0'
                   }
   end
   program .set
                   args x y
                   .x = 'x'
                   .y = 'y'
   end
                                            end coordinate.class
```

With this addition, we could type

```
.coord = .coordinate.new
.coord.set 2 4
```

or we could type

```
.coord = .coordinate.new 2 4
```

We have arranged .new to take arguments—optional ones here—that specify where the new point is to be located. We wrote the code so that .new calls .set, although we could just as well have written the code so that the lines in .set appeared in .new and then deleted the .set program. In fact, the two-part construction can be desirable because then we have a function that will reset the contents of an existing class as well.

In any case, by defining your own .new, you can arrange for any sort of complicated initialization of the class, and that initialization can be a function of arguments specified if that is necessary.

The .new program need not return anything; see *6. Member programs' return values*.

.new programs are not restricted just to filling in initial values. They are programs that you can code however you wish. .new is run every time a new instance of a class is created with one exception: when an instance is created as a member of another instance (in which case, the results are prerecorded).

4.5 Another way of declaring

In addition to the syntax

type   name $\left[\ =\ initialization\right]$

where *type* is one of double, string, *classname*, or array, there is an alternative syntax that reads

name = *initialization*

That is, you may omit specifying *type* when you specify how the member variable is to be initialized because, then, the type of the member variable can be inferred from the initialization.

4.6 Scope

In the examples we have seen so far, the member variables are unique to the instance. For example, if we have

```
.coord1 = .coordinate.new
.coord2 = .coordinate.new
```

then the member variables of .coord1 have nothing to do with the member variables of .coord2. If we were to change .coord1.x, then .coord2.x would remain unchanged.

Classes can also have variables that are shared across all instances of the class. Consider

——— begin coordinate2.class ———————

```
version 11
class coordinate2 {
            classwide:
                    double x_origin = 0
                    double y_origin = 0
            instancespecific:
                    double x = 0
                    double y = 0
}
```

——— end coordinate2.class ———————

In this class definition, .x and .y are as they were in coordinate.class—they are unique to the instance. .x_origin and .y_origin, however, are shared across all instances of the class. That is, if we were to type

```
.ac = .coordinate2.new
.bc = .coordinate2.new
```

there would be only one copy of .x_origin and of .y_origin. If we changed .x_origin in .ac,

```
.ac.x_origin = 2
```

we would find that .bc.x_origin had similarly been changed. That is because .ac.x_origin and .bc.x_origin are, in fact, the same variable.

The effects of initialization are a little different for classwide variables. In coordinate2.class, we specified that .origin_x and .origin_y both be initialized as 0, and so they were when we typed ".ac = .coordinate2.new", creating the first instance of the class. After that, however, .origin_x and .origin_y will never be reinitialized because they need not be recreated, being shared. (That is not exactly accurate because, once the last instance of a coordinate2 has been destroyed, the variables will need to be reinitialized the next time a new first instance of coordinate2 is created.)

Classwide variables, just as with instance-specific variables, can be of any type. We can define

——— begin supercoordinate.class ———————

```
version 11
class supercoordinate {
            classwide:
                    coordinate   origin
            instancespecific:
                    coordinate   pt
}
```

——— end supercoordinate.class ———————

The qualifiers classwide: and instancespecific: are used to designate the scope of the member variables that follow. When neither is specified, instancespecific: is assumed.

4.7 Adding dynamically

Once an instance of a class exists, you can add new (instance-specific) member variables to it. The syntax for doing this is

>   *name* .Declare   *attribute_declaration*

where *name* is the identifier of an instance and *attribute_declaration* is any valid attribute declaration such as

>   double   *varname*
>   string   *varname*
>   array   *varname*
>   *classname* *varname*

and, on top of that, we can include = and initializer information as defined in *4.3 Specifying initialization* above.

For example, we might start with

>   .coord = .coordinate.new

and discover that there is some extra information that we would like to carry around with the particular instance .coord. Here we want to carry around some color information that we will use later, and we have at our fingertips color.class, which defines what we mean by color. We can type

>   .coord.Declare color mycolor

or even

>   .coord.Declare color mycolor = .color.new, color(default)

to cause the new class instance to be initialized the way we want. After that command, .coord now contains .coord.color and whatever third-level or higher identifiers color provides. We can still invoke the member programs of coordinate on .coord, and to them, .coord will look just like a coordinate because they will know nothing about the extra information (although if they were to make a copy of .coord, then the copy would include the extra information). We can use the extra information in our main program and even in subroutines that we write.

❏ Technical note

Just as with the declaration of member variables inside the class {} statement, you can omit specifying the *type* when you specify the initialization. In the above, the following would also be allowed:

>   .coord.Declare mycolor = .color.new, color(default)

❏

4.8 Advanced initialization, .oncopy

Advanced initialization is an advanced concept, and we need concern ourselves with it only when our class is storing references to items outside the class system. In such cases, the class system knows nothing about these items other than their names. We must manage the contents of these items.

Assume that our coordinates class was storing not scalar coordinates but rather the names of Stata variables that contained coordinates. When we create a copy of such a class,

```
.coord = .coordinate.new 2 4
.coordcopy = .coord
```

.coordcopy will contain copies of the names of the variables holding the coordinates, but the variables themselves will not be copied. To be consistent with how all other objects are treated, we may prefer that the contents of the variables be copied to new variables.

As with .new we can define an .oncopy member program that will be run after the default copy operation has been completed. We will probably need to refer to the source object of the copy with the built-in .oncopy_src, which returns a key to the source object.

Let's write the beginnings of a coordinate class that uses Stata variables to store vectors of coordinates.

─────────────────────── begin varcoordinate.class ───────────

```
version 11
class varcoordinate {
        classwide:
                n = 0
        instancespecific:
                string x
                string y
}
program .new
                .nextnames
                if "'0'" != "" {
                        .set '0'
                }
end
program .set
                args x y
                replace '.x' = 'x'
                replace '.y' = 'y'
end
program .nextnames
                .n = '.n' + 1
                .x = "__varcorrd_vname_'.n'"
                .n = '.n' + 1
                .y = "__varcorrd_vname_'.n'"
                gen '.x' = .
                gen '.y' = .
end
program .oncopy
                .nextnames
                .set '.'.oncopy_src'.x' '.'.oncopy_src'.y'
end
```

─────────────────────── end varcoordinate.class ───────────

This class is more complicated than what we have seen before. We are going to use our own unique variable names to store the x- and y-coordinate variables. To ensure that we do not try to reuse the same name, we number these variables by using the classwide counting variable .n. Every time a new instance is created, unique x- and y-coordinate variables are created and filled in with missing. This work is done by .nextnames.

The .set looks similar to the one from .varcoordinates except that now we are holding variable names in '.x' and '.y', and we use `replace` to store the values from the specified variables into our coordinate variables.

The .oncopy member function creates unique names to hold the variables, using .nextnames, and then copies the contents of the coordinate variables from the source object, using .set.

Now, when we type

```
.coordcopy = .coord
```

the x- and y-coordinate variables in .coordcopy will be different variables from those in .coord with copies of their values.

The `varcoordinate` class does not yet do anything interesting, and other than the example in the following section, we will not develop it further.

4.9 Advanced cleanup, destructors

We rarely need to concern ourselves with objects being removed when they are deleted or replaced.

When we type

```
.a = .classname.new
.b = .classname.new
.a = .b
```

the last command causes the original object, .a, to be destroyed and replaces it with .b. The class system handles this task, which is usually all we want done. An exception is objects that are holding onto items outside the class system, such as the coordinate variables in our `destructor` class.

When we need to perform actions before the system deletes an object, we write a .destructor member program in the class file. The .destructor for our `varcoordinate` class is particularly simple; it drops the coordinate variables.

———————————————————— begin varcoordinate.class -- destructor ————————

```
program .destructor
            capture drop '.x'
            capture drop '.y'
    end
```

———————————————————— end varcoordinate.class -- destructor ————————

5. Inheritance

One class definition can inherit from other class definitions. This is done by including the `inherit`(*classnamelist*) option:

———————————————————————————————— begin *newclassname*.class ————————

```
version 11
class newclassname {
            . . .
}, inherit(classnamelist)
program . . .
            . . .
end
. . .
```

———————————————————————————————— end *newclassname*.class ————————

newclassname inherits the member variables and member programs from *classnamelist*. In general, *classnamelist* contains one class name. When *classnamelist* contains more than one class name, that is called *multiple inheritance*.

To be precise, *newclassname* inherits all the member variables from the classes specified except those that are explicitly defined in *newclassname*, in which case the definition provided in *newclassname*.class takes precedence. It is considered bad style to name member variables that conflict.

For multiple inheritance, it is possible that, although a member variable is not defined in *newclassname*, it is defined in more than one of the "parents" (*classnamelist*). Then it will be the definition in the rightmost parent that is operative. This too is to be avoided, because it almost always results in programs' breaking.

newclassname also inherits all the member programs from the classes specified. Here name conflicts are not considered bad style, and in fact, redefinition of member programs is one of the primary reasons to use inheritance.

newclassname inherits all the programs from *classnamelist*—even those with names in common— and a way is provided to specify which of the programs you wish to run. For single inheritance, if member program .zifl is defined in both classes, then .zifl is taken as the instruction to run .zifl as defined in *newclassname*, and .Super.zifl is taken as the instruction to run .zifl as defined in the parent.

For multiple inheritance, .zifl is taken as the instruction to run .zifl as defined in *newclassname*, and .Super(*classname*).zifl is taken as the instruction to run .zifl as defined in the parent *classname*.

A good reason to use inheritance is to "steal" a class and to modify it to suit your purposes. Pretend that you have alreadyexists.class and from that you want to make alternative.class, something that is much like alreadyexists.class—so much like it that it could be used wherever alreadyexists.class is used—but it does one thing a little differently. Perhaps you are writing a graphics system, and alreadyexists.class defines everything about the little circles used to mark points on a graph, and now you want to create alternate.class that does the same, but this time for solid circles. Hence, there is only one member program of alreadyexists.class that you want to change: how to draw the symbol.

In any case, we will assume that alternative.class is to be identical to alreadyexists.class, except that it has changed or improved member function .zifl. In such a circumstance, it would not be uncommon to create

──────────────────────────────── begin alternative.class ─────────

```
version 11
class alternative {
}, inherit(alreadyexists)
program .zifl
            . . .
end
```

──────────────────────────────── end alternative.class ─────────

Moreover, in writing .zifl, you might well call .Super.zifl so that the old .zifl performed its tasks, and all you had to do was code what was extra (filling in the circles, say). In the example above, we added no member variables to the class.

Perhaps the new `.zifl` needs a new member variable—a `double`—and let's call it `.sizeofresult`. Then we might code

── begin alternative.class ────────

```
version 11
class alternative {
                double    sizeofresult
}, inherit(alreadyexists)
program .zifl
                . . .
end
```

── end alternative.class ────────

Now let's consider initialization of the new variable, `.sizeofresult`. Perhaps having it initialized as missing is adequate. Then our code above is adequate. Suppose that we want to initialize it to 5. Then we could include an initializer statement. Perhaps we need something more complicated that must be handled in a `.new`. In this final case, we must call the inherited classes' `.new` programs by using the `.Super` modifier:

── begin alternative.class ────────

```
version 11
class alternative {
                double    sizeofresult
}, inherit(alreadyexists)
program .new
                . . .
                .Super.new
                . . .
end
program .zifl
                . . .
end
```

── end alternative.class ────────

6. Member programs' return values

Member programs may optionally return "values", and those can be doubles, `strings`, `arrays`, or class instances. These return values can be used in assignment, and thus you can code

```
.len    = .li.length
.coord3 = .li.midpoint
```

Just because a member program returns something, it does not mean it has to be consumed. The programs `.li.length` and `.li.midpoint` can still be executed directly,

```
.li.length
.li.midpoint
```

and then the return value is ignored. (`.midpoint` and `.length` are member programs that we included in `line.class`. `.length` returns a `double`, and `.midpoint` returns a `coordinate`.)

You cause member programs to return values by using the `class exit` command; see [P] **class exit**.

Do not confuse returned values with return codes, which all Stata programs set, even member programs. Member programs exit when they execute.

Condition	Returned value	Return code
`class exit` with arguments	as specified	0
`class exit` without arguments	nothing	0
`exit` without arguments	nothing	0
`exit` with arguments	nothing	as specified
`error`	nothing	as specified
command having error	nothing	as appropriate

Any of the preceding are valid ways of exiting a member program, although the last is perhaps best avoided. `class exit` without arguments has the same effect as `exit` without arguments; it does not matter which you code.

If a member program returns nothing, the result is as if it returned `string` containing "" (nothing).

Member programs may also return values in `r()`, `e()`, and `s()`, just like regular programs. Using `class exit` to return a class result does not prevent member programs from also being r-class, e-class, or s-class.

7. Assignment

Consider `.coord` defined

```
.coord = .coordinate.new
```

That is an example of assignment. A new instance of class `coordinate` is created and assigned to `.coord`. In the same way,

```
.coord2 = .coord
```

is another example of assignment. A copy of `.coord` is made and assigned to `.coord2`.

Assignment is not allowed just with top-level names. The following are also valid examples of assignment:

```
.coord.x = 2
.li.c0 = .coord
.li.c0.x = 2+2
.todo.name = "Jane Smith"
.todo.n = 2
.todo.list[1] = "Turn in report"
.todo.list[2] = .li.c0
```

In each case, what appears on the right is evaluated, and a copy is put into the specified place. Assignment based on the returned value of a program is also allowed, so the following are also valid:

```
.coord.x = .li.length
.li.c0 = .li.midpoint
```

`.length` and `.midpoint` are member programs of `line.class`, and `.li` is an instance of `line`. In the first example, `.li.length` returns a `double`, and that `double` is assigned to `.coord.x`. In the second example, `.li.midpoint` returns a `coordinate`, and that `coordinate` is assigned to `li.c0`.

Also allowed would be

```
.todo.list[3] = .color.cvalue, color(green)
.todo.list = {"Turn in report", .li.c0, [.color.cvalue, color(green)]}
```

In both examples, the result of running `.color.cvalue, color(green)` is assigned to the third array element of `.todo.list`.

7.1 Type matching

All the examples above are valid because either a new identifier is being created or the identifier previously existed and was of the same type as the identifier being assigned.

For example, the following would be invalid:

```
.newthing = 2           // valid so far . . .
.newthing = "new"       // . . . invalid
```

The first line is valid because `.newthing` did not previously exist. After the first assignment, however, `.newthing` did exist and was of type `double`. That caused the second assignment to be invalid, the error being "type mismatch"; r(109).

The following are also invalid:

```
.coord.x = .li.midpoint
.li.c0 = .li.length
```

They are invalid because `.li.midpoint` returns a `coordinate`, and `.coord.x` is a `double`, and because `.li.length` returns a `double`, and `.li.c0` is a `coordinate`.

7.2 Arrays and array elements

The statements

```
.todo.list[1] = "Turn in report"
.todo.list[2] = .li.c0
.todo.list[3] = .color.cvalue, color(green)
```

and

```
.todo.list = {"Turn in report", .li.c0, [.color.cvalue, color(green)]}
```

do not have the same effect. The first set of statements reassigns elements 1, 2, and 3 and leaves any other defined elements unchanged. The second statement replaces the entire array with an array that has only elements 1, 2, and 3 defined.

After an element has been assigned, it may be unassigned (cleared) using `.Arrdropel`. For example, to unassign `.todo.list[1]`, you would type

```
.todo.list[1].Arrdropel
```

Clearing an element does not affect the other elements of the array. In the above example, `.todo.list[2]` and `.todo.list[3]` continue to exist.

New and existing elements may be assigned and reassigned freely, except that if an array element already exists, it may be reassigned only to something of the same type.

```
.todo.list[2] = .coordinate[2]
```

would be allowed, but

```
.todo.list[2] = "Clear the coordinate"
```

would not be allowed because .todo.list[2] is a coordinate and "Clear the coordinate" is a string. If you wish to reassign an array element to a different type, you first drop the existing array element and then assign it.

```
.todo.list[2].Arrdropel
.todo.list[2] = "Clear the coordinate"
```

7.3 lvalues and rvalues

Notwithstanding everything that has been said, the syntax for assignment is

lvalue = *rvalue*

lvalue stands for what may appear to the left of the equal sign, and *rvalue* stands for what may appear to the right.

The syntax for specifying an *lvalue* is

$.id\big[.id\big[\dots\big]\big]$

where *id* is either a *name* or *name*[*exp*], the latter being the syntax for specifying an array element, and *exp* must evaluate to a number; if *exp* evaluates to a noninteger number, it is truncated.

Also an *lvalue* must be assignable, meaning that *lvalue* cannot refer to a member program; i.e., an *id* element of *lvalue* cannot be a program name. (In an *rvalue*, if a program name is specified, it must be in the last *id*.)

The syntax for specifying an *rvalue* is any of the following:

$"\big[string\big]"$

$`"\big[string\big]"'$

#

exp

(*exp*)

$.id\big[.id\big[\dots\big]\big]$ $\big[program\_arguments\big]$

{}

$\{el\big[,el\big[,\dots\big]\big]\}$

The last two syntaxes concern assignment to arrays, and *el* may be any of the following:

nothing

$"\big[string\big]"$

$`"\big[string\big]"'$

#

(*exp*)

$.id\big[.id\big[\dots\big]\big]$

$[.id\big[.id\big[\dots\big]\big]\ \big[program\_arguments\big]]$

Let's consider each of the syntaxes for an *rvalue* in turn:

$"\big[string\big]"$ and $`"\big[string\big]"'$

> If the *rvalue* begins with a double quote (simple or compound), a string containing *string* will be returned. *string* may be long—up to the length of a macro.

#

If the *rvalue* is a number excluding missing values ., .a, ..., and .z, a double equal to the number specified will be returned.

exp and (*exp*)

If the *rvalue* is an expression, the expression will be evaluated and the result returned. A double will be returned if the expression returns a numeric result and a string will be returned if expression returns a string. Expressions returning matrices are not allowed.

The expression need not be enclosed in parentheses if the expression does not begin with simple or compound double quotes and does not begin with a period followed by nothing or a letter. In the cases just mentioned, the expression must be enclosed in parentheses. All expressions may be enclosed in parentheses.

An implication of the above is that missing value literals must be enclosed in parentheses: *lvalue* = (.).

.*id*[.*id*[...]] [*program_arguments*]

If the *rvalue* begins with a period, it is interpreted as an object reference. The object is evaluated and returned. .*id*[.*id*[...]] may refer to a member variable or a member program.

If .*id*[.*id*[...]] refers to a member variable, the value of the variable will be returned.

If .*id*[.*id*[...]] refers to a member program, the program will be executed and the result returned. If the member program returns nothing, a string containing "" (nothing) will be returned.

If .*id*[.*id*[...]] refers to a member program, arguments may be specified following the program name.

{} and {*el*[,*el*[,...]]}

If the *rvalue* begins with an open brace, an array will be returned.

If the *rvalue* is {}, an empty array will be returned.

If the *rvalue* is {*el*[,*el*[,...]]}, an array containing the specified elements will be returned.

If an *el* is nothing, the corresponding array element will be left undefined.

If an *el* is "[*string*]" or '"[*string*]"', the corresponding array element will be defined as a string containing *string*.

If an *el* is # excluding missing values ., .a, ..., .z, the corresponding array element will be defined as a double containing the number specified.

If an *el* is (*exp*), the expression is evaluated, and the corresponding array element will be defined as a double if the expression returns a numeric result or as a string if the expression returns a string. Expressions returning matrices are not allowed.

If an *el* is .*id*[.*id*[...]] or [.*id*[.*id*[...]] [*program_arguments*]], the object is evaluated, and the corresponding array element will be defined according to what was returned. If the object is a member program and arguments need to be specified, the *el* must be enclosed in square brackets.

Recursive array definitions are not allowed.

Finally, in *4.3 Specifying initialization*—where we discussed member variable initialization—what actually appears to the right of the equal sign is an *rvalue*, and everything just said applies. The previous discussion was incomplete.

7.4 Assignment of reference

Consider two different identifiers, $.a.b.c$ and $.d.e$, that are of the same type. For example, perhaps both are `doubles` or both are `coordinates`. When you type

$.a.b.c$ = $.d.e$

the result is to copy the values of $.d.e$ into $.a.b.c$. If you type

$.a.b.c$.`ref` = $.d.e$.`ref`

the result is to make $.a.b.c$ and $.d.e$ be the same object. That is, if you were later to change some element of $.d.e$, the corresponding element of $.a.b.c$ would change, and vice versa.

To understand this, think of member values as each being written on an index card. Each instance of a class has its own collection of cards (assuming no classwide variables). When you type

$.a.b.c$.`ref` = $.d.e$.`ref`

the card for $.a.b.c$ is removed and a note is substituted that says to use the card for $.d.e$. Thus both $.a.b.c$ and $.d.e$ become literally the same object.

More than one object can share references. If we were now to code

$.i$.`ref` = $.a.b.c$.`ref`

or

$.i$.`ref` = $.d.e$.`ref`

the result would be the same: $.i$ would also share the already-shared object.

We now have $.a.b.c$, $.d.e$, and $.i$ all being the same object. Say that we want to make $.d.e$ into its own unique object again. We type

$.d.e$.`ref` = *anything evaluating to the right type not ending in* `.ref`

We could, for instance, type any of the following:

$.d.e$.`ref` = *.classname*.`new`
$.d.e$.`ref` = *.j.k*
$.d.e$.`ref` = $.d.e$

All the above will make $.d.e$ unique because what is returned on the right is a copy. The last of the three examples is intriguing because it results in $.d.e$ not changing its values but becoming once again unique.

8. Built-ins

`.new` and `.ref` are examples of built-in member programs that are included in every class. There are other built-ins as well.

Built-ins may be used on any object except programs and other built-ins. Let $.B$ refer to a built-in. Then

- If $.a.b.myprog$ refers to a program, $.a.b.myprog.B$ is an error (and, in fact, $.a.b.myprog.anything$ is also an error).

- $.a.b.B.anything$ is an error.

Built-ins come in two forms: built-in functions and built-in modifiers. Built-in functions return information about the class or class instance on which they operate but do not modify the class or class instance. Built-in modifiers might return something—in general they do not—but they modify (change) the class or class instance.

Except for .new (and that was covered in *4.4 Specifying initialization 2, .new*), built-ins may not be redefined.

8.1 Built-in functions

In the documentation below, *object* refers to the context of the built-in function. For example, if .*a*.*b*.*F* is how the built-in function .*F* was invoked, then .*a*.*b* is the object on which it operates.

The built-in functions are

.new

returns a new instance of *object*. .new may be used whether the *object* is a class name or an instance, although it is most usually used with a class name. For example, if coordinate is a class, .coordinate.new returns a new instance of coordinate.

If .new is used with an instance, a new instance of the class of the object is returned; the current instance is not modified. For example, if .*a*.*b* is an instance of coordinate, then .*a*.*b*.new does exactly what .coordinate.new would do; .*a*.*b* is not modified in any way.

If you define your own .new program, it is run after the built-in .new is run.

.copy

returns a new instance—a copy—of *object*, which must be an instance. .copy returns a new object that is a copy of the original.

.ref

returns a reference to the object. See *7.4 Assignment of reference.*

.objtype

returns a string indicating the type of *object*. Returned is one of "double", "string", "array", or "*classname*".

.isa

returns a string indicating the category of *object*. Returned is one of "double", "string", "array", "class", or "classtype". "classtype" is returned when *object* is a class definition; "class" is returned when the object is an instance of a class *(sic)*.

.classname

returns a string indicating the name of the class. Returned is "*classname*" or, if *object* is of type double, string, or array, returned is "".

.isofclass *classname*

returns a double. Returns 1 if *object* is of class type *classname* and 0 otherwise. To be of a class type, *object* must be an instance of *classname*, inherited from the class *classname*, or inherited from a class that inherits anywhere along its inheritance path from *classname*.

.objkey

returns a string that can be used to reference an object outside the implied context. See *12.1 Keys.*

.uname

returns a string that can be used as a *name* throughout Stata that corresponds to the object. See *12.2 Unames.*

`.ref_n`
> returns a double. Returned is the total number of identifiers sharing *object*. Returned is 1 if the object is unshared. See *7.4 Assignment of reference*.

`.arrnels`
> returns a double. `.arrnels` is for use with `arrays`; it returns the largest index of the array that has been assigned data. If *object* is not an array, it returns an error.

`.arrindexof "string"`
> returns a double. `.arrindexof` is for use with `arrays`; it searches the array for the first element equal to *string* and returns the index of that element. If *string* is not found, `.arrindexof` returns 0. If *object* is not an array, it returns an error.

`.classmv`
> returns an `array` containing the `.refs` of each classwide member variable in *object*. See *12.3 Arrays of member variables*.

`.instancemv`
> returns an `array` containing the `.refs` of each instance-specific member variable in *object*. See *12.3 Arrays of member variables*.

`.dynamicmv`
> returns an `array` containing the `.refs` of each dynamically allocated member variable in *object*. See *12.3 Arrays of member variables*.

`.superclass`
> returns an `array` containing the `.refs` of each of the classes from which the specified object inherited. See *12.3 Arrays of member variables*.

8.2 Built-in modifiers

Modifiers are built-ins that change the object to which they are applied. All built-in modifiers have names beginning with a capital letter. The built-in modifiers are

`.Declare` *declarator*
> returns nothing. `.Declare` may be used only when *object* is a class instance. `.Declare` adds the specified new member variable to the class instance. See *4.7 Adding dynamically*.

`.Arrdropel #`
> returns nothing. `.Arrdropel` may be used only with array elements. `.Arrdropel` drops the specified array element, making it as if it was never defined. `.arrnels` is, of course, updated. See *7.2 Arrays and array elements*.

`.Arrdropall`
> returns nothing. `.Arrdropall` may be used only with `arrays`. `.Arrdropall` drops all elements of an array. `.Arrdropall` is the same as *.arrayname* = {}. If *object* is not an array, `.Arrdropall` returns an error.

`.Arrpop`
> returns nothing. `.Arrpop` may be used only with `arrays`. `.Arrpop` finds the top element of an array (largest index) and removes it from the array. To access the top element before popping, use *.arrayname*[`'.arrayname.arrnels'`]. If *object* is not an array, `.Arrpop` returns an error.

`.Arrpush "string"`
> returns nothing. `.Arrpush` may be used only with `arrays`. `.Arrpush` pushes *string* onto the end of the array, where end is defined as `.arrnels`+1. If *object* is not an array, `.Arrpush` returns an error.

9. Prefix operators

There are three prefix operators:

```
.Global
.Local
.Super
```

Prefix operators determine how object names such as *.a*, *.a.b*, *.a.b.c*, ... are resolved.

Consider a program invoked by typing .alpha.myprog. In program .myprog, any lines such as

```
.a = .b
```

are interpreted according to the implied context, if that is possible. .a is interpreted to mean .alpha.a if .a exists in .alpha; otherwise, it is taken to mean .a in the global context, meaning that it is taken to mean just .a. Similarly, .b is taken to mean .alpha.b if .b exists in .alpha; otherwise, it is taken to mean .b.

What if .myprog wants .a to be interpreted in the global context even if .a exists in .alpha? Then the code would read

```
.Global.a = .b
```

If instead .myprog wanted .b to be interpreted in the global context (and .a to be interpreted in the implied context), the code would read

```
.a = .Global.b
```

Obviously, if the program wanted both to be interpreted in the global context, the code would read

```
.Global.a = .Global.b
```

.Local is the reverse of .Global: it ensures that the object reference is interpreted in the implied context. .Local is rarely specified because the local context is searched first, but if there is a circumstance where you wish to be certain that the object is not found in the global context, you may specify its reference preceded by .Local. Understand, however, that if the object is not found, an error will result, so you would need to precede commands containing such references with capture; see [P] **capture**.

In fact, if it is used at all, .Local is nearly always used in a macro-substitution context—something discussed in the next section—where errors are suppressed and where nothing is substituted when errors occur. Thus in advanced code, if you were trying to determine whether member variable .addedvar exists in the local context, you could code

```
if "`Local.addedvar.objtype'" == "" {
                /* it does not exist */
}
else {
                /* it does */
}
```

The .Super prefix is used only in front of program names and concerns inheritance when one program occults another. This was discussed in *5. Inheritance*.

10. Using object values

We have discussed definition and assignment of objects, but we have not yet discussed how you might use class objects in a program. How do you refer to their values in a program? How do you find out what a value is, skip some code if the value is one thing, and loop if it is another?

The most common way to refer to objects (and the returned results of member programs) is through macro substitution; for example,

```
local x = '.li.c0.x'
local clr "'.color.cvalue, color(green)'"
scalar len = '.coord.length'
forvalues i=1(1)'.todo.n' {
            Mysub "'todo.list['i']'"
}
```

When a class object is quoted, its printable form is substituted. This is defined as

Object type	Printable form
string	contents of the string
double	number printed using %18.0g, spaces stripped
array	nothing
classname	nothing or, if member program .macroexpand is defined, then string or double returned

Any object may be quoted, including programs. If the program takes arguments, they are included inside the quotes:

```
scalar len = '.coord.length'
local clr "'.color.cvalue, color(green)'"
```

If the quoted reference results in an error, the error message is suppressed, and nothing is substituted.

Similarly, if a class instance is quoted—or a program returning a class instance is quoted—nothing is substituted. That is, nothing is substituted, assuming that the member program .macroexpand has not been defined for the class, as is usually the case. If .macroexpand has been defined, however, it is executed, and what macroexpand returns—which may be a string or a double—is substituted.

For example, say that we wanted to make all objects of type coordinate substitute (#,#) when they were quoted. In the class definition for coordinate, we could define .macroexpand,

(Continued on next page)

————————————————————————————————— begin `coordinate.class` ————————

```
version 11
class coordinate {
            [ declaration of member variables omitted ]
        }
[ definitions of class programs omitted ]
program .macroexpand
                local tosub : display "(" '.x' "," '.y' ")"
                class exit "'tosub'"
end
```

————————————————————————————————— end `coordinate.class` ————————

---

and now `coordinates` will be substituted. Say that `.mycoord` is a `coordinate` currently set to (2,3). If we did not include `.macroexpand` in the `coordinate.class` file, typing

> ... '`.mycoord`'...

would not be an error but would merely result in

> · · · · · ·

Having defined `.macroexpand`, it will result in

> ... (2,3)...

A `.macroexpand` member function is intended as a utility for returning the printable form of a class instance and nothing more. In fact, the class system prevents unintended corruption of class-member variables by making a copy, returning the printable form, and then destroying the copy. These steps ensure that implicitly calling `.macroexpand` has no side effects on the class instance.

11. Object destruction

To create an instance of a class, you type

> `.name` = `.classname`.`new` [*arguments*]

To destroy the resulting object and thus release the memory associated with it, you type

> `classutil drop` `.name`

(See [P] **classutil** for more information on the `classutil` command.) You can drop only top-level instances. Objects deeper than that are dropped when the higher-level object containing them is dropped, and classes are automatically dropped when the last instance of the class is dropped.

Also any top-level object named with a name obtained from `tempname`—see [P] **macro**—is automatically dropped when the program concludes. Even so, `tempname` objects may be returned by `class exit`. The following is valid:

```
program .tension
                ...
                tempname a b
                .'a' = .bubble.new
                .'b' = .bubble.new
                ...
                class exit .'a'
end
```

The program creates two new class instances of `bubbles` in the global context, both with temporary names. We can be assured that .'a' and .'b' are global because the names 'a' and 'b' were obtained from `tempname` and therefore cannot already exist in whatever context in which .`tension` runs. Therefore, when the program ends, .'a' and .'b' will be automatically dropped. Even so, .`tension` can return .'a'. It can do that because, at the time `class exit` is executed, the program has not yet concluded and .'a' still exists. You can even code

```
program .tension
                ...
                tempname a b
                .'a' = .bubble.new
                .'b' = .bubble.new
                ...
                class exit .'a'.ref
        end
```

and that also will return .a and, in fact, will be faster because no extra copy will be made. This form is recommended when returning an object stored in a temporary name. Do not, however, add .`refs` on the end of "real" (nontemporary) objects being returned because then you would be returning not just the same values as in the real object but the object itself.

You can clear the entire class system by typing `discard`; see [P] **discard**. There is no `classutil drop _all` command: Stata's graphics system also uses the class system, and dropping all the class definitions and instances would cause `graph` difficulty. `discard` also clears all open graphs, so the disappearance of class definitions and instances causes `graph` no difficulty.

During the development of class-based systems, you should type `discard` whenever you make a change to any part of the system, no matter how minor or how certain you are that no instances of the definition modified yet exist.

12. Advanced topics

12.1 Keys

The .`objkey` built-in function returns a `string` called a key that can be used to reference the object as an *rvalue* but not as an *lvalue*. This would typically be used in

```
local k = '.a.b.objkey'
```

or

```
.c.k = .a.b.objkey
```

where .c.k is a `string`. Thus the keys stored could be then used as follows:

.d = .'k'.x	meaning to assign .a.b.x to .d
.d = .'.c.k'.x	(same)
local z = '.'k'.x'	meaning to put value of .a.b.x in 'z'
local z = '.'.c.k'.x'	(same)

It does not matter if the key is stored in a macro or a string member variable—it can be used equally well—and you always use the key by macro quoting.

A key is a special string that stands for the object. Why not, you wonder, simply type .a.b rather than .'.c.k' or .'k'? The answer has to do with implied context.

Pretend that .myvar.bin.myprogram runs .myprogram. Obviously, it runs .myprogram in the context .myvar.bin. Thus .myprogram can include lines such as

    .x = 5

and that is understood to mean that .myvar.bin.x is to be set to 5. .myprogram, however, might also include a line that reads

    .Global.utility.setup '.x.objkey'

Here .myprogram is calling a utility that runs in a different context (namely, .utility), but myprogram needs to pass .x—of whatever type it might be—to the utility as an argument. Perhaps .x is a coordinate, and .utility.setup expects to receive the identifier of a coordinate as its argument. .myprogram, however, does not know that .myvar.bin.x is the full name of .x, which is what .utility.setup will need, so .myprogram passes '.x.objkey'. Program .utility.setup can use what it receives as its argument just as if it contained .myvar.bin.x, except that .utility.setup cannot use that received reference on the left-hand side of an assignment.

If myprogram needed to pass to .utility.setup a reference to the entire implied context (.myvar.bin), the line would read

    .Global.utility.setup '.objkey'

because .objkey by itself means to return the key of the implied context.

12.2 Unames

The built-in function .uname returns a *name* that can be used throughout Stata that uniquely corresponds to the object. The mapping is one way. Unames can be obtained for objects, but the original object's name cannot be obtained from the uname.

Pretend that you have object .$a.b.c$, and you wish to obtain a name you can associate with that object because you want to create a variable in the current dataset, or a value label, or whatever else, to go along with the object. Later, you want to be able to reobtain that name from the object's name. .$a.b.c$.uname will provide that name. The name will be ugly, but it will be unique. The name is not temporary: you must drop whatever you create with the name later.

Unames are, in fact, based on the object's .ref. That is, consider two objects, .$a.b.c$ and .$d.e$, and pretend that they refer to the same data; i.e., you have previously executed

    .$a.b.c$.ref = .$d.e$.ref

    or

    .$d.e$.ref = .$a.b.c$.ref

Then .$a.b.c$.uname will equal .$d.e$.uname. The names returned are unique to the data being recorded, not the identifiers used to arrive to the data.

As an example of use, within Stata's graphics system sersets are used to hold the data behind a graph; see [P] **serset**. An overall graph might consist of several graphs. In the object nesting for a graph, each individual graph has its own object holding a serset for its use. The individual objects, however, are shared when the same serset will work for two or more graphs, so that the same data are not recorded again and again. That is accomplished by simply setting their .refs equal. Much later in the graphics code, when that code is writing a graph out to disk for saving, it needs to figure out which sersets need to be saved, and it does not wish to write shared sersets out multiple times. Stata finds out what sersets are shared by looking at their unames and, in fact, uses the unames to help it keep track of which sersets go with which graph.

12.3 Arrays of member variables

Note: The following functions are of little use in class programming. They are of use to those writing utilities to describe the contents of the class system, such as the features documented in [P] **classutil**.

The built-in functions .classmv, .instancemv, and .dynamicmv each return an array containing the .refs of each classwide, instance-specific, and dynamically declared member variables. These array elements may be used as either *lvalues* or *rvalues*.

.superclass also returns an array containing .refs, these being references to the classes from which the current object inherited. These array elements may be used as *rvalues* but should not be used as lvalues because they refer to underlying class definitions themselves.

.classmv, .instancemv, .dynamicmv, and .superclass, although documented as built-in functions, are not really functions, but instead are built-in member variables. This means that, unlike built-in functions, their references may be followed by other built-in functions, and it is not an error to type, for instance,

        ... .li.instancemv.arrnels ...

and it would be odd (but allowed) to type

        .myarray = .li.instancemv

It would be odd simply because there is no reason to copy them because you can use them in place.

Each of the above member functions are a little sloppy in that they return nothing (produce an error) if there are no classwide, instance-specific, and dynamically declared member variables, or no inherited classes. This sloppiness has to do with system efficiency, and the proper way to work around the sloppiness is to obtain the number of elements in each array as 0'.classmv.arrnels', 0'.instancemv.arrnels', 0'.dynamicmv.arrnels', and 0'.superclass.arrnels'. If an array does not exist, then nothing will be substituted, and you will still be left with the result 0.

For example, assume that .my.c is of type coordinate2, defined as

──────────────────────────────────── begin coordinate2.class ────────────

```
version 11
class coordinate2 {
            classwide:
                    double x_origin = 0
                    double y_origin = 0
            instancespecific:
                    double x = 0
                    double y = 0
}
```

──────────────────────────────────── end coordinate2.class ────────────

Then

referring to ...	is equivalent to referring to ...
.my.c.classmv[1]	.my.c.c.x_origin
.my.c.classmv[2]	.my.c.c.y_origin
.my.c.instancemv[1]	.my.c.c.x
.my.c.instancemv[2]	.my.c.c.y

If any member variables were added dynamically using .Dynamic, they could equally well be accessed via .my.c.dynamicmv[] or their names. Either of the above could be used on the left or right of an assignment.

If coordinate2.class inherited from another class (it does not), referring to .coordinate2.superclass[1] would be equivalent to referring to the inherited class; .coordinate2.superclass[1].new, for instance, would be allowed.

These "functions" are mainly of interest to those writing utilities to act on class instances as a general structure.

Appendix A. Finding, loading, and clearing class definitions

The definition for class *xyz* is located in file *xyz*.class.

Stata looks for *xyz*.class along the ado-path in the same way that it looks for ado-files; see [U] **17.5 Where does Stata look for ado-files?** and see [P] **sysdir**.

Class definitions are loaded automatically, as they are needed, and are cleared from memory as they fall into disuse.

When you type discard, all class definitions and all existing instances of classes are dropped; see [P] **discard**.

Appendix B. Jargon

built-in: a member program that is automatically defined, such as .new. A **built-in function** is a member program that returns a result without changing the object on which it was run. A **built-in modifier** is a member program that changes the object on which it was run and might return a result as well.

class: a name for which there is a class definition. If we say that coordinate is a class, then *coordinate*.class is the name of the file that contains its definition.

class instance: a "variable"; a specific, named copy (instance) of a class with its member values filled in; an identifier that is defined to be of *type classname*.

classwide variable: a member variable that is shared by all instances of a class. Its alternative is an instance-specific variable.

inheritance: the ability to define a class in terms of one (single inheritance) or more (multiple inheritance) existing classes. The existing class is typically called the base or super class, and by default, the new class inherits all the member variables and member programs of the base class.

identifier: the name by which an object is identified, such as .mybox or .mybox.x.

implied context: the instance on which a member program is run. For example, in .*a*.*b*.myprog, .*a*.*b* is the implied context, and any references to, say, .*x* within the program, are first assumed to, in fact, be references to .*a*.*b*.*x*.

instance: a class instance.

instance-specific variable: a member variable that is unique to each instance of a class; each instance has its own copy of the member variable. Its alternative is a classwide variable.

lvalue: an identifier that may appear to the left of the = assignment operator.

member program: a program that is a member of a class or of an instance.

member variable: a variable that is a member of a class or of an instance.

object: a class or an instance; this is usually a synonym for an instance, but in formal syntax definitions, if something is said to be allowed to be used with an object, that means it may be used with a class or with an instance.

polymorphism: when a system allows the same program name to invoke different programs according to the class of the object. For example, `.draw` might invoke one program when used on a star object, `.mystar.draw`, and a different program when used on a box object, `.mybox.draw`.

reference: most often the word is used according to its English-language definition, but a `.ref` reference can be used to obtain the data associated with an object. If two identifiers have the same reference, then they are the same object.

return value: what an object returns, which might be of type `double`, `string`, `array`, or *classname*. Generally, return value is used in discussions of member programs, but all objects have a return value; they typically return a copy of themselves.

rvalue: an identifier that may appear to the right of the = assignment operator.

scope: how it is determined to what object an identifier references. `.a.b` might be interpreted in the global context and literally mean `.a.b`, or it might be interpreted in an implied context to mean `.impliedcontext.a.b`.

shared object: an object to which two or more different identifiers refer.

type: the type of a member variable or of a return value, which is `double`, `string`, `array`, or *classnam*.

Appendix C. Syntax diagrams

Appendix C.1 Class declaration

class $[newclassname]$ {

   $[\underline{\text{class}}\text{wide:}]$

      $[type\ mvname\ [= rvalue]]$

      $[mvname = rvalue]$

      $[\ldots]$

   $[\underline{\text{instance}}\text{specific:}]$

      $[type\ mvname\ [= rvalue]]$

      $[mvname = rvalue\ ]$

      $[\ldots]$

} $[,\ \text{inherit}(classnamelist)]$

where

   mvname stands for member variable name;

   rvalue is defined in *Appendix C.2 Assignment*; and

   type is $\{classname \mid \text{double} \mid \text{string} \mid \text{array}\}$.

The .Declare built-in may be used to add a member variable to an existing class instance,

> .*id*[.*id*[...]] .Declare *type newmvname* [= *rvalue*]
>
> .*id*[.*id*[...]] .Declare *newmvname* = *rvalue*

where *id* is {*name* | *name*[*exp*]}, the latter being how you refer to an array element; *exp* must evaluate to a number. If *exp* evaluates to a noninteger number, it is truncated.

Appendix C.2 Assignment

> *lvalue* = *rvalue*
>
> *lvalue*.ref = *lvalue*.ref   (*sic*)
>
> *lvalue*.ref = *rvalue*

where

> *lvalue* is .*id*[.*id*[...]]
>
> *rvalue* is
>
> > "[*string*]"
> >
> > '"[*string*]"'
> >
> > #
> >
> > *exp*
> >
> > (*exp*)
> >
> > .*id*[.*id*[...]]
> >
> > [.*id*[.*id*[...]]].*pgmname* [*pgm_arguments*]
> >
> > [.*id*[.*id*[...]]].Super[(*classname*)].*pgmname* [*pgm_arguments*]
> >
> > {}
> >
> > {*el* [,*el* [,...]]}

The last two syntaxes concern assignment to arrays; *el* may be

> > *nothing*
> >
> > "[*string*]"
> >
> > '"[*string*]"'
> >
> > #
> >
> > (*exp*)
> >
> > .*id*[.*id*[...]]
> >
> > [.*id*[.*id*[...]]].*pgmname*
> >
> > [[.*id*[.*id*[...]]].*pgmname* [*pgm_arguments*]]
> >
> > [[.*id*[.*id*[...]]].Super[(*classname*)].*pgmname* [*pgm_arguments*]]

id is {*name* | *name*[*exp*]}, the latter being how you refer to an array element; *exp* must evaluate to a number. If *exp* evaluates to a noninteger number, it is truncated.

Appendix C.3 Macro substitution

Values of member variables or values returned by member programs can be substituted in any Stata command line in any context using macro quoting. The syntax is

... ` .id[.id[...]] '...

... ` [.id[.id[...]]] .pgmname '...

... ` [.id[.id[...]]] .pgmname pgm_arguments '...

... ` [.id[.id[...]]] .Super[(classname)] .pgmname '...

... ` [.id[.id[...]]] .Super[(classname)] .pgmname pgm_arguments '...

Nested substitutions are allowed. For example,

... ` . `tmpname'.x '...

... ` `ref' '...

In the above, perhaps local tmpname was obtained from tempname, and perhaps local ref contains `` .myobj.cvalue ''.

When a class object is quoted, its printable form is substituted. This is defined as

Object type	Printable form
string	contents of the string
double	number printed using %18.0g, spaces stripped
array	nothing
classname	nothing or, if member program .macroexpand is defined, then string or double returned

If the quoted reference results in an error, the error message is suppressed and nothing is substituted.

Appendix C.4 Quick summary of built-ins

Built-ins come in two forms: 1) built-in functions—built-ins that return a result but do not change the object on which they are run, and 2) built-in modifiers—built-ins that might return a result but more importantly modify the object on which they are run.

(Continued on next page)

Built-in functions (may be used as *rvalues*)

.object.id	creates new instance of *.object*
.instance.copy	makes a copy of *.instance*
.instance.ref	for use in assignment by reference
.object.objtype	returns "double", "string", "array", or "*classname*"
.object.isa	returns "double", "string", "array", "class", or "classtype"
.object.classname	returns "*classname*" or ""
.object.isofclass *classname*	returns 1 if *.object* is of class type *classname*
.object.objkey	returns a string that can be used to refer to an object outside the implied context
.object.uname	returns a string that can be used as *name* throughout Stata; *name* corresponds to *.object*'s .ref.
.object.ref_n	returns number (double) of total number of identifiers sharing object
.array.arrnels	returns number (double) corresponding to largest index of the array assigned
.array.arrindexof "*string*"	searches array for first element equal to *string* and returns the index (double) of element or returns 0
.object.classmv	returns array containing the .refs of each classwide member of *.object*
.object.instancemv	returns array containing the .refs of each instance-specific member of *.object*
.object.dynamicmv	returns array containing the .refs of each dynamically added member of *.object*
.object.superclass	returns array containing the .refs of each of the classes from which *.object* inherited

Built-in modifiers

.instance.Declare *declarator*	returns nothing; adds member variable to instance; see *Appendix C.1 Class declaration*
.array[*exp*].Arrdropel #	returns nothing; drops the specified array element
.array.Arrpop	returns nothing; finds the top element and removes it
.array.Arrpush "*string*"	returns nothing; adds string to end of array

Also see

[P] **class exit** — Exit class-member program and return result

[P] **classutil** — Class programming utility

[P] **sysdir** — Query and set system directories

[U] **17.5 Where does Stata look for ado-files?**

Title

| class exit — Exit class-member program and return result |

Syntax

```
class exit [ rvalue ]
```

where *rvalue* is

$$" \lceil string \rceil "$$
$$` " \lceil string \rceil " \text{'}$$
$$\#$$
$$exp$$
$$(exp)$$
$$.id \lceil .id \lceil \dots \rceil \rceil \quad \lceil program\_arguments \rceil$$
$$\{\}$$
$$\{el \lceil ,el \lceil ,\dots \rceil \rceil\}$$

See [P] **class** for more information on *rvalues*.

Description

`class exit` exits a class-member program and optionally returns the specified result.

`class exit` may be used only from class-member programs; see [P] **class**.

Remarks

Do not confuse returned values with return codes, which all Stata programs set, including member programs. Member programs exit when they execute.

condition	returned value	return code
class exit with arguments	as specified	0
class exit without arguments	nothing	0
exit without arguments	nothing	0
exit with arguments	nothing	as specified
error	nothing	as specified
command having error	nothing	as appropriate

Any of the preceding are valid ways of exiting a member program, although the last is perhaps best avoided. `class exit` without arguments has the same effect as `exit` without arguments; it does not matter which you use.

Examples

```
class exit sqrt((`.c0.y1'-`.c1.y0')^2 + (`.c0.y1'-`.c1.y0')^2)
class exit "`myresult'"
class exit (.)
class exit "true"
class exit { 'one', 'two'}
class exit .coord
class exit .coord.x
tempname a
...
class exit .'a'
```

Warning: Distinguish carefully between "class exit .a" and "class exit (.a)". The first returns a copy of the instance .a. The second returns a double equal to the extended missing value .a.

Also see

[P] **class** — Class programming

[P] **exit** — Exit from a program or do-file

[M-2] **class** — Classes

Title

| classutil — Class programming utility |

Syntax

Drop class instances from memory

    classutil drop *instance* [*instance* [...]]

Describe object

    classutil d̲escribe *object* [, r̲ecurse n̲ewok]

List all defined objects

    classutil dir [*pattern*] [, all d̲etail]

Display directory of available classes

    classutil cdir [*pattern*]

List .class file corresponding to classname

    classutil which *classname* [, all]

where

> *object*, *instance*, and *classname* may be specified with or without a leading period.
>
> *instance* and *object* are as defined in [P] **class**: *object* is an *instance* or a *classname*.
>
> *pattern* is as allowed with the strmatch() function: * means that 0 or more characters go here, and ? means that exactly one character goes here.

Command cutil is a synonym for classutil.

Description

If you have not yet read [P] **class**, please do so. classutil stands outside the class system and provides utilities for examining and manipulating what it contains.

classutil drop drops the specified top-level class instances from memory. To drop all class objects, type discard; see [P] **discard**.

classutil describe displays a description of an object.

classutil dir displays a list of all defined objects.

classutil cdir displays a directory of all classes available.

classutil which lists which .class file corresponds to the class specified.

61

Options for classutil describe

recurse specifies that classutil describe be repeated on any class instances or definitions that occur within the specified object. Consider the case where you type classutil describe .myobj, and myobj contains myobj.c0, which is a coordinate. Without the recurse option, you will be informed that myobj.c0 is a coordinate, and classutil describe will stop right there.

With the recurse option, you will be informed that myobj.c0 is a coordinate, and then classutil describe will proceed to describe .myobj.c0, just as if you had typed "classutil describe .myobj.c". If .myobj.c0 itself includes classes or class instances, they too will be described.

newok is relevant only when describing a class, although it is allowed—and ignored—at other times. newok allows classes to be described even when no instances of the class exist.

When asked to describe a class, Stata needs to access information about that class, and Stata knows the details about a class only when one or more instances of the class exist. If there are no instances, Stata is stuck—it does not know anything other than that a class of that name exists. newok specifies that, in such a circumstance, Stata may temporarily create an instance of the class by using .new. If Stata is not allowed to do this, then Stata cannot describe the class. The only reason you are being asked to specify newok is that in some complicated systems, running .new can have side effects, although in most complicated and well-written systems, that will not be the case.

Options for classutil dir

all specifies that class definitions (classes) be listed, as well as top-level instances.

detail specifies that a more detailed description of each of the top-level objects be provided. The default is simply to list the names of the objects in tabular form.

Option for classutil which

all specifies that classutil which list all files along the search path with the specified name, not just the first one (the one Stata will use).

Remarks

Remarks are presented under the following headings:

>*classutil drop*
>*classutil describe*
>*classutil dir*
>*classutil cdir*
>*classutil which*

classutil drop

classutil drop may be used only with top-level instances, meaning objects other than classes having names with no dots other than the leading dot. If .mycoord is of type coordinate (or of type double), it would be allowed to drop .mycoord but not coordinate (or double). Thus each of the following would be valid, assuming that each is not a class definition:

```
. classutil drop .this
. classutil drop .mycolor
. classutil drop .this .mycolor
```

The following would be invalid, assuming that `coordinate` is a class:

```
. classutil drop coordinate
```

There is no need to drop classes because they are automatically dropped when the last instance of them is dropped.

The following would not be allowed because they are not top-level objects:

```
. classutil drop .this.that
. classutil drop .mycolor.color.rgb[1]
```

Second-, third-, and higher-level objects are dropped when the top-level objects containing them are dropped.

In all the examples above, we have shown objects identified with leading periods, as is typical. The period may, however, be omitted.

```
. classutil drop this mycolor
```

❏ Technical note

Stata's graphics are implemented using classes. If you have a graph displayed, be careful not to drop objects that are not yours. If you drop a system object, Stata will not crash, but `graph` may produce some strange error messages. If you are starting a development project, it is best to `discard` (see [P] **discard**) before starting—that will eliminate all objects and clear any graphs. This way, the only objects defined will be the objects you have created.

❏

classutil describe

`classutil describe` presents a description of the object specified. The object may be a class or an instance and may be of any depth. The following are all valid:

```
. classutil describe coordinate
. classutil describe .this
. classutil describe .color.rgb
. classutil describe .color.rgb[1]
```

The object may be specified with or without a leading period; it makes no difference.

Also see above the descriptions of the `recurse` and `newok` options. The following would also be allowed:

```
. classutil describe coordinate, newok
. classutil describe line, recurse
. classutil describe line, recurse newok
```

classutil dir

classutil dir lists all top-level instances currently defined. Note the emphasis on instances: class definitions (*classes*) are not listed. classutil dir, all will list all objects, including the class definitions.

If the detail option is specified, a more detailed description is presented, but it is still less detailed than that provided by classutil describe.

pattern, if specified, is as defined for Stata's strmatch() function: * means that 0 or more characters go here, and ? means that exactly one character goes here. If *pattern* is specified, only top-level instances or objects matching the pattern will be listed. Examples include

```
. classutil dir
. classutil dir, detail
. classutil dir, detail all
. classutil dir c*
. classutil dir *_g, detail
```

classutil cdir

classutil cdir lists the available classes. Without arguments, all classes are listed. If *pattern* is specified, only classes matching the pattern are listed:

```
. classutil cdir
. classutil cdir c*
. classutil cdir coord*
. classutil cdir *_g
. classutil cdir color_?_?_*
```

pattern is as defined for Stata's strmatch() function: * means that 0 or more characters go here, and ? means that exactly one character goes here.

classutil cdir obtains the list by searching for *.class files along the ado-path; see [P] **sysdir**.

classutil which

classutil which identifies the .class file associated with class *classname* and displays lines from the file that begin with *!. For example,

```
. classutil which mycolortype
C:\ado\personal\mycolortype.class
*! version 1.0.1
. classutil which badclass
file "badclass.class" not found
r(611);
```

classutil which searches in the standard way for the .class files, i.e., by looking for them along the ado-path; see [P] **sysdir**.

With the all option, classutil which lists all files along the search path with the specified name, not just the first one found (the one Stata would use):

```
. classutil which mycolortype
C:\ado\personal\mycolortype.class
*! version 1.0.1
C:\ado\plus\m\mycolortype.class
*! version 1.0.0
```

*! lines have to do with versioning. * is one of Stata's comment markers, so *! lines are comment lines. *! is a convention that some programmers use to record version or author information. If there are no *! lines, then only the filename is listed.

Saved results

classutil drop returns nothing.

classutil describe returns macro r(type) containing double, string, *classname*, or array and returns r(bitype) containing the same, except that if r(type)=="*classname*", r(bitype) contains class or instance, depending on whether the object is the definition or an instance of the class.

classutil cdir returns in macro r(list) the names of the available classes matching the pattern specified. The names will not be preceded by a period.

classutil dir returns in macro r(list) the names of the top-level instances matching the pattern specified as currently defined in memory. The names will be preceded by a period if the corresponding object is an instance and will be unadorned if the corresponding object is a class definition.

classutil which without the all option returns in r(fn) the name of the file found; the name is not enclosed in quotes. With the all option, classutil which returns in r(fn) the names of all the files found, listed one after the other and each enclosed in quotes.

Methods and formulas

classutil is implemented as an ado-file.

Also see

[P] **class** — Class programming

Title

> **comments** — Add comments to programs

Description

This entry provides a quick reference for how to specify comments in programs. See [U] **16.1.2 Comments and blank lines in do-files** for more details.

Remarks

Comments may be added to programs in three ways:

- begin the line with *;
- begin the comment with //; or
- place the comment between /* and */ delimiters.

Here are examples of each:

```
* a sample analysis job
version 11
use census
/* obtain the summary statistics */
tabulate region  // there are 4 regions in this dataset
summarize marriage

* a sample analysis job
version 11
use /* obtain the summary statistics */ census
tabulate region
//  there are 4 regions in this dataset
summarize marriage
```

The comment indicator * may be used only at the beginning of a line, but it does have the advantage that it can be used interactively. * indicates that the line is to be ignored. The * comment indicator may not be used within Mata.

The // comment indicator may be used at the beginning or at the end of a line. However, if the // indicator is at the end of a line, it must be preceded by one or more blanks. That is, you cannot type the following:

```
tabulate region// there are 4 regions in this dataset
```

// indicates that the rest of the line is to be ignored.

The /* and */ comment delimiter has the advantage that it may be used in the middle of a line, but it is more cumbersome to type than the other two comment indicators. What appears inside /* */ is ignored.

❑ Technical note

There is a fourth comment indicator, ///, that instructs Stata to view from /// to the end of a line as a comment and to join the next line with the current line. For example,

```
args a          /// input parameter for a
     b          /// input parameter for b
     c          //  input parameter for c
```

is equivalent to

```
args a b c
```

/// is one way to make long lines more readable:

```
replace final_result =                      ///
       sqrt(first_side^2 + second_side^2)  ///
       if type == "rectangle"
```

Another popular method is

```
replace final_result =                      /*
       */ sqrt(first_side^2 + second_side^2)  /*
       */ if type == "rectangle"
```

Like the // comment indicator, the /// indicator must be preceded by one or more blanks.

❑

Also see

[P] **#delimit** — Change delimiter

[U] **16.1.2 Comments and blank lines in do-files**

[U] **18.11.2 Comments and long lines in ado-files**

Title

confirm — Argument verification

Syntax

<u>conf</u>irm <u>e</u>xistence *string*

<u>conf</u>irm [new] <u>f</u>ile *filename*

<u>conf</u>irm [numeric | <u>str</u>ing | date] <u>fo</u>rmat *string*

<u>conf</u>irm <u>name</u>s *names*

<u>conf</u>irm [integer] <u>n</u>umber *string*

<u>conf</u>irm <u>mat</u>rix *string*

<u>conf</u>irm <u>sca</u>lar *string*

<u>conf</u>irm [new | numeric | <u>str</u>ing | *type*] <u>v</u>ariable *varlist* [, <u>ex</u>act]

where *type* is { byte | int | long | float | double | str# }

Description

confirm verifies that the arguments following confirm ... are of the claimed type and issues the appropriate error message and nonzero return code if they are not.

Option

exact specifies that a match be declared only if the names specified in *varlist* match. By default, names that are abbreviations of variables are considered to be a match.

Remarks

Remarks are presented under the following headings:

> confirm *existence*
> confirm *file*
> confirm *format*
> confirm *names*
> confirm *number*
> confirm *matrix*
> confirm *scalar*
> confirm *variable*

confirm is useful in *do-files* and *programs* when you do not want to bother issuing your own error message. confirm can also be combined with capture to detect and handle error conditions before they arise; also see [P] **capture**.

68

confirm existence

confirm existence displays the message " '' found where something expected" and produces a return code of 6 if *string* does not exist.

confirm file

confirm file verifies that *filename* exists and is readable and issues the appropriate error message and return code if not.

confirm new file verifies that *filename* does not exist and that *filename* could be opened for writing, and issues the appropriate error message and return code if not.

The possible error messages and return codes are

Message	Return code
___ found where filename expected	7
file ___ not found	601
file ___ already exists	602
file ___ could not be opened	603

Return codes of 7 and 603 are possible for both confirm file and confirm new file. For confirm new file, a return code of 603 indicates that the filename is invalid, the specified directory does not exist, or the directory permissions do not allow you to create a new file. For instance, even if *filename* does not exist, confirm new file *newdir\newfile* will generate an error if *newdir* does not exist and if you do not have permissions to create a file in *newdir*. confirm new file *filename* will fail if you do not have adequate permissions to create a new file in the current working directory.

confirm format

confirm format verifies that *string* is a valid variable display format. It produces the message

'*string*' found where format expected

with a return code of 7 if the format is not valid. It produces the message

'' found where format expected

with a return code of 7 if the format is empty.

confirm numeric format specifies that the argument must be a valid numeric format. Valid numeric formats are general, fixed, and exponential. If not, it produces a return code of 7 and the message

'*string*' found where numeric format expected

or

'' found where numeric format expected

if *string* is empty.

confirm `string format` specifies that the argument must be a valid string format. If not, it produces a return code of 7 and the message

> *'string'* `found where string format expected`

or

> `'' found where string format expected`

if *string* is empty.

confirm `date format` specifies that the argument must be a valid date format. If not, it produces a return code of 7 and the message

> *'string'* `found where date format expected`

or

> `'' found where date format expected`

if *string* is empty.

confirm names

confirm `names` verifies that the argument or arguments are valid names according to Stata's naming conventions. It produces the message

> {*name* | `nothing`} `invalid name`

with a return code of 7 if the names are not valid.

confirm number

confirm `number` verifies that the argument can be interpreted as a number, such as `1`, `5.2`, `-5.2`, or `2.5e+10`. It produces the message

> {*string* | `nothing`} `found where number expected`

with a return code of 7 if not.

confirm `integer number` specifies that the argument must be an integer, such as 1 or 2.5e+10, but not 5.2 or −5.2. If not, it produces a return code of 7 and a slight variation on the message above:

> {*string* | `nothing`} `found where integer expected`

confirm matrix

`confirm matrix` verifies that *string* is a matrix. It produces the message

`matrix` *string* `not found`

with a return code of 111 if *string* is not a matrix.

confirm scalar

`confirm scalar` verifies that *string* is a scalar. It produces the message

`scalar` *string* `not found`

with a return code of 111 if *string* is not a scalar.

confirm variable

`confirm variable` verifies that *varlist* can be interpreted as an existing varlist of any types of variables. If not, the appropriate error message and nonzero return code are returned:

Message	Return code
___ found where numeric variable expected	7
___ found where string variable expected	7
no variables defined	111
variable ___ not found	111
___ invalid name	198

`confirm numeric variable` specifies that all the variables are numeric. If the variable exists but is not numeric, Stata displays the message

`'`*varname*`' found where numeric variable expected`

or

`'' found where numeric variable expected`

with a return code of 7 if *varlist* is not specified.

`confirm string variable` specifies that all the variables are strings. If the variable exists but is not a string variable, Stata displays the message

`'`*varname*`' found where string variable expected`

or

`'' found where string variable expected`

with a return code of 7 if *varlist* is not specified.

`confirm` *type* `variable` specifies that all variables are of the indicated storage type. For instance, `confirm int variable myvar` or `confirm float variable myvar thatvar`. As with `confirm string variable`, the appropriate message and return code of 7 are possible.

confirm new variable verifies that *varlist* can be interpreted as a new varlist. The possible messages and return codes are

Message	Return code
____ found where varname expected	7
____ already defined	110
____ invalid name	198

> ## Example 1

confirm is a cheap way to include minimal syntax checking in your programs. For instance, you have written a program that is supposed to take a one-integer argument. Although you do not have to include any syntax checking at all—the program will probably fail with some error if the argument is incorrect—it is safer to add one line at the top of the program:

```
confirm integer number '1'
```

Now if the first argument is not an integer, you will get a reasonable error message, and the program will stop automatically.

◁

> ## Example 2

More sophisticated programs often combine the confirm and capture commands. For instance, ttest has a complex syntax: if the user types ttest var=5, it tests that the mean of var is 5 using one set of formulas, and if the user types ttest var=var2, it tests equality of means by using another set of formulas. Whether there is a number or a variable to the right of the equal sign determines which set of formulas ttest uses. This choice was done by

```
capture confirm number 'exp'
if _rc==0 {
        (code for test against a constant )
        exit
}
(code for test of two variables )
```

◁

Also see

[P] **capture** — Capture return code

Title

continue — Break out of loops

Syntax

continue $\left[\, , \underline{br}eak \right]$

Description

The continue command within a foreach, forvalues, or while loop breaks execution of the current loop iteration and skips the remaining commands within the loop. Execution resumes at the top of the loop unless the break option is specified, in which case execution resumes with the command following the looping command. See [P] **foreach**, [P] **forvalues**, and [P] **while** for a discussion of the looping commands.

Option

break indicates that the loop is to be exited. The default is to skip the remaining steps of the current iteration and to resume loop execution again at the top of the loop.

Remarks

We illustrate continue with the forvalues command, but it can be used in the same way with the foreach and while commands.

▷ Example 1

The following forvalues loop lists the odd and even numbers from one to four:

```
. forvalues x = 1(1)4 {
  2.          if mod('x',2) {
  3.                  display "'x' is odd"
  4.          }
  5.          else {
  6.                  display "'x' is even"
  7.          }
  8. }
1 is odd
2 is even
3 is odd
4 is even
```

It could be coded using the continue command instead of else:

```
. forvalues x = 1(1)4 {
  2.          if mod('x',2) {
  3.                  display "'x' is odd"
  4.                  continue
  5.          }
  6.          display "'x' is even"
  7. }
1 is odd
2 is even
3 is odd
4 is even
```

When continue is executed, any remaining statements that exist in the loop are ignored. Execution continues at the top of the loop where, here, forvalues sets the next value of 'x', compares that with 4, and then perhaps begins the loop again.

◁

▷ Example 2

continue, break causes execution of the loop to stop; it prematurely exits the loop.

```
. forvalues x = 6/1000 {
  2.          if mod('x',2)==0 & mod('x',3)==0 & mod('x',5)==0 {
  3.                  display "The least common multiple of 2, 3, and 5 is 'x'"
  4.                  continue, break
  5.          }
  6. }
The least common multiple of 2, 3, and 5 is 30
```

Although the forvalues loop was scheduled to go over the values 6–1,000, the continue, break statement forced it to stop after 30.

◁

Also see

[P] **foreach** — Loop over items

[P] **forvalues** — Loop over consecutive values

[P] **while** — Looping

[P] **if** — if programming command

[P] **exit** — Exit from a program or do-file

[U] **18 Programming Stata**

Title

creturn — Return c-class values

Syntax

```
creturn list
```

Menu

Data > Other utilities > List constants and system parameters

Description

Stata's c-class, c(), contains the values of system parameters and settings, along with certain constants such as the value of pi. c() values may be referred to but may not be assigned.

Remarks

The c-class values are presented under the following headings:

> *System values*
> *Directories and paths*
> *System limits*
> *Numerical and string limits*
> *Current dataset*
> *Memory settings*
> *Output settings*
> *Interface settings*
> *Graphics settings*
> *Efficiency settings*
> *Network settings*
> *Update settings*
> *Trace (program debugging) settings*
> *Mata settings*
> *Other settings*
> *Other*

There may be other c-class values that have been added since the printing of this manual. Type `help creturn` for up-to-date information.

System values

c(current_date) returns the current date as a string in the format "*dd Mon yyyy*", where *dd* is the day of the month (if day is less than 10, a space and one digit are used); *Mon* is one of Jan, Feb, Mar, Apr, May, Jun, Jul, Aug, Sep, Oct, Nov, or Dec; and *yyyy* is the four-digit year.

Examples:
```
 1 Jan 2003
26 Mar 2007
10 Feb 2005
```

c(current_time) returns the current time as a string in the format "*hh*:*mm*:*ss*", where *hh* is the hour 00–23, *mm* is the minute 00–59, and *ss* is the second 00–59.

Examples:
09:42:55
13:02:01
21:15:59

c(rmsg_time) returns a numeric scalar equal to the elapsed time last reported as a result of set rmsg on; see [P] **rmsg**.

c(stata_version) returns a numeric scalar equal to the version of Stata that you are running. In Stata 11, this number is 11; in Stata 11.1, 11.1; and in Stata 12, 12. This is the version of Stata that you are running, not the version being mimicked by the version command.

c(version) returns a numeric scalar equal to the version currently set by the version command; see [P] **version**.

c(born_date) returns a string in the same format as c(current_date) containing the date of the Stata executable that you are running; see [R] **update**.

c(flavor) returns a string containing "Small" or "IC", according to the version of Stata that you are running. c(flavor) == "IC" for Stata/MP and Stata/SE, as well as for Stata/IC.

c(SE) returns a numeric scalar equal to 1 if you are running Stata/SE and 0 otherwise.

c(MP) returns a numeric scalar equal to 1 if you are running Stata/MP and 0 otherwise.

c(processors) returns a numeric scalar equal to the number of processors/cores that Stata/MP is currently set to use. It returns 1 if you are not running Stata/MP.

c(processors_lic) returns a numeric scalar equal to the number of processors/cores that your Stata/MP license allows. It returns 1 if you are not running Stata/MP.

c(processors_mach) returns a numeric scalar equal to the number of processors/cores that your computer has if you are running Stata/MP. It returns missing value (.) if you are not running Stata/MP.

c(processors_max) returns a numeric scalar equal to the maximum number of processors/cores that Stata/MP could use, which is equal to the minimum of c(processors_lic) and c(processors_mach). It returns 1 if you are not running Stata/MP.

c(mode) returns a string containing "" or "batch", depending on whether Stata was invoked in interactive mode (the usual case) or batch mode (using, perhaps, the -b option of Stata for Unix).

c(console) returns a string containing "" or "console", depending on whether you are running a windowed version of Stata or Stata(console).

c(os) returns a string containing "MacOSX", "Unix", or "Windows", depending on the operating system that you are using. The list of alternatives, although complete as of the date of this writing, may not be complete.

c(osdtl) returns an additional string, depending on the operating system, providing the release number or other details about the operating system. c(osdtl) is often "".

c(machine_type) returns a string that describes the hardware platform, such as "PC", "Mac", and "Sun SPARC".

c(byteorder) returns a string containing "lohi" or "hilo", depending on the byte order of the hardware. Consider a two-byte integer. On some computers, the most significant byte is written first, so x'0001' (meaning the byte 00 followed by 01) would mean the number 1. Such computers are designated "hilo". Other computers write the least-significant byte first, so x'0001' would be 256, and 1 would be x'0100'. Such computers are designated "lohi".

c(username) returns the user ID (provided by the operating system) of the user currently using Stata.

Directories and paths

Note: The directory paths returned below usually end in a directory separator, so if you wish to construct the full path name of file abc.def in directory c(...), you code

> ...'c(...)'abc.def...

and not

> ...'c(...)'/abc.def...

If c(...) returns a directory name that does not end in a directory separator, a special note of the fact is made.

c(sysdir_stata) returns a string containing the name of the directory (folder) in which Stata is installed. More technically, c(sysdir_stata) returns the STATA directory as defined by sysdir; see [P] **sysdir**.

Example: C:\Program Files\Stata11/

The above example contains no typographical errors. Under Windows, the directory name will end in forward slash. That is so you can code things such as 'c(sysdir_stata)''filename'. If c(sysdir_stata) ended in backslash, Stata's macro expander would interpret the backslash as an escape character and so not expand 'filename'.

c(sysdir_updates) returns a string containing the name of the directory (folder) in which Stata is to find the official ado-file updates. More technically, c(sysdir_updates) returns the UPDATES directory as defined by sysdir; see [P] **sysdir**.

Example: C:\Program Files\Stata11\ado\updates/

c(sysdir_base) returns a string containing the name of the directory (folder) in which the original official ado-files that were shipped with Stata were installed.

c(sysdir_site) returns a string containing the name of the directory (folder) in which user-written additions may be installed for sitewide use. More technically, c(sysdir_site) returns the SITE directory as defined by sysdir; see [P] **sysdir**.

Example: C:\Program Files\Stata11\ado\site/

c(sysdir_plus) returns a string containing the name of the directory (folder) in which additions written by others may be installed for personal use. More technically, c(sysdir_plus) returns the PLUS directory, as defined by sysdir; see [P] **sysdir**.

Example: C:\ado\plus/

c(sysdir_personal) returns a string containing the name of the directory (folder) in which additions written by you may be installed. More technically, c(sysdir_personal) returns the PERSONAL directory, as defined by sysdir; see [P] **sysdir**.

Example: C:\ado\personal/

c(sysdir_oldplace) identifies another directory in which user-written ado-files might be installed. c(sysdir_oldplace) maintains compatibility with very ancient versions of Stata.

c(tmpdir) returns a string containing the name of the directory (folder) used by Stata for temporary files.

Example: /tmp

c(adopath) returns a string containing the directories that are to be searched when Stata is attempting to locate an ado-file. The path elements are separated by a semicolon (;), and the elements themselves may be directory names, "." to indicate the current directory, or sysdir references.

Example: UPDATES;BASE;SITE;.;PERSONAL;PLUS;OLDPLACE

c(pwd) returns a string containing the current (working) directory.

Example: C:\data

Notice that c(pwd) does not end in a directory separator, so in a program, to save the name of the file abc.def prefixed by the current directory (for example, because you were about to change directories and still wanted to refer to the file), you would code

```
local file "`c(pwd)'/abc.def"
```

or

```
local file "`c(pwd)'`c(dirsep)'abc.def"
```

The second form is preferred if you want to construct "pretty" filenames, but the first form is acceptable because Stata understands a forward slash (/) as a directory separator.

c(dirsep) returns a string containing "/".

Example: /

For Windows operating systems, a forward slash (/) is returned rather than a backslash (\). Stata for Windows understands both, but in programs, use of the forward slash is recommended because the backslash can interfere with Stata's interpretation of macro expansion characters. Do not be concerned if the result of your code is a mix of backslash and forward slash characters, such as \a\b/myfile.dta; Stata will understand it just as it would understand /a/b/myfile.dta or \a\b\myfile.dta.

System limits

c(max_N_theory) and c(max_N_current) each return a numeric scalar reporting the maximum number of observations allowed. c(mac_N_theory) and c(max_N_current) are seldom equal.

c(max_N_theory) reports the maximum number of observations that Stata can process if it has enough memory. This is usually 2,147,483,647.

c(max_N_current) reports the maximum number of observations that Stata can process given the current amount of memory allocated to Stata. You can change the amount of memory, and hence this number, with the set memory command; see [D] **memory**.

c(max_k_theory) and c(max_k_current) each return a numeric scalar reporting the maximum number of variables allowed. c(max_k_theory) returns the theoretical maximum number of variables allowed. c(max_k_current) returns the current maximum possible due to the number of observations you currently have in memory and may be the same as or less than, but never more than, c(max_k_theory). For Stata/SE, c(max_k_theory) is determined by the set maxvar command.

c(max_width_theory) and c(max_width_current) each return a numeric scalar equal to the maximum width of an observation, which is defined as the sum of the byte lengths of its individual variables. If you had a dataset with two int variables, three floats, one double, and a str20 variable, the width of the dataset would be $2*2 + 3*4 + 8 + 20 = 44$ bytes.

c(max_width_theory) returns the theoretical maximum width allowed.

c(max_width_current) returns the current maximum possible due to the number of observations you currently have in memory and may be the same as or less than, but never more than, c(max_width_theory). For Stata/SE, c(max_width_theory) is affected by the set maxvar command.

c(max_matsize) and c(min_matsize) each return a numeric scalar reporting the maximum and minimum values to which matsize may be set. If the version of Stata you are running does not allow the setting of matsize, the two values will be equal. c(matsize), documented under *Memory settings* below, returns the current value of matsize.

c(max_macrolen) and c(macrolen) each return a numeric scalar reporting the maximum length of macros. c(max_macrolen) and c(macrolen) may not be equal under Stata/SE and will be equal otherwise. For Stata/SE, macrolen is set according to maxvar: the length is long enough to hold a macro referring to every variable in the dataset.

c(max_cmdlen) and c(cmdlen) each return a numeric scalar reporting the maximum length of a Stata command. c(max_cmdlen) and c(cmdlen) may not be equal under Stata/SE and will be equal otherwise. For Stata/SE, cmdlen is set according to maxvar: the length is long enough to hold a command referring to every variable in the dataset.

c(namelen) returns a numeric scalar equal to 32, which is the current maximum length of names in Stata.

c(eqlen) returns the maximum length that Stata allows for equation names.

Numerical and string limits

c(mindouble), c(maxdouble), and c(epsdouble) each return a numeric scalar. c(mindouble) is the largest negative number that can be stored in the 8-byte double storage type. c(maxdouble) is the largest positive number that can be stored in a double. c(epsdouble) is the smallest nonzero, positive number (epsilon) that, when added to 1 and stored as a double, does not equal 1.

c(smallestdouble) returns a numeric scalar containing the smallest full-precision double that is bigger than zero. There are smaller positive values that can be stored; these are denormalized numbers. Denormalized numbers do not have full precision.

c(minfloat), c(maxfloat), and c(epsfloat) each return a numeric scalar that reports for the 4-byte float storage type what c(mindouble), c(maxdouble), and c(epsdouble) report for double.

c(minlong) and c(maxlong) return scalars reporting the largest negative number and the largest positive number that can be stored in the 4-byte, integer long storage type. There is no c(epslong), but if there were, it would return 1.

c(minint) and c(maxint) return scalars reporting the largest negative number and the largest positive number that can be stored in the 2-byte, integer int storage type.

c(minbyte) and c(maxbyte) return scalars reporting the largest negative number and the largest positive number that can be stored in the 1-byte, integer byte storage type.

c(maxstrvarlen) returns the longest str# string storage type allowed, which is 244. Do not confuse c(maxstrvarlen) with c(macrolen). c(maxstrvarlen) corresponds to string variables stored in the data.

Current dataset

c(N) returns a numeric scalar equal to _N, the number of observations in the dataset in memory. In an expression, it makes no difference whether you refer to _N or c(N). However, when used in expressions with the by prefix, c(N) does not change with the by-group like _N.

The advantage of c(N) is in nonexpression contexts. Say that you are calling a subroutine, mysub, which takes as an argument the number of observations in the dataset. Then you could code

```
local nobs = _N
mysub 'nobs'
```

or

```
mysub 'c(N)'
```

The second requires less typing.

c(k) returns a numeric scalar equal to the number of variables in the dataset in memory. c(k) is equal to r(k), which is returned by describe.

c(width) returns a numeric scalar equal to the width, in bytes, of the dataset in memory. If you had a dataset with two int variables, three floats, one double, and a str20 variable, the width of the dataset would be $2*2 + 3*4 + 8 + 20 = 44$ bytes. c(width) is equal to r(width), which is returned by describe.

c(changed) returns a numeric scalar equal to 0 if the dataset in memory has not changed since it was last saved and 1 otherwise. c(changed) is equal to r(changed), which is returned by describe.

c(filename) returns a string containing the filename last specified with a use or save, such as "http://www.stata-press.com/data/r11/auto.dta". c(filename) is equal to $S_FN.

c(filedate) returns a string containing the date and time the file in c(filename) was last saved, such as "7 Jul 2006 13:51". c(filedate) is equal to $S_FNDATE.

Memory settings

c(memory) returns a numeric scalar reporting the amount of memory, in bytes, allocated to Stata's data area, as set by set memory.

c(maxvar) returns a numeric scalar reporting the maximum number of variables currently allowed in a dataset, as set by set maxvar if you are running Stata/SE. Otherwise, c(maxvar) is a constant.

c(matsize) returns a numeric scalar reporting the current value of matsize, as set by set matsize.

Output settings

c(more) returns a string containing "on" or "off", according to the current set more setting.

c(rmsg) returns a string containing "on" or "off", according to the current set rmsg setting.

c(dp) returns a string containing "period" or "comma", according to the current set dp setting.

c(linesize) returns a numeric scalar equal to the current set linesize setting.

c(pagesize) returns a numeric scalar equal to the current set pagesize setting.

c(logtype) returns a string containing "smcl" or "text", according to the current set logtype setting.

c(noisily) returns a numeric scalar equal to 0 if output is being suppressed and 1 if output is being displayed; see [P] **quietly**.

c(eolchar) (Mac only) returns a string containing "mac" or "unix", according to the current set eolchar setting.

c(notifyuser) (Mac only) returns a string containing "on" or "off", according to the current set notifyuser setting.

c(playsnd) (Mac only) returns a string containing "on" or "off", according to the current set playsnd setting.

Interface settings

c(dockable) (Windows only) returns a string containing "on" or "off", according to the current set dockable setting.

c(dockingguides) (Windows only) returns a string containing "on" or "off", according to the current set dockingguides setting.

c(locksplitters) (Windows only) returns a string containing "on" or "off", according to the current set locksplitters setting.

c(persistfv) (Windows only) returns a string containing "on" or "off", according to the current set persistfv setting.

c(persistvtopic) (Windows only) returns a string containing "on" or "off", according to the current set persistvtopic setting.

c(pinnable) (Windows only) returns a string containing "on" or "off", according to the current set pinnable setting.

c(doublebuffer) (Windows only) returns a string containing "on" or "off", according to the current set doublebuffer setting.

c(reventries) returns a numeric scalar containing the maximum number of commands stored by the Review window.

c(fastscroll) (Mac and Unix only) returns a string containing "on" or "off", according to the current set fastscroll setting.

c(revwindow) (Mac only) returns a string containing "float" or "nofloat", according to the current set revwindow settings.

c(revkeyboard) (Mac only) returns a string containing "on" or "off", according to the current set revkeyboard settings.

c(varwindow) (Mac only) returns a string containing "float" or "nofloat", according to the current set varwindow settings.

c(varkeyboard) (Mac only) returns a string containing "on" or "off", according to the current set varkeyboard settings.

c(smoothfonts) (Mac only) returns a string containing "on" or "off", according to the current set smoothfonts setting.

c(use_qd_text) (Mac only) returns a string containing "on" or "off", according to the current set use_qd_text setting.

c(smoothsize) (Mac only) returns a numeric scalar equal to the current set smoothsize setting. If set smoothsize is irrelevant under the version of Stata that you are running, c(smoothsize) returns a system missing value.

c(use_atsui_graph) (Mac only) returns a string containing "on" or "off", according to the current set use_atsui_graph setting.

c(linegap) returns a numeric scalar equal to the current set linegap setting. If set linegap is irrelevant under the version of Stata that you are running, c(linegap) returns a system missing value.

c(scrollbufsize) returns a numeric scalar equal to the current set scrollbufsize setting. If set scrollbufsize is irrelevant under the version of Stata that you are running, c(scrollbufsize) returns a system missing value.

c(varlabelpos) (Unix only) returns a numeric scalar equal to the current set varlabelpos setting. If set varlabelpos is irrelevant under the version of Stata that you are running, c(varlabelpos) returns a system missing value.

c(maxdb) returns a numeric scalar containing the maximum number of dialog boxes whose contents are remembered from one invocation to the next during a session; see [R] **db**.

Graphics settings

c(graphics) returns a string containing "on" or "off", according to the current set graphics setting.

c(autotabgraphs) (Windows only) returns a string containing "on" or "off", according to the current set autotabgraphs setting.

c(scheme) returns the name of the current set scheme.

c(printcolor) returns "automatic", "asis", "gs1", "gs2", or "gs3", according to the current set printcolor setting.

c(copycolor) returns "automatic", "asis", "gs1", "gs2", or "gs3", according to the current set copycolor setting.

c(macgphengine) (Mac only) returns a string containing "quartz" or "quickdraw", according to the current set graphics setting.

Efficiency settings

c(adosize) returns a numeric scalar equal to the current set adosize setting.

c(virtual) returns a string containing "on" or "off", according to the current set virtual setting.

Network settings

c(checksum) returns a string containing "on" or "off", according to the current set checksum setting.

c(timeout1) returns a numeric scalar equal to the current set timeout1 setting.

c(timeout2) returns a numeric scalar equal to the current set timeout2 setting.

c(httpproxy) returns a string containing "on" or "off", according to the current set httpproxy setting.

c(httpproxyhost) returns a string containing the name of the proxy host or "" if no proxy host is set. c(httpproxyhost) is relevant only if c(httpproxy) = "on".

c(httpproxyport) returns a numeric scalar equal to the proxy port number. c(httpproxyport) is relevant only if c(httpproxy) = "on".

c(httpproxyauth) returns a string containing "on" or "off", according to the current set httpproxyauth setting. c(httpproxyauth) is relevant only if c(httpproxy) = "on".

c(httpproxyuser) returns a string containing the name of the proxy user, if one is set, or "" otherwise. c(httpproxyuser) is relevant only if c(httpproxy) = "on" and c(httpproxyauth) = "on".

c(httpproxypw) returns a string containing "*" if a password is set or "" otherwise. c(httpproxypw) is relevant only if c(httpproxy) = "on" and c(httpproxyauth) = "on".

Update settings

c(update_query) (Mac and Windows only) returns a string containing "on" or "off", according to the current set update_query setting.

c(update_interval) (Mac and Windows only) returns a numeric scalar containing the current set update_interval setting.

c(update_prompt) (Mac and Windows only) returns a string containing "on" or "off", according to the current set update_prompt setting.

Trace (program debugging) settings

c(trace) returns a string containing "on" or "off", according to the current set trace setting.

c(tracedepth) returns a numeric scalar reporting the current set tracedepth setting.

c(tracesep) returns a string containing "on" or "off", according to the current set tracesep setting.

c(traceindent) returns a string containing "on" or "off", according to the current set traceindent setting.

c(traceexpand) returns a string containing "on" or "off", according to the current set traceexpand setting.

c(tracenumber) returns a string containing "on" or "off", according to the current set tracenumber setting.

c(tracehilite) returns a string containing "*pattern*", according to the current set tracehilite setting.

Mata settings

c(matastrict) returns a string containing "on" or "off", according to the current set matastrict setting.

c(matalnum) returns a string containing "on" or "off", according to the current set matalnum setting.

c(mataoptimize) returns a string containing "on" or "off", according to the current set mataoptimize setting.

c(matafavor) returns a string containing "space" or "speed", according to the current set matafavor setting.

c(matacache) returns a numeric scalar containing the maximum amount of memory, in kilobytes, that may be consumed before Mata starts looking to drop autoloaded functions that are not currently being used.

c(matalibs) returns a string containing the names in order of the .mlib libraries to be searched; see [M-1] **how**.

c(matamofirst) returns a string containing "on" or "off", according to the current set matamofirst setting.

Other settings

c(type) returns a string containing "float" or "double", according to the current set type setting.

c(level) returns a numeric scalar equal to the current set level setting.

c(maxiter) returns a numeric scalar equal to the current set maxiter setting.

c(searchdefault) returns a string containing "local", "net", or "all", according to the current search default setting.

c(seed) returns a string containing the current set seed setting. This records the current state of the random-number generator runiform().

c(varabbrev) returns a string containing "on" or "off", according to the current set varabbrev setting.

c(odbcmgr) (Unix only) returns a string containing "iodbc" or "unixodbc", according to the current set odbcmgr setting.

Other

c(pi) returns a numerical scalar equal to _pi, the value of the ratio of the circumference to the diameter of a circle. In an expression context, it makes no difference whether you use c(pi) or _pi. c(pi), however, may be used (enclosed in single quotes) in other contexts.

c(alpha) returns a string containing "a b c d e f g h i..".

c(ALPHA) returns a string containing "A B C D E F G H I..".

c(Mons) returns a string containing "Jan Feb Mar Apr M..".

c(Months) returns a string containing "January February ..".

c(Wdays) returns a string containing "Sun Mon Tue Wed T..".

c(Weekdays) returns a string containing "Sunday Monday Tue..".

c(rc) returns a numerical scalar equal to _rc, the value set by the capture command. In an expression context, it makes no difference whether you use c(rc) or _rc. c(rc), however, may be used (enclosed in single quotes) in other contexts. This is less important than it sounds because you could just as easily type '=_rc'.

Also see

[P] **return** — Return saved results

[R] **query** — Display system parameters

[R] **set** — Overview of system parameters

Title

_datasignature — Determine whether data have changed

Syntax

_datasignature [*varlist*] [*if*] [*in*] [, *options*]

options	description
f̲ast	perform calculation in machine-dependent way
e̲sample	restrict to estimation sample
non̲ames	do not include checksum for variable names
nodef̲ault	treat empty *varlist* as null

Description

_datasignature calculates, displays, and saves in r(_datasignature) checksums of the data, forming a signature. A signature might be

162:11(12321):2725060400:4007406597

The signature can be saved and later used to determine whether the data have changed.

Options

fast specifies that the checksum calculation be made in a faster, less computationally intensive, and machine-dependent way. With this option, _datasignature runs faster on all computers and can run in less than one-third of the time on some computers. The result can be compared with other fast computations made on the same computer, and computers of the same make, but not across computers of different makes. See *Remarks* below.

esample specifies that the checksum be calculated on the data for which e(sample) = 1. Coding

    _datasignature 'varlist', esample

or

    _datasignature 'varlist' if e(sample)

produces the same result. The former is a little quicker. If the esample option is specified, if *exp* may not be specified.

nonames specifies that the variable-names checksum in the signature be omitted. Rather than the signature being 74:12(71728):2814604011:3381794779, it would be 74:12:2814604011:3381794779. This option is useful when you do not care about the names or you know that the names have changed, such as when using temporary variables.

nodefault specifies that when *varlist* is not specified, it be taken to mean no variables rather than all variables in the dataset. Thus you may code

    _datasignature 'modelvars', nodefault

and obtain desired results even if 'modelvars' expands to nothing.

Remarks

For an introduction to data signatures, see [D] **datasignature**. To briefly summarize:

- A signature is a short string that is calculated from a dataset, such as 74:12(71728):3831085005:1395876116. If a dataset has the same signature at two different times, then it is highly likely that the data have not changed. If a dataset has a different signature, then it is certain that the data have changed.

- An example data signature is 74:12(71728):3831085005:1395876116. The components are

    a. 74, the number of observations;

    b. 12, the number of variables;

    c. 71728, a checksum function of the variable names and the order in which they occur; and

    d. 3831085005 and 1395876116, checksum functions of the values of the variables, calculated two different ways.

- Signatures are functions of

    a. the number of observations and number of variables in the data;

    b. the values of the variables;

    c. the names of the variables;

    d. the order in which the variables occur in the dataset if *varlist* is not specified, or in *varlist* if it is; and

    e. the storage types of the variables.

    If any of these change, the signature changes. The signature is not a function of the sort order of the data. The signature is not a function of variable labels, value labels, contents of characteristics, and the like.

Programs sometimes need to verify that they are running on the same data at two different times. This verification is especially common with estimation commands, where the estimation is performed by one command and postestimation analyses by another. To ensure that the data have not changed, one obtains the signature at the time of estimation and then compares that with the signature obtained when the postestimation command is run. See [P] **signestimationsample** for an example.

If you are producing signatures for use within a Stata session—signatures that will not be written to disk and thus cannot possibly be transferred to different computers—specify _datasignature's fast option. On some computers, _datasignature can run in less than one-third of the time if this option is specified.

_datasignature, fast is faster for two reasons: (1) the option uses a less computationally intensive algorithm and (2) the computation is made in a machine-dependent way. The first affects the quality of the signature, and the second does not.

Remember that signatures have two checksums for the data. When fast is specified, a different, inferior algorithm is substituted for the second checksum. In the fast case, the second signature is not conditionally independent of the first and thus does not provide 48 bits of additional information; it probably provides around 24 bits. The default second checksum calculation was selected to catch problems that the first calculation does not catch. In the fast case, the second checksum does not have that property. These details make the fast signature sound markedly inferior. Nevertheless, the first checksum calculation, which is used both in the default and the fast cases, is good, and when _datasignature was written, we considered using only the first calculation in both cases. We believe that, for within-session testing, where one does not have to guard against changes produced by an intelligent enemy who may be trying to fool you, the first checksum alone is adequate. The inferior second checksum we include in the `fast` case provides more protection than we think necessary.

The second difference has nothing to do with quality. Modern computers come in two types: those that record least-significant bytes (LSBs) first and those that record most-significant bytes (MSBs) first. Intel-based computers, for instance, are usually LSB, whereas Sun computers are MSB.

By default, _datasignature makes the checksum calculation in an LSB way, even on MSB computers. MSB computers must therefore go to extra work to emulate the LSB calculation, and so _datasignature runs slower on them.

When you specify `fast`, _datasignature calculates the checksum the native way. The checksum is every bit as good, but the checksum produced will be different on MSB computers. If you merely store the signature in memory for use later in the session, however, that does not matter.

Saved results

_datasignature saves the following in r():

Macros
r(datasignature)   the signature

Reference

Gould, W. W. 2006. Stata tip 35: Detecting whether data have changed. *Stata Journal* 6: 428–429.

Also see

[D] **datasignature** — Determine whether data have changed

[P] **signestimationsample** — Determine whether the estimation sample has changed

[D] **compare** — Compare two variables

[D] **cf** — Compare two datasets

Title

> **#delimit** — Change delimiter

Syntax

#<u>d</u>elimit $\{$ cr | ; $\}$

Description

The #delimit command resets the character that marks the end of a command. It can be used only in do-files or ado-files.

Remarks

#delimit (pronounced *pound-delimit*) is a Stata preprocessor command. #*commands* do not generate a return code, nor do they generate ordinary Stata errors. The only error message associated with #*commands* is "unrecognized #command".

Commands given from the console are always executed when you press the *Enter*, or *Return*, key. #delimit cannot be used interactively, so you cannot change Stata's interactive behavior.

Commands in a do-file, however, may be delimited with a carriage return or a semicolon. When a do-file begins, the delimiter is a carriage return. The command '#delimit ;' changes the delimiter to a semicolon. To restore the carriage return delimiter inside a file, use #delimit cr.

When a do-file begins execution, the delimiter is automatically set to carriage return, even if it was called from another do-file that set the delimiter to semicolon. Also, the current do-file need not worry about restoring the delimiter to what it was because Stata will do that automatically.

> ## Example 1

```
/*
      When the do-file begins, the delimiter is carriage return:
*/
use basedata, clear
/*
      The last command loaded our data.
      Let's now change the delimiter:
*/
#delimit ;
summarize sex
            salary ;
/*
      Because the delimiter is semicolon, it does not matter that our
      command took two lines.
      We can change the delimiter back:
*/
```

```
#delimit cr
summarize sex salary
/*
     Now our lines once again end on return.  The semicolon delimiter
     is often used when loading programs:
*/
capture program drop fix
program fix
     confirm var '1'
     #delimit ;
     replace '1' = .  if salary>=. | salary==0 |
                         hours>=.  | hours==0 ;
     #delimit cr
end
fix var1
fix var2
```
◁

❑ Technical note

Just because you have long lines does not mean that you must change the delimiter to semicolon. Stata does not care that the line is long. There are also other ways to indicate that more than one physical line is one logical line. One popular choice is ///:

```
replace '1' = .  if salary>=. | salary==0 | ///
                    hours>=.  | hours==0
```

See [P] **comments**.

❑

Also see

[U] **16.1.3 Long lines in do-files**

[U] **18.11.2 Comments and long lines in ado-files**

[P] **comments** — Add comments to programs

Title

dialog programming — Dialog programming

Description

You can add new dialog boxes to Stata by creating a `.dlg` file containing a description of the dialog box. These files are called "dialog-box programs", or sometimes "dialog resource files". Running most dialog boxes creates and executes a Stata command.

In a `.dlg` file, you can define the appearance of a dialog box, specify how the dialog-box controls interact with user input (such as hiding or disabling specific areas), and specify the ultimate action to be taken (such as running a Stata command) when the user presses **OK**, **Submit**, **Copy**, or **Cancel**.

Like ado-files, dialog-box files should be placed on the ado-path (see [U] **17.5 Where does Stata look for ado-files?**) so that they can be automatically found and launched. For example, you can launch the dialog box defined in `xyz.dlg` by typing

. db xyz

See [R] **db** for details. You can also add dialog boxes to Stata's menu; type `help dialog programming`.

Remarks

To see the complete documentation for dialog-box programming, type

. help dialog programming

The online help file contains all the details on creating and programming dialog boxes.

You can print the documentation directly from the Viewer by selecting **File > Print**.

Also see

[P] **window programming** — Programming menus and windows

[R] **db** — Launch dialog

Title

> **discard** — Drop automatically loaded programs

Syntax

```
discard
```

Description

discard drops all automatically loaded programs (see [U] **17.2 What is an ado-file?**); clears e(), r(), and s() saved results (see [P] **return**); eliminates information stored by the most recent estimation command and any other saved estimation results (see [P] **ereturn**); closes any open graphs and drops all sersets (see [P] **serset**); clears all class definitions and instances (see [P] **classutil**); and closes all dialogs and clears their remembered contents (see [P] **dialog programming**).

In short, discard causes Stata to forget everything current without forgetting anything important, such as the data in memory.

Remarks

Use discard to debug ado-files. Making a change to an ado-file will not cause Stata to update its internal copy of the changed program. discard clears all automatically loaded programs from memory, forcing Stata to refresh its internal copies with the versions residing on disk.

Also all of Stata's estimation commands can display their previous output when the command is typed without arguments. They achieve this by storing information on the problem in memory. predict calculates various statistics (predictions, residuals, influence statistics, etc.), estat vce shows the covariance matrix, lincom calculates linear combinations of estimated coefficients, and test and testnl perform hypotheses tests, all using that stored information. discard eliminates that information, making it appear as if you never fit the model.

Also see

[D] **clear** — Clear memory

[P] **class** — Class programming

[P] **classutil** — Class programming utility

[P] **dialog programming** — Dialog programming

[U] **17 Ado-files**

Title

> **display** — Display strings and values of scalar expressions

Syntax

<u>di</u>splay $\left[\,\textit{display\_directive}\,\left[\,\textit{display\_directive}\,\left[\,\ldots\,\right]\,\right]\,\right]$

where *display_directive* is

"*double-quoted string*"

' "*compound double-quoted string*" '

$\left[\,\%\textit{fmt}\,\left[\,=\,\right]\textit{exp}\,\right]$

as $\left\{\,\texttt{text}\,|\,\texttt{txt}\,|\,\underline{\texttt{res}}\texttt{ult}\,|\,\underline{\texttt{error}}\,|\,\underline{\texttt{input}}\,\right\}$

in smcl

_asis

_<u>s</u>kip(*#*)

_<u>col</u>umn(*#*)

_<u>n</u>ewline$\left[\,(\textit{\#})\,\right]$

_continue

_<u>d</u>up(*#*)

_<u>r</u>equest(*macname*)

_char(*#*)

,

, ,

Description

`display` displays strings and values of scalar expressions. `display` produces output from the programs that you write.

Remarks

Remarks are presented under the following headings:

> *Introduction*
> *Styles*
> *display used with quietly and noisily*
> *Columns*
> *display and SMCL*
> *Displaying variable names*
> *Obtaining input from the terminal*

Introduction

Interactively, display can be used as a substitute for a hand calculator; see [R] **display**. You can type things such as 'display 2+2'.

display's *display_directive*s are used in do-files and programs to produce formatted output. The directives are

"*double-quoted string*"	displays the string without the quotes
'"*compound double-quoted string*"'	displays the string without the outer quotes; allows embedded quotes
$\left[\,\%\,fmt\,\right]\ \left[\,=\,\right]$exp	allows results to be formatted; see [U] **12.5 Formats: Controlling how data are displayed**
as *style*	sets the style ("color") for the directives that follow; there may be more than one as *style* per display
in smcl	switches from _asis mode to smcl mode
_asis	switches from smcl mode to _asis mode
_skip(*#*)	skips *#* columns
_column(*#*)	skips to the *#*th column
_newline	goes to a new line
_newline(*#*)	skips *#* lines
_continue	suppresses automatic newline at end of display command
_dup(*#*)	repeats the next directive *#* times
_request(*macname*)	accepts input from the console and places it into the macro *macname*
_char(*#*)	displays the character for ASCII code *#*
,	displays one blank between two directives
,,	places no blanks between two directives

▷ Example 1

Here is a nonsense program called `silly` that illustrates the directives:

```
. program list silly
silly:
    1.      set obs 10
    2.      gen myvar=runiform()
    3.      di as text _dup(59) "-"
    4.      di "hello, world"
    5.      di %~59s "This is centered"
    6.      di "myvar[1] = " as result myvar[1]
    7.      di _col(10) "myvar[1] = " myvar[1] _skip(10) "myvar[2] = " myvar[2]
    8.      di "myvar[1]/myvar[2] = " %5.4f myvar[1]/myvar[2]
    9.      di "This" _newline _col(5) "That" _newline _col(10) "What"
   10.      di `"She said, "Hello""'
   11.      di substr("abcI can do string expressionsXYZ",4,27)
   12.      di _char(65) _char(83) _char(67) _char(73) _char(73)
   13.      di _dup(59) "-" " (good-bye)"
```

Here is the result of running it:

```
. silly
obs was 0, now 10
-----------------------------------------------------------
hello, world
                        This is centered
myvar[1] = .13698408
         myvar[1] = .13698408            myvar[2] = .64322066
myvar[1]/myvar[2] = 0.2130
This
    That
         What
She said, "Hello"
I can do string expressions
ASCII
----------------------------------------------------------- (good-bye)
```

◁

Styles

Stata has four styles: `text` (synonym `txt`), `result`, `error`, and `input`. Typically, these styles are rendered in terms of color,

$$\text{text} = \text{black}$$

$$\text{result} = \text{black and bold}$$

$$\text{error} = \text{red}$$

$$\text{input} = \text{black and bold}$$

or, at least, that is the default in the Results window when the window has a white background. On a black background, the defaults are

$$\text{text} = \text{green}$$

$$\text{result} = \text{yellow}$$

$$\text{error} = \text{red}$$

$$\text{input} = \text{white}$$

In any case, users can reset the styles by selecting **Edit > Preferences > General Preferences** in Windows or Unix(GUI) or by selecting **Preferences > General Preferences** in Mac.

The display directives as text, as result, as error, and as input allow you, the programmer, to specify in which rendition subsequent items in the display statement are to be displayed. So if a piece of your program reads

```
quietly summarize mpg
display as text "mean of mpg = " as result r(mean)
```

what might be displayed is

```
mean of mpg = 21.432432
```

where, above, our use of boldface for the 21.432432 is to emphasize that it would be displayed differently from the "mean of mpg =" part. In the Results window, if we had a black background, the "mean of mpg =" part would be in green and the 21.432432 would be in yellow.

You can switch back and forth among styles within a display statement and between display statements. Here is how we recommend using the styles:

as result should be used to display things that depend on the data being used. For statistical output, think of what would happen if the names of the dataset remained the same but all the data changed. Clearly, calculated results would change. That is what should be displayed as result.

as text should be used to display the text around the results. Again think of the experiment where you change the data but not the names. Anything that would not change should be displayed as text. This will include not just the names but also table lines and borders, variable labels, etc.

as error should be reserved for displaying error messages. as error is special in that it not only displays the message as an error (probably meaning that the message is displayed in red) but also forces the message to display, even if output is being suppressed. (There are two commands for suppressing output: quietly and capture. quietly will not suppress as error messages but capture will, the idea being that capture, because it captures the return code, is anticipating errors and will take the appropriate action.)

as input should never be used unless you are creating a special effect. as input (white on a black background) is reserved for what the user types, and the output your program is producing is by definition not being typed by the user. Stata uses as input when it displays what the user types.

display used with quietly and noisily

display's output will be suppressed by quietly at the appropriate times. Consider the following:

```
. program list example1
example1:
  1. di "hello there"
. example1
hello there
. quietly example1

. _
```

The output was suppressed because the program was run quietly. Messages displayed as error, however, are considered error messages and are always displayed:

```
. program list example2
example2:
  1.       di as error "hello there"
. example2
hello there
. quietly example2
hello there
```

Even though the program was run `quietly`, the message as error was displayed. Error messages should always be displayed as error so that they will always be displayed at the terminal.

Programs often have parts of their code buried in `capture` or `quietly` blocks. `displays` inside such blocks produce no output:

```
. program list example3
example3:
  1. quietly {
  2.       display "hello there"
  3. }
. example3

. _
```

If the `display` had included as error, the text would have been displayed, but only error output should be displayed that way. For regular output, the solution is to precede the `display` with `noisily`:

```
. program list example4
example4:
  1. quietly {
  2.       noisily display "hello there"
  3. }
. example4
hello there
```

This method also allows Stata to correctly treat a `quietly` specified by the caller:

```
. quietly example4

. _
```

Despite its name, `noisily` does not really guarantee that the output will be shown—it restores the output only if output would have been allowed at the instant the program was called.

For more information on `noisily` and `quietly`, see [P] **quietly**.

Columns

`display` can move only forward and downward. The directives that take a numeric argument allow only nonnegative integer arguments. It is not possible to back up to make an insertion in the output.

```
. program list cont
cont:
  1.       di "Stuff" _column(9) "More Stuff"
  2.       di "Stuff" _continue
  3.       di _column(9) "More Stuff"
. cont
Stuff    More Stuff
Stuff    More Stuff
```

display and SMCL

Stata Markup and Control Language (SMCL) is Stata's output formatter, and all Stata output passes through SMCL. See [P] **smcl** for a description. All the features of SMCL are available to `display` and so motivate you to turn to the SMCL section of this manual.

In our opening silly example, we included the line

```
di as text _dup(59) "-"
```

That line would have better read

```
di as text "{hline 59}"
```

The first `display` produces this:

```
-----------------------------------------------------------
```

and the second produces this:

```
_____
```

It was not `display` that produced that solid line—`display` just displayed the characters {hline 59}. Output of Stata, however, passes through SMCL, and SMCL interprets what it hears. When SMCL heard {hline 59}, SMCL drew a horizontal line 59 characters wide.

SMCL has many other capabilities, including creating clickable links in your output that, when you click on them, can even execute other Stata commands.

If you carefully review the SMCL documentation, you will discover many overlap in the capabilities of SMCL and `display` that will lead you to wonder whether you should use `display`'s capabilities or SMCL's. For instance, in the section above, we demonstrated the use of `display`'s `_column()` feature to skip forward to a column. If you read the SMCL documentation, you will discover that SMCL has a similar feature, {col}. You can type

```
display "Stuff" _column(9) "More Stuff"
```

or you can type

```
display "Stuff{col 9}More Stuff"
```

So, which should you type? The answer is that it makes no difference and that when you use `display`'s `_column()` directive, `display` just outputs the corresponding SMCL {col} directive for you. This rule generalizes beyond `_column()`. For instance,

```
display as text "hello"
```

and

```
display "{text}hello"
```

are equivalent. There is, however, one important place where `display` and SMCL are different:

```
display as error "error message"
```

is not the same as

```
display "{error}error message"
```

Use `display as error`. The SMCL {error} directive sets the rendition to that of errors, but it does not tell Stata that the message is to be displayed, even if output is otherwise being suppressed. `display as error` both sets the rendition and tells Stata to override output suppression if that is relevant.

❏ Technical note

All Stata output passes through SMCL, and one side effect of that is that open and close brace characters, { and }, are treated oddly by `display`. Try the following:

```
display as text "{1, 2, 3}"
{1, 2, 3}
```

The result is just as you expect. Now try

```
display as text "{result}"
```

The result will be to display nothing because {result} is a SMCL directive. The first displayed something, even though it contained braces, because {1, 2, 3} is not a SMCL directive.

You want to be careful when displaying something that might itself contain braces. You can do that by using `display`'s _asis directive. Once you specify _asis, whatever follows in the display will be displayed exactly as it is, without SMCL interpretation:

```
display as text _asis "{result}"
{result}
```

You can switch back to allowing SMCL interpretation within the line by using the in smcl directive:

```
display as text _asis "{result}" in smcl "is a {bf:smcl} directive"
{result} is a smcl directive
```

Every `display` command in your program starts off in SMCL mode unless the program is running with `version` set to 6 or before, in which case each `display` starts off in _asis mode. If you want to use SMCL in old programs without otherwise updating them, you can include `display`'s in smcl directive.

❏

Displaying variable names

Let's assume that a program we are writing is to produce a table that looks like this:

Variable	Obs	Mean	Std. Dev.	Min	Max
mpg	74	21.2973	5.785503	12	41
weight	74	3019.459	777.1936	1760	4840
displ	74	197.2973	91.83722	79	425

Putting out the header in our program is easy enough:

```
di as text "    Variable {c |}     Obs" /*
    */ _col(37) "Mean    Std. Dev.      Min       Max"
di as text "{hline 13}{c +}{hline 53}"
```

We use the SMCL directive {hline} to draw the horizontal line, and we use the SMCL characters {c |} and {c +} to output the vertical bar and the "plus" sign where the lines cross.

Now let's turn to putting out the rest of the table. Variable names can be of unequal length and can even be long. If we are not careful, we might end up putting out something that looks like this:

Variable	Obs	Mean	Std. Dev.	Min	Max
miles_per_gallon	74	21.2973	5.785503	12	41
weight	74	3019.459	777.1936	1760	4840
displacement	74	197.2973	91.83722	79	425

If it were not for the too-long variable name, we could avoid the problem by displaying our lines with something like this:

```
display as text %12s "'vname'" " {c |}" /*
        */ as result /*
        */ %8.0g 'n' "    " /*
        */ %9.0g 'mean' "  " %9.0g 'sd'    "  " /*
        */ %9.0g 'min' "  " %9.0g 'max'
```

What we are imagining here is that we write a subroutine to display a line of output and that the display line above appears in that subroutine:

```
program output_line
        args n mean sd min max
        display as text %12s "'vname'" " {c |}" /*
                */ as result /*
                */ %8.0g 'n' "    " /*
                */ %9.0g 'mean' "  " %9.0g 'sd'    "  " /*
                */ %9.0g 'min' "  " %9.0g 'max'
end
```

In our main routine, we would calculate results and then just call output_line with the variable name and results to be displayed. This subroutine would be sufficient to produce the following output:

Variable	Obs	Mean	Std. Dev.	Min	Max
miles_per_gallon	74	21.2973	5.785503	12	41
weight	74	3019.459	777.1936	1760	4840
displacement	74	197.2973	91.83722	79	425

The short variable name weight would be spaced over because we specified the %12s format. The right way to handle the miles_per_gallon variable is to display its abbreviation with Stata's abbrev() function:

```
program output_line
        args n mean sd min max
        display as text %12s abbrev("'vname'",12) " {c |}" /*
                */ as result /*
                */ %8.0g 'n' "    " /*
                */ %9.0g 'mean' "  " %9.0g 'sd'    "  " /*
                */ %9.0g 'min' "  " %9.0g 'max'
end
```

With this improved subroutine, we would get the following output:

Variable	Obs	Mean	Std. Dev.	Min	Max
miles_per_~n	74	21.2973	5.785503	12	41
weight	74	3019.459	777.1936	1760	4840
displacement	74	197.2973	91.83722	79	425

The point of this is to persuade you to learn about and use Stata's abbrev() function. abbrev("'vname'",12) returns 'vname' abbreviated to 12 characters.

If we now wanted to modify our program to produce the following output,

Variable	Obs	Mean	Std. Dev.	Min	Max
miles_per_~n	74	21.2973	5.785503	12	41
weight	74	3019.459	777.1936	1760	4840
displacement	74	197.2973	91.83722	79	425

all we would need to do is add a `display` at the end of the main routine that reads

```
di as text "{hline 13}{c BT}{hline 53}"
```

Note the use of `{c BT}`. The characters that we use to draw lines in and around tables are summarized in [P] **smcl**.

❑ Technical note

Let's now consider outputting the table in the form

```
     Variable |     Obs      Mean  Std. Dev.       Min       Max
--------------+--------------------------------------------------
  miles_per_~n |      74   21.2973   5.785503        12        41
        weight |      74  3019.459   777.1936      1760      4840
  displacement |      74  197.2973   91.83722        79       425
```

where the boldfaced entries are clickable and, if you click on them, the result is to execute `summarize` followed by the variable name. We assume that you have already read [P] **smcl** and so know that the relevant SMCL directive to create the link is `{stata}`, but continue reading even if you have not read [P] **smcl**.

The obvious fix to our subroutine would be simply to add the `{stata}` directive, although to do that we will have to store `abbrev("'vname'",12)` in a macro so that we can refer to it:

```
program output_line
        args n mean sd min max
        local abname = abbrev("'vname'",12)
        display as text %12s "{stata summarize 'vname':'abname'}" /*
              */ " {c |}" /*
              */ as result /*
              */ %8.0g 'n' "   " /*
              */ %9.0g 'mean' "  " %9.0g 'sd' "   " " /*
              */ %9.0g 'min' "  " %9.0g 'max'
end
```

The SMCL directive `{stata summarize 'vname':'abname'}` says to display `'abname'` as clickable, and, if the user clicks on it, to execute `summarize 'vname'`. We used the abbreviated name to display and the unabbreviated name in the command.

The one problem with this fix is that our table will not align correctly because `display` does not know that "`{stata summarize 'vname':'abname'}`" displays only `'abname'`. To `display`, the string looks long and is not going to fit into a `%12s` field. The solution to that problem is

```
program output_line
        args n mean sd min max
        local abname = abbrev("'vname'",12)
        display as text "{ralign 12:{stata summarize 'vname':'abname'}}" /*
              */ " {c |}" /*
              */ as result /*
              */ %8.0g 'n' "   " /*
              */ %9.0g 'mean' "  " %9.0g 'sd' "   " " /*
              */ %9.0g 'min' "  " %9.0g 'max'
end
```

The SMCL `{ralign #:text}` macro right-aligns *text* in a field 12 wide and so is equivalent to `%12s`. The *text* that we are asking be aligned is "`{stata summarize 'vname':'abname'}`", but SMCL understands that the only displayable part of the string is `'abname'` and so will align it correctly.

If we wanted to duplicate the effect of a %-12s format by using SMCL, we would use {lalign 12:*text*}.

❏

Obtaining input from the terminal

display's _request(*macname*) option accepts input from the console and places it into the macro *macname*. For example,

```
. display "What is Y? " _request(yval)
What is Y? i don't know
. display "$yval"
i don't know
```

If yval had to be a number, the code fragment to obtain it might be

```
global yval "junk"
capture confirm number $yval
while _rc!=0 {
        display "What is Y? " _request(yval)
        capture confirm number $yval
}
```

You will typically want to store such input into a local macro. Local macros have names that really begin with a '_':

```
local yval "junk"
capture confirm number `yval'
while _rc!=0 {
        display "What is Y? " _request(_yval)
        capture confirm number `yval'
}
```

Also see

[P] **capture** — Capture return code

[P] **quietly** — Quietly and noisily perform Stata command

[P] **smcl** — Stata Markup and Control Language

[P] **return** — Return saved results

[D] **list** — List values of variables

[D] **outfile** — Write ASCII-format dataset

[U] **12.5 Formats: Controlling how data are displayed**

[U] **18 Programming Stata**

Title

---

ereturn — Post the estimation results

Syntax

Set macro returned by estimation command

> ereturn local *name* ...   (see [P] **macro**)

Set scalar returned by estimation command

> ereturn scalar *name* = *exp*

Set matrix returned by estimation command

> ereturn matrix *name* [=] *matname* [, copy]

Clear e() saved results

> ereturn clear

List e() saved results

> ereturn list

Save coefficient vector and variance–covariance matrix

> ereturn post [b [V [Cns]]] [*weight*] [, depname(*string*) obs(*#*) dof(*#*)
> esample(*varname*) properties(*string*)]

Change coefficient vector and variance–covariance matrix

> ereturn repost [b = b] [V = V] [Cns = Cns] [*weight*] [, esample(*varname*)
> properties(*string*) rename]

Display coefficient table

> ereturn display [, eform(*string*) first neq(*#*) plus level(*#*)]

where *name* is the name of the macro, scalar, or matrix that will be returned in e(*name*) by the estimation program; *matname* is the name of an existing matrix; **b** is a $1 \times p$ coefficient vector (matrix); **V** is a $p \times p$ covariance matrix; and **Cns** is a $c \times (p + 1)$ constraint matrix.

fweights, aweights, iweights, and pweights are allowed; see [U] **11.1.6 weight**.

Description

ereturn local, ereturn scalar, and ereturn matrix set the e() macros, scalars, and matrices other than b, V, and Cns returned by estimation commands. See [P] **return** for more discussion on returning results.

ereturn clear clears the e() saved results.

ereturn list lists the names and values of the e() returned macros and scalars, and the names and sizes of the e() returned matrices from the last estimation command.

ereturn post clears all existing e-class results and saves the coefficient vector (b), variance–covariance matrix (V), and constraint matrix (Cns) in Stata's system areas, making available all the postestimation features described in [U] **20 Estimation and postestimation commands**. b, V, and Cns are optional for ereturn post; some commands (such as factor; see [MV] **factor**) do not have a b, V, or Cns but do set the estimation sample, e(sample), and properties, e(properties). You must use ereturn post before setting other e() macros, scalars, and matrices.

ereturn repost changes the b, V, or Cns matrix (allowed only after estimation commands that posted their results with ereturn post) or changes the declared estimation sample or the contents of e(properties). The specified matrices cease to exist after post or repost; they are moved into Stata's system areas. The resulting b, V, and Cns matrices in Stata's system areas can be retrieved by reference to e(b), e(V), and e(Cns). ereturn post and repost deal with only the coefficient and variance–covariance matrices, whereas ereturn matrix is used to save other matrices associated with the estimation command.

ereturn display displays or redisplays the coefficient table corresponding to results that have been previously posted using ereturn post or repost.

For a discussion of posting results with constraint matrices (**Cns** in the syntax diagram above), see [P] **makecns**, but only after reading this entry.

Options

copy specified with ereturn matrix indicates that the matrix is to be copied; that is, the original matrix should be left in place.

depname(*string*) specified with ereturn post supplies a name that should be that of the dependent variable but can be anything; that name is saved and added to the appropriate place on the output whenever ereturn display is executed.

obs(#) specified with ereturn post supplies the number of observations on which the estimation was performed; that number is saved and stored in e(N).

dof(#) specified with ereturn post supplies the number of (denominator) degrees of freedom that is to be used with t and f statistics and is saved and stored in e(df_r). This number is used in calculating significance levels and confidence intervals by ereturn display and by subsequent test commands performed on the posted results. If the option is not specified, normal (Z) and χ^2 statistics are used.

esample(*varname*) specified with ereturn post or ereturn repost gives the name of the 0/1 variable indicating the observations involved in the estimation. The variable is removed from the dataset but is available for use as e(sample); see [U] **20.6 Specifying the estimation subsample**. If the esample() option is not specified with ereturn post, it is set to all zeros (meaning no estimation sample). See [P] **mark** for details of the marksample command that can help create *varname*.

properties(*string*) specified with `ereturn post` or `ereturn repost` sets the `e(properties)` macro. By default, `e(properties)` is set to b V if `properties()` is not specified.

rename is allowed only with the b = b syntax of `ereturn repost` and tells Stata to use the names obtained from the specified b matrix as the labels for both the b and V estimation matrices. These labels are subsequently used in the output produced by `ereturn display`.

eform(*string*) specified with `ereturn display` indicates that the exponentiated form of the coefficients is to be output and that reporting of the constant is to be suppressed. *string* is used to label the exponentiated coefficients; see [R] *eform_option*.

first requests that Stata display only the first equation and make it appear as if only one equation were estimated.

neq(*#*) requests that Stata display only the first *#* equations and make it appear as if only *#* equations were estimated.

plus changes the bottom separation line produced by `ereturn display` to have a + symbol at the position of the dividing line between variable names and results. This is useful if you plan on adding more output to the table.

level(*#*), an option of `ereturn display`, supplies the significance level for the confidence intervals of the coefficients; see [U] **20 Estimation and postestimation commands**.

Remarks

Remarks are presented under the following headings:

> *Estimation-class programs*
> *Setting individual estimation results*
> *Posting estimation coefficient and variance–covariance matrices*
> > *Single-equation models*
> > *Multiple-equation models*
> > *Single-equation models masquerading as multiple-equation models*
> *Setting the estimation sample*
> *Setting estimation-result properties*
> *Reposting results*
> *Minor details: The depname() and dof() options*

For a summary of the `ereturn` command, see [P] **return**.

Estimation-class programs

After any estimation command, you can obtain individual coefficients and standard errors by using _b[] and _se[] (see [U] **13.5 Accessing coefficients and standard errors**); list the coefficients by using `matrix list e(b)`; list the variance–covariance matrix of the estimators by using `matrix list e(V)` or in a table by using `estat vce` (see [R] **estat**); obtain the linear prediction and its standard error by using `predict` (see [R] **predict**); and test linear hypotheses about the coefficients by using `test` (see [R] **test**). Other important information from an estimation command can be obtained from the returned e() results. (For example, the estimation command name is returned in e(cmd). The dependent variable name is returned in e(depvar).) The e() results from an estimation command can be listed by using the `ereturn list` command. All these features are summarized in [U] **20 Estimation and postestimation commands**.

If you decide to write your own estimation command, your command can share all these features as well. This is accomplished by posting the results you calculate to Stata. The basic outline of an estimation command is

```
program myest, eclass
      version 11
      if !replay() {
              syntax whatever [, whatever Level(cilevel)]
              marksample touse       // see [P] mark
              perform any other parsing of the user's estimation request;
              local depn "dependent variable name"
              local nobs = number of observations in estimation
              tempname b V
              produce coefficient vector 'b' and variance–covariance matrix 'V'
              ereturn post 'b' 'V', obs('nobs') depname('depn') esample('touse')
              ereturn local depvar "'depn'"
              store whatever else you want in e()
              ereturn local cmd "myest"       // set e(cmd) last
      }
      else {    // replay
              if "'e(cmd)'"!="myest" error 301
              syntax [, Level(cilevel)]
      }
      output any header above the coefficient table;
      ereturn display, level('level')
end
```

We will not discuss here how the estimates are formed; see [P] **matrix** for an example of programming linear regression, and see [R] **ml** for examples of programming maximum likelihood estimators. However the estimates are formed, our interest is in posting those results to Stata.

When programming estimation commands, remember to declare them as estimation commands by including the eclass option of program; see [U] **18 Programming Stata**. If you do not declare your program to be eclass, Stata will produce an error if you use ereturn local, ereturn scalar, or ereturn matrix in your program. For more information about saving program results, see [P] **return**.

The estimation program definition statement—program myest, eclass—should also have included a properties() option, but we omitted it because 1) it is not necessary and 2) you might confuse it with ereturn's properties() option.

There are two sets of properties associated with estimation commands: program properties and estimation-result properties. The first are set by the properties() option of the program definition statement. The second are set by ereturn's properties() option. The first tell Stata's prefix commands, such as stepwise and svy, whether they should work with this new estimation command. The second tell Stata's postestimation commands, such as predict and test, whether they should work after this new estimation command.

The first is discussed in [P] **program properties**. The second will be discussed below.

❑ Technical note

Notice the use of the replay() function in our estimation program example. This function is not like other Stata functions; see [D] **functions**. replay() simply returns 1 if the command line is empty or begins with a comma, and 0 otherwise. More simply: replay() indicates whether the command is an initial call to the estimation program (replay() returns 0) or a call to redisplay past estimation results (replay() returns 1).

In fact,

```
if !replay() {
```

is equivalent to

```
if trim(`"`0'"') == "" | substr((trim(`"`0'"')),1,1) == "," {
```

but is easier to read.

❑

The `ereturn local`, `ereturn scalar`, `ereturn matrix`, `ereturn clear`, and `ereturn list` commands are discussed in *Setting individual estimation results*. The `ereturn post`, `ereturn repost`, and `ereturn display` commands are discussed in *Posting estimation coefficient and variance–covariance matrices*.

Setting individual estimation results

Stata's estimation commands save the command name in the returned macro `e(cmd)` and save the name of the dependent variable in `e(depvar)`. Other macros and scalars are also saved. For example, the estimation sample size is saved in the returned scalar `e(N)`. The model and residual degrees of freedom are saved in `e(df_m)` and `e(df_r)`.

These `e()` macro and scalar results are saved using the `ereturn local` and `ereturn scalar` commands. Matrices may be saved using the `ereturn matrix` command. The coefficient vector `e(b)` and variance–covariance matrix `e(V)`, however, are handled differently and are saved using only the `ereturn post` and `ereturn repost` commands, which are discussed in the next section.

▷ Example 1

Assume that we are programming an estimation command called `xyz` and that we have the dependent variable in `'depname'`, the estimation sample size in `'nobs'`, and other important information stored in other local macros and scalars. We also wish to save an auxiliary estimation matrix that our program has created called `lam` into the saved matrix `e(lambda)`. We would save these results by using commands such as the following in our estimation program:

```
...
ereturn local depvar "'depname'"
ereturn scalar N = 'nobs'
ereturn matrix lambda lam
...
ereturn local cmd "xyz"
```

◁

The matrix given to the `ereturn matrix` command is removed, and the new `e()` matrix is then made available. For instance, in this example, we have the line

```
ereturn matrix lambda lam
```

After this line has executed, the matrix `lam` is no longer available for use, but you can instead refer to the newly created `e(lambda)` matrix.

The `e()` results from an estimation command can be viewed using the `ereturn list` command.

▷ Example 2

We regress automobile weight on length and engine displacement by using the auto dataset.

```
. use http://www.stata-press.com/data/r11/auto
(1978 Automobile Data)
. regress weight length displ
```

Source	SS	df	MS			
Model	41063449.8	2	20531724.9			
Residual	3030728.55	71	42686.3176			
Total	44094178.4	73	604029.841			

	Number of obs =	74
	F(2, 71) =	480.99
	Prob > F =	0.0000
	R-squared =	0.9313
	Adj R-squared =	0.9293
	Root MSE =	206.61

weight	Coef.	Std. Err.	t	P>|t|	[95% Conf. Interval]	
length	22.91788	1.974431	11.61	0.000	18.98097	26.85478
displacement	2.932772	.4787094	6.13	0.000	1.978252	3.887291
_cons	-1866.181	297.7349	-6.27	0.000	-2459.847	-1272.514

```
. ereturn list
scalars:
                 e(N) =  74
              e(df_m) =  2
              e(df_r) =  71
                 e(F) =  480.9907735088092
                e(r2) =  .9312669232040125
              e(rmse) =  206.6066736285299
               e(mss) =  41063449.82964132
               e(rss) =  3030728.548737055
              e(r2_a) =  .9293307801956748
                e(ll) =  -497.9506459758983
              e(ll_0) =  -597.0190609278627
              e(rank) =  3

macros:
           e(cmdline) : "regress weight length displ"
             e(title) : "Linear regression"
         e(marginsok) : "XB default"
               e(vce) : "ols"
            e(depvar) : "weight"
               e(cmd) : "regress"
        e(properties) : "b V"
           e(predict) : "regres_p"
             e(model) : "ols"
         e(estat_cmd) : "regress_estat"

matrices:
                 e(b) :  1 x 3
                 e(V) :  3 x 3

functions:
             e(sample)
```

In addition to listing all the e() results after an estimation command, you can access individual e() results.

```
. display "The command is: `e(cmd)'"
The command is: regress
. display "The adjusted R-squared is: `e(r2_a)'"
The adjusted R-squared is: .9293307801956748
. display "The residual sums-of-squares is: `e(rss)'"
The residual sums-of-squares is: 3030728.548737053
```

```
. matrix list e(V)

symmetric e(V)[3,3]
                     length  displacement           _cons
       length     3.8983761
 displacement    -.78935643     .22916272
        _cons    -576.89342     103.13249       88646.064

. matrix list e(b)

e(b)[1,3]
           length  displacement         _cons
   y1    22.917876     2.9327718    -1866.1807
```

For more information on referring to e() results, see [P] **return**.   ◁

The reference manuals' entries for Stata's estimation commands have a *Saved results* section describing the e() results that are returned by the command. If you are writing an estimation command, we recommend that you save the same kind of estimation results by using the same naming convention as Stata's estimation commands. This is important if you want postestimation commands to work after your estimation command. See [U] **20 Estimation and postestimation commands** and [P] **return** for details.

When programming your estimation command, you will want to issue either an ereturn clear command or an ereturn post command before you save any estimation results. The ereturn clear command clears all e() results. The ereturn post command, which is discussed in the next section, first clears all previous e() results and then performs the post.

We recommend that you postpone clearing past estimation results and setting new e() results until late in your program. If an error occurs early in your program, the last successful estimation results will remain intact. The best place in your estimation program to set the e() results is after all other calculations have been completed and before estimation results are displayed.

We also recommend that you save the command name in e(cmd) as your last act of saving results. This ensures that if e(cmd) is present, then all the other estimation results were successfully saved. Postestimation commands assume that if e(cmd) is present, then the estimation command completed successfully and all expected results were saved. If you saved e(cmd) early in your estimation command and the user pressed *Break* before the remaining e() results were saved, postestimation commands operating on the partial results will probably produce an error.

Posting estimation coefficient and variance–covariance matrices

The most important estimation results are the coefficient vector b and the variance–covariance matrix V. Because these two matrices are at the heart of most estimation commands, for increased command execution speed, Stata handles these matrices in a special way. The ereturn post, ereturn repost, and ereturn display commands work on these matrices. The ereturn matrix command discussed in the last section cannot be used to save or to post the b and V matrices.

Single-equation models

Before posting, the coefficient vector is stored as a $1 \times p$ matrix and the corresponding variance–covariance matrix as a $p \times p$ matrix. The names bordering the coefficient matrix and those bordering the variance–covariance matrix play an important role. First, they must be the same. Second, it is these names that tell Stata how the results link to Stata's other features.

Estimation results come in two forms: those for single-equation models and those for multiple-equation models. The absence or presence of equation names in the names bordering the matrix (see [P] **matrix rownames**) tells Stata which form it is.

▷ Example 3

For instance, consider

```
. use http://www.stata-press.com/data/r11/auto
(1978 Automobile Data)
. regress price weight mpg
 (output omitted )
. matrix b = e(b)
. matrix V = e(V)
. matrix list b
b[1,3]
        weight        mpg       _cons
y1    1.7465592  -49.512221   1946.0687
. matrix list V
symmetric V[3,3]
             weight         mpg        _cons
weight    .41133468
   mpg    44.601659    7422.863
 _cons  -2191.9032  -292759.82    12938766
```

If these were our estimation results, they would correspond to a single-equation model because the names bordering the matrices have no equation names. Here we post these results:

```
. ereturn post b V
. ereturn display
```

	Coef.	Std. Err.	z	P>|z|	[95% Conf. Interval]	
weight	1.746559	.6413538	2.72	0.006	.4895288	3.003589
mpg	-49.51222	86.15604	-0.57	0.566	-218.375	119.3505
_cons	1946.069	3597.05	0.54	0.588	-5104.019	8996.156

Once the results have been posted, anytime the `ereturn display` command is executed, Stata will redisplay the coefficient table. Moreover, all of Stata's other postestimation features work. For instance,

```
. correlate, _coef
            weight      mpg     _cons
  weight    1.0000
     mpg    0.8072   1.0000
   _cons   -0.9501  -0.9447   1.0000
. test weight
 ( 1)  weight = 0
           chi2(  1) =    7.42
         Prob > chi2 =   0.0065
. test weight = mpg/50
 ( 1)  weight - .02*mpg = 0
           chi2(  1) =    4.69
         Prob > chi2 =   0.0303
```

If the user were to type predict pred, then predict would create a new variable based on

$$1.746559 \, \text{weight} - 49.51222 \, \text{mpg} + 1946.069$$

except that it would carry out the calculation by using the full, double-precision values of the coefficients. All determinations are made by Stata on the basis of the names bordering the posted matrices.

◁

Multiple-equation models

If the matrices posted using the ereturn post or ereturn repost commands have more than one equation name, the estimation command is treated as a multiple-equation model.

▷ Example 4

Consider the following two matrices before posting:

```
. mat list b

b[1,6]
           price:      price:      price:      displ:      displ:      displ:
           weight         mpg       _cons      weight     foreign       _cons
y1      1.7417059   -50.31993   1977.9249   .09341608  -35.124241  -74.326413

. mat list V

symmetric V[6,6]
                       price:      price:      price:      displ:      displ:
                       weight         mpg       _cons      weight     foreign
price:weight        .38775906
  price:mpg         41.645165   6930.8263
  price:_cons      -2057.7522  -273353.75    12116943
 displ:weight       .00030351   -.01074361  -.68762197   .00005432
displ:foreign      -.18390487     -30.6065    1207.129   .05342871   152.20821
 displ:_cons       -.86175743    41.539129   1936.6875   -.1798972  -206.57691
                       displ:
                       _cons
 displ:_cons        625.79842
```

The row and column names of the matrices include equation names. Here we post these matrices to Stata and then use the posted results:

```
. ereturn post b V

. ereturn display
```

	Coef.	Std. Err.	z	P>|z|	[95% Conf. Interval]	
price						
weight	1.741706	.622703	2.80	0.005	.5212304	2.962181
mpg	-50.31993	83.25158	-0.60	0.546	-213.49	112.8502
_cons	1977.925	3480.94	0.57	0.570	-4844.592	8800.442
displ						
weight	.0934161	.0073701	12.67	0.000	.0789709	.1078612
foreign	-35.12424	12.33727	-2.85	0.004	-59.30484	-10.94364
_cons	-74.32641	25.01596	-2.97	0.003	-123.3568	-25.29603

```
. test [price]weight

( 1)  [price]weight = 0

            chi2(  1) =     7.82
          Prob > chi2 =    0.0052

. test weight

( 1)  [price]weight = 0
( 2)  [displ]weight = 0

            chi2(  2) =   164.51
          Prob > chi2 =    0.0000
```

Stata determined that this was a multiple-equation model because equation names were present. All Stata's equation-name features (such as those available with the test command) are then made available. The user could type predict pred to obtain linear predictions of the [price] equation (because predict defaults to the first equation) or type predict pred, equation(displ) to obtain predictions of the [displ] equation:

$$.0934161\,weight - 35.12424\,foreign - 74.32641$$

◁

Single-equation models masquerading as multiple-equation models

▷ Example 5

Sometimes, it may be convenient to program a single-equation model as if it were a multiple-equation model. This occurs when there are ancillary parameters. Think of linear regression: in addition to the parameter estimates, there is s, which is an estimate of σ, the standard error of the residual. This can be calculated on the side in that you can calculate $\mathbf{b} = (\mathbf{X}'\mathbf{X})^{-1}\mathbf{X}'\mathbf{y}$ independently of s and then calculate s given $\mathbf{b}$. Pretend that were not the case—think of a straightforward maximum likelihood calculation where s is just one more parameter (in most models, ancillary parameters and the coefficients must be solved for jointly). The right thing to do would be to give s its own equation:

```
. mat list b

b[1,4]
          price:       price:       price:       _anc:
          weight          mpg        _cons        sigma
y1    1.7465592   -49.512221    1946.0687         2514

. matrix list V
(output omitted )

. ereturn post b V

. ereturn display
```

		Coef.	Std. Err.	z	P>|z|	[95% Conf.	Interval]
price							
	weight	1.746559	.6413538	2.72	0.006	.4895288	3.003589
	mpg	-49.51222	86.15604	-0.57	0.566	-218.375	119.3505
	_cons	1946.069	3597.05	0.54	0.588	-5104.019	8996.156
_anc							
	sigma	2514	900	2.79	0.005	750.0324	4277.968

Now consider the alternative, which would be simply to add *s* to the estimated parameters without equation names:

```
. matrix list b
b[1,4]
        weight       mpg      _cons      sigma
y1   1.7465592  -49.512221  1946.0687     2514
. matrix list V
  (output omitted)
. ereturn post b V
. ereturn display
```

	Coef.	Std. Err.	z	P>|z|	[95% Conf. Interval]
weight	1.746559	.6413538	2.72	0.006	.4895288 3.003589
mpg	-49.51222	86.15604	-0.57	0.566	-218.375 119.3505
_cons	1946.069	3597.05	0.54	0.588	-5104.019 8996.156
sigma	2514	900	2.79	0.005	750.0324 4277.968

This second solution is inferior because, if the user typed `predict pred`, then `predict` would attempt to form the linear combination:

$$1.746559 \, \texttt{weight} - 49.51222 \, \texttt{mpg} + 1946.069 + 2514 \, \texttt{sigma}$$

There are only two possibilities, and neither is good: either `sigma` does not exist in the dataset—which is to be hoped—and `predict` produces the error message "variable sigma not found", or something called `sigma` does exist, and `predict` goes on to form this meaningless combination.

◁

On the other hand, if the parameter estimates are separated from the ancillary parameter (which could be parameters) by the equation names, the user can type `predict pred, equation(price)` to obtain a meaningful result. Moreover, the user can omit `equation(price)` partly because `predict` (and Stata's other postestimation commands) defaults to the first equation.

We recommend that ancillary parameters be collected together and given their own equation and that the equation be called `_anc`.

Setting the estimation sample

In our previous examples, we did not indicate the estimation sample as specified with the `esample(varname)` option. In general, you provide this either with your initial `ereturn post` command or with a subsequent `ereturn repost` command. Some postestimation commands automatically restrict themselves to the estimation sample, and if you do not provide this information, they will complain that there are no observations; see [U] **20.6 Specifying the estimation subsample**. Also, users of your estimation command expect to use `if e(sample)` successfully in commands that they execute after your estimation command.

▷ Example 6

Returning to our first example:

```
. ereturn post b V
. ereturn display
  (output omitted)
```

```
. summarize price if e(sample)
    Variable |     Obs      Mean    Std. Dev.      Min       Max
-------------+-----------------------------------------------------
       price |       0
```

does not produce what the user expects. Specifying the estimation sample with the esample() option of ereturn post produces the expected result:

```
. ereturn post b V, esample(estsamp)
. ereturn display
```
(*output omitted*)
```
. summarize price if e(sample)
    Variable |     Obs      Mean    Std. Dev.      Min       Max
-------------+-----------------------------------------------------
       price |      74   6165.257   2949.496      3291     15906
```

◁

The marksample command (see [P] **mark**) is a useful programming command that aids in creating and setting up an estimation sample indicator variable, such as estsamp.

Setting estimation-result properties

The properties() option of ereturn post and repost allows you to set e(properties). By default, ereturn post sets e(properties) to b V when you supply a b and V argument. If you supply the b, but not the V, it defaults to b. If you do not supply the b and V, it defaults to being empty. Using the properties() option, you can augment or override the default setting. You are also free to use ereturn local to set e(properties).

e(properties) is used as a signal to postestimation commands. A b in e(properties) is a signal that the e(b) returned matrix can be interpreted as a coefficient vector. A V in e(properties) indicates that e(V) can be interpreted as a VCE matrix. An e(properties) containing eigen indicates that the estimation command has placed eigenvalues in e(Ev) and eigenvectors in e(L). A command, such as screeplot (see [MV] **screeplot**), that plots the eigenvalues and can be used as a postestimation command looks to see if eigen is found in e(properties). If so, it then looks for e(Ev) to contain the eigenvalues.

▷ Example 7

We demonstrate by interactively posting a b vector without posting a V matrix. Even without a V matrix, the available information provided by b is used appropriately.

```
. use http://www.stata-press.com/data/r11/auto
(1978 Automobile Data)
. matrix b=(2,-1)
. matrix colnames b = turn trunk
. ereturn post b
. ereturn display
```

	Coef.
turn	2
trunk	-1

```
. predict myxb, xb
. list turn trunk myxb in 1/4
```

	turn	trunk	myxb
1.	40	11	69
2.	40	11	69
3.	35	12	58
4.	40	16	64

The estimation table produced by `ereturn display` omits the standard errors, tests, and confidence intervals because they rely on having a VCE matrix. `predict` with the xb option produces the linear predictions. If you tried to use the `stdp` option of `predict`, you would get an error message indicating that the requested action was not valid.

◁

The `has_eprop()` programmer's function is useful for determining if `e(properties)` contains a particular property; see [D] **functions**.

❏ Technical note

Do not confuse the properties set with the `properties()` option of `ereturn post` and `ereturn repost`, which are placed in `e(properties)` and used by postestimation commands, with the `properties()` option of the `program` command; see [P] **program**. The properties set by `program` indicate to other programs before the command is executed that certain features have been implemented, e.g., the `svyr` property indicates to the `svy` prefix command that the requirements to use the `vce(linearized)` variance estimation method have been satisfied. On the other hand, the properties set by `ereturn` are for use after the program has run and may depend on the data and options of the program.

❏

Reposting results

In certain programming situations, only a small part of a previous estimation result needs to be altered. `ereturn repost` allows us to change five parts of an estimation result that was previously posted with `ereturn post`. We can change the coefficient vector, the variance–covariance matrix, and the declared estimation sample by using the `esample()` option; we can change the declared properties by using the `properties()` option; and we can change the variable names for the coefficients by using the `rename` option. A programmer might, for instance, simply replace the variance–covariance matrix provided by a previous `ereturn post` with a robust covariance matrix to create a new estimation result.

Sometimes a programmer might preserve the data, make major alterations to the data (using drop, reshape, etc.) to perform needed computations, post the estimation results, and then finally restore the data. Here, when `ereturn post` is called, the correct estimation sample indicator variable is unavailable. `ereturn repost` with the `esample()` option allows us to set the estimation sample without changing the rest of our posted estimation results.

▷ Example 8

For example, inside an estimation command program, we might have

```
...
ereturn post b V
...
ereturn repost, esample(estsamp)
...
```
◁

❏ Technical note

ereturn repost may be called only from within a program that has been declared an estimation class program by using the eclass option of the program statement. The same is not true of ereturn post. We believe that the only legitimate uses of ereturn repost are in a programming context. ereturn post, on the other hand, may be important for some non–e-class programming situations.
❏

Minor details: The depname() and dof() options

Single-equation models may have one dependent variable; in those that do, you should specify the identity of this one dependent variable in the depname() option with ereturn post. The result is simply to add a little more labeling to the output.

If you do not specify the dof(#) option at the time of posting or set e(df_r) equal to the degrees of freedom, normal (Z) statistics will be used to calculate significance levels and confidence intervals on subsequent ereturn display output. If you do specify dof(#) or set e(df_r) equal to #, t statistics with # degrees of freedom will be used. Similarly, if you did not specify dof(#) or set e(df_r), any subsequent test commands will present a χ^2 statistic; if you specify dof(#) or set e(df_r), subsequent test commands will use the f statistic with # denominator degrees of freedom.

▷ Example 9

Let's add the dependent variable name and degrees of freedom to example 3.

```
. ereturn post b V, depname(price) dof(71)
. ereturn display
```

price	Coef.	Std. Err.	t	P>|t|	[95% Conf. Interval]	
weight	1.746559	.6413538	2.72	0.008	.467736	3.025382
mpg	-49.51222	86.15604	-0.57	0.567	-221.3025	122.278
_cons	1946.069	3597.05	0.54	0.590	-5226.245	9118.382

Note the addition of the word price at the top of the table. This was produced because of the depname(price) option specification. Also t statistics were used instead of normal (Z) statistics because the dof(71) option was specified.
◁

Saved results

`ereturn post` saves the following in `e()`:

Scalars
e(N)	number of observations
e(df_r)	degrees of freedom, if specified

Macros
e(wtype)	weight type
e(wexp)	weight expression
e(properties)	estimation properties; typically b V

Matrices
e(b)	coefficient vector
e(Cns)	constraints matrix
e(V)	variance–covariance matrix of the estimators

Functions
e(sample)	marks estimation sample

`ereturn repost` saves the following in `e()`:

Macros
e(wtype)	weight type
e(wexp)	weight expression
e(properties)	estimation properties; typically b V

Matrices
e(b)	coefficient vector
e(Cns)	constraints matrix
e(V)	variance–covariance matrix of the estimators

Functions
e(sample)	marks estimation sample

With `ereturn post`, all previously stored estimation results—`e()` items—are removed. `ereturn repost`, however, does not remove previously stored estimation results. `ereturn clear` removes the current `e()` results.

Also see

[P] _estimates — Manage estimation results

[P] **return** — Return saved results

[R] **estimates** — Save and manipulate estimation results

[U] **18 Programming Stata**

[U] **18.9 Accessing results calculated by estimation commands**

[U] **18.10.2 Saving results in e()**

[U] **20 Estimation and postestimation commands**

Title

error — Display generic error message and exit

Syntax

error *exp*

Description

error displays the most generic form of the error message associated with expression and sets the return code to the evaluation of the expression. If expression evaluates to 0, error does nothing. Otherwise, the nonzero return code will force an exit from the program or capture block in which it occurs. error sets the return code to 197 if there is an error in using error itself.

Remarks

Remarks are presented under the following headings:

> *Introduction*
> *Summary*
> *Other messages*

Introduction

error is used in two ways inside programs. In the first case, you want to display a standard error message so that users can look up your message by using search:

```
if ('nvals'>100) error 134
```

According to [R] **search**, return code 134 is associated with the message "too many values". During program development, you can verify that by typing the error command interactively:

```
. error 134
too many values
r(134);
```

Below we list the individual return codes so that you can select the appropriate one for use with error in your programs.

error is also used when you have processed a block of code in a capture block, suppressing all output. If anything has gone wrong, you want to display the error message associated with whatever the problem was:

```
capture {
        code continues
}
local rc=_rc                          preserve return code from capture
cleanup code
error 'rc'                            present error message and exit if necessary
code could continue
```

Usually, one hopes that the return code will be zero so that error does nothing.

You can interrogate the built-in variable _rc to determine the type of error that occurred and then take the appropriate action. Also see [U] **16.1.4 Error handling in do-files**.

The return codes are numerically grouped, which is a feature that you may find useful when you are writing programs. The groups are

Return codes	Meaning
1–99	sundry "minor" errors
100–199	syntax errors
300–399	failure to find previously stored result
400–499	statistical problems
500–599	matrix-manipulation errors
600–699	file errors
700–799	operating-system errors
900–999	insufficient-memory errors
1000–1999	system-limit-exceeded errors
2000–2999	nonerrors (continuation of 400–499)
3000–3999	Mata run-time errors; see [M-2] **errors** for codes
4000–4999	class system errors
9000–9999	system-failure errors

Summary

1. You pressed *Break*. This is not considered an error.

2. `connection timed out -- see help r(2) for troubleshooting`
   An Internet connection has timed out. This can happen when the initial attempt to make a connection over the Internet has not succeeded within a certain time limit. You can change the time limit that Stata uses under this condition by typing set timeout1 *#seconds*. Or, the initial connection was successful, but a subsequent attempt to send or receive data over the Internet has timed out. You can also change this time limit by typing set timeout2 *#seconds*.

3. `no dataset in use`
   You attempted to perform a command requiring data and have no data in memory.

4. `no; data in memory would be lost`
   You attempted to perform a command that would substantively alter or destroy the data, and the data have not been saved, at least since the data were last changed. If you wish to continue anyway, add the clear option to the end of the command. Otherwise, save the data first.

5. `not sorted`
   `master data not sorted`
   `using data not sorted`
   The observations of the data are not in the order required. To solve the problem, use sort to sort the data then reissue the command; see [D] **sort**.

   In the second and third cases, both the dataset in memory and the dataset on disk must be sorted by the variables specified in the varlist of merge before they can be merged. merge automatically sorts the datasets for you, unless you specify the sorted option. You specified sorted, but your dataset is not sorted on the variables in varlist. Do not specify sorted.

6. Return code from confirm existence when *string* does not exist.

7. '_____' found where _____ expected
   You are using a program that is using the confirm command to verify that what you typed makes sense. The messages indicate what you typed and what the program expected to find instead of what you typed.

9. `assertion is false`
   `no action taken`
   Return code and message from assert when the assertion is false; see [D] **assert**.
   Or, you were using mvencode and requested that Stata change '.' to # in the specified varlist, but # already existed in the varlist, so Stata refused; see [D] **mvencode**.

18. `you must start with an empty dataset`
    The command (e.g., `infile`) requires that no data be in memory—you must `drop _all` first. You are probably using `infile` to append additional data to the data in memory. Instead, `save` the data in memory, `drop _all`, `infile` the new data, and then `append` the previously saved data; see [D] **append**.

100. `varlist required`
     `= exp required`
     `using required`
     `by() option required`
     Certain commands require a varlist or another element of the language. The message specifies the required item that was missing from the command you gave. See the command's syntax diagram. For example, `merge` requires `using` to be specified; perhaps you meant to type `append`. Or, `ranksum` requires a `by()` option; see [R] **ranksum**.

101. `varlist not allowed`
     `weights not allowed`
     `in range not allowed`
     `if not allowed`
     `= exp not allowed`
     `using not allowed`
     Certain commands do not allow an `if` qualifier or other elements of the language. The message specifies which item in the command is not allowed. See the command's syntax diagram. For example, `append` does not allow a varlist; perhaps you meant to type `merge`.

102. `too few variables specified`
     The command requires more variables than you specified. For instance, `stack` requires at least two variables. See the syntax diagram for the command.

103. `too many variables specified`
     The command does not allow as many variables as you specified. For example, `tabulate` takes only one or two variables. See the syntax diagram for the command.

104. `nothing to input`
     You gave the `input` command with no varlist. Stata will input onto the end of the dataset, but there is no existing dataset here. You must specify the variable names on the `input` command.

106. `_____ is _____ in using data`
     You have attempted to match-merge two datasets, but one of the key variables is a string in one dataset and a numeric in the other. The first blank is filled in with the variable name and the second blank with the storage type. It is logically impossible to fulfill your request. Perhaps you meant another variable.

107. `not possible with numeric variable`
     You have requested something that is logically impossible with a numeric variable, such as encoding it. Perhaps you meant another variable or typed `encode` when you meant `decode`.

108. `not possible with string variable`
     You have requested something that is logically impossible with a string variable, such as decoding it. Perhaps you meant another variable or typed `decode` when you meant `encode`.

109. `type mismatch`
     In an expression, you attempted to combine a string and numeric subexpression in a logically impossible way. For instance, you attempted to subtract a string from a number or you attempted to take the substring of a number.

110. `_____ already defined`
     A variable or a value label has already been defined, and you attempted to redefine it. This occurs most often with `generate`. If you really intend to replace the values, use `replace`. If you intend to replace a value label, specify the `replace` option with the `label define` command. If you are attempting to alter an existing label, specify the `add` or `modify` option with the `label define` command.

111. _____ not found
no variables defined
The variable does not exist. You may have mistyped the variable's name.

variables out of order
You specified a varlist containing *varname1–varname2*, yet *varname1* occurs after *varname2*. Reverse the order of the variables if you did not make some other typographical error. Remember, *varname1–varname2* is taken by Stata to mean *varname1*, *varname2*, and all the variables in *dataset order* in between. Type describe to see the order of the variables in your dataset.

_____ not found in using data
You specified a varlist with merge, but the variables on which you wish to merge are not found in the using dataset, so the merge is not possible.

_____ ambiguous abbreviation
You typed an ambiguous abbreviation for a variable in your data. The abbreviation could refer to more than one variable. Use a nonambiguous abbreviation, or if you intend all the variables implied by the ambiguous abbreviation, append a '*' to the end of the abbreviation.

119. statement out of context
This is the generic form of this message; more likely, you will see messages such as "may not streset after ...". You have attempted to do something that, in this context, is not allowed or does not make sense.

120. invalid %format
You specified an invalid *%fmt*; see [U] **12.5 Formats: Controlling how data are displayed**.

Return codes 121–127 are errors that might occur when you specify a numlist. For details about *numlist*, see [U] **11.1.8 numlist**.

121. invalid numlist

122. invalid numlist has too few elements

123. invalid numlist has too many elements

124. invalid numlist has elements out of order

125. invalid numlist has elements outside of allowed range

126. invalid numlist has noninteger elements

127. invalid numlist has missing values

130. expression too long
too many SUMs
In the first case, you specified an expression that is too long for Stata to process—the expression contains more than 249 pairs of nested parentheses or more than 800 dyadic operators. (For Small Stata, the limit is 66 dyadic operators.) Break the expression into smaller parts. In the second case, the expression contains more than 5 sum() functions. This expression, too, will have to be broken into smaller parts.

131. not possible with test
You requested a test of a hypothesis that is nonlinear in the variables. test tests only linear hypotheses. Use testnl.

132. too many '(' or '['
too many ')' or ']'
You specified an expression with unbalanced parentheses or brackets.

133. unknown function _____()
You specified a function that is unknown to Stata; see [D] **functions**. Or you may have meant to subscript a variable and accidentally used parentheses rather than square brackets; see [U] **13.7 Explicit subscripting**.

134. too many values
1) You attempted to encode a string variable that takes on more than 65,536 unique values. 2) You attempted to tabulate a variable or pair of variables that take on too many values. If you specified two variables, try interchanging them. 3) You issued a graph command using the by option. The by-variable takes on too many different values to construct a readable chart.

135. not possible with weighted data
You attempted to predict something other than the prediction or residual, but the underlying model was weighted. Stata cannot calculate the statistic you requested using weighted data.

140. `repeated categorical variable in term`
At least one of the terms in your `anova` model or `test` statement has a repeated categorical variable, such as `reg#div#reg`. Either you forgot to specify that the variable is continuous or the second occurrence of the variable is unnecessary.

141. `repeated term`
In the list of terms in your `anova` model or `test` statement is a duplicate of another term, although perhaps ordered differently. For instance, `X#A#X` and `A#X#X`. Remove the repeated term.

145. `term contains more than 8 variables`
One of the terms in your `anova` model `test` statement contains more than eight variables. Stata cannot fit such models.

146. `too many variables or values  (matsize too small)`
You can increase matsize using the set matsize command; see help matsize.
Your `anova` model resulted in a specification containing more than $matsize - 2$ explanatory variables; see [R] **matsize**.

147. `term not in model`
Your `test` command refers to a term that was not contained in your `anova` model.

148. `too few categories`
You attempted to fit a model such as `mlogit`, `ologit`, or `oprobit` when the number of outcomes is smaller than 3. Check that the dependent variable is the variable you intend. If it takes on exactly two values, use `logit` or `probit`.

149. `too many categories`
You attempted to fit an `mprobit` or `slogit` model with a dependent variable that takes on more than 30 categories.

151. `non r-class program may not set r()`
Perhaps you specified `return local` in your program but forgot to declare the program `rclass` in the `program define` statement.

152. `non e-class program may not set e()`
Perhaps you specified `estimates local` in your program but forgot to declare the program `eclass` in the `program define` statement.

153. `non s-class program may not set s()`
Perhaps you specified `sreturn local` in your program but forgot to declare the program `sclass` in the `program define` statement.

161. `ado-file has commands outside of program define ...end`
All commands in ado-files must be part of Stata programs. That is, all commands must be between a `program define` that begins a program definition and an `end` that concludes a program definition. The command you typed automatically loaded an ado-file that violates this rule.

162. `ado-file does not define command`
`xyz.ado` is supposed to define `xyz` and, perhaps, subroutines for use by `xyz`, in which case file `xyz.ado` did not define anything named `xyz`.

170. `unable to chdir`
(*Unix and Mac.*) `cd` was unable to change to the directory you typed because it does not exist, it is protected, or it is not a directory.

175. `factor level out of range`
You specified an invalid value for the level of a factor variable.

180. `invalid attempt to modify label`
You are attempting to modify the contents of an existing value label by using the `label define` command. If you mean to completely replace the existing label, specify the `replace` option with the `label define` command. If you wish to modify the existing label, be sure to specify either the `add` option or the `modify` option on the `label define` command. `add` lets you add new entries but not change existing ones, and `modify` lets you do both. You will get this error if you specify `add` and then attempt to modify an existing entry. Then edit the command and substitute `modify` for the `add` option.

181. `may not label strings`
You attempted to assign a value label to a string variable, which makes no sense.

182. `_____ not labeled`
The indicated variable has no value label, yet your request requires a labeled variable. You may, for instance, be attempting to decode a numeric variable.

184. `options _____ and _____ may not be combined`
For instance, you issued the `regress` command and tried to specify both the `beta` and the `vce(cluster clustvar)` options.

190. `request may not be combined with by`
Certain commands may not be combined with by, and you constructed such a combination. See the syntax diagram for the command.
`in may not be combined with by`
in may never be combined with by. Use if instead; see [U] **11.5 by varlist: construct**.

191. `request may not be combined with by() option`
Certain commands may not be combined with the by() option, and you constructed such a combination. See the syntax diagram for the command.

`in may not be combined with by`
in may never be combined with by. Use if instead; see [U] **11.5 by varlist: construct**.

196. `could not restore sort order because variables were dropped`
You ran an ado-file program that has an error, and the program dropped the temporary marker variables that allow the sort order to be restored.

197. `invalid syntax`
This error is produced by `syntax` and other parsing commands when there is a syntax error in the use of the command itself rather than in what is being parsed.

198. `invalid syntax`
`option _____ incorrectly specified`
`option _____ not allowed`
`_____ invalid`
`range invalid`
`_____ invalid obs no`
`invalid filename`
`_____ invalid varname`
`_____ invalid name`
`multiple by's not allowed`
`_____ found where number expected`
`on or off required`
All items in this list indicate invalid syntax. These errors are often, but not always, due to typographical errors. Stata attempts to provide you with as much information as it can. Review the syntax diagram for the designated command.

In giving the message "invalid syntax", Stata is not helpful. Errors in specifying expressions often result in this message.

199. `unrecognized command`
Stata failed to recognize the command, program, or ado-file name, probably because of a typographical or abbreviation error.

301. `last estimates not found`
You typed an estimation command, such as `regress`, without arguments or attempted to perform a `test` or typed `predict`, but there were no previous estimation results.

302. `last test not found`
You have requested the redisplay of a previous `test`, yet you have not run a `test` previously.

303. `equation not found`
You referred to a coefficient or stored result corresponding to an equation or outcome that cannot be found. For instance, you estimated an `mlogit` model and the outcome variable took on the values 1, 3, and 4. You referred to `[2]_b[var]` when perhaps you meant `[#2]_b[var]` or `[3]_b[var]`.

304. `ml model not found`
You have used `mleval`, `mlsum`, or `mlmatsum` without having first used the other `ml` commands to define the model.

305. `ml model not found`
Same as 304.

310. not possible because object(s) in use
    This can occur with mata describe and mata drop and indicates that the objects referred to cannot be described or eliminated because an earlier iteration of Mata is currently using them.

321. requested action not valid after most recent estimation command
    This message can be produced by predict or test and indicates that the requested action cannot be performed.

322. something that should be true of your estimation results is not
    This error is used by prefix commands and postestimation commands to indicate that the estimation command returned an unexpected result and that the prefix or postestimation command does not know how to proceed.

399. may not drop constant
    You issued a logistic or logit command and the constant was dropped. Your model may be underidentified; try removing one or more of the independent variables.

401. may not use noninteger frequency weights
    You specified an fweight frequency weight with noninteger weights, telling Stata that your weights are to be treated as replication counts. Stata encountered a weight that was not an integer, so your request made no sense. You probably meant to specify aweight analytic weights; see [U] **11.1.6 weight**.

402. negative weights encountered
    negative weights not allowed
    You specified a variable that contains negative values as the weighting variable, so your request made no sense. Perhaps you meant to specify another variable.

404. not possible with pweighted data
    You requested a statistic that Stata cannot calculate with pweighted data, either because of a shortcoming in Stata or because the statistics of the problem have not been worked out. For example, perhaps you requested the standard error of the Kaplan–Meier survival curve, and you had previously specified pweight when you stset your data (a case where no one has worked out the statistics).

406. not possible with analytic weights
    You specified a command that does not allow analytic weights. See the syntax diagram for the command to see which types of weights are allowed.

407. weights must be the same for all observations in a group
    weights not constant for same observation across repeated variables
    For some commands, weights must be the same for all observations in a group for statistical or computational reasons. For the anova command with the repeated() option, weights must be constant for an observation across the repeated variables.

409. no variance
    You were using lnskew0 or bcskew0, for instance, but the *exp* that you specified has no variance.

411. nonpositive values encountered
    _____ has negative values
    time variable has negative values
    For instance, you have used graph with the xlog or ylog options, requesting log scales, and yet some of the data or the labeling you specified is negative or zero.
    Or perhaps you were using ltable and specified a time variable that has negative values.

412. redundant or inconsistent constraints
    For instance, you are estimating a constrained model with mlogit. Among the constraints specified is at least one that is redundant or inconsistent. A redundant constraint might constrain a coefficient to be zero that some other constraint also constrains to be zero. An inconsistent constraint might constrain a coefficient to be 1 that some other constraint constrains to be zero. List the constraints, find the offender, and then reissue the mlogit command omitting it.

416. missing values encountered
    You were using a command that requires that no values be missing.

420. _____ groups found, 2 required
    You used a command (such as ttest), and the grouping variable you specified does not take on two unique values.

421. could not determine between-subject error term; use bse() option
    You specified the repeated() option to anova, but Stata could not automatically determine certain terms that are needed in the calculation; see [R] **anova**.

422. `could not determine between-subject basic unit; use bseunit() option`
You specified the `repeated()` option to `anova`, but Stata could not automatically determine certain terms that are needed in the calculation; see [R] **anova**.

430. `convergence not achieved`
You have estimated a maximum likelihood model, and Stata's maximization procedure failed to converge to a solution; see [R] **maximize**. Check if the model is identified.

450. `_____ is not a 0/1 variable`
`number of successes invalid`
`p invalid`
`_____ takes on _____ values, not 2`
You have used a command, such as `bitest`, that requires the variable take on only the values 0, 1, or missing, but the variable you specified does not meet that restriction. (You can also get this message from, for example, `bitesti`, when you specify a number of successes greater than the number of observations or a probability not between 0 and 1.)

451. `invalid values for time variable`
For instance, you specified `mytime` as a time variable, and `mytime` contains noninteger values.

452. `invalid values for factor variable`
You specified a variable that does not meet the factor-variable restrictions. Factor variables are assumed to take on only nonnegative integer values.

459. `something that should be true of your data is not`
`data have changed since estimation`
This is the generic form of this message; more likely, you will see messages such as "y must be between 0 and 1" or "x not positive". You have attempted to do something that, given your data, does not make sense.

460. `only one cluster detected`
`only one PSU detected`
`stratum with only one PSU detected`
`stratum with only one observation detected`
You were using the `cluster()` option and you had only one cluster; you must have at least two clusters—preferably much more than two. Or you were using an `svy` command, and you had only one PSU in one stratum; the `svydescribe` command will determine which stratum, and the [SVY] **svydescribe** entry shows how to deal with the situation.

461. `number of obs must be greater than # for robust variance computation`
`number of obs in subpopulation must be greater than #`
`no observations in subpopulation`
You had insufficient observations for the robust variance estimator. Or you were trying to produce estimates for a subpopulation and had insufficient observations in the subpopulation.

462. `fpc must be >= 0`
`fpc for all observations within a stratum must be the same`
`fpc must be <= 1 if a rate, or >= no. sampled PSUs per stratum if PSU totals`
There is a problem with your `fpc` variable; see [SVY] **svyset**.

463. `sum of weights equals zero`
`sum of weights for subpopulation equals zero`
When weights sum to zero, the requested statistic cannot be computed.

464. `poststratum weights must be constant within poststrata`
You have `svyset` your data and specified the `poststrata()` and `postweight()` options. The variable containing poststratum population sizes must be constant within each poststratum to be valid.

465. `poststratum weights must be >= 0`
You have svyset your data and specified the `postweight()` option. Poststratum population sizes cannot be negative.

466. `standardization weights must be constant within standard strata`
You are using the mean, proportion, or ratio command, and you specified the `stdweight()` option. The weight variable for standardization must be constant within each standard stratum.

467. `standardization weights must be >= 0`
You are using the mean, proportion, or ratio command, and you specified the `stdweight()` option. The standardization weights cannot be negative.

471. esample() invalid
This concerns ereturn post. The *varname* variable specified by the esample(*varname*) option must contain exclusively 0 and 1 values (never, for instance, 2 or missing). *varname* contains invalid values.

480. starting values invalid or some RHS variables have missing values
You were using nl and specified starting values that were infeasible, or you have missing values for some of your independent variables.

481. equation/system not identified
cannot calculate derivatives
You were using reg3, for instance, and the system that you have specified is not identified.

You specified an nl *fcn* for which derivatives cannot be calculated.

482. nonpositive value(s) among _____, cannot log transform
You specified an lnlsq option in nl that attempts to take the log of a nonpositive value.

491. could not find feasible values
You are using ml and it could not find starting values for which the likelihood function could be evaluated. You could try using ml search with the repeat() option to randomly try more values, or you could use ml init to specify valid starting values.

498. *various messages*
The statistical problem described in the message has occurred. The code 498 is not helpful, but the message is supposed to be. Return code 498 is reserved for messages that are unique to a particular situation.

499. *various messages*
The statistical problem described in the message has occurred. The code 499 is not helpful, but the message is supposed to be. Return code 499 is reserved for messages that are unique to a particular situation.

501. matrix operation not found
You have issued an unknown matrix subcommand or used matrix define with a function or operator that is unknown to Stata.

503. conformability error
You have issued a matrix command attempting to combine two matrices that are not conformable, for example, multiplying a 3×2 matrix by a 3×3 matrix. You will also get this message if you attempt an operation that requires a square matrix and the matrix is not square.

504. matrix has missing values
This return code is now infrequently used because, beginning with version 8, Stata now permits missing values in matrices.

505. matrix not symmetric
You have issued a matrix command that can be performed only on a symmetric matrix, and your matrix is not symmetric. While fixing their code, programmers are requested to admire our choice of the "symmetric" number 505—it is symmetric about the zero—for this error.

506. matrix not positive definite
You have issued a matrix command that can be performed only on a positive-definite matrix, and your matrix is not positive definite.

507. name conflict
You have issued a matrix post command, and the variance–covariance matrix of the estimators does not have the same row and column names, or if it does, those names are not the same as for the coefficient vector.

508. matrix has zero values
matrix has zero values on diagonal
matrix has zero or negative values
matrix has zero or negative values on diagonal
A matrix is being used or produced that has zero or negative values where it should not. For instance, you used the matrix sweep() function, but the matrix had zero values on the diagonal.

509. matrix operators that return matrices not allowed in this context
Expressions returning nonmatrices, such as those in generate and replace, may use matrix functions returning scalars, such as trace(A), but may not include subexpressions evaluating to matrices, such as trace(A+B), which requires evaluating the matrix expression A + B. (Such subexpressions are allowed in the context of expressions returning matrices, such as those in matrix.)

601. `file _____ not found`
The filename you specified cannot be found. Perhaps you mistyped the name, or it may be on another CD or directory. If you are a Mac user, perhaps you had an unintentional blank at the beginning or ending of your filename when it was created. In Finder, click on the file to blacken the name. If you see anything other than a thin, even space on each side of the name, rename the file to eliminate the leading and trailing space characters.

602. `file _____ already exists`
You attempted to write over a file that already exists. Stata will never let you do this accidentally. If you really intend to overwrite the previous file, reissue the last command, specifying the `replace` option.

603. `file _____ could not be opened`
This file, although found, failed to open properly. This error is unlikely to occur. You will have to review your operating system's manual to determine why it occurred.

604. `log file already open`
You attempted to open a `log` file when one is already open. Perhaps you forgot that you have the file open or forgot to close it.

606. `no log file open`
You have attempted to `close`, turn `on`, or turn `off` logging when no log file was open. Perhaps you forgot to open the log file.

607. `no cmdlog file open`
You have attempted to `close`, turn `on`, or turn `off` logging when no cmdlog file was open. Perhaps you forgot to open the cmdlog file.

608. `file is read-only; cannot be modified or erased`
The operating system has the file marked as read-only, meaning that changes cannot be made.

609. `file xp format`
The designated file is stored in an unsupported cross-product format.

610. `file _____ not Stata format`
The designated file is not a Stata-format file. This occurs most often with use, append, and merge. You probably typed the wrong filename.

611. `record too long`
You have attempted to process a record that exceeds 524,275 characters by using formatted `infile` (i.e., `infile` with a dictionary). When reading formatted data, records may not exceed this maximum. If the records are not formatted, you can read these data by using the standard `infile` command (i.e., without a dictionary). There is no maximum record length for unformatted data.

612. `unexpected end of file`
You used `infile` with a dictionary, and the file containing the dictionary ended before the '}' character. Perhaps you forgot to type the closing brace, or perhaps you are missing a hard return at the end of your file. You may also get this message if you issued the command `#delimit ;` in a do-file and then subsequently forgot to use ';' before the 'end' statement.

613. `file does not contain dictionary`
You used `infile` with a dictionary, yet the file you specified does not begin with the word 'dictionary'. Perhaps you are attempting to `infile` data without using a dictionary and forgot to specify the varlist on the `infile` command. Or you forgot to include the word dictionary at the top of the dictionary file or typed DICTIONARY in uppercase.

614. `dictionary invalid`
You used `infile` with a dictionary, and the file appears to contain a dictionary. Nevertheless, you have made some error in specifying the dictionary, and Stata does not understand your intentions. The contents of the dictionary are listed on the screen, and the last line is the line that gave rise to the problem.

615. `cannot determine separator -- use tab or comma option`
You used the `insheet` command to read a file, but Stata is having trouble determining whether the file is tab- or comma-separated. Reissue the `insheet` command, and specify the `comma` or `tab` option.

616. `wrong number of values in checksum file`
The checksum file being used to verify integrity of another file does not contain values in the expected checksum format.

621. `already preserved`
You specified `preserve`, but you have already `preserve`d the data.

622. nothing to restore
You issued the restore command, but you have not previously specified preserve.

Return codes 630–696 are all messages that you might receive when executing any command with a file over the network.

631. host not found

632. web filename not supported in this context

633. may not write files over Internet

639. file transmission error (checksums do not match)

640. package file too long

641. package file invalid

651. may not seek past end of file
may not seek in write-append file
You may not seek past the end of a file; if your desire is to increase the file's length, you must seek to the end and then write.

660. proxy host not found
The host name specified as a proxy server cannot be mapped to an IP address. Type query to determine the host you have set.

662. proxy server refused request to send
Stata was able to contact the proxy server, but the proxy server refused to send data back to Stata. The proxy host or port specified may be incorrect. Type query to determine your settings.

663. remote connection to proxy failed
Although you have set a proxy server, it is not responding to Stata. The likely problems are that you specified the wrong port, you specified the wrong host, or the proxy server is down. Type query to determine the host and port that you have set.

665. could not set socket nonblocking

667. wrong version winsock.dll

668. could not find a valid winsock.dll

669. invalid URL

670. invalid network port number

671. unknown network protocol

672. server refused to send file

673. authorization required by server

674. unexpected response from server

675. server reported server error

676. server refused request to send

677. remote connection failed
You requested that something be done over the web, but Stata could not contact the specified host. Perhaps the host is down; try again later.

If all your web access results in this message, perhaps your network connection is via a proxy server. If it is, you must tell Stata. Contact your system administrator and ask for the name and port of the "http proxy server". See *Using the Internet* in the *Getting Started* manual for details on how to inform Stata.

678. could not open local network socket

681. too many open files

682. could not connect to odbc dsn
This typically occurs because of incorrect permissions, such as a bad *User Name* or *Password*. Use set debug on to display the actual error message generated by the ODBC driver.

683. `could not fetch variable in odbc table`
This error usually occurs when a requested variable is not found in the current ODBC data table. Other scenarios can generate this error, however, so use `set debug on` to display the error message generated by the ODBC driver.

688. `file is corrupt`

691. `I/O error`
A filesystem error occurred during input or output. This typically indicates a hardware or operating system failure, although it is possible that the disk was merely full and this state was misinterpreted as an I/O error.

692. `file I/O error on read`

693. `file I/O error on write`

694. `could not rename file`
The file is in a directory that is marked by the operating system as read-only, and therefore files in that directory cannot be modified.

695. `could not copy file`
You tried to perform an `update swap` but Stata could not make a backup copy of the Stata executable, so the update was not performed.

696. `_____ is temporarily unavailable`

699. `insufficient disk space`
You ran out of disk space while writing a file to disk. The file is now closed and is probably erased. Review your operating system documentation to determine how to proceed.

702. `op. sys. refused to start new process`

703. `op. sys. refused to open pipe`

900. `no room to add more variables`
The maximum number of variables allowed by Small Stata is 99. The maximum number of variables allowed by Stata/IC is 2,047. The maximum number of variables allowed by Stata/MP and Stata/SE is 32,766. If you are using Stata/IC and have fewer than 2,047 variables (or Stata/MP and Stata/SE and have fewer than 32,766 variables), you are short on memory; see [U] **6 Setting the size of memory**.

901. `no room to add more observations`
The maximum number of observations allowed by Small Stata is *approximately* 1,200. The maximum number of observations allowed by Stata/MP, Stata/SE, or Stata/IC is 2,147,483,647. If you are using Stata/IC, you are short on memory; see [U] **6 Setting the size of memory**.

902. `no room to add more variables due to width`
Try typing compress; see [D] **compress**.

903. `no room to promote variable (e.g., change int to float) due to width`

908. `matsize too small`

909. `op. sys. refuses to provide memory`
You have attempted to `set memory` or `set matsize`, and although the request seems reasonable to Stata, the operating system has refused to provide the extra memory.

910. `value too small`
You attempted to change the size of memory but specified values for memory, maximum observations, maximum width, or maximum variables that are too small. Stata wants to allocate a minimum of 300 K.

912. `value too large`
You attempted to change the size of memory but specified values for memory, maximum observations, maximum width, or maximum variables that are too large.

913. `op. sys. refuses to provide sufficient memory`
`op. sys. provided base request, but then refused to provide`
`sufficient memory for matsize`
You attempted to `set memory` or `set matsize`, and, although the request seems reasonable to Stata, the operating system refused to provide the memory for matsize (although the operating system would provide memory for the data).

This return code has the same implications as r(909). Stata allocates memory separately for the data and for matsize. r(913) merely indicates that it was the second rather than the first request that failed. Typically, the first request fails because it is the request for additional memory.

914. op. sys. refused to allow Stata to open a temporary file
    To honor your request for memory, Stata needed to open a temporary disk file, and the operating system said that
    it could not do so. This most often occurs under Unix, and then the text of the error message provided more
    information on how to repair the problem.

920. too many macros
    You specified a line containing recursive macro substitutions. An example of single-level recursion is referring to
    "$this" when $this contains "$that" and $that contains "result". The result of evaluating "$this" is to
    produce "result". Double-level recursion would be when $this contains "$that" and $that contains "$what"
    and $what contains "result". Error 920 arises when the recursion level is greater than 20.

950. insufficient memory
    There is insufficient memory to fulfill the request. Type discard, press *Return*, and try the command again. If
    that fails, consider dropping value labels, variable labels, or macros.

1000. system limit exceeded - see manual
    Type help limits.

1001. too many values
    You have attempted to create a table that has too many rows or columns. For a one-way table, the maximum
    number of rows is 12,000 for Stata/MP and Stata/SE, 3,000 for Stata/IC, and 500 for Small Stata. For a two-way
    table, the maximum number of rows and columns is 1,200 by 80 for Stata/MP and Stata/SE, 300 by 20 for Stata/IC,
    and 160 by 20 for Small Stata. Thus tabulate y x may not result in too many values even if tabulate x y
    does.

1002. too many by variables
    The number of by variables exceeded 32,766 for Stata/SE, 2,047 for Stata/IC, or 99 for Small Stata. You cannot
    exceed these maximums.

1003. too many options
    The number of options specified exceeded 70. You cannot exceed this maximum.

1004. command too long
    You attempted to issue a Stata command in a do-file, ado-file, or program, and the command exceeded 165,216
    characters for Stata/IC or 8,697 for Small Stata. For Stata/MP and Stata/SE, the limit is 33*c(max_k_theory) +
    216, which for the default setting of 5,000 is 165,216.

1010. system limit exceeded -- width shortage
    An attempt was made to add a variable that would have increased the memory required to store an observation
    beyond the maximum width allowed, which is 800 bytes for Small Stata, 24,564 bytes for Stata/IC, and 393,192
    bytes for Stata/SE and Stata/MP. You have the following alternatives:

    1. Store existing variables more efficiently; see [D] **compress**. Also consider using factor variables where
       possible; see [U] **11.4.3 Factor variables**.

    2. Drop some variables; see [D] **drop**.

    3. If you are using Stata/MP or Stata/SE, increase the maximum width by increasing maxvar; see [D] **memory**.
       The maximum width is set to 12×maxvar.

1400. numerical overflow
    You have attempted something that, in the midst of the necessary calculations, has resulted in something too large
    for Stata to deal with accurately. Most commonly, this is an attempt to estimate a model (say, with regress) with
    more than 2,147,483,647 effective observations. This effective number could be reached with far fewer observations
    if you were running a frequency-weighted model.

2000. no observations
    You have requested some statistical calculation and there are no observations on which to perform it. Perhaps you
    specified if or in and inadvertently filtered all the data.

2001. insufficient observations
    You have requested some statistical calculation, and although there are some observations, the number is not
    sufficient to carry out your request.

3000–3999. Mata run-time errors; see [M-2] **errors** for codes.

9xxx. Various messages, all indicating an unexpected system failure. You should never see such a message. If one occurs,
    save your data, and exit Stata immediately. Please email tech-support@stata.com to report the problem.

Other messages

`no observations`
`insufficient observations`
You have requested something when there are either no observations or insufficient observations in memory to carry forth your request.

`(_____ not found)`
You referred to the indicated value name in an expression, and no such value label existed. A missing value was substituted.

`(eof before end of obs)`
`infile` was reading your data and encountered the end-of-file marker before it had completed reading the current observation. Missing values are filled in for the remaining variables. This message indicates that the dataset may contain more or fewer variables than you expected.

`(_____ missing values generated)`
The command created the indicated number of missing values. Missing values occur when a mathematical operation is performed on a missing value or when a mathematical operation is infeasible.

`(note: file _____ not found)`
You specified the `replace` option on a command, yet no such file was found. The file was saved anyway.

`(note: ____ is ____ in using data but will be ____ now)`
Occurs during `append` or `merge` when there is a type mismatch between the data in memory and the data on disk and you used the `force` option to perform the `append` or `merge` anyway. The first blank is filled in with a variable name, and the second and third blanks with a storage type (`byte`, `int`, `long`, `float`, `double`, or `str#`). For instance, you might receive the message "myvar is str5 in using data but will be float now". This means that `myvar` is of type `float` in the *master dataset* but that a variable of the same name was found in the *using dataset* with type `str5`. You will receive this message when one variable is a string and the other is numeric.

`(label _____ already defined)`
Occurs during `append` or `merge`. The *using* data has a label definition for one of its variables. A label with the same name exists in the *master* dataset. Thus you are warned that the label already exists, and the previous definition (the one from the *master* dataset) is retained.

`(note: hascons false)`
You specified the `hascons` option on `regress`, yet an examination of the data revealed that there is no effective constant in your varlist. Stata added a constant to your regression.

`____ real changes made`
You used `replace`. This is the actual number of changes made to your data, not counting observations that already contained the replaced value.

`____ was ____ now ____`
Occurs during `replace`, `append`, or `merge`. The first blank is filled in with a variable name, and the second and third blanks are filled in with a numeric storage type (`byte`, `int`, `long`, `float`, or `double`). For instance, you might receive the message "myvar was byte now float". Stata automatically promoted `myvar` to a `float` to prevent truncation.

Also see

[P] **break** — Suppress Break key

[P] **capture** — Capture return code

[R] **search** — Search Stata documentation

[P] **exit** — Exit from a program or do-file

[U] **16.1.4 Error handling in do-files**

Title

---

estat programming — Controlling estat after user-written commands

---

Description

This entry discusses how programmers of estimation commands can customize how estat works after their commands. If you want to use only the standard estat subcommands, ic, summarize, and vce, your program may not need any modifications.

Remarks

Remarks are presented under the following headings:

> *Standard subcommands*
> *Adding subcommands to estat*
> *Overriding standard behavior of a subcommand*

Standard subcommands

For estat to work, your estimation command must be implemented as an e-class program, and it must save its name in e(cmd).

estat vce requires that the covariance matrix be stored in e(V), and estat summarize requires that the estimation sample be marked by the function e(sample). Both requirements can be met by using ereturn post with the esample() option in your program.

Finally, estat ic requires that your program store the final log likelihood in e(ll) and the sample size in e(N). If your program also stores the log likelihood of the null (constant only) model in e(ll_0), it will appear in the output of estat ic, as well.

Adding subcommands to estat

To add new features (subcommands) to estat for use after a particular estimation command, you write a handler, which is nothing more than an ado-file command. The standard is to name the new command *cmd*_estat, where *cmd* is the name of the corresponding estimation command. For instance, the handler that provides the special estat features after regress is named regress_estat, and the handler that provides the special features after pca is named pca_estat.

Next you must let estat know about your new handler, which you do by filling in e(estat_cmd) in the corresponding estimation command. For example, in the code that implements pca is the line

```
ereturn local estat_cmd "pca_estat"
```

Finally, you must write *cmd*_estat. The syntax of estat is

```
estat subcmd ...
```

When the estat command is invoked, the first and only thing it does is call 'e(estat_cmd)' if 'e(estat_cmd)' exists. This way, your handler can even do something special in the standard cases, if that is necessary. We will get to that, but in the meantime, understand that the handler receives just what estat received, which is exactly what the user typed. The outline for a handler is

—————————————————————————— begin *cmd*_estat.ado ——————————

```
program cmd_estat, rclass
        version 11
        if "`e(cmd)'" != "cmd" {
                error 301
        }
        gettoken subcmd rest : 0, parse(" ,")
        if "`subcmd'"=="first_special_subcmd" {
                First_special_subcmd `rest'
        }
        else if "`subcmd'"=="second_special_subcmd" {
                Second_special_subcmd `rest'
        }
        ...
        else {
                estat_default `0'
        }
        return add
end
program First_special_subcmd, rclass
        syntax ...
        ...
end
program Second_special_subcmd, rclass
        syntax ...
        ...
end
```

—————————————————————————————— end *cmd*_estat.ado ——————————

The ideas underlying the above outline are simple:

1. You check that e(cmd) matches *cmd*.

2. You isolate the *subcmd* that the user typed and then see if it is one of the special cases that you wish to handle.

3. If *subcmd* is a special case, you call the code you wrote to handle it.

4. If *subcmd* is not a special case, you let Stata's estat_default handle it.

When you check for the special cases, those special cases can be new *subcmd*s that you wish to add, or they can be standard *subcmd*s whose default behavior you wish to override.

▷ Example 1

Suppose that we have written the estimation command myreg and want the estat subcommands fit and sens to work after it, in addition to the standard subcommands. Moreover, we want to be able to abbreviate sens as se or sen. The following code fragment illustrates the structure of our myreg_estat handler program:

(Continued on next page)

```
                                                          begin myreg_estat.ado
    program myreg_estat, rclass
            version 11

            gettoken subcmd rest : 0 , parse(", ")
            local lsubcmd= length("'subcmd'")

            if "'subcmd'" == "fit" {
                    Fit 'rest'
            }
            else if "'subcmd'" == substr("sens",1,max(2,'lsubcmd')) {
                    Sens 'rest'
            }
            else {
                    estat_default '0'
            }

            return add
    end
    program Fit, rclass
            syntax ...
            ...
    end
    program Sens, rclass
            syntax ...
            ...
    end
                                                          end myreg_estat.ado
```

Say that we issue the command

```
    estat sen, myoption("Circus peanuts")
```

The only way that the above differs from the standard outline is the complication we added to handle the abbreviation of *subcmd* sens. Rather than asking if `"'subcmd'"=="sens"`, we asked if `"'subcmd'"==substr("sens",1,max(2,'lsubcmd'))`, where `'lsubcmd'` was previously filled in with `length("'subcmd'")`.

◁

Overriding standard behavior of a subcommand

Occasionally, you may want to override the behavior of a subcommand normally handled by estat_default. This is accomplished by providing a local handler. Consider, for example, summarize after pca. The standard way of invoking estat summarize is not appropriate here—estat summarize extracts the list of variables to be summarized from e(b). This does not work after pca. Here the varlist has to be extracted from the column names of the correlation or covariance matrix e(C). This varlist is transferred to estat summarize (or more directly to estat_summ) as the argument of the standard estat_summ program.

```
    program Summarize
            syntax [, *]
            tempname C
            matrix 'C' = e(C)
            estat_summ ':colnames 'C'', 'options'
    end
```

You add the local handler by inserting an additional switch in *cmd_*estat to ensure that the summarize subcommand is not handled by the default handler estat_default. As a detail, we have to make sure that the minimal abbreviation is s̲ummarize.

── begin pca_estat.ado ──────────

```
program pca_estat, rclass
        version 11

        gettoken subcmd rest : 0 , parse(", ")
        local lsubcmd= length("`subcmd'")

        if '"`subcmd'"' == substr("summarize", 1, max(2, `lsubcmd')) {
                Summarize `rest'
        }
        else {
                estat_default `0'
        }

        return add
end
program Summarize
        syntax ...
        ...
end
```

─── end pca_estat.ado ──────────

Also see

[R] **estat** — Postestimation statistics

Title

_estimates — Manage estimation results

Syntax

Move estimation results into holdname

    _estimates hold *holdname* [, copy restore nullok varname(*newvar*)]

Restore estimation results

    _estimates unhold *holdname* [, not]

List names holding estimation results

    _estimates dir

Eliminate estimation results

    _estimates clear

Eliminate specified estimation results

    _estimates drop { *holdnames* | _all }

where *holdname* is the name under which estimation results will be held.

Description

_estimates hold, _estimates unhold, _estimates dir, _estimates clear, and _estimates drop provide a low-level mechanism for saving and later restoring up to 300 estimation results.

_estimates hold moves, or copies if the copy option is specified, all information associated with the last estimation command into *holdname*. If *holdname* is a temporary name, it will automatically be deleted when you exit from the current program.

_estimates unhold restores the information from the estimation command previously moved into *holdname* and eliminates *holdname*.

_estimates dir lists the *holdnames* under which estimation results are currently held.

_estimates clear eliminates all stored results. Also, if the restore option is specified when the estimates are held, those estimates will be automatically restored when the program concludes. It is not necessary to perform an _estimates unhold in that case.

_estimates drop eliminates the estimation results stored under the specified *holdnames*.

_estimates is a programmer's command designed to be used within programs. estimates is a user's command to manage multiple estimation results. estimates uses _estimates to hold and unhold results, and it adds features such as model-selection indices and looping over results. Postestimation commands, such as suest and lrtest, assume that estimation results are stored using estimates rather than _estimates.

136

Options

copy requests that all information associated with the last estimation command be copied into *holdname*. By default, it is moved, meaning that the estimation results temporarily disappear. The default action is faster and uses less memory.

restore requests that the information in *holdname* be automatically restored when the program ends, regardless of whether that occurred because the program exited normally, the user pressed *Break*, or there was an error.

nullok specifies that it is valid to store null results. After restoring a null result, no estimation results are active.

varname(*newvar*) specifies the variable name under which esample() will be held. If varname() is not specified, *holdname* is used. If the variable already exists in the data, an error message is shown. This variable is visible to users. If it is dropped, _estimates unhold will not be able to restore the estimation sample e(sample) and sets e(sample) to 1.

not specifies that the previous _estimates hold, restore request for automatic restoration be canceled. The previously held estimation results are discarded from memory without restoration, now or later.

Remarks

_estimates hold and _estimates unhold are typically used in programs and ado-files, although they can be used interactively. After fitting, say, a regression by using regress, you can replay the regression by typing regress without arguments, and you can obtain predicted values with predict, and the like; see [U] **20 Estimation and postestimation commands**. This is because Stata stored information associated with the regression in what we will call the "last estimation results". The last estimation results include the coefficient vector and the variance–covariance matrix, as well as the other e() saved results.

When you type _estimates hold myreg, Stata moves the last estimation results to a holding area named myreg. After issuing this command, you can no longer replay the regression, calculate predicted values, etc. From Stata's point of view, the estimates are gone. When you type _estimates unhold myreg, however, Stata moves the estimates back. You can once again type regress without arguments, calculate predicted values, and everything else just as if the last estimation results were never disturbed.

If you instead type _estimates hold myreg, copy, Stata copies, rather than moves, the results, meaning that you can still redisplay results. Obviously, you hold estimates because you want to fit some other model and then get these estimates back, so generally, holding by moving works as well as holding by copying. Sometimes, however, you may want to hold by copy so that you can modify the estimates in memory and still retrieve the original.

(Continued on next page)

▷ Example 1

You could run a regression, hold the results, run another regression, and then unhold the original results. One method you could use is

```
regress y x1 x2 x3                    (fit first model)
_estimates hold model1                (and save it)
regress y x1 x2 x3 x4                  (fit the second model)
_estimates hold model2                (and save it, too)
use newdata                           (use another dataset)
_estimates unhold model1              (get the first model)
predict yhat1                         (predict using first regression)
_estimates unhold model2              (get the second model)
predict yhat2                         (predict using second regression)
```

You are not limited to doing this with regression; you can do this with any estimation command.

◁

❑ Technical note

Warning: Holding estimation results can tie up considerable amounts of memory, depending on the kind of model and the number of variables in it. This is why there is a limit of 300 held estimation results.

❑

_estimates dir, _estimates drop, and _estimates clear are utilities associated with _estimates hold and _estimates unhold. _estimates dir lists the names of held estimation results. _estimates drop drops held estimation results. _estimates clear is equivalent to _estimates drop _all.

❑ Technical note

Despite our interactive example, _estimates hold and _estimates unhold are typically used inside programs. For instance, linktest fits a model of the dependent variable, the prediction, and the prediction squared and shows the result. Yet when it is over, the user's original model remains as the last estimation result just as if no intervening model had been estimated. linktest does this by holding the original model, performing its task, and then restoring the original model.

In addition to moving Stata's last estimation result matrices, e(b) and e(V), _estimates hold and _estimates unhold also move the other e() results. When you hold the current estimates, e(b), e(V), e(cmd), e(depvar), and the other e() results disappear. When you unhold them, they are restored.

To avoid naming conflicts, we recommend that estimates be held under a name created by tempvar or tempname; see [P] **macro**. Thus the code fragment is

```
tempvar est
_estimates hold 'est'
(code including new estimation)
_estimates unhold 'est'
```

❑

Estimates held under a temporary name will automatically be discarded when the program ends. You can also specify _estimates hold's restore option when you hold the estimates, and then the held estimates will be restored when the program ends, too.

Saved results

_estimates hold removes the estimation results—e() items.

_estimates unhold restores the previously held e() results.

_estimates clear permanently removes all held e() results.

_estimates dir returns the names of the held estimation results in the local r(names), separated by single spaces.

_estimates dir also returns r(varnames), which has the corresponding variable names for esample().

Also see

[P] **makecns** — Constrained estimation

[P] **mark** — Mark observations for inclusion

[P] **matrix** — Introduction to matrix commands

[P] **matrix rownames** — Name rows and columns

[R] **estimates** — Save and manipulate estimation results

[R] **ml** — Maximum likelihood estimation

[P] **return** — Return saved results

[R] **saved results** — Saved results

[U] **13.5 Accessing coefficients and standard errors**

[U] **18 Programming Stata**

[U] **20 Estimation and postestimation commands**

Title

exit — Exit from a program or do-file

Syntax

exit [[=]*exp*] [, clear STATA noprefs]

Description

exit, when typed from the keyboard, causes Stata to terminate processing and returns control to the operating system. If the dataset in memory has changed since the last save command, you must specify the clear option before Stata will let you leave. Use of the command in this way is discussed in [R] **exit**.

More generally, exit causes Stata to terminate the current process and returns control to the calling process. The return code is set to the value of the expression or to zero if no expression is specified. Thus exit can be used to exit a program or do-file and return control to Stata. With an option, exit can even be used to exit Stata from a program or do-file. Such use of exit is the subject of this entry.

Options

clear permits you to exit, even if the current dataset has not been saved.

STATA exits Stata and returns control to the operating system, even when given from a do-file or program. The STATA option is implied when exit is issued from the keyboard.

noprefs, available only for Unix(GUI), indicates that any preference changes are to be ignored upon exit. The default is to save the preferences when Stata is exited.

Remarks

exit can be used at the terminal, from do-files, or from programs. From the terminal, it allows you to leave Stata. Given from a do-file or program without the STATA option, it causes the do-file or program to terminate and return control to the calling process, which might be the keyboard or another do-file or program.

Caution should be used if exit is included to break execution within a loop. A more suitable command is continue or continue, break; see [P] **continue**. continue is used to explicitly break execution of the current loop iteration with execution resuming at the top of the loop unless the break option is specified, in which case execution resumes with the command following the looping command.

140

▷ Example 1

Here is a useless program that will tell you whether a variable exists:

```
. program check
1. capture confirm variable '1'
2. if _rc!=0 {
3.     display "'1' not found"
4.     exit
5. }
6. display "The variable '1' exists."
7. end
. check median_age
The variable median_age exists.
. check age
age not found
```

exit did not close Stata and cause a return to the operating system; it instead terminated the program.

◁

▷ Example 2

You type exit from the keyboard to leave Stata and return to the operating system. If the dataset in memory has changed since the last time it was saved, however, Stata will refuse. At that point, you can either save the data and then exit or type exit, clear:

```
. exit
no; data in memory would be lost
r(4);
. exit, clear
```

(*Operating system prompts you for next command*)

◁

❏ Technical note

You can also exit Stata and return to the operating system from a do-file or program by including the line exit, STATA in your do-file or program. To return to the operating system regardless of whether the dataset in memory has changed, you include the line exit, STATA clear.

❏

❏ Technical note

When using exit to force termination of a program or do-file, you may specify an expression following the exit, and the resulting value of that expression will be used to set the return code. Not specifying an expression is equivalent to specifying exit 0.

❏

Also see

[P] **capture** — Capture return code

[P] **class exit** — Exit class-member program and return result

[P] **continue** — Break out of loops

[P] **error** — Display generic error message and exit

[R] **error messages** — Error messages and return codes

[R] **exit** — Exit Stata

Title

file — Read and write ASCII text and binary files

Syntax

Open file

    file open *handle* using *filename* , { read | write | read write }

      [[text | binary] [replace | append] all]

Read file

    file read *handle* [*specs*]

Write to file

    file write *handle* [*specs*]

Change current location in file

    file seek *handle* { query | tof | eof | # }

Set byte order of binary file

    file set *handle* byteorder { hilo | lohi | 1 | 2 }

Close file

    file close { *handle* | _all }

List file type, status, and name of handle

    file query

where *specs* for ASCII text output is

"*string*" or ' "*string*" '	
(*exp*)	(parentheses are required)
%*fmt* (*exp*)	(see [D] **format** about %*fmt*)
_skip(#)	
_column(#)	
_newline [(#)]	
_char(#)	($0 \leq \# \leq 255$)
_tab [(#)]	
_page [(#)]	
_dup(#)	

specs for ASCII text input is *localmacroname*,

specs for binary output is

$$\%\{8|4\}z \qquad\qquad (exp)$$
$$\%\{4|2|1\}b[s|u] \qquad (exp)$$
$$\%\#s \qquad\qquad\qquad \textit{"text"} \qquad (1 \le \# \le \texttt{max\_macrolen})$$
$$\%\#s \qquad\qquad\qquad `\textit{"text"}\,{}'$$
$$\%\#s \qquad\qquad\qquad (exp)$$

and *specs* for binary input is

$$\%\{8|4\}z \qquad\qquad \textit{scalarname}$$
$$\%\{4|2|1\}b[s|u] \qquad \textit{scalarname}$$
$$\%\#s \qquad\qquad\qquad \textit{localmacroname} \qquad (1 \le \# \le \texttt{max\_macrolen})$$

Description

file is a programmer's command and should not be confused with [D] **insheet**, [D] **infile**, and [D] **infix (fixed format)**, which are the usual ways that data are brought into Stata. file allows programmers to read and write both ASCII text and binary files, so file could be used to write a program to input data in some complicated situation, but that would be an arduous undertaking.

Files are referred to by a file *handle*. When you open a file, you specify the file handle that you want to use; for example, in

```
. file open myfile using example.txt, write
```

myfile is the file handle for the file named example.txt. From that point on, you refer to the file by its handle. Thus

```
. file write myfile "this is a test" _n
```

would write the line "this is a test" (without the quotes) followed by a new line into the file, and

```
. file close myfile
```

would then close the file. You may have multiple files open at the same time, and you may access them in any order.

For information on reading and writing sersets, see [P] **serset**.

Options

read, write, or read write is required; they specify how the file is to be opened. If the file is opened read, you can later use file read but not file write; if the file is opened write, you can later use file write but not file read. If the file is opened read write, you can then use both.

read write is more flexible, but most programmers open files purely read or purely write because that is all that is necessary; it is safer and it is faster.

When a file is opened read, the file must already exist, or an error message will be issued. The file is positioned at the top (tof), so the first file read reads at the beginning of the file. Both local files and files over the net may be opened for read.

When a file is opened write and the replace or append option is not specified, the file must not exist, or an error message will be issued. The file is positioned at the top (tof), so the first file write writes at the beginning of the file. Net files may not be opened for write.

When a file is opened write and the replace option is also specified, it does not matter whether the file already exists; the existing file, if any, is erased beforehand.

When a file is opened write and the append option is also specified, it also does not matter whether the file already exists; the file will be reopened or created if necessary. The file will be positioned at the append point, meaning that if the file existed, the first file write will write at the first byte past the end of the previous file; if there was no previous file, file write begins writing at the first byte in the file. file seek may not be used with write append files.

When a file is opened read write, it also does not matter whether the file exists. If the file exists, it is reopened. If the file does not exist, a new file is created. Regardless, the file will be positioned at the top of the file. You can use file seek to seek to the end of the file or wherever else you desire. Net files may not be opened for read write.

Before opening a file, you can determine whether it exists by using confirm file; see [P] **confirm**.

text and binary determine how the file is to be treated once it is opened. text, the default, means ASCII text files. In ASCII text, files are assumed to be composed of lines of characters, with each line ending in a line-end character. The character varies across operating systems, being line feed under Unix, carriage return under Mac, and carriage return/line feed under Windows. file understands all the ways that lines might end when reading and assumes that lines are to end in the usual way for the computer being used when writing.

The alternative to text is binary, meaning that the file is to be viewed merely as a stream of bytes. In binary files, there is an issue of byte order; consider the number 1 written as a 2-byte integer. On some computers (called hilo), it is written as "00 01", and on other computers (called lohi), it is written as "01 00" (with the least significant byte written first). There are similar issues for 4-byte integers, 4-byte floats, and 8-byte floats.

file assumes that the bytes are ordered in the way natural to the computer being used. file set can be used to vary this assumption. file set can be issued immediately after file open, or later, or repeatedly.

replace and append are allowed only when the file is opened for write (which does not include read write). They determine what is to be done if the file already exists. The default is to issue an error message and not open the file. See the description of the options read, write, and read write above for more details.

all is allowed when the file is opened for write or for read write. It specifies that, if the file needs to be created, the permissions on the file are to be set so that it is readable by everybody.

ASCII text output specifications

"*string*" and ' "*string*" ' write *string* into the file, without the surrounding quotes.

(*exp*) evaluates the expression *exp* and writes the result into the file. If the result is numeric, it is written with a %10.0g format, but with leading and trailing spaces removed. If *exp* evaluates to a string, the resulting string is written, with no extra leading or trailing blanks.

%fmt (*exp*) evaluates expression *exp* and writes the result with the specified *%fmt*. If *exp* evaluates to a string, *%fmt* must be a string format, and, correspondingly, if *exp* evaluates to a real, a numeric format must be specified. Do not confuse Stata's standard display formats with the binary formats %b and %z described elsewhere in this entry. file write here allows Stata's display formats described in [D] **format** and allows the centering extensions (e.g., %~20s) described in [P] **display**.

_skip(*#*) inserts *#* blanks into the file. If *# ≤* 0, nothing is written; *# ≤* 0 is not considered an error.

_column(*#*) writes enough blanks to skip forward to column *#* of the line; if *#* refers to a prior column, nothing is displayed. The first column of a line is numbered 1. Referring to a column less than 1 is not considered an error; nothing is displayed then.

_newline[(*#*)], which may be abbreviated _n[(*#*)], outputs one end-of-line character if *#* is not specified or outputs the specified number of end-of-line characters. The end-of-line character varies according to your operating system, being line feed under Unix, carriage return under Mac, and the two characters carriage return/line feed under Windows. If *# ≤* 0, no end-of-line character is output.

_char(*#*) outputs one character, being the one given by the ASCII code *#* specified. *#* must be between 0 and 255, inclusive.

_tab[(*#*)] outputs one tab character if *#* is not specified or outputs the specified number of tab characters. Coding _tab is equivalent to coding _char(9).

_page[(*#*)] outputs one page feed character if *#* is not specified or outputs the specified number of page feed characters. Coding _page is equivalent to coding _char(12). The page feed character is often called *Control-L*.

_dup(*#*) specified that the next directive is to be executed (duplicated) *#* times. *#* must be greater than or equal to 0. If *#* is equal to zero, the next element is not displayed.

Remarks

Remarks are presented under the following headings:

> *Use of file*
> *Use of file with tempfiles*
> *Writing ASCII text files*
> *Reading ASCII text files*
> *Use of seek when writing or reading ASCII text files*
> *Writing and reading binary files*
> *Writing binary files*
> *Reading binary files*
> *Use of seek when writing or reading binary files*
> *Appendix A.1 Useful commands and functions for use with file*
> *Appendix A.2 Actions of binary output formats with out-of-range values*

Use of file

file provides low-level access to file I/O. You open the file, use file read or file write repeatedly to read or write the file, and then close the file with file close:

```
file open ...
...
file read   or   file write ...
...
file read   or   file write ...
...
file close ...
```

Do not forget to close the file. Open files tie up system resources. Also, for files opened for writing, the contents of the file probably will not be fully written until you close the file.

Typing `file close _all` will close all open files, and the `clear all` command closes all files as well. These commands, however, should not be included in programs that you write; they are included to allow the user to reset Stata when programmers have been sloppy.

If you use file handles obtained from `tempname`, the file will be automatically closed when the ado-file terminates:

```
tempname myfile
file open 'myfile' using ...
```

This is the only case when not closing the file is appropriate. Use of temporary names for file handles offers considerable advantages because programs can be stopped because of errors or because the user presses *Break*.

Use of file with tempfiles

In the rare event that you `file open` a `tempfile`, you must obtain the handle from `tempname`. Temporary files are automatically deleted when the ado- or do-file ends. If the file is erased before it is closed, significant problems are possible. Using a tempname will guarantee that the file is properly closed beforehand:

```
tempname myfile
tempfile tfile
file open 'myfile' using "'tfile'" ...
```

Writing ASCII text files

This is easy to do:

```
file open handle using filename, write text
file write handle ...
...
file close handle
```

The syntax of `file write` is similar to that of `display`; see [R] **display**. The significant difference is that expressions must be bound in parentheses. In `display`, you can code

```
display 2+2
```

but using `file write`, you must code

file write *handle* (2+2)

The other important difference between `file write` and `display` is that `display` assumes you want the end-of-line character output at the end of each `display` (and `display` provides _continue for use when you do not want this), but `file write` assumes you want an end-of-line character only when you specify it. Thus rather than coding "file write *handle* (2+2)", you probably want to code

file write *handle* (2+2) _n

Because Stata outputs end-of-line characters only where you specify, coding

file write *handle* "first part is " (2+2) _n

has the same effect as coding

file write *handle* "first part is "
file write *handle* (2+2) _n

or even

file write *handle* "first part is "
file write *handle* (2+2)
file write *handle* _n

There is no limit to the line length that `file write` can write because, as far as `file write` is concerned, _n is just another character. The _col(#) directive, however, will lose count if you write lines of more than 2,147,483,646 characters (_col(#) skips forward to the specified column). In general, we recommend that you do not write lines longer than 165,199 characters because reading lines longer than that is more difficult using `file read`.

We say that _n is just another character, but we should say character or characters. _n outputs the appropriate end-of-line character for your operating system, meaning the two-character carriage return followed by line feed under Windows, the one-character carriage return under Mac, and the one-character line feed under Unix.

Reading ASCII text files

The commands for reading text files are similar to those for writing them:

file open *handle* using *filename*, read text
file read *handle* *localmacroname*
. . .
file close *handle*

The `file read` command has one syntax:

    file read *handle localmacroname*

One line is read from the file, and it is put in *localmacroname*. For instance, to read a line from the file `myfile` and put it in the local macro line, you code

    file read myfile line

Thereafter in your code, you can refer to 'line' to obtain the contents of the line just read. The following program will do a reasonable job of displaying the contents of the file, putting line numbers in front of the lines:

```
program ltype
        version 11
        local 0 '"using '0'"'
        syntax using/
        tempname fh
        local linenum = 0
        file open 'fh' using '"'using'"'', read
        file read 'fh' line
        while r(eof)==0 {
                local linenum = 'linenum' + 1
                display %4.0f 'linenum' _asis '"  'macval(line)'"'
                file read 'fh' line
        }
        file close 'fh'
end
```

In the program above, we used `tempname` to obtain a temporary name for the file handle. Doing that, we ensure that the file will be closed, even if the user presses *Break* while our program is displaying lines, and so never executes `file close 'fh'`. In fact, our `file close 'fh'` line is unnecessary.

We also used `r(eof)` to determine when the file ends. `file read` sets `r(eof)` to contain 0 before end of file and 1 once end of file is encountered; see *Saved results* below.

We included `_asis` in the `display` in case the file contained braces or SMCL commands. These would be interpreted, and we wanted to suppress that interpretation so that `ltype` would display lines exactly as stored; see [P] **smcl**. We also used the `macval()` macro function to obtain what was in 'line' without recursively expanding the contents of line.

Use of seek when writing or reading ASCII text files

You may use `file seek` when reading or writing text files, although, in fact, it is seldom used, except with read write files, and even then, it is seldom used with ASCII text files.

See *Use of seek when writing or reading binary files* below for a description of `file seek`—seek works the same way with both text and binary files—and then bear the following in mind:

- The # in "file seek *handle* #" refers to byte position, not line number. "file seek *handle* 5" means to seek to the fifth byte of the file, not the fifth line.

- When calculating byte offsets by hand, remember that the end-of-line character is 1 byte under Mac and Unix but is 2 bytes under Windows.

- Rewriting a line of an ASCII text file works as expected only if the new and old lines are of the same length.

Writing and reading binary files

Consider whether you wish to read this section. There are many potential pitfalls associated with binary files, and, at least in theory, a poorly written binary-I/O program can cause Stata to crash.

Binary files are made up of binary elements, of which Stata can understand the following:

Element	Corresponding format
single- and multiple-character strings	%1s and %#s
signed and unsigned 1-byte binary integers	%1b, %1bs, and %1bu
signed and unsigned 2-byte binary integers	%2b, %2bs, and %2bu
signed and unsigned 4-byte binary integers	%4b, %4bs, and %4bu
4-byte IEEE floating-point numbers	%4z
8-byte IEEE floating-point numbers	%8z

The differences between all these types are only of interpretation. For instance, the decimal number 72, stored as a 1-byte binary integer, also represents the character H. If a file contained the 1-byte integer 72 and you were to read the byte by using the format %1s, you would get back the character "H", and if a file contained the character "H" and you were to read the byte by using the format %1bu, you would get back the number 72; 72 and H are indistinguishable in that they represent the same bit pattern. Whether that bit pattern represents 72 or H depends on the format you use, meaning the interpretation you give to the field.

Similar equivalence relations hold between the other elements. A binary file is nothing more than a sequence of unsigned 1-byte integers, where those integers are sometimes given different interpretations or are grouped and given an interpretation. In fact, all you need is the format %1bu to read or write anything. The other formats, however, make programming more convenient.

Format	Length	Type	Minimum	Maximum	Missing values?
%1bu	1	unsigned byte	0	255	no
%1bs	1	signed byte	-127	127	no
%1b	1	Stata byte	-127	100	yes
%2bu	2	unsigned short int	0	65,535	no
%2bs	2	signed short int	$-32,767$	32,767	no
%2b	2	Stata int	$-32,767$	32,740	yes
%4bu	4	unsigned int	0	4,294,967,295	no
%4bs	4	signed int	$-2,147,483,647$	2,147,483,647	no
%4b	4	Stata long	$-2,147,483,647$	2,147,483,620	yes
%4z	4	float	-10^{38}	10^{38}	yes
%8z	8	double	-10^{307}	10^{307}	yes

When you write a binary file, you must decide on the format that you will use for every element that you will write. When you read a binary file, you must know ahead of time the format that was used for each element.

Writing binary files

As with ASCII text files, you open the file, write repeatedly, and then close the file:

> file open *handle* using *filename*, write binary
> file write *handle* ...
> ...
> file close *handle*

The file write command may include the following elements:

> %{8|4}z   (*exp*)
> %{4|2|1}b[s|u]   (*exp*)
> %#s   "*text*"   ($1 \leq \# \leq$ max_macrolen)
> %#s   ' "*text*" '
> %#s   (*exp*)

For instance, to write "test file" followed by 2, $2 + 2$, and 3×2 represented in its various forms, you could code

> . file write *handle* %9s "test file" %8z (2) %4b (2+2) %1bu (3*2)

or

> . file write *handle* %9s "test file"
> . file write *handle* %8z (2) %4b (2+2) %1bu (3*2)

or even

> . file write *handle* %9s "test file"
> . file write *handle* %8z (2)
> . file write *handle* %4b (2+2) %1bu (3*2)

etc.

You write strings with the %#s format and numbers with the %b or %z formats. Concerning strings, the # in %#s should be greater than or equal to the length of the string to be written. If # is too small, only that many characters of the string will be written. Thus

> . file write *handle* %4s "test file"

would write "test" into the file and leave the file positioned at the fifth byte. There is nothing wrong with coding that (the "test" can be read back easily enough), but this is probably not what you intended to write.

Also concerning strings, you can output string literals—just enclose the string in quotes—or you can output the results of string expressions. Expressions, as for using file write to output text files, must be enclosed in parentheses:

> . file write *handle* %4s (substr(a,2,6))

The following program will output a user-specified matrix to a user-specified file; the syntax of the command being implemented is

> mymatout1 *matname* using *filename* [, replace]

and the code is

```
program mymatout1
        version 11
        gettoken mname 0 : 0
        syntax using/ [, replace]

        local r = rowsof('mname')
        local c = colsof('mname')

        tempname hdl
        file open 'hdl' using '"'using'"', 'replace' write binary

        file write 'hdl' %2b ('r') %2b ('c')
        forvalues i=1(1)'r' {
                forvalues j=1(1)'c' {
                        file write 'hdl' %8z ('mname'['i','j'])
                }
        }
        file close 'hdl'
end
```

A significant problem with `mymatout1` is that, if we wrote a matrix on our Unix computer (an Intel-based computer) and copied the file to a PowerPC-based Mac, we would discover that we could not read the file. Intel computers write multiple-byte numbers with the least-significant byte first; PowerPC-based computers write the most-significant byte first. Who knows what your computer does? Thus even though there is general agreement across computers on how numbers and characters are written, this byte-ordering difference is enough to stop binary files.

`file` can handle this problem for you, but you have to insert a little code. The recommended procedure is this: before writing any numbers in the file, write a field saying which byte order this computer uses (see `byteorder()` in [D] **functions**). Later, when we write the command to read the file, it will read the ordering that we recorded. We will then tell `file` which byte ordering the file is using, and `file` itself will reorder the bytes if that is necessary. There are other ways that we could handle this—such as always writing in a known byte order—but the recommended procedure is better because it is, on average, faster. Most files are read on the same computer that wrote them, and thus the computer wastes no time rearranging bytes then.

The improved version of `mymatout1` is

```
program mymatout2
        version 11
        gettoken mname 0 : 0
        syntax using/ [, replace]

        local r = rowsof('mname')
        local c = colsof('mname')

        tempname hdl
        file open 'hdl' using '"'using'"', 'replace' write binary
/* new */  file write 'hdl' %1b (byteorder())

        file write 'hdl' %2b ('r') %2b ('c')
        forvalues i=1(1)'r' {
                forvalues j=1(1)'c' {
                        file write 'hdl' %8z ('mname'['i','j'])
                }
        }
        file close 'hdl'
end
```

`byteorder()` returns 1 if the machine is hilo and 2 if lohi, but all that matters is that it is small enough to fit in a byte. The important thing is that we write this number using %1b, about which there is no byte-ordering disagreement. What we do with this number we will deal with later.

The second significant problem with our program is that it does not write a signature. Binary files are difficult to tell apart: they all look like binary junk. It is important that we include some sort of marker at the top saying who wrote this file and in what format it was written. That is called a signature. The signature that we will use is

mymatout 1.0.0

We will write that 14-character-long string first thing in the file so that later, when we write mymatin, we can read the string and verify that it contains what we expect. Signature lines should always contain a generic identity (mymatout here) along with a version number, which we can change if we modify the output program to change the output format. This way, the wrong input program cannot be used with a more up-to-date file format.

Our improved program is

```
          program mymatout3
                  version 11
                  gettoken mname 0 : 0
                  syntax using/ [, replace]

                  local r = rowsof('mname')
                  local c = colsof('mname')

                  tempname hdl
                  file open 'hdl' using '"'using'"', 'replace' write binary
/* new */         file write 'hdl' %14s "mymatout 1.0.0"
                  file write 'hdl' %1b (byteorder())

                  file write 'hdl' %2b ('r') %2b ('c')
                  forvalues i=1(1)'r' {
                          forvalues j=1(1)'c' {
                                  file write 'hdl' %8z ('mname'['i','j'])
                          }
                  }
                  file close 'hdl'
          end
```

This program works well. After we wrote the corresponding input routine (see *Reading binary files* below), however, we noticed that our restored matrices lacked their original row and column names, which led to a final round of changes:

```
              program mymatout4
                      version 11
                      gettoken mname 0 : 0
                      syntax using/ [, replace]

                      local r = rowsof('mname')
                      local c = colsof('mname')

                      tempname hdl

                      file open 'hdl' using '"'using'"', 'replace' write binary
/* changed */ file write 'hdl' %14s "mymatout 1.0.1"
                      file write 'hdl' %1b (byteorder())
                      file write 'hdl' %2b ('r') %2b ('c')

/* new */             local names : rownames 'mname'
/* new */             local len : length local names
/* new */             file write 'hdl' %4b ('len') %'len's '"'names'"'

/* new */             local names : colnames 'mname'
/* new */             local len : length local names
/* new */             file write 'hdl' %4b ('len') %'len's '"'names'"'
```

```
            forvalues i=1(1)'r' {
                    forvalues j=1(1)'c' {
                            file write 'hdl' %8z ('mname'['i','j'])
                    }
            }
            file close 'hdl'
    end
```

In this version, we added the lines necessary to write the row and column names into the file. We write the row names by coding

```
    local names : rownames 'mname'
    local len : length local names
    file write 'hdl' %4b ('len') %'len's '"'names'"'
```

and we similarly write the column names. The interesting thing here is that we need to write a string into our binary file for which the length of the string varies. One solution would be

```
    file write 'hdl' %165199s '"'mname'"'
```

but that would be inefficient because, in general, the names are much shorter than 165,199 characters. The solution is to obtain the length of the string to be written and then write the length into the file. In the above code, macro 'len' contains the length, we write 'len' as a 4-byte integer, and then we write the string using a %'len's format. Consider what happens when 'len' is, say, 50. We write 50 into the file, and then we write the string using a %50s format. Later, when we read back the file, we can reverse this process, reading the length and then using the appropriate format.

We also changed the signature from "mymatout 1.0.0" to "mymatout 1.0.1" because the file format changed. Making that change ensures that an old read program does not attempt to read a more modern format (and so produce incorrect results).

❑ **Technical note**

You may write strings using %#s formats that are narrower than, equal to, or wider than the length of the string being written. When the format is too narrow, only that many characters of the string are written. When the format and string are of the same width, the entire string is written. When the format is wider than the string, the entire string is written, and then the excess positions in the file are filled with binary zeros.

Binary zeros are special in strings because binary denotes the end of the string. Thus when you read back the string, even if it was written in a field that was too wide, it will appear exactly as it appeared originally.

❑

Reading binary files

You read binary files just as you wrote them,

```
    file open handle using filename, read binary
    file read handle ...
    ...
    file close handle
```

When reading them, you must be careful to specify the same formats as you did when you wrote the file.

The program that will read the matrices written by mymatout1, presented below, has the syntax

```
    mymatin1 matname filename
```

and the code is

```
program mymatin1
        version 11
        gettoken mname 0 : 0
        syntax using/
        tempname hdl
        file open 'hdl' using '"'using'"', read binary
        tempname val
        file read 'hdl' %2b 'val'
        local r = 'val'
        file read 'hdl' %2b 'val'
        local c = 'val'
        matrix 'mname' = J('r', 'c', 0)
        forvalues i=1(1)'r' {
                forvalues j=1(1)'c' {
                        file read 'hdl' %8z 'val'
                        matrix 'mname'['i','j'] = 'val'
                }
        }
        file close 'hdl'
end
```

When `file read` reads numeric values, they are always stored into `scalars` (see [P] **scalar**), and you specify the name of the scalar directly after the binary numeric format. Here we are using the scalar named 'val', where 'val' is a name that we obtained from `tempname`. We could just as well have used a fixed name, say, `myscalar`, so the first `file read` would read

```
file read 'hdl' %2b myscalar
```

and we would similarly substitute `myscalar` everywhere 'val' appears, but that would make our program less elegant. If the user had previously stored a value under the name `myscalar`, our values would replace it.

In the second version of `mymatout`, we included the byte order. The correspondingly improved version of `mymatin` is

```
            program mymatin2
                    version 11
                    gettoken mname 0 : 0
                    syntax using/
                    tempname hdl
                    file open 'hdl' using '"'using'"', read binary
                    tempname val
/* new */           file read 'hdl' %1b 'val'
/* new */           local border = 'val'
/* new */           file set 'hdl' byteorder 'border'
                    file read 'hdl' %2b 'val'
                    local r = 'val'
                    file read 'hdl' %2b 'val'
                    local c = 'val'
                    matrix 'mname' = J('r', 'c', 0)
                    forvalues i=1(1)'r' {
                            forvalues j=1(1)'c' {
                                    file read 'hdl' %8z 'val'
                                    matrix 'mname'['i','j'] = 'val'
                            }
                    }
                    file close 'hdl'
            end
```

We simply read back the value we recorded and then `file set` it. We cannot directly `file set` *handle* byteorder 'val' because 'val' is a scalar, and the syntax for `file set byteorder` is

$$\text{file set } \textit{handle} \text{ byteorder } \{\text{hilo}|\text{lohi}|1|2\}$$

That is, `file set` is willing to see a number (1 and `hilo` mean the same thing, as do 2 and `lohi`), but that number must be a literal (the character 1 or 2), so we had to copy 'val' into a macro before we could use it. Once we set the byte order, however, we could from then on depend on `file` to reorder the bytes for us should that be necessary.

In the third version of `mymatout`, we added a signature. In the modification below, we read the signature by using a `%14s` format. Strings are copied into local macros, and we must specify the name of the local macro following the format:

```
          program mymatin3
                  version 11
                  gettoken mname 0 : 0
                  syntax using/

                  tempname hdl
                  file open 'hdl' using '"'using'"', read binary
/* new */         file read 'hdl' %14s signature
/* new */         if "'signature'" != "mymatout 1.0.0" {
/* new */                 disp as err "file not mymatout 1.0.0"
/* new */                 exit 610
/* new */         }

                  tempname val
                  file read 'hdl' %1b 'val'
                  local border = 'val'
                  file set 'hdl' byteorder 'border'

                  file read 'hdl' %2b 'val'
                  local r = 'val'
                  file read 'hdl' %2b 'val'
                  local c = 'val'

                  matrix 'mname' = J('r', 'c', 0)
                  forvalues i=1(1)'r' {
                          forvalues j=1(1)'c' {
                                  file read 'hdl' %8z 'val'
                                  matrix 'mname'['i','j'] = 'val'
                          }
                  }
                  file close 'hdl'
          end
```

In the fourth and final version, we wrote the row and column names. We wrote the names by first preceding them with a 4-byte integer recording their width:

```
            program mymatin4
                    version 11
                    gettoken mname 0 : 0
                    syntax using/

                    tempname hdl
                    file open 'hdl' using '"'using'"', read binary

                    file read 'hdl' %14s signature
/* changed */ if "'signature'" != "mymatout 1.0.1" {
/* changed */         disp as err "file not mymatout 1.0.1"
                      exit 610
                    }

                    tempname val
                    file read 'hdl' %1b 'val'
                    local border = 'val'
                    file set 'hdl' byteorder 'border'

                    file read 'hdl' %2b 'val'
                    local r = 'val'
                    file read 'hdl' %2b 'val'
                    local c = 'val'

                    matrix 'mname' = J('r', 'c', 0)

/* new */           file read 'hdl' %4b 'val'
/* new */           local len = 'val'
/* new */           file read 'hdl' %'len's names
/* new */           matrix rownames 'mname' = 'names'

/* new */           file read 'hdl' %4b 'val'
/* new */           local len = 'val'
/* new */           file read 'hdl' %'len's names
/* new */           matrix colnames 'mname' = 'names'

                    forvalues i=1(1)'r' {
                            forvalues j=1(1)'c' {
                                    file read 'hdl' %8z 'val'
                                    matrix 'mname'['i','j'] = 'val'
                            }
                    }
                    file close 'hdl'
            end
```

Use of seek when writing or reading binary files

Nearly all I/O programs are written without using file seek. file seek changes your location in the file. Ordinarily, you start at the beginning of the file and proceed sequentially through the bytes. file seek lets you back up or skip ahead.

file seek *handle* query actually does not change your location in the file; it merely returns in scalar r(loc) the current position, with the first byte in the file being numbered 0, the second 1, and so on. In fact, all the file seek commands return r(loc), but file seek query is unique because that is all it does.

file seek *handle* tof moves to the beginning (top) of the file. This is useful with read files when you want to read the file again, but you can seek to tof even with write files and, of course, with read write files. (Concerning read files: you can seek to top, or any point, before or after the end-of-file condition is raised.)

file seek *handle* eof moves to the end of the file. This is useful only with write files (or read write files) but may be used with read files, too.

file seek *handle* # moves to the specified position. # is measured in bytes from the beginning of the file and is in the same units as reported in r(loc). 'file seek *handle* 0' is equivalent to 'file seek *handle* tof'.

❏ Technical note

When a file is opened write append, you may not use file seek. If you need to seek in the file, open the file read write instead.

❏

Appendix A.1   Useful commands and functions for use with file

- When opening a file read write or write append, file's actions differ depending upon whether the file already exists. confirm file (see [P] **confirm**) can tell you whether a file exists; use it before opening the file.

- To obtain the length of strings when writing binary files, use the macro extended function length:

        local length : length local mystr
        file write *handle* %'length's '"'mystr'"'

  See *Macro extended functions for parsing* in [P] **macro** for details.

- To write portable binary files, we recommend writing in natural byte order and recording the byte order in the file. Then the file can be read by reading the byte order and setting it:

  Writing:

        file write handle %1b (byteorder())

  Reading:

        tempname mysca
        file read handle %1b 'mysca'
        local b_order = 'mysca'
        file set handle byteorder 'b_order'

  The byteorder() function returns 1 or 2, depending on whether the computer being used records data in hilo or lohi format. See [D] **functions**.

Appendix A.2   Actions of binary output formats with out-of-range values

Say that you write the number 2,137 with a %1b format. What value will you later get back when you read the field with a %1b format? Here the answer is ., Stata's missing value, because the %1b format is a variation of %1bs that supports Stata's missing value. If you wrote 2,137 with %1bs, it would read back as 127; if you wrote it with %1bu, it would read back as 255.

In general, in the Stata variation, missing values are supported, and numbers outside the range are written as missing. In the remaining formats, the minimum or maximum is written as

Format	Min value	Max value	Value written when value is ... Too small	Too large
%1bu	0	255	0	255
%1bs	−127	127	−127	127
%1b	−127	100	.	.
%2bu	0	65,535	0	65,535
%2bs	−32,767	32,767	−32,767	32,767
%2b	−32,767	32,740	.	.
%4bu	0	4,294,967,295	0	4,294,967,295
%4bs	−2,147,483,647	2,147,483,647	−2,147,483,647	2,147,483,647
%4b	−2,147,483,647	2,147,483,620	.	.
%4z	-10^{38}	10^{38}	.	.
%8z	-10^{307}	10^{307}	.	.

In the above table, if you write a missing value, take that as writing a value larger than the maximum allowed for the type.

If you write a noninteger value with an integer format, the result will be truncated to an integer. For example, writing 124.75 with a %2b format is the same as writing 124.

Saved results

file read saves the following in r():

Scalars
    r(eof)   1 on end of file; 0 otherwise

Macros
    r(status) (if text file)

win	line read; line ended in cr-lf
mac	line read; line ended in cr
unix	line read; line ended in lf
split	line read; line was too long and so split
none	line read; line was not terminated
eof	line not read because of end of file

r(status)=split indicates that max_macrolen − 1 (33 maxvar + 199 for Stata/MP and Stata/SE, 165,199 for Stata/IC, 8,680 for Small Stata) characters of the line were returned and that the next file read will pick up where the last read left off.

r(status)=none indicates that the entire line was returned, that no line-end character was found, and the next file read will return r(status)=eof.

If r(status)=eof (r(eof)=1), then the local macro into which the line was read contains "". The local macro containing "", however, does not imply end of file because the line might simply have been empty.

`file seek` saves the following in `r()`:

Scalars
    `r(loc)` current position of the file

`file query` saves the following in `r()`:

Scalars
    `r(N)` number of open files

Reference

Slaymaker, E. 2005. Using the file command to produce formatted output for other applications. *Stata Journal* 5: 239–247.

Also see

[P] **display** — Display strings and values of scalar expressions

[P] **serset** — Create and manipulate sersets

[D] **filefilter** — Convert ASCII text or binary patterns in a file

[D] **hexdump** — Display hexadecimal report on file

[D] **infile** — Overview of reading data into Stata

[D] **infix (fixed format)** — Read ASCII (text) data in fixed format

[D] **insheet** — Read ASCII (text) data created by a spreadsheet

[M-4] **io** — I/O functions

Title

> **file formats .dta** — Description of .dta file format

Description

Stata's .dta datasets record data in a way generalized to work across computers that do not agree on how data are recorded. Thus the same dataset may be used, without translation, on different computers (Windows, Unix, and Mac computers). Given a computer, datasets are divided into two categories: native-format and foreign-format datasets. Stata uses the following two rules:

R1. On any computer, Stata knows how to write only native-format datasets.

R2. On all computers, Stata can read foreign-format as well as native-format datasets.

Rules R1 and R2 ensure that Stata users need not be concerned with dataset formats.

Stata is also continually being updated, and these updates sometimes require that changes be made to how Stata records .dta datasets. Stata can read older formats, but whenever it writes a dataset, it writes in the modern format.

Remarks

For up-to-date documentation on the Stata .dta file format, type `help dta`. The online help file contains all the details a programmer will need. To obtain a copy of the help file in PostScript format, which you can then print, type

```
. which dta.sthlp
. translate help_file dta.ps, translator(smcl2ps)
```

The first command will show you where the help file is, and then you can type that name in the `translate` command. Even easier is

```
. findfile dta.sthlp
. translate "`r(fn)'" dta.ps, translator(smcl2ps)
```

Either way, you can then print the new file `dta.ps` from your current directory.

Also see

[R] **translate** — Print and translate logs

161

Title

findfile — Find file in path

Syntax

findfile *filename* $\left[\right.$, path(*path*) <u>nodes</u>cend all $\left.\right]$

where *filename* and *path* may optionally be enclosed in quotes, and the default is to look over the ado-path if option `path()` is not specified.

Description

`findfile` looks for a file along a specified path and, if the file is found, displays the fully qualified name and returns the name in `r(fn)`. If the file is not found, the file-not-found error, r(601), is issued.

Unless told otherwise, `findfile` looks along the ado-path, the same path that Stata uses for searching for ado-files, help files, etc.

In programming contexts, `findfile` is usually preceded by `quietly`; see [P] **quietly**.

Options

path(*path*) specifies the path over which `findfile` is to search. Not specifying this option is equivalent to specifying `path('"'c(adopath)'"')`.

If specified, *path* should be a list of directory (folder) names separated by semicolons; for example,

```
path('".;~/bin;"~/data/my data";~"')
path('".;\bin;"\data\my data";~"')
```

The individual directory names may be enclosed in quotes, but if any are, remember to enclose the entire path argument in compound quotes.

Also any of the directory names may be specified as STATA, UPDATES, BASE, SITE, PLUS, PERSONAL, or OLDPLACE, which are indirect references to directories recorded by `sysdir`:

```
path(UPDATES;BASE;SITE;.;PERSONAL;PLUS)
path(\bin:SITE;.;PERSONAL;PLUS)
path('"\bin;.;"\data\my data";PERSONAL;PLUS"')
path('".;'c(adopath)'"')
```

nodescend specifies that `findfile` not follow Stata's normal practice of searching in letter subdirectories of directories in the path, as well as in the directories themselves. nodescend is rarely specified, and, if it is specified, `path()` would usually be specified, too.

all specifies that all files along the path with the specified name are to be found and then listed and saved in r(fn). When all is not specified, the default is to stop the search when the first instance of the specified name is found.

When all is specified, the fully qualified names of the files found are returned in r(fn), listed one after the other, and each enclosed in quotes. Thus when all is specified, if you later need to quote the returned list, you must use compound double quotes. Also remember that findfile issues a file-not-found error if no files are found. If you wish to suppress that and want r(fn) returned containing nothing, precede findfile with capture. Thus the typical usage of findfile, all is

```
. capture findfile filename, all
. local filelist `"`r(fn)'"'
```

Remarks

findfile is not a utility to search everywhere for a file that you have lost. findfile is for use in those rare ado-files that use prerecorded datasets and for which you wish to place the datasets along the ado-path, along with the ado-file itself.

For instance, Stata's icd9 command performs a mapping, and that mapping is in fact stored in a dataset containing original values and mapped values. Thus along with icd9.ado is dataset icd9_cod.dta, and that dataset is stored along the ado-path, too. Users of icd9 know nothing about the dataset. In icd9.ado, the icd9_cod.dta is merged with the data in memory. The code fragment that does that reads

```
. quietly findfile icd9_cod.dta
. merge ... using `"`r(fn)'"'
```

It would not have been possible to code simply

```
. merge ... using icd9_cod.dta
```

because icd9_cod.dta is not in the current directory.

Saved results

findfile saves the following in r():

Macros
r(fn)   (all not specified)   name of the file found; name not enclosed in quotes
         (all specified)   names of the files found, listed one after the other,
                               each enclosed in quotes

Methods and formulas

findfile is implemented as an ado-file.

Also see

[P] **sysdir** — Query and set system directories

[P] **unabcmd** — Unabbreviate command name

[R] **which** — Display location and version for an ado-file

[D] **sysuse** — Use shipped dataset

Title

> **foreach** — Loop over items

Syntax

```
foreach lname { in | of listtype } list {
        Stata commands referring to 'lname'
}
```

Allowed are

```
foreach lname in anylist
```

```
foreach lname of local lmacname {
```

```
foreach lname of global gmacname {
```

```
foreach lname of varlist varlist {
```

```
foreach lname of newlist newvarlist {
```

```
foreach lname of numlist numlist {
```

Braces must be specified with `foreach`, and

1. the open brace must appear on the same line as `foreach`;
2. nothing may follow the open brace except, of course, comments; the first command to be executed must appear on a new line;
3. the close brace must appear on a line by itself.

Description

`foreach` repeatedly sets local macro *lname* to each element of the list and executes the commands enclosed in braces. The loop is executed zero or more times; it is executed zero times if the list is null or empty. Also see [P] **forvalues**, which is the fastest way to loop over consecutive values, such as looping over numbers from 1 to k.

`foreach lname in list {...}` allows a general list. Elements are separated from each other by one or more blanks.

`foreach lname of local list {...}` and `foreach lname of global list {...}` obtain the list from the indicated place. This method of using `foreach` produces the fastest executing code.

foreach *lname* of varlist *list* {...}, foreach *lname* of newlist *list* {...}, and foreach *lname* of numlist *list* {...} are much like foreach *lname* in *list* {...}, except that the *list* is given the appropriate interpretation. For instance,

```
foreach x in mpg weight-turn {
    ...
}
```

has two elements, mpg and weight-turn, so the loop will be executed twice.

```
foreach x of varlist mpg weight-turn {
    ...
}
```

has four elements, mpg, weight, length, and turn, because *list* was given the interpretation of a varlist.

foreach *lname* of varlist *list* {...} gives *list* the interpretation of a varlist. The *list* is expanded according to standard variable abbreviation rules, and the existence of the variables is confirmed.

foreach *lname* of newlist *list* {...} indicates that the *list* is to be interpreted as new variable names; see [U] **11.4.2 Lists of new variables**. A check is performed to see that the named variables could be created, but they are not automatically created.

foreach *lname* of numlist *list* {...} indicates a number list and allows standard number-list notation; see [U] **11.1.8 numlist**.

Remarks

Remarks are presented under the following headings:

> *Introduction*
> *foreach ... of local and foreach ... of global*
> *foreach ... of varlist*
> *foreach ... of newlist*
> *foreach ... of numlist*
> *Use of foreach with continue*
> *The unprocessed list elements*

Introduction

foreach has many forms, but it is just one command, and what it means is

```
foreach  value of a list of things, set x equal to each and {
             execute these instructions once per value
             and in the loop we can refer to 'x' to refer to the value
}
```

and this is coded

```
foreach x ... {
        ... 'x' ...
}
```

We use the name x for illustration; you may use whatever name you like. The list itself can come from a variety of places and can be given a variety of interpretations, but foreach x in is easiest to understand:

```
foreach x in a b mpg 2 3 2.2 {
        ... 'x' ...
}
```

The list is a, b, mpg, 2, 3, and 2.2, and appears right in the command. In some programming instances, you might know the list ahead of time, but often what you know is that you want to do the loop for each value of the list contained in a macro, for instance, 'varlist'. Then you could code

```
foreach x in 'varlist' {
        ... 'x' ...
}
```

but your code will execute more quickly if you code

```
foreach x of local varlist {
        ... 'x' ...
}
```

Both work, but the second is quicker to execute. In the first, Stata has to expand the macro and substitute it into the command line, whereupon foreach must then pull back the elements one at a time and store them. In the second, all of that is already done, and foreach can just grab the local macro varlist.

The two forms we have just shown,

```
foreach x in ... {
        ... 'x' ...
}
```

and

```
foreach x of local ... {
        ... 'x' ...
}
```

are the two ways foreach is most commonly used. The other forms are for special occasions.

In the event that you have something that you want to be given the interpretation of a varlist, newvarlist, or numlist before it is interpreted as a list, you can code

```
foreach x of varlist mpg weight-turn g* {
        ... 'x' ...
}
```

or

```
foreach x of newlist id values1-values9 {
        ... 'x' ...
}
```

or

```
foreach x of numlist 1/3 5 6/10 {
        ... 'x' ...
}
```

Just as with foreach x in ..., you put the list right on the command line, and, if you have the list in a macro, you can put 'macroname' on the command line.

If you have the list in a macro, you have no alternative but to code 'macroname'; there is no special foreach x of local macroname variant for varlist, newvarlist, and numlist because, in those cases, foreach x of local macroname itself is probably sufficient. If you have the list in a macro, then how did it get there? Well, it probably was something that the user typed and that your program has already parsed. Then the list has already been expanded, and treating the list as a general list is adequate; it need not be given the special interpretation again, at least as far as foreach is concerned.

▷ Example 1: Using foreach, interactively

foreach is generally used in programs, but it may be used interactively, and for illustration we will use it that way. Three files are appended to the dataset in memory. The dataset currently in memory and each of the three files has only one string observation.

```
. list
                          x
   1.           data in memory
. foreach file in this.dta that.dta theother.dta {
   2.           append using "'file'"
   3. }
. list
                          x
   1.           data in memory
   2.      data from this.dta
   3.      data from that.dta
   4. data from theother.dta
```

Quotes may be used to allow elements with blanks.

```
. foreach name in "Annette Fett" "Ashley Poole" "Marsha Martinez" {
   2.           display length("'name'") " characters long -- 'name'"
   3. }
12 characters long -- Annette Fett
12 characters long -- Ashley Poole
15 characters long -- Marsha Martinez
```

◁

foreach ... of local and foreach ... of global

foreach *lname* of local *lmacname* obtains the blank-separated list (which may contain quotes) from local macro *lmacname*. For example,

```
foreach file of local flist {
       ...
}
```

produces the same results as typing

```
foreach file in 'flist' {
       ...
}
```

except that foreach file of local flist is faster, uses less memory, and allows the list to be modified in the body of the loop.

If the contents of flist are modified in the body of foreach file in 'flist', foreach will not notice, and the original list will be used. The contents of flist may, however, be modified in foreach file of local flist, but only to add new elements onto the end.

foreach *lname* of global *gmacname* is the same as foreach *lname* in $*gmacname*, with the same three caveats as to speed, memory use, and modification in the loop body.

▷ Example 2: Looping over the elements of local and global macros

```
. local grains "rice wheat flax"

. foreach x of local grains {
  2.          display "`x'"
  3. }
rice
wheat
flax

. global money "Dollar Lira Pound"

. foreach y of global money {
  2.          display "`y'"
  3. }
Dollar
Lira
Pound
```

◁

foreach ... of varlist

foreach *lname* of varlist *varlist* allows specifying an existing variable list.

▷ Example 3: Looping over existing variables

```
. foreach var of varlist pri-rep t* {
  2.          quietly summarize `var'
  3.          summarize `var' if `var' > r(mean)
  4. }
```

Variable	Obs	Mean	Std. Dev.	Min	Max
price	22	9814.364	3022.929	6229	15906

Variable	Obs	Mean	Std. Dev.	Min	Max
mpg	31	26.67742	4.628802	22	41

Variable	Obs	Mean	Std. Dev.	Min	Max
rep78	29	4.37931	.493804	4	5

Variable	Obs	Mean	Std. Dev.	Min	Max
trunk	40	17.1	2.351214	14	23

Variable	Obs	Mean	Std. Dev.	Min	Max
turn	41	43.07317	2.412367	40	51

◁

foreach *lname* of varlist *varlist* can be useful interactively but is rarely used in programming contexts. You can code

```
syntax [varlist] ...
foreach var of varlist `varlist' {
       ...
}
```

but that is not as efficient as coding

```
syntax [varlist] ...
foreach var of local varlist {
        ...
}
```

because 'varlist' has already been expanded by the syntax command according to the macro rules.

❏ Technical note

```
syntax [varlist] ...
foreach var of local varlist {
        ...
}
```

is also preferable to

```
syntax [varlist] ...
tokenize 'varlist'
while "'1'" != "" {
        ...
        macro shift
}
```

or

```
syntax [varlist] ...
tokenize 'varlist'
local i = 1
while "''i''" != "" {
        ...
        local i = 'i' + 1
}
```

because it is not only more readable but also faster.

❏

foreach ... of newlist

newlist signifies to foreach that the list is composed of new variables. foreach verifies that the list contains valid new variable names, but it does not create the variables. For instance,

```
. foreach var of newlist z1-z4 {
2.          gen 'var' = runiform()
3. }
```

would create variables z1, z2, z3, and z4.

foreach ... of numlist

foreach *lname* of numlist *numlist* provides a method of looping through a list of numbers. Standard number-list notation is allowed; see [U] **11.1.8 numlist**. For instance,

```
. foreach num of numlist 1/4 8 103 {
2.          display 'num'
3. }
1
2
3
4
8
103
```

If you wish to loop over many equally spaced values, do not code, for instance,

```
foreach x in 1/1000 {
    ...
}
```

Instead, code

```
forvalues x = 1/1000 {
    ...
}
```

foreach must store the list of elements, whereas forvalues obtains the elements one at a time by calculation; see [P] **forvalues**.

Use of foreach with continue

The *lname* in foreach is defined only in the loop body. If you code

```
foreach x ... {
        // loop body, 'x' is defined
}
// 'x' is now undefined, meaning it contains ""
```

'x' is defined only within the loop body, which is the case even if you use continue, break (see [P] **continue**) to exit the loop early:

```
foreach x ... {
        ...
        if ... {
                continue, break
        }
}
// 'x' is still undefined, even if continue, break is executed
```

If you later need the value of 'x', code

```
foreach x ... {
        ...
        if ... {
                local lastx '""'x'"'
                continue, break
        }
}
// 'lastx' defined
```

The unprocessed list elements

The macro 'ferest()' may be used in the body of the foreach loop to obtain the unprocessed list elements.

▷ Example 4

```
. foreach x in alpha "one two" three four {
  2.          display
  3.          display `"        x is |`x'|"'
  4.          display `"ferest() is |`ferest()'|"'
  5. }

         x is |alpha|
ferest() is |"one two" three four|

         x is |one two|
ferest() is |three four|

         x is |three|
ferest() is |four|

         x is |four|
ferest() is ||
```
◁

'ferest()' is available only within the body of the loop; outside that, 'ferest()' evaluates to "". Thus you might code

```
foreach x ... {
        ...
        if ... {
                local lastx `""`x'""'
                local rest `""`ferest()'""'
                continue, break
        }
}
// `lastx' and `rest' are defined
```

Also see

[P] **continue** — Break out of loops

[P] **forvalues** — Loop over consecutive values

[P] **if** — if programming command

[P] **levelsof** — Levels of variable

[P] **while** — Looping

[U] **18 Programming Stata**

[U] **18.3 Macros**

Title

> **forvalues** — Loop over consecutive values

Syntax

<u>forv</u>alues *lname* = *range* {

        Stata commands referring to '*lname*'

}

where *range* is

$\#_1(\#_d)\#_2$	meaning $\#_1$ to $\#_2$ in steps of $\#_d$
$\#_1/\#_2$	meaning $\#_1$ to $\#_2$ in steps of 1
$\#_1 \ \#_t$ to $\#_2$	meaning $\#_1$ to $\#_2$ in steps of $\#_t - \#_1$
$\#_1 \ \#_t : \#_2$	meaning $\#_1$ to $\#_2$ in steps of $\#_t - \#_1$

The loop is executed as long as calculated values of '*lname*' are $\leq \#_2$, assuming that $\#_d > 0$.

Braces must be specified with `forvalues`, and

1. the open brace must appear on the same line as `forvalues`;

2. nothing may follow the open brace except, of course, comments; the first command to be executed must appear on a new line;

3. the close brace must appear on a line by itself.

Description

`forvalues` repeatedly sets local macro *lname* to each element of *range* and executes the commands enclosed in braces. The loop is executed zero or more times.

Remarks

`forvalues` is the fastest way to execute a block of code for different numeric values of *lname*.

> ## Example 1

With `forvalues` *lname* = $\#_1(\#_d)\#_2$, the loop is executed zero or more times, once for *lname* = $\#_1$, once for *lname* = $\#_1 + \#_d$, once for *lname* = $\#_1 + \#_d + \#_d$, and so on, as long as *lname* $\leq \#_2$ (assuming $\#_d$ is positive) or as long as *lname* $\geq \#_2$ (assuming $\#_d$ is negative). Specifying $\#_d$ as 0 is an error.

```
. forvalues i = 1(1)5 {
  2.          display 'i'
  3. }
1
2
3
4
5
```

lists the numbers 1–5, stepping by 1, whereas

```
. forvalues i = 10(-2)1 {
  2.          display 'i'
  3. }
10
8
6
4
2
```

lists the numbers starting from 10, stepping down by 2 until it reaches 2. It stops at 2 instead of at 1 or 0.

```
. forvalues i = 1(1)1 {
  2.          display 'i'
  3. }
1
```

displays 1, whereas

```
. forvalues i = 1(1)0 {
  2.          display 'i'
  3. }
```

displays nothing.

◁

forvalues *lname* = $\#_1/\#_2$ is the same as using forvalues *lname* = $\#_1(1)\#_2$. Using / does not allow counting backward.

▷ Example 2

```
. forvalues i = 1/3 {
  2.          display 'i'
  3. }
1
2
3
```

lists the three values from 1 to 3, but

```
. forvalues i = 3/1 {
  2.          display 'i'
  3. }
```

lists nothing because using this form of the forvalues command allows incrementing only by 1.

◁

The forvalues *lname* = $\#_1$ $\#_t$ to $\#_2$ and forvalues *lname* = $\#_1$ $\#_t$: $\#_2$ forms of the forvalues command are equivalent to computing $\#_d = \#_t - \#_1$ and then using the forvalues *lname* = $\#_1(\#_d)\#_2$ form of the command.

▷ Example 3

```
. forvalues i = 5 10 : 25 {
  2.          display 'i'
  3. }
5
10
15
20
25
. forvalues i = 25 20 to 5 {
  2.          display 'i'
  3. }
25
20
15
10
5
```

◁

❑ Technical note

It is not legal syntax to type

```
. scalar x = 3
. forvalues i = 1(1)'x' {
  2.          local x = 'x' + 1
  3.          display 'i'
  4. }
```

forvalues requires literal numbers. Using macros, as shown in the following technical note, is allowed.

❑

❑ Technical note

The values of the loop bounds are determined once and for all the first time the loop is executed. Changing the loop bounds will have no effect. For instance,

```
. local n 3
. forvalues i = 1(1)'n' {
  2.          local n = 'n' + 1
  3.          display 'i'
  4. }
1
2
3
```

will not create an infinite loop. With 'n' originally equal to 3, the loop will be performed three times.

Similarly, modifying the loop counter will not affect `forvalues`' subsequent behavior. For instance,

```
. forvalues i = 1(1)3 {
  2.          display "Top of loop  i = `i'"
  3.          local i = `i' * 4
  4.          display "After change i = `i'"
  5. }
Top of loop  i = 1
After change i = 4
Top of loop  i = 2
After change i = 8
Top of loop  i = 3
After change i = 12
```

will still execute three times, setting 'i' to 1, 2, and 3 at the beginning of each iteration.

❏

Also see

[P] **continue** — Break out of loops

[P] **foreach** — Loop over items

[P] **if** — if programming command

[P] **while** — Looping

[U] **18 Programming Stata**

[U] **18.3 Macros**

Title

---

fvexpand — Expand factor varlists

Syntax

fvexpand [*varlist*] [*if*] [*in*]

varlist may contain factor variables and time-series operators; see [U] **11.4.3 Factor variables** and [U] **11.4.4 Time-series varlists**.

Description

fvexpand expands a factor varlist to the corresponding expanded, specific varlist. *varlist* may be general or specific and even may already be expanded.

Remarks

An example of a general factor varlist is mpg i.foreign. The corresponding specific factor varlist would be mpg i(0 1)b0.foreign if foreign took on the values 0 and 1 in the data.

A specific factor varlist is specific with respect to a given problem, which is to say, a given dataset and subsample. The specific varlist identifies the values taken on by factor variables and the base.

Factor varlist mpg i(0 1)b0.foreign is specific. The same varlist could be written as mpg i0b.foreign i1.foreign, so that is specific, too. The first is unexpanded and specific. The second is expanded and specific.

fvexpand takes a general or specific (expanded or unexpanded) factor varlist, along with an optional if or in, and returns a fully expanded, specific varlist.

Saved results

fvexpand saves the following in r():

Macros
    r(varlist)   the expanded, specific varlist

Also see

[U] **11.4.3 Factor variables**

Title

gettoken — Low-level parsing

Syntax

gettoken *emname1* [*emname2*] : *emname3* [, p̲arse("*pchars*") q̲uotes

q̲ed(*lmacname*) m̲atch(*lmacname*) bind]

where *pchars* are the parsing characters, *lmacname* is a local macro name, and *emname* is described in the following table:

emname is . . .	Refers to a . . .
macroname	local macro
(local) *macroname*	local macro
(global) *macroname*	global macro

Description

gettoken is a low-level parsing command designed for programmers who wish to parse input for themselves. The syntax command (see [P] **syntax**) is an easier-to-use, high-level parsing command.

gettoken obtains the next token from the macro *emname3* and stores it in the macro *emname1*. If macro *emname2* is specified, the rest of the string from *emname3* is stored in the *emname2* macro. *emname1* and *emname3*, or *emname2* and *emname3*, may be the same name. The first token is determined based on the parsing characters *pchars*, which default to a space if not specified.

Options

parse("*pchars*") specifies the parsing characters. If parse() is not specified, parse(" ") is assumed, meaning that tokens are identified by blanks.

quotes indicates that the outside quotes are not to be stripped in what is stored in *emname1*. This option has no effect on what is stored in *emname2* because it always retains outside quotes. quotes is a rarely specified option; usually you want the quotes stripped. You would not want the quotes stripped if you wanted to make a perfect copy of the contents of the original macro for parsing at a later time.

qed(*lmacname*) specifies a local macroname that is to be filled in with 1 or 0 according to whether the returned token was enclosed in quotes in the original string. qed() does not change how parsing is done; it merely returns more information.

match(*lmacname*) specifies that parentheses be matched in determining the token. The outer level of parentheses, if any, are removed before the token is stored in *emname1*. The local macro *lmacname* is set to "(" if parentheses were found; otherwise, it is set to an empty string.

bind specifies that expressions within parentheses and those within brackets are to be bound together, even when not parsing on () and [].

Remarks

Often we apply `gettoken` to the macro '0' (see [U] **18.4.6 Parsing nonstandard syntax**), as in

```
gettoken first : 0
```

which obtains the first token (with spaces as token delimiters) from '0' and leaves '0' unchanged. Or, alternatively,

```
gettoken first 0 : 0
```

which obtains the first token from '0' and saves the rest back in '0'.

▷ Example 1

Even though `gettoken` is typically used as a programming command, we demonstrate its use interactively:

```
. local str "cat+dog   mouse++horse"
. gettoken left : str
. display '"'left'"'
cat+dog
. display '"'str'"'
cat+dog   mouse++horse
. gettoken left str : str, parse(" +")
. display '"'left'"'
cat
. display '"'str'"'
+dog   mouse++horse
. gettoken next str : str, parse(" +")
. display '"'next'"'
+
. display '"'str'"'
dog   mouse++horse
```

Both global and local variables may be used with `gettoken`. Strings with nested quotes are also allowed, and the `quotes` option may be specified if desired. For more information on compound double quotes, see [U] **18.3.5 Double quotes**.

```
. global weird '"'""some" strings"' are '"within "strings""'"'
. gettoken (local)left (global)right : (global)weird
. display '"'left'"'
"some" strings
. display '"$right"'
 are '"within "strings""'
. gettoken left (global)right : (global)weird , quotes
. display '"'left'"'
'""some" strings"'
. display '"$right"'
 are '"within "strings""'
```

The `match()` option is illustrated below.

```
. local pstr "(a (b c)) ((d e f) g h)"

. gettoken left right : pstr

. display '"'left'"'
(a

. display '"'right'"'
 (b c)) ((d e f) g h)

. gettoken left right : pstr , match(parns)

. display '"'left'"'
a (b c)

. display '"'right'"'
 ((d e f) g h)

. display '"'parns'"'
(
```

◁

▷ Example 2

One use of `gettoken` is to process two-word commands. For example, `mycmd list` does one thing and `mycmd generate` does another. We wish to obtain the word following `mycmd`, examine it, and call the appropriate subroutine with a perfect copy of what followed.

```
program mycmd
        version 11
        gettoken subcmd 0 : 0
        if "'subcmd'" == "list" {
                mycmd_l '0'
        }
        else if "'subcmd'" == "generate" {
                mycmd_g '0'
        }
        else    error 199
end

program mycmd_l
        ...
end

program mycmd_g
        ...
end
```

◁

▷ Example 3

Suppose that we wish to create a general prefix command with the syntax

```
newcmd ... : stata_command
```

where ... represents some possibly complicated syntax. We want to split this entire command line at the colon, making a perfect copy of what precedes the colon, which will be parsed by our program, and what follows the colon, which will be passed along to *stata_command*.

```
program newcmd
        version 11
        gettoken part 0 : 0, parse(" :") quotes
        while `"`part'"' != ":" & `"`part'"' != "" {
                local left `"`left' `part'"'
                gettoken part 0 : 0, parse(" :") quotes
        }
```

(`left` *now contains what followed* newcmd *up to the colon*)
(`0` *now contains what followed the colon*)

. . .

```
end
```

Notice the use of the quotes option. We also used compound double quotes when accessing `part` and `left` because these macros might contain embedded quotation marks.

◁

□ Technical note

We strongly encourage you to specify space as one of your parsing characters. For instance, with the last example, you may have been tempted to use gettoken but to parse only on colon instead of on colon and space, as in

```
gettoken left 0 : 0, parse(":") quotes
gettoken colon 0 : 0, parse(":")
```

and thereby avoid the while loop. This is not guaranteed to work for two reasons. First, if the length of the string up to the colon is large, then you run the risk of having it truncated. Second, if `left` begins with a quotation mark, then the result will not be what you expect.

Our recommendation is always to specify a space as one of your parsing characters and to grow your desired macro as demonstrated in our last example.

□

□ Technical note

If one of the parsing characters specified is the equal sign, e.g., parse("= "), then not only is the equal sign treated as one token, but so is Stata's equality operator, ==. For instance, parsing "y=x if z==3" results in the tokens "y", "=", "x", "if", "z", "==", and "3".

□

Also see

[P] **syntax** — Parse Stata syntax

[P] **tokenize** — Divide strings into tokens

[P] **while** — Looping

[U] **18 Programming Stata**

Title

if — if programming command

Syntax

if *exp* {   or   if *exp single_command*
    multiple_commands
}

which, in either case, may be followed by

else {   or   else *single_command*
    multiple_commands
}

If you put braces following the if or else,

1. the open brace must appear on the same line as the if or else;

2. nothing may follow the open brace except, of course, comments; the first command to be executed must appear on a new line;

3. the close brace must appear on a line by itself.

Description

The if command (not to be confused with the if qualifier; see [U] **11.1.3 if exp**) evaluates *exp*. If the result is *true* (nonzero), the commands inside the braces are executed. If the result is *false* (zero), those statements are ignored, and the statement (or statements if enclosed in braces) following the else is executed.

Remarks

Remarks are presented under the following headings:

    Introduction
    Avoid single-line if and else with ++ and -- macro expansion

Introduction

The if command is intended for use inside programs and do-files; see [U] **18.3.4 Macros and expressions** for examples of its use.

▷ Example 1

Do not confuse the if command with the if qualifier. Typing if (age>21) summarize age will summarize *all* the observations on age if the first observation on age is greater than 21. Otherwise, it will do nothing. Typing summarize age if age>21, on the other hand, summarizes all the observations on age that are greater than 21.

◁

181

▷ Example 2

if is typically used in do-files and programs. For instance, let's write a program to calculate the Tukey (1977, 90–91) "power" function of a variable, x:

```
. program power
        if '2'>0 {
                generate z='1'^'2'
                label variable z "'1'^'2'"
        }
        else if '2'==0 {
                generate z=log('1')
                label variable z "log('1')"
        }
        else {
                generate z=-('1'^('2'))
                label variable z "-'1'^('2')"
        }
        end
```

This program takes two arguments. The first argument is the name of an existing variable, x. The second argument is a number, which we will call n. The program creates the new variable z. If $n > 0$, z is x^n; if $n = 0$, z is $\log x$; and if $n < 0$, z is $-x^n$. No matter which path the program follows through the code, it labels the variable appropriately:

```
. power age 2
. describe z
```

variable name	storage type	display format	value label	variable label
z	float	%9.0g		age^2

◁

❑ Technical note

If the expression refers to any variables, their values in the first observation are used unless explicit subscripts are specified.

❑

Avoid single-line if and else with ++ and -- macro expansion

Do not use the single-line forms of if and else—do not omit the braces—when the action includes the '++' or '--' macro-expansion operators. For instance, do not code

```
if (...) somecommand '++i'
```

Code instead,

```
if (...) {
        somecommand '++i'
}
```

In the first example, i will be incremented regardless of whether the condition is true or false because macro expansion occurs before the line is interpreted. In the second example, if the condition is false, the line inside the braces will not be macro expanded and so i will not be incremented.

The same applies to the else statement; do not code

```
else somecommand '++i'
```

Code instead,

```
else {
        somecommand '++i'
}
```

❏ Technical note

What was just said also applies to macro-induced execution of class programs that have side effects. Consider

```
if (...) somecommand '.clspgm.getnext'
```

Class-member program .getnext would execute regardless of whether the condition were true or false. Here code

```
if (...) {
        somecommand '.clspgm.getnext'
}
```

Understand that the problem arises only when macro substitution causes the invocation of the class program. There would be nothing wrong with coding

```
if (...) '.clspgm.getnext'
```

❏

Reference

Tukey, J. W. 1977. *Exploratory Data Analysis.* Reading, MA: Addison–Wesley.

Also see

[P] **continue** — Break out of loops

[P] **foreach** — Loop over items

[P] **forvalues** — Loop over consecutive values

[P] **while** — Looping

[U] **18 Programming Stata**

Title

include — Include commands from file

Syntax

include *filename*

Description

include is a variation on do and run—see [R] **do**—that causes Stata to execute the commands stored in *filename* just as if they were entered from the keyboard.

include differs from do and run in that any local macros (changed settings, etc.) created by executing the file are not dropped or reset when execution of the file concludes. Rather, results are just as if the commands in *filename* appeared in the session or file that included *filename*.

If *filename* is specified without an extension, .do is assumed.

Remarks

Remarks are presented under the following headings:

Use with do-files
Use with Mata
Warning

Use with do-files

include can be used in advanced programming situations where you have several do-files among which you wish to share common definitions. Say that you have do-files step1.do, step2.do, and step3.do that perform a data-management task. You want the do-files to include a common definition of the local macros 'inname' and 'outname', which are, respectively, the names of the files to be read and created. One way to do this is

```
──────────────────────────────────────────── begin step1.do ───────────
...
include common.doh
...
──────────────────────────────────────────── end step1.do ───────────
```

```
──────────────────────────────────────────── begin step2.do ───────────
...
include common.doh
...
──────────────────────────────────────────── end step2.do ───────────
```

184

```
——————————————————————————— begin step3.do ———————
...
include common.doh
...
——————————————————————————————— end step3.do ———————

——————————————————————————— begin common.doh ———————
local inname   "inputdata.dta"
local outname "outputdata.dta"
——————————————————————————————— end common.doh ———————
```

Presumably, files step1.do, step2.do, and step3.do include lines such as

```
. use 'inname', clear
```

and

```
. save 'outname', replace
```

Our use of the .doh suffix in naming file common.doh is not a typo. We called the file .doh to emphasize that it is a header for do-files, but you can name the file as you wish, including common.do.

You could call the file common.do, but you could not use the do command to run it because the local macros that the file defines would automatically be dropped when the file finished executing, and thus in step1.do, step2.do, and step3.do, the macros would be undefined.

Use with Mata

include is sometimes used in advanced Mata situations where you are creating a library of routines with shared concepts:

```
——————————————————————————— begin inpivot.mata ———————
version 11
include limits.matah

mata:
real matrix inpivot(real matrix X)
{
        real matrix     y1, yz
        real scalar     n

        if (rows(X)>'MAXDIM' | cols(X)>'MAXDIM') {
                errprintf("inpivot:  matrix too large\n")
                exit(1000)
        }
        ...
}
end
——————————————————————————————— end inpivot.mata ———————

——————————————————————————— begin limits.matah ———————
...
local MAXDIM    800
...
——————————————————————————————— end limits.matah ———————
```

Presumably, many .mata files include limits.matah.

Warning

Do not use command `include` in the body of a Stata program:

```
program ...
        ...
        include ...
        ...
end
```

The `include` will not be executed, as you might have hoped, when the program is compiled. Instead, the `include` will be stored in your program and executed every time your program is run. The result will be the same as if the lines had been included at compile time, but the execution will be slower.

Also see

[R] **do** — Execute commands from a file

[R] **doedit** — Edit do-files and other text files

Title

levelsof — Levels of variable

Syntax

levelsof *varname* [*if*] [*in*] [*, options*]

options	description
<u>c</u>lean	display string values without compound double quotes
<u>l</u>ocal(*macname*)	insert the list of values in the local macro *macname*
<u>mis</u>sing	include missing values of *varname* in calculation
<u>s</u>eparate(*separator*)	separator to serve as punctuation for the values of returned list; default is a space

Description

levelsof displays a sorted list of the distinct values of *varname*.

Options

clean displays string values without compound double quotes. By default, each distinct string value is displayed within compound double quotes, as these are the most general delimiters. If you know that the string values in *varname* do not include embedded spaces or embedded quotes, this is an appropriate option. **clean** does not affect the display of values from numeric variables.

local(*macname*) inserts the list of values in local macro *macname* within the calling program's space. Hence, that macro will be accessible after **levelsof** has finished. This is helpful for subsequent use, especially with **foreach**.

missing specifies that missing values of *varname* be included in the tabulation. The default is to exclude them.

separate(*separator*) specifies a separator to serve as punctuation for the values of the returned list. The default is a space. A useful alternative is a comma.

Remarks

levelsof serves two different functions. First, it provides a compact list of the distinct values of *varname*. More commonly, it is useful when you desire to cycle through the distinct values of *varname* with (say) **foreach**; see [P] **foreach**. **levelsof** leaves behind a list in **r(levels)** that may be used in a subsequent command.

levelsof may hit the limits imposed by your Stata. However, it is typically used when the number of distinct values of *varname* is modest.

The terminology of levels of a factor has long been standard in experimental design. See Cochran and Cox (1957, 148), Fisher (1942), or Yates (1937, 5).

▷ Example 1

```
. use http://www.stata-press.com/data/r11/auto
(1978 Automobile Data)
. levelsof rep78
1 2 3 4 5
. display "'r(levels)'"
1 2 3 4 5
. levelsof rep78, miss local(mylevs)
1 2 3 4 5 .
. display "'mylevs'"
1 2 3 4 5 .
. levelsof rep78, sep(,)
1,2,3,4,5
. display "'r(levels)'"
1,2,3,4,5
```

Showing value labels when defined:

```
. levelsof factor, local(levels)
. foreach l of local levels {
.         di "-> factor = ': label (factor) 'l''"
.         whatever if factor == 'l'
. }
```

◁

Saved results

levelsof saves the following in r():

Macros
r(levels)   list of distinct values

Methods and formulas

levelsof is implemented as an ado-file.

Acknowledgments

levelsof was written by Nicholas J. Cox, Durham University, who in turn thanks Christopher F. Baum, Boston College, and Nicholas Winter, University of Virginia, for their input.

References

Cochran, W. G., and G. M. Cox. 1957. *Experimental Designs*. 2nd ed. New York: Wiley.

Cox, N. J. 2001. dm90: Listing distinct values of a variable. *Stata Technical Bulletin* 60: 8–11. Reprinted in *Stata Technical Bulletin Reprints*, vol. 10, pp. 46–49. College Station, TX: Stata Press.

Fisher, R. A. 1942. The theory of confounding in factorial experiments in relation to the theory of groups. *Annals of Eugenics* 11: 341–353.

Yates, F. 1937. *The Design and Analysis of Factorial Experiments*. Harpenden, England: Technical Communication 35, Imperial Bureau of Soil Science.

Also see

[P] **foreach** — Loop over items

[D] **codebook** — Describe data contents

[D] **inspect** — Display simple summary of data's attributes

[R] **tabulate oneway** — One-way tables of frequencies

Title

> **macro** — Macro definition and manipulation

Syntax

<u>gl</u>obal *mname* $\left[\,=exp\ \mid\ :extended\_fcn\ \mid\ "\left[\,string\,\right]"\ \mid\ ‘"\left[\,string\,\right]"’\,\right]$

<u>loc</u>al *lclname* $\left[\,=exp\ \mid\ :extended\_fcn\ \mid\ "\left[\,string\,\right]"\ \mid\ ‘"\left[\,string\,\right]"’\,\right]$

tempvar *lclname* $\left[\,lclname\ \left[\,\ldots\,\right]\,\right]$

tempname *lclname* $\left[\,lclname\ \left[\,\ldots\,\right]\,\right]$

tempfile *lclname* $\left[\,lclname\ \left[\,\ldots\,\right]\,\right]$

<u>loc</u>al $\left\{\,++lclname\ \mid\ --lclname\,\right\}$

<u>ma</u>cro <u>dir</u>

<u>ma</u>cro <u>drop</u> $\left\{\,mname\ \left[\,mname\ \left[\,\ldots\,\right]\,\right]\ \mid\ mname*\ \mid\ \_all\,\right\}$

<u>ma</u>cro <u>list</u> $\left[\,mname\ \left[\,mname\ \left[\,\ldots\,\right]\,\right]\ \mid\ \_all\,\right]$

<u>ma</u>cro <u>sh</u>ift $\left[\,\#\,\right]$

$\left[\,\ldots\,\right]$ *‘expansion_optr’* $\left[\,\ldots\,\right]$

where *expansion_optr* is

> *lclname* $\mid$ *++lclname* $\mid$ *lclname++* $\mid$ *--lclname* $\mid$ *lclname--* $\mid$ *=exp* $\mid$
>
> *:extended_fcn* $\mid$ *.class_directive* $\mid$ macval(*lclname*)

and where *extended_fcn* is any of the following:

> *Macro extended function for extracting program properties*
>
> properties *command*

Macro extended functions for extracting data attributes

$\left\{ \underline{\text{type}} \,|\, \underline{\text{f}}\text{ormat} \,|\, \underline{\text{val}}\text{ue label} \,|\, \underline{\text{var}}\text{iable} \,\underline{\text{l}}\text{abel} \right\}$ *varname*

data $\underline{\text{l}}$abel

$\underline{\text{sort}}$edby

$\underline{\text{l}}$abel $\left\{ valuelabelname \,|\, (varname) \right\}$ $\left\{ \texttt{maxlength} \,|\, \# \left[\#_2 \right] \right\}$ $\left[\,, \text{strict} \right]$

constraint $\left\{ \# \,|\, \text{dir} \right\}$

char $\left\{ varname[\,] \,|\, varname[charname] \right\}$ or   char $\left\{ \_\text{dta}[\,] \,|\, \_\text{dta}[charname] \right\}$

Macro extended function for naming variables

permname *suggested_name* $\left[\,, \underline{\text{l}}\text{ength}(\#) \right]$

Macro extended functions for filenames and file paths

adosubdir $\left[{}^{\text{"}} \right]$*filename*$\left[{}^{\text{"}} \right]$

dir $\left[{}^{\text{"}} \right]$*dir*$\left[{}^{\text{"}} \right]$ $\left\{ \underline{\text{files}} \,|\, \underline{\text{dirs}} \,|\, \text{other} \right\}$$\left[{}^{\text{"}} \right]$*pattern*$\left[{}^{\text{"}} \right]$ $\left[\,, \text{nofail} \,\underline{\text{respect}}\text{case} \right]$

sysdir $\left[\text{STATA} \,|\, \text{UPDATES} \,|\, \text{BASE} \,|\, \text{SITE} \,|\, \text{PLUS} \,|\, \text{PERSONAL} \,|\, dirname \right]$

Macro extended function for accessing operating-system parameters

$\underline{\text{env}}$ironment *name*

Macro extended functions for names of saved results

e(scalars $|$ macros $|$ matrices $|$ functions)

r(scalars $|$ macros $|$ matrices $|$ functions)

s(macros)

all $\left\{ \text{globals} \,|\, \text{scalars} \,|\, \text{matrices} \right\}$ $\left[{}^{\text{"}}\textit{pattern}{}^{\text{"}} \right]$

all $\left\{ \text{numeric} \,|\, \text{string} \right\}$ scalars $\left[{}^{\text{"}}\textit{pattern}{}^{\text{"}} \right]$

Macro extended function for formatting results

$\underline{\text{di}}$splay ...

Macro extended function for manipulating lists

list ...

Macro extended functions related to matrices

{ <u>row</u>names | <u>col</u>names | <u>rowf</u>ullnames | <u>colf</u>ullnames } *matname*

{ <u>row</u>eq | <u>col</u>eq } *matname* [, <u>q</u>uoted]

Macro extended function related to time-series operators

tsnorm *string* [, <u>v</u>arname]

Macro extended function for copying a macro

copy { local | global } *macname*

Macro extended functions for parsing

word { count | # of } *string*

piece *#piece_number* *#length_of_pieces* of ['] "*string*" ['] [, <u>no</u>break]

length { local | global } *macname*

subinstr { <u>gl</u>obal *mname2* | <u>loc</u>al *lclname2* }

{ "*from*" | ' "*from*" ' } { "*to*" | ' "*to*" ' }

[, all <u>c</u>ount(<u>gl</u>obal *mname3* | <u>loc</u>al *lclname3*) <u>w</u>ord]

Description

global assigns strings to specified global macro names (*mnames*). local assigns strings to local macro names (*lclnames*). Both double quotes (" and ") and compound double quotes (' " and " ') are allowed; see [U] **18.3.5 Double quotes**. If the *string* has embedded quotes, compound double quotes are needed.

tempvar assigns names to the specified local macro names that may be used as temporary variable names in the dataset. When the program or do-file concludes, any variables in the dataset with these assigned names are dropped.

tempname assigns names to the specified local macro names that may be used as temporary scalar or matrix names. When the program or do-file concludes, any scalars or matrices with these assigned names are dropped.

tempfile assigns names to the specified local macro names that may be used as names for temporary files. When the program or do-file concludes, any datasets created with these assigned names are erased.

macro manipulates global and local macros.

See [U] **18.3 Macros** for information on macro substitution.

Remarks

Remarks are presented under the following headings:

Formal definition of a macro
Global and local macro names
Macro assignment
Macro extended functions
Macro extended function for extracting program properties
Macro extended functions for extracting data attributes
Macro extended function for naming variables
Macro extended functions for filenames and file paths
Macro extended function for accessing operating-system parameters
Macro extended functions for names of saved results
Macro extended function for formatting results
Macro extended function for manipulating lists
Macro extended functions related to matrices
Macro extended function related to time-series operators
Macro extended function for copying a macro
Macro extended functions for parsing
Macro expansion operators and function
The tempvar, tempname, and tempfile commands
    Temporary variables
    Temporary scalars and matrices
    Temporary files
Manipulation of macros
Macros as arguments

Macros are a tool used in programming Stata, and this entry assumes that you have read [U] **18 Programming Stata** and especially [U] **18.3 Macros**. This entry concerns advanced issues not previously covered.

Formal definition of a macro

A *macro* has a *macro name* and *macro contents*. Everywhere a punctuated macro name appears in a command—punctuation is defined below—the macro contents are substituted for the macro name.

Macros come in two types, global and local. Macro names are up to 32 characters long for global macros and up to 31 characters long for local macros. The contents of global macros are defined with the `global` command and those of local macros with the `local` command. Global macros, once defined, are available anywhere in Stata. Local macros exist solely within the program or do-file in which they are defined. If that program or do-file calls another program or do-file, the local macros previously defined temporarily cease to exist, and their existence is reestablished when the calling program regains control. When a program or do-file ends, its local macros are permanently deleted.

To substitute the macro contents of a global macro name, the macro name is typed (punctuated) with a dollar sign ($) in front. To substitute the macro contents of a local macro name, the macro name is typed (punctuated) with surrounding left and right single quotes (` '). In either case, braces ({ }) can be used to clarify meaning and to form nested constructions. When the contents of an undefined macro are substituted, the macro name and punctuation are removed, and nothing is substituted in its place.

For example,

The input ...	is equivalent to ...
```global a "myvar"```	
```gen $a = oldvar```	```gen myvar = oldvar```
```gen a = oldvar```	```gen a = oldvar```
```local a "myvar"```	
```gen 'a' = oldvar```	```gen myvar = oldvar```
```gen a = oldvar```	```gen a = oldvar```
```global a "newvar"```	
```global i = 2```	
```gen ai = oldvar```	```gen newvar2 = oldvar```
```local a "newvar"```	
```local i = 2```	
```gen 'a''i' = oldvar```	```gen newvar2 = oldvar```
```global b1 "newvar"```	
```global i=1```	
```gen ${b$i} = oldvar```	```gen newvar = oldvar```
```local b1 "newvar"```	
```local i=1```	
```gen 'b'i'' = oldvar```	```gen newvar = oldvar```
```global b1 "newvar"```	
```global a "b"```	
```global i = 1```	
```gen ${$a$i} = oldvar```	```gen newvar = oldvar```
```local b1 "newvar"```	
```local a "b"```	
```local i = 1```	
```gen ''a''i'' = oldvar```	```gen newvar = oldvar```

Global and local macro names

What we say next is an exceedingly fine point: global macro names that begin with an underscore are really local macros; this is why local macro names can have only 31 characters. The `local` command is formally defined as equivalent to `global _`. Thus the following are equivalent:

```
local x                     global _x
local i=1                   global _i=1
local name "Bill"           global _name "Bill"
local fmt : format myvar    global _fmt : format myvar
local 3 '2'                 global _3 $_2
```

`tempvar` is formally defined as equivalent to `local` *name* `: tempvar` for each name specified after `tempvar`. Thus

```
tempvar a b c
```

is equivalent to

```
local a : tempvar
local b : tempvar
local c : tempvar
```

which in turn is equivalent to

```
global _a : tempvar
global _b : tempvar
global _c : tempvar
```

`tempfile` is defined similarly.

Macro assignment

When you type

```
. local name "something"
```

or

```
. local name '"something"'
```

something becomes the contents of the macro. The compound double quotes (' " and " ') are needed when *something* itself contains quotation marks. When you type

```
. local name = something
```

something is evaluated as an expression, and the result becomes the contents of the macro. Note the presence and lack of the equal sign. That is, if you type

```
. local problem "2+2"
. local result = 2+2
```

then `problem` contains 2+2, whereas `result` contains 4.

Finally, when you type

```
. local name : something
```

something is interpreted as an extended macro function. (Note the colon rather than nothing or the equal sign.) Of course, all of this applies to `global` as well as to `local`.

`local ++`*lclname*, or `local --`*lclname*, is used to increment, or decrement, *lclname*.

For instance, typing

```
. local ++x
```

is equivalent to typing

```
. local x = 'x' + 1
```

Macro extended functions

Macro extended functions are of the form

```
. local macname : ...
```

For instance,

```
. local x : type mpg
. local y : matsize
. local z : display %9.4f sqrt(2)
```

We document the macro extended functions below. Macro extended functions are typically used in programs, but you can experiment with them interactively. For instance, if you are unsure what 'local x : type mpg' does, you could type

```
. local x : type mpg
. display "'x'"
int
```

Macro extended function for extracting program properties

`properties` *command*
    returns the properties declared for *command*; see [P] **program properties**.

Macro extended functions for extracting data attributes

`type` *varname*
    returns the storage type of *varname*, which might be `int`, `long`, `float`, `double`, `str1`, `str2`, etc.

`format` *varname*
    returns the display format associated with *varname*, for instance, `%9.0g` or `%12s`.

`value label` *varname*
    returns the name of the value label associated with *varname*, which might be " " (meaning no label), or, for example, `make`, meaning that the value label's name is `make`.

`variable label` *varname*
    returns the variable label associated with *varname*, which might be " " (meaning no label), or, for example, `Repair Record 1978`.

`data label`
    returns the dataset label associated with the dataset currently in memory, which might be " " (meaning no label), or, for example, `1978 Automobile Data`. See [D] **label**.

`sortedby`
    returns the names of the variables by which the data in memory are currently sorted, which might be " " (meaning not sorted), or, for example, `foreign mpg`, meaning that the data are in the order of the variable `foreign`, and, within that, in the order of `mpg` (the order that would be obtained from the Stata command `sort foreign mpg`). See [D] **sort**.

`label` *valuelabelname* { `maxlength` | # [#₂] } [, `strict`]
    returns the label value of # in *valuelabelname*. For instance, `label forlab 1` might return `Foreign cars` if `forlab` were the name of a value label and 1 mapped to "Foreign cars". If 1 did not correspond to any mapping within the value label, or if the value label `forlab` were not defined, 1 (the # itself) would be returned.

    #₂ optionally specifies the maximum length of the label to be returned. If `label forlab 1` would return `Foreign cars`, then `label forlab 1 6` would return `Foreig`.

    `maxlength` specifies that, rather than looking up a number in a value label, `label` return the maximum length of the labelings. For instance, if value label `yesno` mapped 0 to `no` and 1 to `yes`, then its `maxlength` would be 3 because `yes` is the longest label and it has three characters.

    `strict` specifies that nothing is to be returned if there is no value label for #.

`label` (*varname*) { `maxlength` | # [#₂] } [, `strict`]
    works exactly as the above, except that rather than specifying the *valuelabelname* directly, you indirectly specify it. The value label name associated with *varname* is used, if there is one. If not, it is treated just as if *valuelabelname* were undefined, and the number itself is returned.

`constraint` { # | `dir` }
    gives information on constraints.

    `constraint` # puts constraint # in *macroname* or returns " " if constraint # is not defined.
    `constraint` # for # < 0 is an error.

constraint dir returns an unsorted numerical list of those constraints that are currently defined. For example,

```
. constraint 1 price = weight
. constraint 2 mpg > 20
. local myname : constraint 2
. macro list _myname
_myname         mpg > 20
. local aname : constraint dir
. macro list _aname
_aname:    2 1
```

char { *varname*[ ] | *varname*[*charname*] }   or   char { _dta[ ] | _dta[*charname*] } returns information on the characteristics of a dataset; see [P] **char**. For instance,

```
. use http://www.stata-press.com/data/r11/auto
(1978 Automobile Data)
. char mpg[one] "this"
. char mpg[two] "that"
. local x : char mpg[one]
. di "`x'"
this
. local x : char mpg[nosuch]
. di "`x'"

. local x : char mpg[]
. di "`x'"
two one
```

Macro extended function for naming variables

permname *suggested_name* [, length(*#*)]
    returns a valid new variable name based on *suggested_name* in *mname*, where *suggested_name* must follow naming conventions but may be too long or correspond to an already existing variable.

    length(*#*) specifies the maximum length of the returned variable name, which must be between 8 and 32. length(32) is the default. For instance,

```
. local myname : permname foreign
. macro list _myname
_myname:        foreign1
.local aname : permname displacement, length(8)
. macro list _aname
_aname:         displace
```

Macro extended functions for filenames and file paths

adosubdir ["]*filename*["]
    puts in *macroname* the subdirectory in which Stata would search for this file along the ado-path. Typically, the directory name would be the first letter of *filename*. However, certain files may result in a different name depending on their extension.

dir ["]*dir*["] { files | dirs | other } ["]*pattern*["] [, nofail respectcase]
    puts in *macroname* the specified files, directories, or entries that are neither files nor directories, from directory *dir* and matching pattern *pattern*, where the pattern matching is defined by Stata's strmatch(s_1, s_2) function; see [D] **functions**. The quotes in the command are optional but

recommended, and they are nearly always required surrounding *pattern*. The returned string will contain each of the names, separated one from the other by spaces and each enclosed in double quotes. If *macroname* is subsequently used in a quoted context, it must be enclosed in compound double quotes: ' " ' *macroname* ' " ' .

The nofail option specifies that if the directory contains too many filenames to fit into a macro, rather than issuing an error, the filenames that fit into *macroname* should be returned. nofail should rarely, if ever, be specified.

In Windows only, the respectcase option specifies that dir respect the case of filenames when performing matches. Unlike other operating systems, Windows has, by default, case-insensitive filenames. respectcase is ignored in operating systems other than Windows.

For example,

local list : dir . files "*" makes a list of all regular files in the current directory. In list might be returned "subjects.dta" "step1.do" "step2.do" "reest.ado".

local list : dir . files "s*", respectcase in Windows makes a list of all regular files in the current directory that begin with a lowercase "s". The case of characters in the filenames is preserved. In Windows, without the respectcase option, all filenames would be converted to lowercase before being compared with *pattern* and possibly returned.

local list : dir . dirs "*" makes a list of all subdirectories of the current directory. In list might be returned "notes" "subpanel".

local list : dir . other "*" makes a list of all things that are neither regular files nor directories. These files rarely occur and might be, for instance, Unix device drivers.

local list : dir "\mydir\data" files "*" makes a list of all regular files that are to be found in \mydir\data. Returned might be "example.dta" "make.do" "analyze.do".

It is the names of the files that are returned, not their full path names.

local list : dir "subdir" files "*" makes a list of all regular files that are to be found in subdir of the current directory.

sysdir [STATA | UPDATES | BASE | SITE | PLUS | PERSONAL]
    returns the various Stata system directory paths; see [P] **sysdir**. The path is returned with a trailing separator; e.g., sysdir STATA might return D:\PROGRAMS\STATA\.

sysdir *dirname*
    returns *dirname*. This function is used to code local x : sysdir 'dir', where 'dir' might contain the name of a directory specified by a user or a keyword, such as STATA or UPDATES. The appropriate directory name will be returned. The path is returned with a trailing separator.

Macro extended function for accessing operating-system parameters

environment *name*
    returns the contents of the operating system's environment variable named *name*, or " " if *name* is undefined.

Macro extended functions for names of saved results

e(scalars | macros | matrices | functions)
    returns the names of all the saved results in e() of the specified type, with the names listed one after the other and separated by one space. For instance, e(scalars) might return N ll_0 ll df_m chi2 r2_p, meaning that scalar saved results e(N), e(ll_0), ... exist.

r(scalars), r(macros), r(matrices), r(functions)
> returns the names of all the saved results in r() of the specified type.

s(macros)
> returns the names of all the saved results in s() of type macro, which is the only type that exists within s().

all { globals | scalars | matrices } [*"pattern"*]
> puts in *macroname* the specified globals, scalars, or matrices that match the *pattern*, where the matching is defined by Stata's strmatch(s_1,s_2) function; see [D] **functions**.

all { numeric | string } scalars [*"pattern"*]
> puts in *macroname* the specified numeric or string scalars that match the *pattern*, where the matching is defined by Stata's strmatch(s_1,s_2) function; see [D] **functions**.

Macro extended function for formatting results

display ...
> returns the results from the display command. The display extended function is the display command, except that the output is rerouted to a macro rather than to the screen.

> You can use all the features of display that make sense. That is, you may not set styles with as *style* because macros do not have colors, you may not use _continue to suppress going to a new line on the real display (it is not being displayed), you may not use _newline (for the same reason), and you may not use _request to obtain input from the console (because input and output have nothing to do with macro definition). Everything else works. See [P] **display**.

> *Example:*
> local x : display %9.4f sqrt(2)

Macro extended function for manipulating lists

list ...
> fills in *macroname* with the *macrolist_directive*, which specifies one of many available commands or operators for working with macros that contain lists; see [P] **macro lists**.

Macro extended functions related to matrices

In understanding the functions below, remember that the *fullname* of a matrix row or column is defined as *eqname:name*. For instance, *fullname* might be outcome:weight, and then the *eqname* is outcome and the *name* is weight. Or the *fullname* might be gnp:L.cpi, and then the *eqname* is gnp and the *name* is L.cpi. Or the *fullname* might be mpg, in which case the *eqname* is "" and the *name* is mpg. Or the *fullname* might be gnp:1.south#1.smsa, and then the *eqname* is gnp and the *name* is 1.south#1.smsa. For more information, see [P] **matrix define**.

rownames *matname*
> returns the names of the rows of *matname*, listed one after another and separated by one space. As many names are listed as there are rows of *matname*.

colnames *matname*
> is like rownames, but returns the names of the columns.

rowfullnames *matname*
> returns the full names of the rows of *matname*, listed one after another and separated by one space. As many full names are listed as there are rows of *matname*.

colfullnames *matname*
> is like rowfullnames, but returns the full names of the columns.

roweq *matname* [, quoted]
> returns the equation names of the columns of *matname*, listed one after another and separated by one space. As many names are listed as there are columns of *matname*. If the eqname of a column is blank, _ (underscore) is substituted. Thus roweq might return "Poor Poor Poor Average Average Average" for one matrix and "_ _ _ _ _ _" for another. quoted specifies that equation names be enclosed in double quotes.

coleq *matname* [, quoted]
> is like roweq, but returns the equation names of the columns.

In all cases, *matname* may be either a Stata matrix name or a matrix stored in e() or r(), such as e(b) or e(V).

Macro extended function related to time-series operators

tsnorm *string*
> returns the canonical form of *string* when *string* is interpreted as a time-series operator. For instance, if *string* is 1d1, then L2D is returned, or if *string* is 1.1d1, then L3D is returned. If *string* is nothing, " " is returned.

tsnorm *string*, varname
> returns the canonical form of *string* when *string* is interpreted as a time-series–operated variable. For instance, if *string* is 1d1.gnp, then L2D.gnp is returned, or if string is 1.1d1.gnp, then L3D.gnp is returned. If *string* is just a variable name, then the variable name is returned.

Macro extended function for copying a macro

copy { local | global } *macname*
> returns a copy of the contents of *macname*, or an empty string if *macname* is undefined.

Macro extended functions for parsing

word count *string*
> returns the number of tokens in *string*. A token is a word (characters separated by spaces) or set of words enclosed in quotes. Do not enclose *string* in double quotes because word count will return 1.

word # of *string*
> returns the #th token of *string*. Do not enclose *string* in double quotes.

piece $\#_1$ $\#_2$ of "*string*" [, nobreak]
> returns a piece of *string*. This macro extended function provides a smart method of breaking a string into pieces of roughly the specified length. $\#_1$ specifies which piece to obtain. $\#_2$ specifies the maximum length of each piece. Each piece is built trying to fill to the maximum length without breaking in the middle of a word. However, when a word is longer than $\#_2$, the word will be split unless nobreak is specified. nobreak specifies that words not be broken, even if that would result in a string longer than $\#_2$ characters.
>
> Compound double quotes may be used around *string* and must be used when *string* itself might contain double quotes.

length { local | global } *macname*
> returns the length of *macname* in characters. If *macname* is undefined, then 0 is returned. For instance,

```
. constraint 1 price = weight
. local myname : constraint 1
. macro list _myname
_myname         price = weight
. local lmyname : length local myname
. macro list _lmyname
_lmyname:       14
```

subinstr local *mname* "*from*" "*to*"
  returns the contents of *mname*, with the first occurrence of "*from*" changed to "*to*".

subinstr local *mname* "*from*" "*to*", all
  does the same thing but changes all occurrences of "*from*" to "*to*".

subinstr local *mname* "*from*" "*to*", word
  returns the contents of *mname*, with the first occurrence of the word "*from*" changed to "*to*". A
  word is defined as a space-separated token or a token at the beginning or end of the string.

subinstr local *mname* "*from*" "*to*", all word
  does the same thing but changes all occurrences of the word "*from*" to "*to*".

subinstr global *mname* ...
  is the same as the above, but obtains the original string from the global macro $mname rather than
  from the local macro *mname*.

subinstr ... global *mname* ..., ... count({global | local} *mname2*)
  in addition to the usual, places a count of the number of substitutions in the specified global or
  in local macro *mname2*.

▷ Example 1

```
. local string "a or b or c or d"
. global newstr : subinstr local string "c" "sand"
. display "$newstr"
a or b or sand or d
. local string2 : subinstr global newstr "or" "and", all count(local n)
. display "'string2'"
a and b and sand and d
. display "'n'"
3
. local string3: subinstr local string2 "and" "x", all word
. display "'string3'"
a x b x sand x d
```

The "and" in "sand" was not replaced by "x" because the word option was specified.

◁

Macro expansion operators and function

There are five macro expansion operators that may be used within references to local (not global)
macros.

'*lclname*++' and '++*lclname*' provide inline incrementation of local macro *lclname*. For example,

```
. local x 5
. display "'x++'"
5
. display "'x'"
6
```

++ can be place before *lclname*, in which case *lclname* is incremented before '*lclname*' is evaluated.

```
. local x 5
. display "'++x'"
6
. display "'x'"
6
```

'*lclname--*' and '*--lclname*' provide inline decrementation of local macro *lclname*.

'*=exp*' provides inline access to Stata's expression evaluator. The Stata expression *exp* is evaluated and the result substituted. For example,

```
. local alpha = 0.05
. regress mpg weight, level('=100*(1-'alpha')')
```

'*:extended_fcn*' provides inline access to Stata's extended macro functions. '*:extended_fcn*' evaluates to the results of the extended macro function *extended_fcn*. For example,

```
. format ':format gear_ratio' headroom
```

will set the display format of headroom to that of gear_ratio, which was obtained via the extended macro function format.

'*.class_directive*' provides inline access to class-object values. See [P] **class** for details.

The macro expansion function 'macval(name)' expands local macro name but not any macros contained within name. For instance, if name contained "example 'of' macval", 'name' would expand to "example macval" (assuming that 'of' is not defined), whereas 'macval(name)' would expand to "example 'of' macval". The 'of' would be left just as it is.

❑ Technical note

To store an unexpanded macro within another macro, use "\" to prevent macro expansion. This is useful when defining a formula with elements that will be substituted later in the program. To save the formula sqrt('A' + 1), where 'A' is a macro you would like to fill in later, you would use the command

```
. local formula sqrt(\'A' + 1)
```

which would produce

```
. macro list _formula
_formula:       sqrt('A' + 1)
```

Because the statement \'A' was used, it prevented Stata from expanding the macro 'A' when it stored it in the macro 'formula'.

Now you can fill in the macro 'A' with different statements and have this be reflected when you call 'formula'.

```
. local A 2^3
. display "formula 'formula': " 'formula'
formula sqrt(2^3 + 1): 3
. local A log10(('A' + 2)^3)
. display "formula 'formula': " 'formula'
formula sqrt(log10((2^3 + 2)^3) + 1): 2
```

❑

The tempvar, tempname, and tempfile commands

The `tempvar`, `tempname`, and `tempfile` commands create names that may be used for temporary variables, temporary scalars and matrices, and temporary files. A temporary element exists while the program or do-file is running but, once it concludes, automatically ceases to exist.

Temporary variables

You are writing a program, and in the middle of it you need to calculate a new variable equal to $var1^2 + var2^2$ for use in the calculation. You might be tempted to write

```
( code omitted )
gen sumsq = var1^2 + var2^2
( code continues )
( code uses sumsq  in subsequent calculations )
drop sumsq
```

This would be a poor idea. First, users of your program might already have a variable called `sumsq`, and if they did, your program would break at the `generate` statement with the error "sumsq already defined". Second, your program in the subsequent code might call some other program, and perhaps that program also attempts (poorly) to create the variable `sumsq`. Third, even if nothing goes wrong, if users press *Break* after your code executes `generate` but before `drop`, you would confuse them by leaving behind the `sumsq` variable.

The way around these problems is to use temporary variables. Your code should read

```
( code omitted )
tempvar sumsq
gen 'sumsq' = var1^2 + var2^2
( code continues )
( code uses 'sumsq'  in subsequent calculations )
( you do not bother to drop 'sumsq' )
```

The `tempvar sumsq` command creates a local macro called `sumsq` and stores in it a name that is different from any name currently in the data. Subsequently, you then use `'sumsq'` with single quotes around it rather than `sumsq` in your calculation, so that rather than naming your temporary variable `sumsq`, you are naming it whatever Stata wants you to name it. With that small change, your program works just as before.

Another advantage of temporary variables is that you do not have to drop them—Stata will do that for you when your program terminates, regardless of the reason for the termination. If a user presses *Break* after the `generate`, your program is stopped, the temporary variables are dropped, and things really are just as if the user had never run your program.

❑ Technical note

What do these temporary variable names assigned by Stata look like? It should not matter to you; however they look, they are guaranteed to be unique (`tempvar` will not hand out the same name to more than one concurrently executing program). Nevertheless, to satisfy your curiosity,

```
. tempvar var1 var2
. display "'var1' 'var2'"
__000009 __00000A
```

Although we reveal the style of the names created by `tempvar`, you should not depend on this style. All that is important is that

- The names are unique; they differ from one call to the next.

- You should not prefix or suffix them with additional characters.

- Stata keeps track of any names created by `tempvar` and, when the program or do-file ends, searches the data for those names. Any variables found with those names are automatically dropped. This happens regardless of whether your program ends with an error.

❏

Temporary scalars and matrices

`tempname` is the equivalent of `tempvar` for obtaining names for scalars and matrices. This use is explained, with examples, in [P] **scalar**.

❏ Technical note

The temporary names created by `tempname` look just like those created by `tempvar`. The same cautions and features apply to `tempname` as `tempvar`:

- The names are unique; they differ from one call to the next.

- You should not prefix or suffix them with additional characters.

- Stata keeps track of any names created by `tempname` and, when the program or do-file ends, searches for scalars or matrices with those names. Any scalars or matrices so found are automatically dropped; see [P] **scalar**. This happens regardless of whether your program ends with an error.

❏

Temporary files

`tempfile` is the equivalent of `tempvar` for obtaining names for disk files. Before getting into that, let's discuss how you should not use `tempfile`. Sometimes, in the midst of your program, you will find it necessary to destroy the user's data to obtain your desired result. You do not want to change the data, but it cannot be helped, and therefore you would like to arrange things so that the user's original data are restored at the conclusion of your program.

You might then be tempted to save the user's data in a (temporary) file, do your damage, and then restore the data. You can do this, but it is complicated, because you then have to worry about the user pressing *Break* after you have stored the data and done the damage but have not yet restored the data. Working with `capture` (see [P] **capture**), you can program all of this, but you do not have to. Stata's `preserve` command (see [P] **preserve**) will handle saving and restoring the user's data, regardless of how your program ends.

Still, there may be times when you need temporary files. For example,

```
( code omitted )
preserve                          // preserve user's data
keep var1 var2 xvar
save master, replace
drop var2
save part1, replace
use master, clear
drop var1
rename var2 var1
append using part1
erase master.dta
erase part1.dta
(code continues)
```

This is poor code, even though it does use `preserve` so that, regardless of how this code concludes, the user's original data will be restored. It is poor because datasets called `master.dta` and `part1.dta` might already exist, and, if they do, this program will replace the user's (presumably valuable) data. It is also poor because, if the user presses *Break* before both (temporary) datasets are erased, they will be left behind to consume (presumably valuable) disk space.

Here is how the code should read:

```
( code omitted )
preserve                          // preserve user's data
keep var1 var2 xvar
tempfile master part1             // declare temporary files
save "'master'"
drop var2
save "'part1'"
use "'master'", clear
drop var1
rename var2 var1
append using "'part1'"
(code continues; temporary files are not erased)
```

In this version, Stata was asked to provide the names of temporary files in local macros named `master` and `part1`. We then put single quotes around `master` and `part1` wherever we referred to them so that, rather than using the names `master` and `part1`, we used the names Stata handed us. At the end of our program, we no longer bother to erase the temporary files. Because Stata gave us the temporary filenames, it knows that they are temporary and erases them for us if our program completes, has an error, or the user presses *Break*.

❏ Technical note

What do the temporary filenames look like? Again it should not matter to you, but for the curious,

```
. tempfile file1 file2
. display "'file1' 'file2'"
/tmp/St13310.0001 /tmp/St13310.0002
```

We were using the Unix version of Stata; had we been using the Windows version, the last line might read

```
. display "'file1' 'file2'"
C:\WIN\TEMP\ST_0a00000c.tmp C:\WIN\TEMP\ST_00000d.tmp
```

Under Windows, Stata uses the environment variable `TEMP` to determine where temporary files are to be located. This variable is typically set in your `autoexec.bat` file. Ours is set to `C:\WIN\TEMP`. If the variable is not defined, Stata places temporary files in your current directory.

Under Unix, Stata uses the environment variable TMPDIR to determine where temporary files are to be located. If the variable is not defined, Stata locates temporary files in /tmp.

Although we reveal the style of the names created by tempfile, just as with tempvar, you should not depend on it. tempfile produces names the operating system finds pleasing, and all that is important is that

- The names are unique; they differ from one call to the next.

- You should assume that they are so long that you cannot prefix or suffix them with additional characters and make use of them.

- Stata keeps track of any names created by tempfile, and, when your program or do-file ends, looks for files with those names. Any files found are automatically erased. This happens regardless of whether your program ends with an error.

❏

Manipulation of macros

macro dir and macro list list the names and contents of all defined macros; both do the same thing:

```
. macro list
S_FNDATE:      13 Apr 2007 17:45
S_FN:          C:\Program Files\Stata11\ado\base/a/auto.dta
tofname:       str18
S_level:       95
F1:            help
F2:            #review;
F3:            describe;
F7:            save
F8:            use
S_ADO:         UPDATES;BASE;SITE;.;PERSONAL;PLUS;OLDPLACE
S_StataSE:     SE
S_FLAVOR:      Intercooled
S_OS:          Windows
S_MACH:        PC
_file2:        C:\WIN\Temp\ST_0a00000d.tmp
_file1:        C:\WIN\Temp\ST_0a00000c.tmp
_var2:         __00000A
_var1:         __000009
_str3:         a x b x sand x d
_dl:           Employee Data
_lbl:          Employee name
_vl:           sexlbl
_fmt:          %9.0g
```

macro drop eliminates macros from memory, although it is rarely used because most macros are local and automatically disappear when the program ends. Macros can also be eliminated by defining their contents to be nothing using global or local, but macro drop is more convenient.

Typing macro drop *base** drops all global macros whose names begin with *base*.

Typing macro drop _all eliminates all macros except system macros—those with names that begin with "S_".

Typing macro drop S_* does not drop all system macros that begin with "S_". It leaves certain macros in place that should not be casually deleted.

▷ Example 2

```
. macro drop _var* _lbl tofname _fmt
. macro list
S_FNDATE:        13 Apr 2007 17:45
S_FN:            C:\Program Files\Stata11\ado\base/a/auto.dta
S_level:         95
F1:              help
F2:              #review;
F3:              describe;
F7:              save
F8:              use
S_ADO:           UPDATES;BASE;SITE;.;PERSONAL;PLUS;OLDPLACE
S_StataSE:       SE
S_FLAVOR:        Intercooled
S_OS:            Windows
S_MACH:          PC
_file2:          C:\WIN\Temp\ST_0a00000d.tmp
_file1:          C:\WIN\Temp\ST_0a00000c.tmp
_str3:           a x b x sand x d
_dl:             Employee Data
_vl:             sexlbl
. macro drop _all
. macro list
S_FNDATE:        13 Apr 2007 17:45
S_FN:            C:\Program Files\Stata11\ado\base/a/auto.dta
S_level:         95
S_ADO:           UPDATES;BASE;SITE;.;PERSONAL;PLUS;OLDPLACE
S_StataSE:       SE
S_FLAVOR:        Intercooled
S_OS:            Windows
S_MACH:          PC
. macro drop S_*
. macro list
S_level:         95
S_ADO:           UPDATES;BASE;SITE;.;PERSONAL;PLUS;OLDPLACE
S_StataSE:       SE
S_FLAVOR:        Intercooled
S_OS:            Windows
S_MACH:          PC
```

◁

❏ Technical note

Stata usually requires that you explicitly drop something before redefining it. For instance, before redefining a value label with the label define command or redefining a program with the program define command, you must type label drop or program drop. This way, you are protected from accidentally replacing something that might require considerable effort to reproduce.

Macros, however, may be redefined freely. It is *not* necessary to drop a macro before redefining it. Macros typically consist of short strings that could be easily reproduced if necessary. The inconvenience of the protection is not justified by the small benefit.

❏

Macros as arguments

Sometimes programs have in a macro a list of things—numbers, variable names, etc.—that you wish to access one at a time. For instance, after parsing (see [U] **18.4 Program arguments**), you might have in the local macro 'varlist' a list of variable names. The tokenize command (see [P] **tokenize**) will take any macro containing a list and assign the elements to local macros named '1', '2', and so on. That is, if 'varlist' contained "mpg weight displ", then coding

```
tokenize 'varlist'
```

will make '1' contain "mpg", '2' contain "weight", '3' contain "displ", and '4' contain "" (nothing). The empty fourth macro marks the end of the list.

macro shift can be used to work through these elements one at a time in constructs like

```
while "'1'" != "" {
        do something based on '1'
        macro shift
}
```

macro shift discards '1', shifts '2' to '1', '3' to '2', and so on. For instance, in our example, after the first macro shift, '1' will contain "weight", '2' will contain "displ", and '3' will contain "" (nothing).

It is better to avoid macro shift and instead code

```
local i = 1
while "''i''" != "" {
        do something based on ''i''
        local i = 'i' + 1
}
```

This second approach has the advantage that it is faster. Also what is in '1', '2', ... remains unchanged so that you can pass through the list multiple times without resetting it (coding "tokenize 'varlist'" again).

It is even better to avoid tokenize and the numbered macros altogether and to instead loop over the variables in 'varlist' directly:

```
foreach var of local varlist {
        do something based on 'var'
}
```

This is easier to understand and executes even more quickly; see [P] **foreach**.

macro shift # performs multiple macro shifts, or if # is 0, none at all. That is, macro shift 2 is equivalent to two macro shift commands. macro shift 0 does nothing.

Also see [P] **macro lists** for other list-processing commands.

Also see

[P] **char** — Characteristics

[P] **display** — Display strings and values of scalar expressions

[D] **functions** — Functions

[P] **gettoken** — Low-level parsing

[P] **macro lists** — Manipulate lists

[P] **matrix** — Introduction to matrix commands

[P] **numlist** — Parse numeric lists

[P] **return** — Return saved results

[P] **creturn** — Return c-class values

[P] **syntax** — Parse Stata syntax

[P] **tokenize** — Divide strings into tokens

[P] **preserve** — Preserve and restore data

[P] **scalar** — Scalar variables

[U] **12.8 Characteristics**

[U] **18 Programming Stata**

[U] **18.3 Macros**

Title

macro lists — Manipulate lists

Syntax

{ <u>lo</u>cal | <u>gl</u>obal } *macname* : list uniq *macname*

{ <u>lo</u>cal | <u>gl</u>obal } *macname* : list dups *macname*

{ <u>lo</u>cal | <u>gl</u>obal } *macname* : list sort *macname*

{ <u>lo</u>cal | <u>gl</u>obal } *macname* : list <u>retok</u>enize *macname*

{ <u>lo</u>cal | <u>gl</u>obal } *macname* : list clean *macname*

{ <u>lo</u>cal | <u>gl</u>obal } *macname* : list *macname* | *macname*

{ <u>lo</u>cal | <u>gl</u>obal } *macname* : list *macname* & *macname*

{ <u>lo</u>cal | <u>gl</u>obal } *macname* : list *macname* - *macname*

{ <u>lo</u>cal | <u>gl</u>obal } *macname* : list *macname* == *macname*

{ <u>lo</u>cal | <u>gl</u>obal } *macname* : list *macname* === *macname*

{ <u>lo</u>cal | <u>gl</u>obal } *macname* : list *macname* in *macname*

{ <u>lo</u>cal | <u>gl</u>obal } *macname* : list sizeof *macname*

{ <u>lo</u>cal | <u>gl</u>obal } *macname* : list posof "*element*" in *macname*

Note: Where *macname* appears above, it is the name of a macro and *not* its contents that you are to type. For example, you are to type

```
local result : list list1 | list2
```

and not

```
local result : list "'list1'" | "'list2'"
```

*macname*s that appear to the right of the colon are also the names of local macros. You may type local(*macname*) to emphasize that fact. Type global(*macname*) if you wish to refer to a global macro.

Description

The extended macro function list manipulates lists.

uniq A returns A with duplicate elements removed. The resulting list has the same ordering of its elements as A; duplicate elements are removed from their rightmost position. If A = "a b a c a", uniq returns "a b c".

dups A returns the duplicate elements of A. If A = "a b a c a", dups returns "a a".

sort A returns A with its elements placed in alphabetical (ascending ASCII) order.

retokenize A returns A with single spaces between elements. Logically speaking, it makes no difference how many spaces a list has between elements, and thus retokenize leaves the list logically unchanged.

clean A returns A retokenized and with each element adorned minimally. An element is said to be unadorned if it is not enclosed in quotes (e.g., a). An element may also be adorned in simple or compound quotes (e.g., $"a"$ or $‘"a"’$). Logically speaking, it makes no difference how elements are adorned, assuming that they are adorned adequately. The list

$$‘"a"’ \quad ‘"b \ c"’ \quad ‘"b \ "c" \ d"’$$

is equal to

$$a \ "b \ c" \ ‘"b \ "c" \ d"’$$

clean, in addition to performing the actions of retokenize, adorns each element minimally: not at all if the element contains no spaces or quotes, in simple quotes (" and ") if it contains spaces but not quotes, and in compound quotes (‘" and "’) otherwise.

A | B returns the union of A and B, the result being equal to A with elements of B not found in A added to the tail. For instance, if A = "a b c" and B = "b d e", A | B is "a b c d e". If you instead want list concatenation, you code,

$$\text{local } newlist \ ‘"‘A’ \ ‘B’"’$$

In the example above, this would return "a b c b d e".

A & B returns the intersection of A and B. If A = "a b c d" and B = "b c f g", then A & B = "b c".

A - B returns a list containing elements of A with the elements of B removed, with the resulting elements in the same order as A. For instance, if A = "a b c d" and B = "b e", the result is "a c d".

A == B returns 0 or 1; it returns 1 if A is equal to B, that is, if A has the same elements as B and in the same order. Otherwise, 0 is returned.

A === B returns 0 or 1; it returns 1 if A is equivalent to B, that is, if A has the same elements as B regardless of the order in which the elements appear. Otherwise, 0 is returned.

A in B returns 0 or 1; it returns 1 if all elements of A are found in B. If A is empty, in returns 1. Otherwise, 0 is returned.

sizeof A returns the number of elements of A. If A = "a b c", sizeof A is 3. (sizeof returns the same result as the extended macro function word count.)

posof "*element*" in A returns the location of *macname* in A or returns 0 if not found. For instance, if A contains "a b c d", then posof "b" in A returns 2. (word # of may be used to extract positional elements from lists, as can tokenize and gettoken.)

It is the element itself and not a macroname that you type as the first argument. In a program where macro tofind contained an element to be found in list (macro) variables, you might code

```
local i : list posof '"'tofind'"' in variables
```

element must be enclosed in simple or compound quotes.

Remarks

Remarks are presented under the following headings:

> *Treatment of adornment*
> *Treatment of duplicate elements in lists*

A *list* is a space-separated set of elements listed one after the other. The individual elements may be enclosed in quotes, and elements containing spaces obviously must be enclosed in quotes. The following are examples of lists:

```
this that what
"first element" second "third element" 4
this that what this that
```

Also a list could be empty.

Do not confuse varlist with list. Varlists are a special notation, such as "id m* pop*", which is a shorthand way of specifying a list of variables. Once expanded, however, a varlist is a list.

Treatment of adornment

An element of a list is said to be adorned if it is enclosed in quotes. Adornment, however, plays no role in the substantive interpretation of lists. The list

a "b" c

is identical to the list

$a\ b\ c$

Treatment of duplicate elements in lists

With the exception of uniq and dups, all list functions treat duplicates as being distinct. For instance, consider the list A,

$$a\ b\ c\ b$$

Notice that b appears twice in this list. You want to think of the list as containing a, the first occurrence of b, c, and the second occurrence of b:

$$a\ b_1\ c\ b_2$$

Do the same thing with the duplicate elements of all lists, carry out the operation on the now unique elements, and then erase the subscripts from the result.

If you were to ask whether $B = $ "$b\ b$" is in A, the answer would be yes, because A contains two occurrences of b. If B contained "$b\ b\ b$", however, the answer would be no because A does not contain three occurrences of b.

Similarly, if $B = $ "$b\ b$", then $A \mid B = $ "$a\ b\ c\ b$", but if $B = $ "$b\ b\ b$", then $A \mid B = $ "$a\ b\ c\ b\ b$".

Also see

[P] **macro** — Macro definition and manipulation

Title

> **makecns** — Constrained estimation

Syntax

Build constraints

> makecns [*clist* | *matname*] [, *options*]

Create constraint matrix

> matcproc **T a C**

where *clist* is a list of constraint numbers, separated by commas or dashes; *matname* is an existing matrix representing the constraints and must have one more column than the e(b) and e(V) matrices.

T, **a**, and **C** are names of new or existing matrices.

options	description
nocnsnotes	do not display notes when constraints are dropped
displaycns	display the system-stored constraint matrix
r	return the accepted constraints in r(); this option overrides displaycns

Description

makecns is a programmer's command that facilitates adding constraints to estimation commands.

makecns will create a constraint matrix and displays a note for each constraint that is dropped because of an error. The constraint matrix is stored in e(Cns).

matcproc returns matrices helpful for performing constrained estimation, including the constraint matrix.

If your interest is simply in using constraints in a command that supports constrained estimation, see [R] **constraint**.

Options

nocnsnotes prevents notes from being displayed when constraints are dropped.

displaycns displays the system-stored constraint matrix in readable form.

r returns the accepted constraints in r(). This option overrides displaycns.

Remarks

Remarks are presented under the following headings:

> *Introduction*
> *Overview*
> *Mathematics*
> *Linkage of the mathematics to Stata*

Introduction

Users of estimation commands that allow constrained estimation define constraints with the `constraint` command; they indicate which constraints they want to use by specifying the constraints(*clist*) option to the estimation command. This entry concerns programming such sophisticated estimators. If you are programming using `ml`, you can ignore this entry. Constraints are handled automatically (and if you were to look inside the `ml` code, you would find that it uses `makecns`).

Before reading this entry, you should be familiar with constraints from a user's perspective; see [R] **constraint**. You should also be familiar with programming estimation commands that do not include constraints; see [P] **ereturn**.

Overview

You have an estimation command and wish to allow a set of linear constraints to be specified for the parameters by the user and then to produce estimates subject to those constraints. Stata will do most of the work for you. First, it will collect the constraints—all you have to do is add an option to your estimation command to allow the user to specify which constraints to use. Second, it will process those constraints, converting them from algebraic form (such as `group1=group2`) to a constraint matrix. Third, it will convert the constraint matrix into two matrices that will, for maximum likelihood estimation, allow you to write your routine almost as if there were no constraints.

There will be a "reduced-form" parameter vector, $\mathbf{b}_c$, which your likelihood-calculation routine will receive. That vector, multiplied by one of the almost magical matrices and then added to the other, can be converted into a regular parameter vector with the constraints applied, so other than the few extra matrix calculations, you can calculate the likelihood function as if there were no constraints. You can do the same thing with respect to the first and second derivatives (if you are calculating them), except that, after getting them, you will need to perform another matrix multiplication or two to convert them into the reduced form.

Once the optimum is found, you will have reduced-form parameter vector $\mathbf{b}_c$ and variance–covariance matrix $\mathbf{V}_c$. Both can be easily converted into full-form-but-constrained $\mathbf{b}$ and $\mathbf{V}$.

Finally, you will `ereturn post` the results along with the constraint matrix Stata made up for you in the first place. You can, with a few lines of program code, arrange it so that, every time results are replayed, the constraints under which they were produced are redisplayed in standard algebraic format.

Mathematics

Let $\mathbf{R}\mathbf{b}' = \mathbf{r}$ be the constraint for $\mathbf{R}$, a $c \times p$ constraint matrix imposing c constraints on p parameters; $\mathbf{b}$, a $1 \times p$ parameter vector; and $\mathbf{r}$, a $c \times 1$ vector of constraint values.

We wish to construct a $p \times k$ matrix, $\mathbf{T}$, that takes $\mathbf{b}$ into a reduced-rank form, where $k = p - c$. There are obviously many $\mathbf{T}$ matrices that will do this; we choose one with the properties

$$\mathbf{b}_c = \mathbf{b}_0 \mathbf{T}$$
$$\mathbf{b} = \mathbf{b}_c \mathbf{T}' + \mathbf{a}$$

where $\mathbf{b}_c$ is a reduced-form projection of any solution $\mathbf{b}_0$; i.e., $\mathbf{b}_c$ is a vector of lesser dimension ($1 \times k$ rather than $1 \times p$) that can be treated as if it were unconstrained. The second equation says that $\mathbf{b}_c$ can be mapped back into a higher-dimensioned, properly constrained $\mathbf{b}$; $1 \times p$ vector $\mathbf{a}$ is a constant that depends only on $\mathbf{R}$ and $\mathbf{r}$.

With such a $\mathbf{T}$ matrix and $\mathbf{a}$ vector, you can engage in unconstrained optimization of $\mathbf{b}_c$. If the estimate $\mathbf{b}_c$ with variance–covariance matrix $\mathbf{V}_c$ is produced, it can be mapped back into $\mathbf{b} = \mathbf{b}_c \mathbf{T}' + \mathbf{a}$ and $\mathbf{V} = \mathbf{T}\mathbf{V}_c\mathbf{T}'$. The resulting $\mathbf{b}$ and $\mathbf{V}$ can then be posted.

❏ Technical note

So, how did we get so lucky? This happy solution arises if

$$\mathbf{T} = \text{first } k \text{ eigenvectors of } \mathbf{I} - \mathbf{R}'(\mathbf{R}\mathbf{R}')^{-1}\mathbf{R} \qquad (p \times k)$$
$$\mathbf{L} = \text{last } c \text{ eigenvectors of } \mathbf{I} - \mathbf{R}'(\mathbf{R}\mathbf{R}')^{-1}\mathbf{R} \qquad (p \times c)$$
$$\mathbf{a} = \mathbf{r}'(\mathbf{L}'\mathbf{R}')^{-1}\mathbf{L}'$$

because

$$(\mathbf{b}_c, \mathbf{r}') = \mathbf{b}(\mathbf{T}, \mathbf{R}')$$

If $\mathbf{R}$ consists of a set of consistent constraints, then it is guaranteed to have rank c. Thus $\mathbf{R}\mathbf{R}'$ is a $c \times c$ invertible matrix.

We will now show that $\mathbf{R}\mathbf{T} = \mathbf{0}$ and $\mathbf{R}(\mathbf{L}\mathbf{L}') = \mathbf{R}$.

Because $\mathbf{R}: c \times p$ is assumed to be of rank c, the first k eigenvalues of $\mathbf{P} = \mathbf{I} - \mathbf{R}'(\mathbf{R}\mathbf{R}')^{-1}\mathbf{R}$ are positive and the last c are zero. Break $\mathbf{R}$ into a basis spanned by these components. If $\mathbf{R}$ had any components in the first k, they could not be annihilated by $\mathbf{P}$, contradicting

$$\mathbf{R}\mathbf{P} = \mathbf{R} - \mathbf{R}\mathbf{R}'(\mathbf{R}\mathbf{R}')^{-1}\mathbf{R} = \mathbf{0}$$

Therefore, $\mathbf{T}$ and $\mathbf{R}$ are orthogonal to each other. Because $(\mathbf{T}, \mathbf{L})$ is an orthonormal basis, $(\mathbf{T}, \mathbf{L})'$ is its inverse, so $(\mathbf{T}, \mathbf{L})(\mathbf{T}, \mathbf{L})' = \mathbf{I}$. Thus

$$\mathbf{T}\mathbf{T}' + \mathbf{L}\mathbf{L}' = \mathbf{I}$$
$$(\mathbf{T}\mathbf{T}' + \mathbf{L}\mathbf{L}')\mathbf{R}' = \mathbf{R}'$$
$$(\mathbf{L}\mathbf{L}')\mathbf{R}' = \mathbf{R}'$$

So we conclude that $\mathbf{r} = \mathbf{b}\mathbf{R}(\mathbf{L}\mathbf{L}')$. $\mathbf{R}\mathbf{L}$ is an invertible $c \times c$ matrix, so

$$\{\mathbf{b}_c, \mathbf{r}'(\mathbf{L}'\mathbf{R})^{-1}\} = \mathbf{b}(\mathbf{T}, \mathbf{L})$$

Remember, $(\mathbf{T}, \mathbf{L})$ is a set of eigenvectors, meaning $(\mathbf{T}, \mathbf{L})^{-1} = (\mathbf{T}, \mathbf{L})'$, so $\mathbf{b} = \mathbf{b}_c\mathbf{T}' + \mathbf{r}'(\mathbf{L}'\mathbf{R}')^{-1}\mathbf{L}'$.

❏

If a solution is found by likelihood methods, the reduced-form parameter vector is passed to the maximizer and from there to the program that computes a likelihood value from it. To find the likelihood value, the inner routines can compute $\mathbf{b} = \mathbf{b}_c\mathbf{T}' + \mathbf{a}$. The routine may then go on to produce a set of $1 \times p$ first derivatives, $\mathbf{d}$, and $p \times p$ second derivatives, $\mathbf{H}$, even though the problem is of lesser dimension. These matrices can be reduced to the k-dimensional space via

$$\mathbf{d}_c = \mathbf{d}\mathbf{T}$$

$$\mathbf{H}_c = \mathbf{T}'\mathbf{H}\mathbf{T}$$

❏ Technical note

Alternatively, if a solution were to be found by direct matrix methods, the programmer must derive a new solution based on $\mathbf{b} = \mathbf{b}_c\mathbf{T}' + \mathbf{a}$. For example, the least-squares normal equations come from differentiating $(\mathbf{y} - \mathbf{X}\mathbf{b})^2$. Setting the derivative with respect to $\mathbf{b}$ to zero results in

$$\mathbf{T}'\mathbf{X}'\left\{\mathbf{y} - \mathbf{X}(\mathbf{T}\mathbf{b}'_c + \mathbf{a}')\right\} = 0$$

yielding

$$\mathbf{b}'_c = (\mathbf{T}'\mathbf{X}'\mathbf{X}\mathbf{T})^{-1}(\mathbf{T}'\mathbf{X}'\mathbf{y} - \mathbf{T}'\mathbf{X}'\mathbf{X}\mathbf{a}')$$

$$\mathbf{b}' = \mathbf{T}\left\{(\mathbf{T}'\mathbf{X}'\mathbf{X}\mathbf{T})^{-1}(\mathbf{T}'\mathbf{X}'\mathbf{y} - \mathbf{T}'\mathbf{X}'\mathbf{X}\mathbf{a}')\right\} + \mathbf{a}'$$

Using the matrices $\mathbf{T}$ and $\mathbf{a}$, the solution is not merely to constrain the $\mathbf{b}'$ obtained from an unconstrained solution $(\mathbf{X}'\mathbf{X})^{-1}\mathbf{X}'\mathbf{y}$, even though you might know that, here, with further substitutions this could be reduced to

$$\mathbf{b}' = (\mathbf{X}'\mathbf{X})^{-1}\mathbf{X}'\mathbf{y} + (\mathbf{X}'\mathbf{X})^{-1}\mathbf{R}'\{\mathbf{R}(\mathbf{X}'\mathbf{X})^{-1}\mathbf{R}'\}^{-1}\{\mathbf{r} - \mathbf{R}(\mathbf{X}'\mathbf{X})^{-1}\mathbf{X}'\mathbf{y}\}$$

❏

Linkage of the mathematics to Stata

Users define constraints using the `constraint` command; see [R] **constraint**. The constraints are numbered, and Stata stores them in algebraic format—the same format in which the user typed them. Stata does this because, until the estimation problem is defined, it cannot know how to interpret the constraint. Think of the constraint `_b[group1]=_b[group2]`, meaning that two coefficients are to be constrained to equality, along with the constraint `_b[group3]=2`. The constraint matrices $\mathbf{R}$ and $\mathbf{r}$ are defined so that $\mathbf{R}\mathbf{b}' = \mathbf{r}$ imposes the constraint. The matrices *might* be

$$\begin{pmatrix} 0 & 0 & 1 & -1 & 0 & 0 \\ 0 & 0 & 0 & 0 & 1 & 0 \end{pmatrix} \begin{pmatrix} b_1 \\ b_2 \\ b_3 \\ b_4 \\ b_5 \\ b_6 \end{pmatrix} = \begin{pmatrix} 0 \\ 2 \end{pmatrix}$$

if it just so happened that the third and fourth coefficients corresponded to `group1` and `group2` and the fifth corresponded to `group3`. Then again, it might look different if the coefficients were organized differently.

Therefore, Stata must wait until estimation begins to define the $\mathbf{R}$ and $\mathbf{r}$ matrices. Stata learns about the organization of a problem from the names bordering the coefficient vector and variance–covariance matrix. Therefore, Stata requires you to `ereturn post` a dummy estimation result that has the correct names. From that, it can now determine the organization of the constraint matrix and make it for you. Once an (dummy) estimation result has been posted, `makecns` can make the constraint matrices, and, once they are built, you can obtain copies of them from `e(Cns)`. Stata stores the constraint matrices $\mathbf{R}$ and $\mathbf{r}$ as a $c \times (p+1)$ matrix $\mathbf{C} = (\mathbf{R}, \mathbf{r})$. Putting them together makes it easier to pass them to subroutines.

The second step in the process is to convert the constrained problem to a reduced-form problem. We outlined the mathematics above; the `matcproc` command will produce the $\mathbf{T}$ and $\mathbf{a}$ matrices. If you are performing maximum likelihood, your likelihood, gradient, and Hessian calculation subroutines can still work in the full metric by using the same $\mathbf{T}$ and $\mathbf{a}$ matrices to translate the reduced-format parameter vector back to the original metric. If you do this, and if you are calculating gradients or Hessians, you must remember to compress them to reduced form using the $\mathbf{T}$ and $\mathbf{a}$ matrices.

When you have a reduced-form solution, you translate this back to a constrained solution using $\mathbf{T}$ and $\mathbf{a}$. You then `ereturn post` the constrained solutions, along with the original Cns matrix, and use `ereturn display` to display the results.

Thus the outline of a program to perform constrained estimation is

```
program myest, eclass properties(...)
        version 11
        if replay() {      // replay the results
                if ("`e(cmd)'" != "myest") error 301
                syntax [, Level(cilevel) ]
                makecns , displaycns
        }
        else {             // fit the model
                syntax whatever  [,                        ///
                        whatever                           ///
                        Constraints(string)                ///
                        Level(cilevel)                     ///
                ]
                // any other parsing of the user's estimate request
                tempname b V C T a bc Vc
                local p=number of parameters
                // define the model  (set the row and column
                // names)  in 'b'
                if "`constraints'" != "" {
                        matrix `V' = `b''*`b'
                        ereturn post `b' `V'          // a dummy solution
                        makecns `constraints', display
                        matcproc `T' `a' `C'
                        // obtain solution in 'bc' and 'Vc'
                        matrix `b' = `bc'*`T' + `a'
                        matrix `V' = `T'*`Vc'*`T''    // note prime
                        ereturn post `b' `V' `C', options
                }
                else {
                        // obtain standard solution in 'b' and 'V'
                        ereturn post `b' `V', options
                }
                // store whatever else you want in e()
                ereturn local cmd "myest"
        }
        // output any header above the coefficient table
        ereturn display, level(`level')
end
```

There is one point that might escape your attention: Immediately after obtaining the constraint, we display the constraints even before we undertake the estimation. This way, a user who has made a mistake may press *Break* rather than waiting until the estimation is complete to discover the error. Our code displays the constraints every time the results are reported, even when typing *myest* without arguments.

Saved results

makecns saves the following in r():

Scalars
    r(k_autoCns) number of base, empty, and omitted constraints
Macros
    r(clist)   constraints used (numlist or matrix name)

Methods and formulas

makecns and matcproc are implemented as ado-files.

Also see

[P] **ereturn** — Post the estimation results

[P] **macro** — Macro definition and manipulation

[P] **matrix get** — Access system matrices

[R] **cnsreg** — Constrained linear regression

[R] **constraint** — Define and list constraints

[P] **matrix** — Introduction to matrix commands

[R] **ml** — Maximum likelihood estimation

Title

> **mark** — Mark observations for inclusion

Syntax

Create marker variable after syntax

    marksample *lmacname* [, <u>no</u>varlist <u>s</u>trok <u>zero</u>weight noby]

Create marker variable

    mark *newmarkvar* [*if*] [*in*] [*weight*] [, <u>zero</u>weight noby]

Modify marker variable

    markout *markvar* [*varlist*] [, <u>s</u>trok <u>sys</u>missok]

Find range containing selected observations

    markin [*if*] [*in*] [, <u>n</u>ame(*lclname*) noby]

Modify marker variable based on survey-characteristic variables

    svymarkout *markvar*

aweights, fweights, iweights, and pweights are allowed; see [U] **11.1.6 weight**.
varlist may contain time-series operators; see [U] **11.4.4 Time-series varlists**.

Description

    marksample, mark, and markout are for use in Stata programs. marksample and mark are alternatives; marksample links to information left behind by syntax, and mark is seldom used. Both create a 0/1 to-use variable that records which observations are to be used in subsequent code. markout sets the to-use variable to 0 if any variables in *varlist* contain missing and is used to further restrict observations.

    markin is for use after marksample, mark, and markout and, sometimes, provides a more efficient encoding of the observations to be used in subsequent code. markin is rarely used.

    svymarkout sets the to-use variable to 0 wherever any of the survey-characteristic variables contain missing values; it is discussed in [SVY] **svymarkout** and is not further discussed here.

Options

    novarlist is for use with marksample. It specifies that missing values among variables in *varlist* not cause the marker variable to be set to 0. Specify novarlist if you previously specified

            syntax newvarlist ...

    or

            syntax newvarname ...

You should also specify `novarlist` when missing values are not to cause observations to be excluded (perhaps you are analyzing the pattern of missing values).

`strok` is used with `marksample` or `markout`. Specify this option if string variables in *varlist* are to be allowed. `strok` changes rule 6 in *Remarks* below to read

"The marker variable is set to 0 in observations for which any of the string variables in *varlist* contain `""`."

`zeroweight` is for use with `marksample` or `mark`. It deletes rule 1 in *Remarks* below, meaning that observations will not be excluded because the weight is zero.

`noby` is used rarely and only in `byable(recall)` programs. It specifies that, in identifying the sample, the restriction to the by-group be ignored. `mark` and `marksample` are to create the marker variable as they would had the user not specified the by prefix. If the user did not specify the by prefix, specifying `noby` has no effect. `noby` provides a way for `byable(recall)` programs to identify the overall sample. For instance, if the program needed to calculate the percentage of observations in the by-group, the program would need to know both the sample to be used on this call and the overall sample. The program might be coded as

```
program ..., byable(recall)
        ...
        marksample touse
        marksample alluse, noby
        ...
        quietly count if 'touse'
        local curN = r(N)
        quietly count if 'alluse'
        local totN = r(N)
        local frac = 'curN'/'totN'
        ...
end
```

See [P] **byable**.

`sysmissok` is used with `markout`. Specify this option if numeric variables in *varlist* equal to system missing (`.`) are to be allowed and only numeric variables equal to extended missing (`.a`, `.b`, ...) are to be excluded. The default is that all missing values (`.`, `.a`, `.b`, ...) are excluded.

`name(`*lclname*`)` is for use with `markin`. It specifies the name of the macro to be created. If `name()` is not specified, the name `in` is used.

Remarks

`marksample`, `mark`, and `markout` are for use in Stata programs. They create a 0/1 variable recording which observations are to be used in subsequent code. The idea is to determine the relevant sample early in the code:

```
program ...
        (parse the arguments)
        (determine which observations are to be used)
        rest of code ... if to be used
end
```

`marksample`, `mark`, and `markout` assist in this.

```
program ...
        (parse the arguments)
        (use mark* to create temporary variable 'touse' containing 0 or 1)
        rest of code ... if 'touse'
end
```

`marksample` is for use in programs where the arguments are parsed using the `syntax` command; see [P] **syntax**. `marksample` creates a temporary `byte` variable, stores the name of the temporary variable in *lmacname*, and fills in the temporary variable with 0s and 1s according to whether the observation should be used. This determination is made by accessing information stored by `syntax` concerning the varlist, `if` *exp*, etc., allowed by the program. Its typical use is

```
program ...
        syntax ...
        marksample touse
        rest of code ... if 'touse'
end
```

`mark` starts with an already created temporary variable name. It fills in *newmarkvar* with 0s and 1s according to whether the observation should be used according to the *weight*, `if` *exp*, and `in` *range* specified. `markout` modifies the variable created by `mark` by resetting it to contain 0 in observations that have missing values recorded for any of the variables in *varlist*. These commands are typically used as

```
program ...
        (parse the arguments)
        tempvar touse
        mark 'touse' ...
        markout 'touse' ...
        rest of code ... if 'touse'
end
```

`marksample` is better than `mark` because there is less chance that you will forget to include some part of the sample restriction. `markout` can be used after `mark` or `marksample` when there are variables other than the varlist and when observations that contain missing values of those variables are also to be excluded. For instance, the following code is common:

```
program ...
        syntax ... [, Denom(varname) ... ]
        marksample touse
        markout 'touse' 'denom'
        rest of code ... if 'touse'
end
```

Regardless of whether you use `mark` or `marksample`, followed or not by `markout`, the following rules apply:

1. The marker variable is set to 0 in observations for which *weight* is 0 (but see the `zeroweight` option).

2. The appropriate error message is issued, and everything stops if *weight* is invalid (such as being less than 0 in some observation or being a noninteger for frequency weights).

3. The marker variable is set to 0 in observations for which `if` *exp* is not satisfied.

4. The marker variable is set to 0 in observations outside `in` *range*.

5. The marker variable is set to 0 in observations for which any of the numeric variables in *varlist* contain a numeric missing value.

6. The marker variable is set to 0 in *all* observations if any of the variables in *varlist* are strings; see the `strok` option for an exception.

7. The marker variable is set to 1 in the remaining observations.

Using the name `touse` is a convention, not a rule, but it is recommended for consistency between programs.

❏ Technical note

markin is for use after marksample, mark, and markout and should be used only with extreme caution. Its use is never necessary, but when it is known that the specified if *exp* will select a small subset of the observations (small being, for example, 6 of 750,000), using markin can result in code that executes more quickly. markin creates local macro *'lclname'* (or 'in' if name() is not specified) containing the smallest in *range* that contains the if *exp*.

❏

By far the most common programming error—made by us at StataCorp and others—is to use different samples in different parts of a Stata program. We strongly recommend that programmers identify the sample at the outset. This is easy with marksample (or alternatively, mark and markout). Consider a Stata program that begins

```
program myprog
        version 11
        syntax varlist [if] [in]
        ...
end
```

Pretend that this program makes a statistical calculation based on the observations specified in *varlist* that do not contain missing values (such as a linear regression). The program must identify the observations that it will use. Moreover, because the user can specify if *exp* or in *range*, these restrictions must also be taken into account. marksample makes this easy:

```
        version 11
        syntax varlist [if] [in]
        marksample touse
        ...
end
```

To produce the same result, we could create the temporary variable touse and then use mark and markout as follows:

```
program myprog
        version 11
        syntax varlist [if] [in]
        tempvar touse
        mark 'touse' 'if' 'in'
        markout 'touse' 'varlist'
        ...
end
```

The result will be the same.

The mark command creates temporary variable 'touse' (temporary because of the preceding tempvar; see [P] **macro**) based on the if *exp* and in *range*. If there is no if *exp* or in *range*, 'touse' will contain 1 for every observation in the data. If if price>1000 was specified by the user, only observations for which price is greater than 1,000 will have touse set to 1; the remaining observations will have touse set to 0.

The markout command updates the 'touse' marker created by mark. For observations where 'touse' is 1—observations that might potentially be used—the variables in *varlist* are checked for missing values. If such an observation has any variables equal to missing, the observation's 'touse' value is reset to 0.

Thus observations to be used all have 'touse' set to 1. Including if 'touse' at the end of statistical or data-management commands will restrict the command to operate on the appropriate sample.

▷ Example 1

Let's write a program to do the same thing as summarize, except that our program will also engage in casewise deletion—if an observation has a missing value in any of the variables, it is to be excluded from all the calculations.

```
program cwsumm
        version 11
        syntax [varlist(fv ts)] [if] [in] [aweight fweight] [, Detail noFormat]
        marksample touse
        summarize 'varlist' ['weight''exp'] if 'touse', 'detail' 'format'
end
```

◁

❏ Technical note

Let's now turn to markin, which is for use in those rare instances where you, as a programmer, know that only a few of the observations are going to be selected, that those small number of observations probably occur close together in terms of observation number, and that speed is important. That is, the use of markin is never required, and a certain caution is required in its use, so it is usually best to avoid it. On the other hand, when the requirements are met, markin can speed programs considerably.

The safe way to use markin is to first write the program without it and then splice in its use. Form a touse variable in the usual way by using marksample, mark, and markout. Once you have identified the touse sample, use markin to construct an in *range* from it. Then add 'in' on every command in which if 'touse' appears, without removing the if 'touse'.

That is, pretend that our original code reads like the following:

```
program ...
        syntax ...
        marksample touse
        mark 'touse' ...               // touse now fully set
        gen ... if 'touse'
        replace ... if 'touse'
        summarize ... if 'touse'
        replace ... if 'touse'
        ...
end
```

We now change our code to read as follows:

```
program ...
        syntax ...
        marksample touse
        mark 'touse' ...               // touse now fully set
        markin if 'touse'              // <- new
                                       // we add 'in':
        gen ... if 'touse' 'in'
        replace ... if 'touse' 'in'
        summarize ... if 'touse' 'in'
        replace ... if 'touse' 'in'
        ...
end
```

This new version will, under certain conditions, run faster. Why? Consider the case when the program is called and there are 750,000 observations in memory. Let's imagine that the 750,000 observations are a panel dataset containing 20 observations each on 37,500 individuals. Let's further imagine that the dataset is sorted by subjectid, the individual identifier, and that the user calls our program and includes the restriction if subject_id==4225.

Thus our program must select 20 observations from the 750,000. That's fine, but think about the work that generate, replace, summarize, and replace must each go to in our original program. Each must thumb through 750,000 observations, asking themselves whether 'touse' is true, and 749,980 times, the answer is no. That will happen four times.

markin will save Stata work here. It creates a macro named 'in' of the form "in j_1/j_2", where j_1 to j_2 is the narrowest range that contains all the 'touse' $\neq 0$ values. Under the assumptions we made, that range will be exactly 20 long; perhaps it will be in 84500/84520. Now the generate, replace, summarize, and replace commands will each restrict themselves to those 20 observations. This will save them much work and the user much time.

Because there is a speed advantage, why not always use markin in our programs? Assume that between the summarize and the replace there was a sort command in our program. The in *range* constructed by markin would be inappropriate for our last replace; we would break our program. If we use markin, we must make sure that the in *range* constructed continues to be valid throughout our program (our construct a new one when it changes). So that is the first answer: you cannot add markin without thinking. The second answer is that markin takes time to execute, albeit just a little, and that time is usually wasted because in *range* will not improve performance because the data are not ordered as required. Taking the two reasons together, adding markin to most programs is simply not worth the effort.

When it is worth the effort, you may wonder why, when we added 'in' to the subsequent commands, we did not simultaneously remove if 'touse'. The answer is that 'in' is not a guaranteed substitute for if. In our example, under the assumptions made, the 'in' happens to substitute perfectly, but that was just an assumption, and we have no guarantees that the user happens to have his or her data sorted in the desired way. If, in our program, we sorted the data, and then we used markin to produce the range, we could omit if 'touse', but even then, we do not recommend it. We always recommend programming defensively, and the cost of evaluating if 'touse', when 'in' really does restrict the sample to the relevant observations, is barely measurable.

❏

Methods and formulas

svymarkout is implemented as an ado-file.

Reference

Jann, B. 2007. Stata tip 34: Get a handle on your sample. *Stata Journal* 7: 266–267.

Also see

[P] **byable** — Make programs byable

[P] **syntax** — Parse Stata syntax

[SVY] **svymarkout** — Mark observations for exclusion on the basis of survey characteristics

[U] **18 Programming Stata**

Title

> **matlist** — Display a matrix and control its format

Syntax

One common display format for every column

> matlist *matrix_exp* $\left[\ ,\ style\_options\ general\_options\right]$

Each column with its own display format

> matlist *matrix_exp* , cspec(*cspec*) rspec(*rspec*) $\left[general\_options\right]$

style_options	description
lines(*lstyle*)	lines style; default between headers/labels and data
border(*bspec*)	border style; default is none
border	same as border(all)
format(%*fmt*)	display format; default is format(%9.0g)
twidth(#)	row-label width; default is twidth(12)
left(#)	left indent for tables; default is left(0)
right(#)	right indent for tables; default is right(0)

lstyle	lines are drawn ...
oneline	between headers/labels and data; default with no equations
eq	between equations; default when equations are present
rowtotal	same as oneline plus line before last row
coltotal	same as oneline plus line before last column
rctotal	same as oneline plus line before last row and column
rows	between all rows; between row labels and data
columns	between all columns; between column header and data
cells	between all rows and columns
none	suppress all lines

bspec	border lines are drawn ...
none	no border lines are drawn; the default
all	around all four sides
rows	at the top and bottom
columns	at the left and right
left	at the left
right	at the right
top	at the top
bottom	at the bottom

general_options	description
<u>titl</u>e(*string*)	title displayed above table
<u>tind</u>ent(*#*)	indent title *#* spaces
<u>row</u>title(*string*)	title to display above row names
<u>names</u>(<u>r</u>ows)	display row names
<u>names</u>(<u>c</u>olumns)	display column names
<u>names</u>(<u>a</u>ll)	display row and column names; the default
<u>names</u>(<u>n</u>one)	suppress row and column names
<u>nonames</u>	same as names(none)
showcoleq(*ceq*)	specify how column equation names are displayed
colorcoleq(<u>t</u>xt | <u>r</u>es)	display mode (color) for column equation names; default is txt
keepcoleq	keep columns of the same equation together
aligncolnames(<u>r</u>align)	right-align column names
aligncolnames(<u>l</u>align)	left-align column names
aligncolnames(<u>c</u>enter)	center column names
<u>nobl</u>ank	suppress blank line before tables
<u>noha</u>lf	display full matrix even if symmetric
nodotz	display missing value .z as blank
<u>under</u>score	display underscores as blanks in row and column names
linesize(*#*)	overrule linesize setting

ceq	equation names are displayed
<u>f</u>irst	over the first column only; the default
<u>e</u>ach	over each column
<u>c</u>ombined	centered over all associated columns
<u>l</u>combined	left-aligned over all associated columns
<u>r</u>combined	right-aligned over all associated columns

Description

matlist displays a matrix, allowing you to control the display format. Row and column names are used as the row and column headers. Equation names are displayed in a manner similar to estimation results.

Columns may have different formats, and lines may be shown between each column. You cannot format rows of the matrix differently.

matlist is an extension of the matrix list command (see [P] **matrix utility**).

Style options

lines(*lstyle*) specifies where lines are drawn in the display of *matrix_exp*. The following values of *lstyle* are allowed:

oneline draws lines separating the row and column headers from the numerical entries. This is the default if the *matrix_exp* has no equation names.

eq draws horizontal and vertical lines between equations. This is the default if the *matrix_exp* has row or column equation names.

rowtotal is the same as oneline and has a line separating the last row (the totals) from the rest.

coltotal is the same as oneline and has a line separating the last column (the totals) from the rest.

rctotal is the same as oneline and has lines separating the last row and column (the totals) from the rest.

rows draws horizontal lines between all rows and one vertical line between the row-label column and the first column with numerical entries.

columns draws vertical lines between all columns and one horizontal line between the headers and the first numeric row.

cells draws horizontal and vertical lines between all rows and columns.

none suppresses all horizontal and vertical lines.

border$\left[\,(bspec)\,\right]$ specifies the type of border drawn around the table. *bspec* is any combination of the following values:

none draws no outside border lines and is the default.

all draws all four outside border lines.

rows draws horizontal lines in the top and bottom margins.

columns draws vertical lines in the left and right margins.

left draws a line in the left margin.

right draws a line in the right margin.

top draws a line in the top margin.

bottom draws a line in the bottom margin.

border without an argument is equivalent to border(all), or, equivalently, border(left right top bottom).

format(%*fmt*) specifies the format for displaying the individual elements of the matrix. The default is format(%9.0g). See [U] **12.5 Formats: Controlling how data are displayed**.

twidth(*#*) specifies the width of the row-label column (first column); the default is twidth(12).

left(*#*) specifies that the table be indented *#* spaces; the default is left(0). To indent the title, see the tindent() option.

right(*#*) specifies that the right margin of the table be *#* spaces in from the page margin. The default is right(0). The right margin affects the number of columns that are displayed before wrapping.

General options

title(*string*) adds *string* as the title displayed before the matrix. matlist has no default title or header.

tindent(#) specifies the indentation for the title; the default is tindent(0).

rowtitle(*string*) specifies that *string* be used as a column header for the row labels. This option is allowed only when both row and column labels are displayed.

names(rows | columns | all | none) specifies whether the row and column names are displayed; the default is names(all), which displays both.

nonames suppresses row and column names and is a synonym for names(none).

showcoleq(*ceq*) specifies how column equation names are displayed. The following *ceq* are allowed:

first displays an equation name over the first column associated with that name; this is the default.

each displays an equation name over each column.

combined displays an equation name centered over all columns associated with that name.

lcombined displays an equation name left-aligned over all columns associated with that name.

rcombined displays an equation name right-aligned over all columns associated with that name.

If necessary, equation names are truncated to the width of the field in which the names are displayed. With combined, lcombined, and rcombined, the field comprises all columns and the associated separators for the equation.

colorcoleq(txt | res) specifies the mode (color) used for the column equation names that appear in the first displayed row. Specifying txt (the default) displays the equation name in the same color used to display text. Specifying res displays the name in the same color used to display results.

keepcoleq specifies that columns of the same equation be kept together if possible.

aligncolnames(ralign | lalign | center) specifies the alignment for the column names. ralign indicates alignment to the right, lalign indicates alignment to the left, and center indicates centering. aligncolnames(ralign) is the default.

noblank suppresses printing a blank line before the matrix. This is useful in programs.

nohalf specifies that, even if the matrix is symmetric, the full matrix be printed. The default is to print only the lower triangle in such cases.

nodotz specifies that .z missing values be listed as a field of blanks rather than as .z.

underscore converts underscores to blanks in row and column names.

linesize(#) specifies the width of the page for formatting the table. Specifying a value of linesize() wider than your screen width can produce truly ugly output on the screen, but that output can nevertheless be useful if you are logging output and later plan to print the log on a wide printer.

(Continued on next page)

Required options for the second syntax

cspec(*cspec*) specifies the formatting of the columns and the separators of the columns, where *cspec* is [*sep* [*qual*] %#s] *sep* *nspec* [*nspec* [...]]

and where *sep* is [o#] &| | [o#]

　　　qual is

qual	Description
s	standard font
b	boldface font
i	italic font
t	text mode
e	error mode
c	command mode
L	left-aligned
R	right-aligned
C	centered
w#	field width #

　　　nspec is [*qual*] *nfmt* *sep*

　　　nfmt is %#.#{f|g}

The first (optional) part, [*sep* [*qual*] %#s], of *cspec* specifies the formatting for the column containing row names. It is required if the row names are part of the display; see the names() option. The number of *nspec*s should equal the number of columns of *matname*.

In a separator specification, *sep*, | specifies that a vertical line be drawn. & specifies that no line be drawn. The number of spaces before and after the separator may be specified with o#; these default to one space, except that by default no spaces are included before the first column and after the last column.

Here are examples for a matrix with two columns (three columns when you count the column containing the row labels):

```
cspec(& %16s & %9.2f & %7.4f &)
```

specifies that the first column, containing row labels, be displayed using 16 characters; the second column, with format %9.2f; and the third column, with format %7.4f. No vertical lines are drawn. The number of spaces before and after the table is 0. Columns are separated with two spaces.

```
cspec(&o2 %16s o2&o2 %9.2f o2&o2 %7.4f o2&)
```

specifies more white space around the columns (two spaces everywhere, for a total of four spaces between columns).

```
cspec(|%16s|%9.2f|%7.4f|)
```

displays the columns in the same way as the first example but draws vertical lines before and after each column.

```
cspec(| b %16s | %9.2f & %7.4f |)
```

specifies that vertical lines be drawn before and after all columns, except between the two columns with numeric entries. The first column is displayed in the boldface font.

rspec(*rspec*) specifies where horizontal lines be drawn. *rspec* consists of a sequence of characters, optionally separated by white space. - (or synonym |) specifies that a line be drawn. & indicates that no line be drawn. When *matname* has r rows, $r + 2$ characters are required if column headers are displayed, and $r + 1$ characters are required otherwise. The first character specifies whether a line is to be drawn before the first row of the table; the second, whether a line is to be drawn between the first and second row, etc.; and the last character, whether a line is to be drawn after the last row of the table.

You cannot add blank lines before or after the horizontal lines.

For example, in a table with column headers and three numeric rows,

> rspec(||&&|)   or equivalently   rspec(--&&-)

specifies that horizontal lines be drawn before the first and second rows and after the last row, but not elsewhere.

Remarks

Remarks are presented under the following headings:

> *All columns with the same format*
> *Different formats for each column*
> *Other output options*

All columns with the same format

The `matrix list` command displays Stata matrices but gives you little control over formatting; see [P] **matrix utility**.

The `matlist` command, on the other hand, offers a wide array of options to give you more detailed control over the formatting of the output.

The output produced by `matlist` is a rectangular table of numbers with an optional row and column on top and to the left of the table. We distinguish two cases. In the first style, all numeric columns are to be displayed in the same format. In the second style, each column and each intercolumn divider is formatted individually.

▷ Example 1

We demonstrate with a simple 3×2 matrix, A.

```
. matrix A = ( 1,2 \ 3,4 \ 5,6 )
. matrix list A
A[3,2]
    c1  c2
r1   1   2
r2   3   4
r3   5   6
```

Like `matrix list`, the `matlist` command displays one matrix but adopts a tabular display style.

```
. matlist A
             |      c1        c2
 ------------+--------------------
          r1 |       1         2
          r2 |       3         4
          r3 |       5         6
```

Other border lines at the left, top, right, and bottom of the table may be specified with the border() option. For instance, border(rows) specifies a horizontal line at the top and bottom margins. rowtitle() specifies a row title. To make it easier to organize output with multiple matrices, you can use the left() option to left-indent the output.

```
. matlist A, border(rows) rowtitle(rows) left(4)
```

rows	c1	c2
r1	1	2
r2	3	4
r3	5	6

The lines() option specifies where internal lines are to be drawn. lines(none) suppresses all internal horizontal and vertical lines. lines(all) displays lines between all rows and columns. twidth() specifies the width of the first column—the column containing the row names. By default, matlist shows row and column names obtained from the matrix resulting from *matrix_exp*. names(rows) specifies that the row names be shown, and the column names be suppressed. names(none) would suppress all row and column names. You may also display a title for the table, displayed in SMCL paragraph mode; see [P] **smcl**. If the table is indented, the title will be shown with a hanging indent. The tindent() option allows you to indent the title as well. Finally, matlist allows a matrix expression—convenient for interactive use. Enclose the matrix expression in parentheses if the expression itself contains commas.

```
. matlist 2*A, border(all) lines(none) format(%6.1f) names(rows) twidth(8)
> left(4) title(Guess what, a title)
```

Guess what, a title

r1	2.0	4.0
r2	6.0	8.0
r3	10.0	12.0

◁

matlist supports equations.

▷ Example 2

By default, matlist draws vertical and horizontal lines between equations.

```
. matrix E = (  1 ,  2 ,    3 ,  4 ,    5 ,  6 ,  7 \
>               8 ,  9 ,   10 , 11 ,   12 , 13 , 14 \
>              15 , 16 ,   17 , 18 ,   19 , 20 , 21 \
>              22 , 23 ,   24 , 25 ,   26 , 27 , 28 \
>              29 , 30 ,   31 , 32 ,   33 , 34 , 35 \
>              36 , 37 ,   38 , 39 ,   40 , 41 , 42 )
. matrix colnames E = A:a1 A:a2 B:b1 B:b2 C:c1 C:c2 C:c3
. matrix rownames E = D:d1 D:d2 E:e1 E:e2 F:f1 F:f2
```

```
. matlist E
```

		A			B			C	
			a1	a2		b1	b2		c1
D									
	d1		1	2		3	4		5
	d2		8	9		10	11		12
E									
	e1		15	16		17	18		19
	e2		22	23		24	25		26
F									
	f1		29	30		31	32		33
	f2		36	37		38	39		40

		C		
			c2	c3
D				
	d1		6	7
	d2		13	14
E				
	e1		20	21
	e2		27	28
F				
	f1		34	35
	f2		41	42

matlist wraps the columns, if necessary. The keepcoleq option keeps all columns of an equation together. By default, matlist shows the equation name left-aligned over the first column associated with the equation. Equation names are truncated, if necessary. We may also display equation names in the field created by combining the columns associated with the equation. In this wider field, truncation of equation names will be rare. The showcoleq(combined) option displays the equation names centered in this combined field. See the description of the showcoleq() option for other ways to format the column equation names. border(right) displays a vertical line to the right of the table. If the table is wrapped, a border line is shown to the right of each panel.

(Continued on next page)

```
. matlist hadamard(E,E)', showcoleq(c) keepcoleq border(right) left(4)
```

		D		E	
		d1	d2	e1	e2
A					
	a1	1	64	225	484
	a2	4	81	256	529
B					
	b1	9	100	289	576
	b2	16	121	324	625
C					
	c1	25	144	361	676
	c2	36	169	400	729
	c3	49	196	441	784

		F	
		f1	f2
A			
	a1	841	1296
	a2	900	1369
B			
	b1	961	1444
	b2	1024	1521
C			
	c1	1089	1600
	c2	1156	1681
	c3	1225	1764

◁

Different formats for each column

matlist allows you to format each column's display format (e.g., %8.2f for the data columns), type style (e.g., boldface font), and alignment. You may also specify whether a vertical line is to be drawn between the columns and the number of spaces before and after the line.

▷ Example 3

We illustrate the different formatting options with the example of a matrix of test results, one row per test, with the last row representing an overall test.

```
. matrix Htest = (  12.30,  2,  .00044642  \
>                    2.17,  1,  .35332874  \
>                    8.81,  3,  .04022625  \
>                   20.05,  6,  .00106763  )
. matrix rownames Htest = trunk length weight overall
. matrix colnames Htest = chi2 df p
```

Again we can display the matrix Htest with matrix list,

```
. matrix list Htest
Htest[4,3]
             chi2          df           p
  trunk      12.3           2   .00044642
 length      2.17           1   .35332874
 weight      8.81           3   .04022625
overall     20.05           6   .00106763
```

or with matlist,

```
. matlist Htest
                  chi2          df           p
    trunk         12.3           2   .0004464
   length         2.17           1   .3533287
   weight         8.81           3   .0402262
  overall        20.05           6   .0010676
```

Neither of these displays of Htest is attractive because all columns are the same width and the numbers are formatted with the same display format. matlist can provide a better display of the matrix Htest.

```
. matlist Htest, rowtitle(Variables) title(Test results)
> cspec(o4& %12s | %8.0g & %5.0f & %8.4f o2&) rspec(&-&&--)
Test results
    Variables         chi2   df          p
        trunk         12.3    2     0.0004
       length         2.17    1     0.3533
       weight         8.81    3     0.0402

      overall        20.05    6     0.0011
```

The cspec() and rspec() options may look somewhat intimidating at first, but they become clear if we examine their parts. The table for matrix Htest has four columns: one string column with the row names and three numeric columns with chi2 statistics, degrees of freedom, and p-values. There are also five separators: one before the first column, three between the columns, and one after the last column. Thus the cspec() specification is made up of $4 + 5 = 9$ elements that are explained in the next table.

Element	Purpose	Description
o4&	before column 1	4 spaces/no vertical line
%12s	display format column 1	string display format %12s
|	between columns 1 and 2	1 space/vertical line/1 space
%8.0g	display format column 2	numeric display format %8.0g
&	between columns 2 and 3	1 space/no vertical line/1 space
%5.0f	display format column 3	numeric display format %5.0f
&	between columns 3 and 4	1 space/no vertical line/1 space
%8.4f	display format column 4	numeric display format %8.4f
o2&	after column 4	2 spaces/no vertical line

Vertical lines are drawn if the separator consists of a | character, whereas no vertical line is drawn with an & specification. By default, one space is displayed before and after the vertical line;

the exception is that, by default, no space is displayed before the first separator and after the last separator. More white space may be added by adding o specifications. For instance, o3 | o2, or more compactly o3|o2, specifies that three spaces be included before the vertical line and two spaces after the line.

The `rspec()` row formatting specification for a table with r rows (including the column headers) comprises a series of $r + 1$ - and & characters, where

- denotes that a horizontal line is to be drawn and

& denotes that no horizontal line is to be drawn.

The table for matrix `Htest` has five rows: the column headers and four data rows. The specification `rspec(&-&&--)` is detailed in the next table.

Element	Purpose	Description
&	before row 1	no line is drawn
-	between rows 1 and 2	a line is drawn
&	between rows 2 and 3	no line is drawn
&	between rows 3 and 4	no line is drawn
-	between rows 4 and 5	a line is drawn
-	after row 5	a line is drawn

Lines are drawn before and after the last row of the table for matrix `Htest` to emphasize that this row is an overall (total) test.

Further formatting is possible. For instance, we can specify that the second column (the first numeric column) be in the boldface font and text mode and that the last column be in italic and command mode. We simply insert appropriate qualifiers in the specification part for the respective columns.

```
. matlist Htest, rowt(Variables) title(Test results (again))
> cspec( o4&o2  %10s  |  b t %8.0g  &  %4.0f  &  i c %7.4f  o2& )
> rspec( &  -  &  &  -  & )

Test results (again)
        Variables |     chi2    df        p
        ----------+--------------------------
            trunk |     12.3     2   0.0004
           length |     2.17     1   0.3533
           weight |     8.81     3   0.0402
        ----------+--------------------------
          overall |    20.05     6   0.0011
```

In this manual, the boldface font is used for the `chi2` column and the italic font is used for the p column, but there is no difference due to the requested text mode and command mode. If we run this example interactively, both the font change and color change due to the requested mode can be seen. Depending on the settings, the `chi2` column might display in the boldface font and the green color (text mode); the `df` column, in the default standard font and the yellow color (result mode); and the p column, in the italic font and the white color (command mode).

◁

Other output options

▷ Example 4

Finally, we illustrate two options for use with the extended missing value .z and with row and column names that contain underscores.

```
. matrix Z = ( .z, 1 \ .c, .z )
. matrix rownames Z = row_1 row_2
. matrix colnames Z = col1 col2
. matlist Z
```

	col1	col2
row_1	.z	1
row_2	.c	.z

The nodotz option displays .z as blanks. Underscores in row names are translated into spaces with the underscore option.

```
. matlist Z, nodotz underscore
```

	col1	col2
row 1		1
row 2	.c	

◁

Methods and formulas

matlist is implemented as an ado-file.

Also see

[P] **matrix utility** — List, rename, and drop matrices

[U] **14 Matrix expressions**

[P] **matrix** — Introduction to matrix commands

Title

matrix — Introduction to matrix commands

Description

An introduction to matrices in Stata is found in [U] **14 Matrix expressions**. This entry provides an overview of the `matrix` commands and provides more background information on matrices in Stata.

Beyond the `matrix` commands, Stata has a complete matrix programming language, Mata, that provides more advanced matrix functions, support for complex matrices, fast execution speed, and the ability to directly access Stata's data, macros, matrices, and returned results. Mata can be used interactively as a matrix calculator, but it is even more useful for programming; see the *Mata Reference Manual*.

Remarks

Remarks are presented under the following headings:

> *Overview of matrix commands*
> *Creating and replacing matrices*
> *Namespace*
> *Naming conventions in programs*

Overview of matrix commands

Documentation on matrices in Stata is grouped below into three categories—Basics, Programming, and Specialized. We recommend that you begin with [U] **14 Matrix expressions** and then read [P] **matrix define**. After that, feel free to skip around.

Basics

[U] **14 Matrix expressions**	Introduction to matrices in Stata
[P] **matrix define**	Matrix definition, operators, and functions
[P] **matrix utility**	List, rename, and drop matrices
[P] **matlist**	Display a matrix and control its format

Programming

[P] **matrix accum**	Form cross-product matrices
[R] **ml**	Maximum likelihood estimation
[P] **ereturn**	Post the estimation results
[P] **matrix rownames**	Name rows and columns
[P] **matrix score**	Score data from coefficient vectors

Specialized

[P] **makecns**	Constrained estimation
[P] **matrix mkmat**	Convert variables to matrix and vice versa
[P] **matrix svd**	Singular value decomposition
[P] **matrix symeigen**	Eigenvalues and eigenvectors of symmetric matrices
[P] **matrix eigenvalues**	Eigenvalues of nonsymmetric matrices
[P] **matrix get**	Access system matrices
[P] **matrix dissimilarity**	Compute similarity or dissimilarity measures

Creating and replacing matrices

Matrices generally do not have to be preallocated or dimensioned before creation, except when you want to create an $r \times c$ matrix and then fill in each element one by one; see the description of the J() function in [P] **matrix define**. Matrices are typically created by matrix define or matrix accum; see [P] **matrix accum**.

Stata takes a high-handed approach to redefining matrices. You know that, when dealing with data, you must distinguish between creating a new variable or replacing the contents of an existing variable—Stata has two commands for this: generate and replace. For matrices, there is no such distinction. If you define a new matrix, it is created. If you give the same command and the matrix already exists, then the currently existing matrix is destroyed and the new one is defined. This treatment is the same as that given to macros and scalars.

❏ Technical note

Beginning with Stata 8, matrices were allowed to contain missing values. If version is set less than 8 (see [P] **version**), sometimes missing values cannot be assigned to matrices; this was done to keep old code working.

❏

Namespace

The term "namespace" refers to how names are interpreted. For instance, the variables in your dataset occupy one namespace—other things, such as value labels, macros, and scalars, can have the same name and not cause confusion.

Macros also have their own namespace; macros can have the same names as other things, and Stata can still tell by context when you are referring to a macro because of the punctuation. When you type gen newvar=myname, myname must refer to a variable. When you type gen newvar=`myname'—note the single quotes around myname—myname must refer to a local macro. When you type gen newvar=$myname, myname must refer to a global macro.

Scalars and matrices share the same namespace; i.e., scalars and matrices may have the same names as variables in the dataset, etc., but they cannot have the same names as each other. Thus when you define a matrix called, say, myres, if a scalar by that name already exists, it is destroyed, and the matrix replaces it. Correspondingly, when you define a scalar called myres, if a matrix by that name exists, it is destroyed, and the scalar replaces it.

Naming conventions in programs

If you are writing Stata programs or ado-files using matrices, you may have some matrices that you wish to leave behind for other programs to build upon, but you will certainly have other matrices that are nothing more than leftovers from calculations. Such matrices are called *temporary*. You should use Stata's tempname facility (see [P] **macro**) to name such matrices. These matrices will automatically be discarded when your program ends. For example, a piece of your program might read

```
tempname YXX XX
matrix accum `YXX' = price weight mpg
matrix `XX' = `YXX'[2...,2...]
```

Note the single quotes around the names after they are obtained from tempname; see [U] **18.3 Macros**.

❑ Technical note

Let's consider writing a regression program in Stata. (There is actually no need for such a program because Stata already has the `regress` command.) A well-written estimation command would allow the `level()` option for specifying the width of confidence intervals, and it would replay results when the command is typed without arguments. Here is a well-written version:

```
program myreg, eclass
        version 11
        if !replay() {
                syntax varlist(min=2 numeric) [if] [in] [, Level(cilevel)]
                marksample touse       // mark the sample
                tempname YXX XX Xy b hat V
                // compute cross products YXX = (Y'Y , Y'X \ X'Y , X'X)
                quietly matrix accum 'YXX' = 'varlist' if 'touse'
                local nobs = r(N)
                local df = 'nobs' - (rowsof('YXX') - 1)
                matrix 'XX' = 'YXX'[2...,2...]
                matrix 'Xy' = 'YXX'[1,2...]
                // compute the beta vector
                matrix 'b' = 'Xy' * invsym('XX')
                // compute the covariance matrix
                matrix 'hat' = 'b' * 'Xy''
                matrix 'V' = invsym('XX') * ('YXX'[1,1] - 'hat'[1,1])/'df'
                // post the beta vector and covariance matrix
                ereturn post 'b' 'V', dof('df') obs('nobs') depname('1') /*
                                */ esample('touse')
                // save estimation information
                tokenize "'varlist'"  // put varlist into numbered arguments
                ereturn local depvar "'1'"
                ereturn local cmd "myreg"
        }
        else {  // replay
                syntax [, Level(cilevel)]
        }
        if "'e(cmd)'"!="myreg" error 301
        // print the regression table
        ereturn display, level('level')
end
```

The syntax of our new command is

$$\text{myreg } depvar\ indepvars \left[if \right] \left[in \right] \left[, \text{level}(\#) \right]$$

`myreg`, typed without arguments, redisplays the output of the last `myreg` command. After estimation with `myreg`, the user may use `correlate` to display the covariance matrix of the estimators, `predict` to obtain predicted values or standard errors of the prediction, and `test` to test linear hypotheses about the estimated coefficients. The command is indistinguishable from any other Stata estimation command.

Despite the excellence of our work, we do have some criticisms:

- `myreg` does not display the ANOVA table, R^2, etc.; it should and could be made to, although we would have to insert our own `display` statements before the `ereturn display` instruction.

- The program makes copious use of matrices with different names, resulting in extra memory use while the estimation is being made; the code could be made more economical, if less readable, by reusing matrices.

- myreg makes the least-squares calculation by using the absolute cross-product matrix, an invitation to numerical problems if the data are not consistently scaled. Stata's own regress command is more careful, and we could be, too: matrix accum does have an option for forming the cross-product matrix in deviation form, but its use would complicate this program. This does not overly concern us, although we should make a note of it when we document myreg. Nowadays, users expect to be protected in linear regression but have no such expectations for more complicated estimation schemes because avoiding the problem can be difficult.

There is one nice feature of our program that did not occur to us when we wrote it. We use invsym() to form the inverse of the cross-product matrix, and invsym() can handle singular matrices. If there is a collinearity problem, myreg behaves just like regress: it omits the offending variables and notes that they are omitted when it displays the output (at the ereturn display step).

❑

❑ Technical note

Our linear regression program is longer than we might have written in an exclusively matrix programming language. After all, the coefficients can be obtained from $(\mathbf{X}'\mathbf{X})^{-1}\mathbf{X}'\mathbf{y}$, and in a dedicated matrix language, we would type nearly that, and obtaining the standard errors would require only a few more matrix calculations. In fact, we did type nearly that to make the calculation; the extra lines in our program have to do mostly with syntax issues and linking to the rest of Stata. In writing your own programs, you might be tempted not to bother linking to the rest of Stata. Fight this temptation.

Linking to the rest of Stata pays off: here we do not merely display the numerical results, but we display them in a readable form, complete with variable names. We made a command that is indistinguishable from Stata's other estimation commands. If the user wants to test _b[denver]=_b[la], the user types literally that; there is no need to remember the matrix equation and to count variables (such as constrain the third minus the 15th variable to sum to zero).

❑

Also see

[P] **ereturn** — Post the estimation results

[P] **matrix define** — Matrix definition, operators, and functions

[R] **ml** — Maximum likelihood estimation

[U] **14 Matrix expressions**

[U] **18 Programming Stata**

Mata Reference Manual

Title

> **matrix accum** — Form cross-product matrices

Syntax

Accumulate cross-product matrices to form $\mathbf{X}'\mathbf{X}$

> matrix accum $\mathbf{A}$ = *varlist* $\big[$ *if* $\big]$ $\big[$ *in* $\big]$ $\big[$ *weight* $\big]$ $\big[$, noconstant
>
> deviations means(m) $\big]$

Accumulate cross-product matrices to form $\mathbf{X}'\mathbf{B}\mathbf{X}$

> matrix glsaccum $\mathbf{A}$ = *varlist* $\big[$ *if* $\big]$ $\big[$ *in* $\big]$ $\big[$ *weight* $\big]$, group(*groupvar*)
>
> glsmat($\mathbf{W}$ | *stringvar*) row(*rowvar*) $\big[$ noconstant $\big]$

Accumulate cross-product matrices to form $\sum \mathbf{X}_i'\mathbf{e}_i\mathbf{e}_i'\mathbf{X}_i$

> matrix opaccum $\mathbf{A}$ = *varlist* $\big[$ *if* $\big]$ $\big[$ *in* $\big]$, group(*groupvar*)
>
> opvar(*opvar*) $\big[$ noconstant $\big]$

Accumulate first variable against remaining variables

> matrix vecaccum $\mathbf{a}$ = *varlist* $\big[$ *if* $\big]$ $\big[$ *in* $\big]$ $\big[$ *weight* $\big]$ $\big[$, noconstant $\big]$

varlist in matrix accum and in matrix vecaccum may contain factor variables (except for the first variable in matrix vecaccum *varlist*); see [U] **11.4.3 Factor variables**.

varlist may contain time-series operators; see [U] **11.4.4 Time-series varlists**.

aweights, fweights, iweights, and pweights are allowed; see [U] **11.1.6 weight**.

Description

matrix accum accumulates cross-product matrices from the data to form $\mathbf{A} = \mathbf{X}'\mathbf{X}$.

matrix glsaccum accumulates cross-product matrices from the data by using a specified inner weight matrix to form $\mathbf{A} = \mathbf{X}'\mathbf{B}\mathbf{X}$, where $\mathbf{B}$ is a block diagonal matrix.

matrix opaccum accumulates cross-product matrices from the data by using an inner weight matrix formed from the outer product of a variable in the data to form

$$\mathbf{A} = \mathbf{X}_1'\mathbf{e}_1\mathbf{e}_1'\mathbf{X}_1 + \mathbf{X}_2'\mathbf{e}_2\mathbf{e}_2'\mathbf{X}_2 + \cdots + \mathbf{X}_K'\mathbf{e}_K\mathbf{e}_K'\mathbf{X}_K$$

where $\mathbf{X}_i$ is a matrix of observations from the ith group of the *varlist* variables and $\mathbf{e}_i$ is a vector formed from the observations in the ith group of the *opvar* variable.

matrix vecaccum accumulates the first variable against remaining variables in *varlist* to form a row vector of accumulated inner products to form $\mathbf{a} = \mathbf{x}_1'\mathbf{X}$, where $\mathbf{X} = (\mathbf{x}_2, \mathbf{x}_3, \dots)$.

Also see [M-5] **cross( )** for other routines for forming cross-product matrices.

Options

noconstant suppresses the addition of a "constant" to the $\mathbf{X}$ matrix. If noconstant is not specified, it is as if a column of 1s is added to $\mathbf{X}$ before the accumulation begins. For instance, for matrix accum without noconstant, $\mathbf{X}'\mathbf{X}$ is really $(\mathbf{X}, \mathbf{1})'(\mathbf{X}, \mathbf{1})$, resulting in

$$\begin{pmatrix} \mathbf{X}'\mathbf{X} & \mathbf{X}'\mathbf{1} \\ \mathbf{1}'\mathbf{X} & \mathbf{1}'\mathbf{1} \end{pmatrix}$$

Thus the last row and column contain the sums of the columns of $\mathbf{X}$, and the element in the last row and column contains the number of observations. If p variables are specified in *varlist*, the resulting matrix is $(p+1) \times (p+1)$. Specifying noconstant suppresses the addition of this row and column (or just the column for matrix vecaccum).

deviations, allowed only with matrix accum, causes the accumulation to be performed in terms of deviations from the mean. If noconstant is not specified, the accumulation of $\mathbf{X}$ is done in terms of deviations, but the added row and column of sums are not in deviation format (in which case they would be zeros). With noconstant specified, the resulting matrix, divided through by $N - 1$, where N is the number of observations, is a covariance matrix.

means(**m**), allowed only with matrix accum, creates matrix **m**: $1 \times (p+1)$ or $1 \times p$ (depending on whether noconstant is also specified) containing the means of $\mathbf{X}$.

group(*groupvar*) is required with matrix glsaccum and matrix opaccum and is not allowed otherwise. In the two cases where it is required, it specifies the name of a variable that identifies groups of observations. The data must be sorted by *groupvar*.

In matrix glsaccum, *groupvar* identifies the observations to be individually weighted by glsmat().

In matrix opaccum, *groupvar* identifies the observations to be weighted by the outer product of opvar().

glsmat(**W** | *stringvar*), required with matrix glsaccum and not allowed otherwise, specifies the name of the matrix or the name of a string variable in the dataset that contains the name of the matrix that is to be used to weight the observations in group(). *stringvar* must be str8 or less.

row(*rowvar*), required with matrix glsaccum and not allowed otherwise, specifies the name of a numeric variable containing the row numbers that specify the row and column of the glsmat() matrix to use in the inner-product calculation.

opvar(*opvar*), required with matrix opaccum, specifies the variable used to form the vector whose outer product forms the weighting matrix.

Remarks

Remarks are presented under the following headings:

> *matrix accum*
> *matrix glsaccum*
> *matrix opaccum*
> *matrix vecaccum*
> *Treatment of user-specified weights*

matrix accum

`matrix accum` is a straightforward command that accumulates one matrix that holds $\mathbf{X}'\mathbf{X}$ and $\mathbf{X}'\mathbf{y}$, which is typically used in $\mathbf{b} = (\mathbf{X}'\mathbf{X})^{-1}\mathbf{X}'\mathbf{y}$. Say that we wish to run a regression of the variable `price` on `mpg` and `weight`. We can begin by accumulating the full cross-product matrix for all three variables:

```
. use http://www.stata-press.com/data/r11/auto
. matrix accum A = price weight mpg
(obs=74)
. matrix list A

symmetric A[4,4]
             price      weight         mpg       _cons
 price   3.448e+09
weight   1.468e+09   7.188e+08
   mpg     9132716     4493720       36008
 _cons      456229      223440        1576          74
```

In our accumulation, `matrix accum` automatically added a constant; we specified three variables and got back a 4×4 matrix. The constant term is always added last. In terms of our regression model, the matrix we just accumulated has $\mathbf{y} = $ `price` and $\mathbf{X} = $ (`weight, mpg, _cons`) and can be written as

$$\mathbf{A} = \left(\mathbf{y}, \mathbf{X}\right)'\left(\mathbf{y}, \mathbf{X}\right) = \begin{pmatrix} \mathbf{y}'\mathbf{y} & \mathbf{y}'\mathbf{X} \\ \mathbf{X}'\mathbf{y} & \mathbf{X}'\mathbf{X} \end{pmatrix}$$

Thus we can extract $\mathbf{X}'\mathbf{X}$ from the submatrix of $\mathbf{A}$ beginning at the second row and column, and we can extract $\mathbf{X}'\mathbf{y}$ from the first column of $\mathbf{A}$, omitting the first row:

```
. matrix XX = A[2...,2...]
. matrix list XX

symmetric XX[3,3]
             weight         mpg       _cons
weight   7.188e+08
   mpg     4493720       36008
 _cons      223440        1576          74
. matrix Xy = A[2...,1]
. matrix list Xy

Xy[3,1]
               price
weight   1.468e+09
   mpg     9132716
 _cons      456229
```

We can now calculate $\mathbf{b} = (\mathbf{X}'\mathbf{X})^{-1}\mathbf{X}'\mathbf{y}$:

```
. matrix b = invsym(XX)*Xy
. matrix list b

b[3,1]
               price
weight   1.7465592
   mpg  -49.512221
 _cons   1946.0687
```

The same result could have been obtained directly from $\mathbf{A}$:

```
. matrix b = invsym(A[2...,2...])*A[2...,1]
```

❑ Technical note

matrix accum, with the deviations and noconstant options, can also be used to obtain covariance matrices. The covariance between variables x_i and x_j is defined as

$$C_{ij} = \frac{\sum_{k=1}^{n}(x_{ik} - \overline{x}_i)(x_{jk} - \overline{x}_j)}{n - 1}$$

Without the deviations option, matrix accum calculates a matrix with elements

$$R_{ij} = \sum_{k=1}^{n} x_{ik}x_{jk}$$

and with the deviations option,

$$A_{ij} = \sum_{k=1}^{n}(x_{ik} - \overline{x}_i)(x_{jk} - \overline{x}_j)$$

Thus the covariance matrix $\mathbf{C} = \mathbf{A}/(n - 1)$.

```
. matrix accum Cov = price weight mpg, deviations noconstant
(obs=74)
. matrix Cov = Cov/(r(N)-1)
. matrix list Cov
symmetric Cov[3,3]
              price       weight          mpg
 price      8699526
weight    1234674.8    604029.84
   mpg   -7996.2829   -3629.4261    33.472047
```

In addition to calculating the cross-product matrix, matrix accum records the number of observations in r(N), a feature we use in calculating the normalizing factor. With the corr() matrix function defined in [P] **matrix define**, we can convert the covariance matrix into a correlation matrix:

```
. matrix P = corr(Cov)
. matrix list P
symmetric P[3,3]
              price       weight          mpg
 price            1
weight    .53861146            1
   mpg   -.46859669   -.80717486            1
```

◁

matrix glsaccum

matrix glsaccum is a generalization of matrix accum useful in producing GLS-style weighted accumulations. Whereas matrix accum produces matrices of the form $\mathbf{X}'\mathbf{X}$, matrix glsaccum produces matrices of the form $\mathbf{X}'\mathbf{B}\mathbf{X}$, where

$$B = \begin{pmatrix} \mathbf{W}_1 & 0 & \cdots & 0 \\ 0 & \mathbf{W}_2 & \cdots & 0 \\ \vdots & \vdots & \ddots & \vdots \\ 0 & 0 & \cdots & \mathbf{W}_K \end{pmatrix}$$

The matrices $\mathbf{W}_k$, $k = 1, \ldots, K$ are called the weighting matrices for observation group k. In the matrices above, each of the $\mathbf{W}_k$ matrices is square, but there is no assumption that they all have the same dimension. By writing

$$\mathbf{X} = \begin{pmatrix} \mathbf{X}_1 \\ \mathbf{X}_2 \\ \vdots \\ \mathbf{X}_K \end{pmatrix}$$

the accumulation made by `matrix glsaccum` can be written as

$$\mathbf{X}'\mathbf{B}\mathbf{X} = \mathbf{X}_1'\mathbf{W}_1\mathbf{X}_1 + \mathbf{X}_2'\mathbf{W}_2\mathbf{X}_2 + \cdots + \mathbf{X}_K'\mathbf{W}_K\mathbf{X}_K$$

`matrix glsaccum` requires you to specify three options: `group(`*groupvar*`)`, `glsmat(`*stringvar*`)` or `glsmat(`*matvar*`)`, and `row(`*rowvar*`)`. Observations sharing the same value of *groupvar* are said to be in the same observation group—this specifies the group, k, in which they are to be accumulated. Before calling `matrix glsaccum`, you must `sort` the data by *groupvar*. How $\mathbf{W}_k$ is assembled is the subject of the other two options.

Think of there being a superweighting matrix for the group, which we will call $\mathbf{V}_k$. $\mathbf{V}_k$ is specified by `glsmat()`. The same supermatrix can be used for all observations by specifying a *matname* as the argument to `glsmat()`, or, if a variable name is specified, different supermatrices can be specified—the contents of the variable will be used to obtain the particular name of the supermatrix. (More correctly, the contents of the variable for the first observation in the group will be used: supermatrices can vary across groups but must be the same within group.)

Weighting matrix $\mathbf{W}_k$ is made from supermatrix $\mathbf{V}_k$ by selecting the rows and columns specified in `row(`*rowvar*`)`. In the simple case, $\mathbf{W}_k = \mathbf{V}_k$. This happens when there are m observations in the group and the first observation in the group has *rowvar* $= 1$, the second has *rowvar* $= 2$, and so on. To fix ideas, let $m = 3$ and write

$$\mathbf{V}_1 = \begin{pmatrix} v_{11} & v_{12} & v_{13} \\ v_{21} & v_{22} & v_{23} \\ v_{31} & v_{32} & v_{33} \end{pmatrix}$$

$\mathbf{V}$ need not be symmetric. Let's pretend that the first 4 observations in our dataset contain

obs. no.	*groupvar*	*rowvar*
1	1	1
2	1	2
3	1	3
4	2	...

In these data, the first 3 observations are in the first group because they share an equal *groupvar*. It is not important that *groupvar* happens to equal 1; it is important that the values are equal. The *rowvars* are, in order, 1, 2, and 3, so $\mathbf{W}_1$ is formed by selecting the first row and column of $\mathbf{V}_1$, then the second row and column of $\mathbf{V}_1$, and finally the third row and column of $\mathbf{V}_1$:

$$\mathbf{W}_1 = \begin{pmatrix} v_{11} & v_{12} & v_{13} \\ v_{21} & v_{22} & v_{23} \\ v_{31} & v_{32} & v_{33} \end{pmatrix}$$

or $\mathbf{W}_1 = \mathbf{V}_1$. Now consider the same data, but reordered:

obs. no.	groupvar	rowvar
1	1	2
2	1	1
3	1	3
4	2	...

$\mathbf{W}_1$ is now formed by selecting the second row and column, then the first row and column, and finally the third row and column of $\mathbf{V}_1$. These steps can be performed sequentially, reordering first the rows and then the columns; the result is

$$\mathbf{W}_1 = \begin{pmatrix} v_{22} & v_{21} & v_{23} \\ v_{12} & v_{11} & v_{13} \\ v_{32} & v_{31} & v_{33} \end{pmatrix}$$

This reorganization of the $\mathbf{W}_1$ matrix exactly undoes the reorganization of the $\mathbf{X}_1$ matrix, so $\mathbf{X}_1'\mathbf{W}_1\mathbf{X}_1$ remains unchanged. Given how $\mathbf{W}_k$ is assembled from $\mathbf{V}_k$, the order of the row numbers in the data does not matter.

matrix glsaccum is willing to carry this concept even further. Consider the following data:

obs. no.	groupvar	rowvar
1	1	1
2	1	3
3	1	3
4	2	...

Now *rowvar* equals 1 followed by 3 twice, so the first row and column of $\mathbf{V}_1$ are selected, followed by the third row and column twice; the second column is never selected. The resulting weighting matrix is

$$\mathbf{W}_1 = \begin{pmatrix} v_{11} & v_{13} & v_{13} \\ v_{31} & v_{33} & v_{33} \\ v_{31} & v_{33} & v_{33} \end{pmatrix}$$

Such odd weighting would not occur in, say, time-series analysis, where the matrix might be weighting lags and leads. It could well occur in an analysis of individuals in families, where 1 might indicate the head of household, 2 a spouse, and 3 a child. In fact, such a case could be handled with a 3×3 superweighting matrix V, even if the family became large: the appropriate weighting matrix $\mathbf{W}_k$ would be assembled, on a group-by-group (family-by-family) basis, from the underlying supermatrix.

matrix opaccum

matrix opaccum is a special case of matrix glsaccum. matrix glsaccum calculates results of the form

$$\mathbf{A} = \mathbf{X}_1'\mathbf{W}_1\mathbf{X}_1 + \mathbf{X}_2'\mathbf{W}_2\mathbf{X}_2 + \cdots + \mathbf{X}_K'\mathbf{W}_K\mathbf{X}_K$$

Often $\mathbf{W}_i$ is simply the outer product of another variable in the dataset; i.e.,

$$\mathbf{W}_i = \mathbf{e}_i\mathbf{e}_i'$$

where $\mathbf{e}_i$ is the $n_i \times 1$ vector formed from the n_i groupvar() observations of the variable specified in opvar(). The data must be sorted by *groupvar*.

▷ Example 1

Suppose that we have a panel dataset that contains five variables: id, t, e (a residual), and covariates x1 and x2. Further suppose that we need to compute

$$\mathbf{A} = \mathbf{X}_1' \mathbf{e}_1 \mathbf{e}_1' \mathbf{X}_1 + \mathbf{X}_2' \mathbf{e}_2 \mathbf{e}_2' \mathbf{X}_2 + \cdots + \mathbf{X}_K' \mathbf{e}_K \mathbf{e}_K' \mathbf{X}_K$$

where $\mathbf{X}_i$ contains the observations on x1 and x2 when id==i and $\mathbf{e}_i$ contains the observations on e when id==i.

Below is the output from xtdescribe for our example data. There are 11 groups and the number of observations per group is not constant.

```
. use http://www.stata-press.com/data/r11/maccumxmpl
. xtdescribe, patterns(11)
    id:  1, 2, ..., 11                                n =          11
     t:  1, 2, ..., 15                                T =          15
         Delta(t) = 1 unit
         Span(t)  = 15 periods
         (id*t uniquely identifies each observation)

Distribution of T_i:   min    5%    25%    50%    75%    95%    max
                         5     5      7     10     13     15     15

      Freq.  Percent    Cum. |  Pattern
  -----------------------------+-----------------
          1     9.09    9.09 |  11111.........
          1     9.09   18.18 |  111111........
          1     9.09   27.27 |  1111111.......
          1     9.09   36.36 |  11111111......
          1     9.09   45.45 |  111111111.....
          1     9.09   54.55 |  1111111111....
          1     9.09   63.64 |  11111111111...
          1     9.09   72.73 |  111111111111..
          1     9.09   81.82 |  1111111111111.
          1     9.09   90.91 |  11111111111111.
          1     9.09  100.00 |  111111111111111
  -----------------------------+-----------------
         11   100.00         |  XXXXXXXXXXXXXXX
```

If we were to calculate $\mathbf{A}$ with matrix glsaccum, we would need to form 11 matrices and store their names in a string variable before calling matrix glsaccum. This step slows down matrix glsaccum when there are many groups. Also all the information contained in the $\mathbf{W}_i$ matrices is contained in the variable e. It is this structure that matrix opaccum exploits to make a faster command for this type of problem:

```
. sort id t
. matrix opaccum  A = x1 x2, group(id) opvar(e)
```

◁

matrix vecaccum

The first variable in *varlist* is treated differently from the others by `matrix vecaccum`. Think of the first variable as specifying vector $\mathbf{y}$ and the remaining variables as specifying matrix $\mathbf{X}$. `matrix vecaccum` makes the accumulation $\mathbf{y}'\mathbf{X}$ to return a row vector with elements

$$a_i = \sum_{k=1}^{n} y_k x_{ki}$$

Like `matrix accum`, `matrix vecaccum` adds a constant, `_cons`, to $\mathbf{X}$ unless `noconstant` is specified.

`matrix vecaccum` serves two purposes. First, terms like $\mathbf{y}'\mathbf{X}$ often occur in calculating derivatives of likelihood functions; `matrix vecaccum` provides a fast way of calculating them. Second, it is useful in time-series accumulations of the form

$$\mathbf{C} = \sum_{t=1}^{T} \sum_{\delta=-k}^{k} \mathbf{x}'_{t-\delta} \mathbf{x}_t W_\delta r_{t-\delta} r_t$$

In this calculation, $\mathbf{X}$ is an observation matrix with elements x_{tj}, with t indexing time (observations) and j variables, $t = 1, \ldots, T$ and $j = 1, \ldots, p$. $\mathbf{x}_t$ ($1 \times p$) refers to the tth row of this matrix. Thus $\mathbf{C}$ is a $p \times p$ matrix.

The Newey–West covariance matrix uses the definition $W_\delta = 1 - |\delta|/(k+1)$ for $\delta \leq k$. To make the calculation, the user (programmer) cycles through each of the j variables, forming

$$z_{tj} = \sum_{\delta=-k}^{k} x_{(t-\delta)j} W_\delta r_{t-\delta} r_t$$

Writing $\mathbf{z}_j = (z_{1j}, z_{2j}, \ldots, z_{Tj})'$, we can then say that $\mathbf{C}$ is

$$\mathbf{C} = \sum_{j=1}^{p} \mathbf{z}'_j \mathbf{X}$$

In this derivation, the user must decide in advance the maximum lag length, k, such that observations that are far apart in time must have increasingly small covariances to establish the convergence results.

The Newey–West estimator is in the class of generalized method-of-moments (GMM) estimators. The choice of a maximum lag length, k, is a reflection of the length in time beyond which the autocorrelation becomes negligible for estimating the variance matrix. The code fragment given below is merely for illustration of the matrix commands, because Stata includes estimation with the Newey–West covariance matrix in the `newey` command. See [TS] **newey** or Greene (2008, 643) for details on this estimator.

Calculations like $\mathbf{z}'_j \mathbf{X}$ are made by `matrix vecaccum`, and $\mathbf{z}_j$ can be treated as a temporary variable in the dataset.

```
            assume '1','2', etc., contain the xs including constant
            assume 'r' contains the r variable
            assume 'k' contains the k range
            tempname C factor t c
            tempvar z

            local p : word count '*'
            matrix 'C' = J('p','p',0)
            gen double 'z' = 0
            forvalues d = 0/'k' {
                            /* Add each submatrix twice except for
                               the lag==0 case */
                scalar 'factor' = cond('d'>0, 1, .5)
```

```
local w = (1 - 'd'/('k'+1))
capture mat drop 't'
forvalues j = 1/'p' {
        replace 'z' = ''j''[_n-'d']*'w'*'r'[_n-'d']*'r'
        mat vecaccum 'c' = 'z' '*', nocons
        mat 't' = 't' \ 'c'
}
mat 'C' = 'C' + ('t' + 't'')*'factor'
}
local 'p' = "_cons"                    // Rename last var to _cons
mat rownames 'C' = '*'
mat colnames 'C' = '*'
```
assume inverse and scaling for standard-error reports

Treatment of user-specified weights

`matrix accum`, `matrix glsaccum`, and `matrix vecaccum` all allow weights. Here is how they are treated:

All three commands can be thought of as returning something of the form $\mathbf{X}_1'\mathbf{B}\mathbf{X}_2$. `matrix accum`, $\mathbf{X}_1 = \mathbf{X}_2$ and $\mathbf{B} = \mathbf{I}$; for `matrix glsaccum`, $\mathbf{X}_1 = \mathbf{X}_2$; and `matrix vecaccum`, $\mathbf{B} = \mathbf{I}$, $\mathbf{X}_1$ is a column vector and $\mathbf{X}_2$ is a matrix.

The commands really calculate $\mathbf{X}_1'\mathbf{W}^{1/2}\mathbf{B}\mathbf{W}^{1/2}\mathbf{X}_2$, where $\mathbf{W}$ is a diagonal matrix. If no weights are specified, $\mathbf{W} = \mathbf{I}$. Now assume that weights are specified, and let $\mathbf{v}: 1 \times n$ be the specified weights. If `fweights` or `pweights` are specified, $\mathbf{W} = \mathrm{diag}(\mathbf{v})$. If `aweights` are specified, $\mathbf{W} = \mathrm{diag}\{\mathbf{v}/(\mathbf{1}'\mathbf{v})(\mathbf{1}'\mathbf{1})\}$, meaning that the weights are normalized to sum to the number of observations. If `iweights` are specified, they are treated like `fweights`, except that the elements of $\mathbf{v}$ are not restricted to be positive integers.

Saved results

`matrix accum`, `matrix glsaccum`, `matrix opaccum`, and `matrix vecaccum` save the number of observations in `r(N)`. `matrix glsaccum` (with `aweights`) and `matrix vecaccum` also store the sum of the weight in `r(sum_w)`, but `matrix accum` does not.

Reference

Greene, W. H. 2008. *Econometric Analysis*. 6th ed. Upper Saddle River, NJ: Prentice–Hall.

Also see

[R] **ml** — Maximum likelihood estimation

[U] **14 Matrix expressions**

[P] **matrix** — Introduction to matrix commands

[M-4] **statistical** — Statistical functions

Title

---
matrix define — Matrix definition, operators, and functions

Syntax

Perform matrix computations

<u>matr</u>ix [<u>def</u>ine] *matname* = *matrix_expression*

Input matrices

<u>matr</u>ix [<u>input</u>] *matname* = (# [,# ...] [\ # [, # ...] [\ [...]]])

Menu

matrix define

Data > Matrices, ado language > Define matrix from expression

matrix input

Data > Matrices, ado language > Input matrix by hand

Description

matrix define performs matrix computations. The word define may be omitted.

matrix input provides a method for inputting matrices. The word input may be omitted (see the discussion that follows).

For an introduction and overview of matrices in Stata, see [U] **14 Matrix expressions**.

See [M-2] **exp** for matrix expressions in Mata.

Remarks

Remarks are presented under the following headings:

> *Introduction*
> *Inputting matrices by hand*
> *Matrix operators*
> *Matrix functions returning matrices*
> *Matrix functions returning scalars*
> *Subscripting and element-by-element definition*
> *Name conflicts in expressions (namespaces)*
> *Macro extended functions*

Introduction

`matrix define` calculates matrix results from other matrices. For instance,

```
. matrix define D = A + B + C
```

creates D containing the sum of A, B, and C. The word `define` may be omitted,

```
. matrix D = A + B + C
```

and the command may be further abbreviated:

```
. mat D=A+B+C
```

The same matrix may appear on both the left and the right of the equal sign in all contexts, and Stata will not become confused. Complicated matrix expressions are allowed.

With `matrix input`, you define the matrix elements rowwise; commas are used to separate elements within a row, and backslashes are used to separate the rows. Spacing does not matter.

```
. matrix input A = (1,2\3,4)
```

The above would also work if you omitted the `input` subcommand.

```
. matrix A = (1,2\3,4)
```

There is a subtle difference: the first method uses the `matrix input` command, and the second uses the matrix expression parser. Omitting `input` allows expressions in the command. For instance,

```
. matrix X = (1+1, 2*3/4 \ 5/2, 3)
```

is understood but

```
. matrix input X = (1+1, 2*3/4 \ 5/2, 3)
```

would produce an error.

`matrix input`, however, has two advantages. First, it allows input of large matrices. (The expression parser is limited because it must "compile" the expressions and, if the result is too long, will produce an error.) Second, `matrix input` allows you to omit the commas.

Inputting matrices by hand

Before turning to operations on matrices, let's examine how matrices are created. Typically, at least in programming situations, you obtain matrices by accessing one of Stata's internal matrices (e(b) and e(V); see [P] **matrix get**) or by accumulating it from the data (see [P] **matrix accum**). Nevertheless, the easiest way to create a matrix is to enter it using `matrix input`—this may not be the normal way to create matrices, but it is useful for performing small, experimental calculations.

⊳ Example 1

To create the matrix

$$\mathbf{A} = \begin{pmatrix} 1 & 2 \\ 3 & 4 \end{pmatrix}$$

type

```
. matrix A = (1,2 \ 3,4)
```

The spacing does not matter. To define the matrix

$$\mathbf{B} = \begin{pmatrix} 1 & 2 & 3 \\ 4 & . & 6 \end{pmatrix}$$

type

```
. matrix B = (1,2,3 \ 4,.,6)
```

To define the matrix

$$\mathbf{C} = \begin{pmatrix} 1 & 2 \\ 3 & 4 \\ 5 & 6 \end{pmatrix}$$

type

```
. matrix C = (1,2 \ 3,4 \ 5,6)
```

If you need more than one line, and you are working interactively, just keep typing; Stata will wrap the line around the screen. If you are working in a do- or ado-file, see [U] **16.1.3 Long lines in do-files**.

To create vectors, you enter the elements, separating them by commas or backslashes. To create the row vector

$$\mathbf{D} = \begin{pmatrix} 1 & 2 & 3 \end{pmatrix}$$

type

```
. matrix D = (1,2,3)
```

To create the column vector

$$\mathbf{E} = \begin{pmatrix} 1 \\ 2 \\ 3 \end{pmatrix}$$

type

```
. matrix E = (1\2\3)
```

To create the 1×1 matrix $\mathbf{F} = (2)$, type

```
. matrix F = (2)
```

In these examples, we have omitted the input subcommand. They would work either way.

◁

Matrix operators

In what follows, uppercase letters $\mathbf{A}$, $\mathbf{B}$, ... stand for matrix names. The matrix operators are

+, meaning addition. matrix $\mathbf{C=A+B}$, $\mathbf{A}$: $r \times c$ and $\mathbf{B}$: $r \times c$, creates $\mathbf{C}$: $r \times c$ containing the elementwise addition $\mathbf{A} + \mathbf{B}$. An error is issued if the matrices are not conformable. Row and column names are obtained from $\mathbf{B}$.

-, meaning subtraction or negation. matrix $\mathbf{C=A-B}$, $\mathbf{A}$: $r \times c$ and $\mathbf{B}$: $r \times c$, creates $\mathbf{C}$ containing the elementwise subtraction $\mathbf{A} - \mathbf{B}$. An error is issued if the matrices are not conformable. matrix $\mathbf{C=-A}$ creates $\mathbf{C}$ containing the elementwise negation of $\mathbf{A}$. Row and column names are obtained from $\mathbf{B}$.

*, meaning multiplication. `matrix C=A*B`, $\mathbf{A}$: $a \times b$ and $\mathbf{B}$: $b \times c$, returns $\mathbf{C}$: $a \times c$ containing the matrix product $\mathbf{AB}$; an error is issued if $\mathbf{A}$ and $\mathbf{B}$ are not conformable. The row names of $\mathbf{C}$ are obtained from the row names of $\mathbf{A}$, and the column names of $\mathbf{C}$ from the column names of $\mathbf{B}$.

`matrix C=A*s` or `matrix C=s*A`, $\mathbf{A}$: $a \times b$ and s a Stata scalar (see [P] **scalar**) or a literal number, returns $\mathbf{C}$: $a \times b$ containing the elements of $\mathbf{A}$ each multiplied by s. The row and column names of $\mathbf{C}$ are obtained from $\mathbf{A}$. For example, `matrix VC=MYMAT*2.5` multiplies each element of `MYMAT` by 2.5 and stores the result in `VC`.

/, meaning matrix division by scalar. `matrix C=A/s`, $\mathbf{A}$: $a \times b$ and s a Stata scalar (see [P] **scalar**) or a literal number, returns $\mathbf{C}$: $a \times b$ containing the elements of $\mathbf{A}$ each divided by s. The row and column names of $\mathbf{C}$ are obtained from $\mathbf{A}$.

#, meaning the Kronecker product. `matrix C=A#B`, $\mathbf{A}$: $a \times b$ and $\mathbf{B}$: $c \times d$, returns $\mathbf{C}$: $ac \times bd$ containing the Kronecker product $\mathbf{A} \otimes \mathbf{B}$, all elementwise products of $\mathbf{A}$ and $\mathbf{B}$. The upper-left submatrix of $\mathbf{C}$ is the product $A_{1,1}\mathbf{B}$; the submatrix to the right is $A_{1,2}\mathbf{B}$; and so on. Row and column names are obtained by using the subnames of $\mathbf{A}$ as resulting equation names and the subnames of $\mathbf{B}$ for the subnames of $\mathbf{C}$ in each submatrix.

Nothing, meaning copy. `matrix B=A` copies $\mathbf{A}$ into $\mathbf{B}$. The row and column names of $\mathbf{B}$ are obtained from $\mathbf{A}$. The `matrix rename` command (see [P] **matrix utility**) will rename instead of copy a matrix.

', meaning transpose. `matrix B=A'`, $\mathbf{A}$: $r \times c$, creates $\mathbf{B}$: $c \times r$ containing the transpose of $\mathbf{A}$. The row names of $\mathbf{B}$ are obtained from the column names of $\mathbf{A}$ and the column names of $\mathbf{B}$ from the row names of $\mathbf{A}$.

,, meaning join columns by row. `matrix C=A,B`, $\mathbf{A}$: $a \times b$ and $\mathbf{B}$: $a \times c$, returns $\mathbf{C}$: $a \times (b+c)$ containing $\mathbf{A}$ in columns 1 through b and $\mathbf{B}$ in columns $b+1$ through $b+c$ (the columns of $\mathbf{B}$ are appended to the columns of $\mathbf{A}$). An error is issued if the matrices are not conformable. The row names of $\mathbf{C}$ are obtained from $\mathbf{A}$. The column names are obtained from $\mathbf{A}$ and $\mathbf{B}$.

\, meaning join rows by column. `matrix C=A\B`, $\mathbf{A}$: $a \times b$ and $\mathbf{B}$: $c \times b$, returns $\mathbf{C}$: $(a+c) \times b$ containing $\mathbf{A}$ in rows 1 through a and $\mathbf{B}$ in rows $a+1$ through $a+c$ (the rows of $\mathbf{B}$ are appended to the rows of $\mathbf{A}$). An error is issued if the matrices are not conformable. The column names of $\mathbf{C}$ are obtained from $\mathbf{A}$. The row names are obtained from $\mathbf{A}$ and $\mathbf{B}$.

`matrix define` allows complicated matrix expressions. Parentheses may be used to control the order of evaluation. The default order of precedence for the matrix operators (from highest to lowest) is

Matrix operator precedence	
Operator	**Symbol**
parentheses	( )
transpose	'
negation	–
Kronecker product	#
division by scalar	/
multiplication	*
subtraction	–
addition	+
column join	,
row join	\

▷ Example 2

The following examples are artificial but informative:

```
. matrix A = (1,2\3,4)
. matrix B = (5,7\9,2)
. matrix C = A+B
. matrix list C

C[2,2]
     c1  c2
r1    6   9
r2   12   6

. matrix B = A-B
. matrix list B

B[2,2]
     c1  c2
r1   -4  -5
r2   -6   2

. matrix X = (1,1\2,5\8,0\4,5)
. matrix C = 3*X*A'*B
. matrix list C

C[4,2]
      c1    c2
r1  -162    -3
r2  -612   -24
r3  -528    24
r4  -744   -18

. matrix D = (X'*X - A'*A)/4
. matrix rownames D = dog cat       // see [P] matrix rownames
. matrix colnames D = bark meow     // see [P] matrix rownames
. matrix list D

symmetric D[2,2]
       bark    meow
dog   18.75
cat    4.25    7.75

. matrix rownames A = aa bb         // see [P] matrix rownames
. matrix colnames A = alpha beta    // see [P] matrix rownames
. matrix list A

A[2,2]
     alpha    beta
aa       1       2
bb       3       4

. matrix D=A#D
. matrix list D

D[4,4]
         alpha:  alpha:   beta:   beta:
          bark    meow    bark    meow
aa:dog   18.75    4.25    37.5     8.5
aa:cat    4.25    7.75     8.5    15.5
bb:dog   56.25   12.75      75      17
bb:cat   12.75   23.25      17      31

. matrix G=A,B\D
```

```
. matrix list G

G[6,4]
           alpha    beta      c1      c2
     aa        1       2      -4      -5
     bb        3       4      -6       2
 aa:dog    18.75    4.25    37.5     8.5
 aa:cat     4.25    7.75     8.5    15.5
 bb:dog    56.25   12.75      75      17
 bb:cat    12.75   23.25      17      31

. matrix Z = (B - A)'*(B + A'*-B)/4

. matrix list Z

Z[2,2]
            c1      c2
 alpha     -81    -1.5
  beta   -44.5     8.5
```

◁

❏ Technical note

Programmers: Watch out for confusion when combining ', meaning to transpose with local macros, where ' is one of the characters that enclose macro names: '*mname*'. Stata will not become confused, but you might. Compare:

```
. matrix 'new1' = 'old'
```

   and

```
. matrix 'new2' = 'old''
```

Matrix 'new2' contains matrix 'old', transposed. Stata will become confused if you type

```
. matrix 'C' = 'A'\'B'
```

because the backslash in front of the 'B' makes the macro processor take the left quote literally. No substitution is ever made for 'B'. Even worse, the macro processor assumes that the backslash was meant for it and so removes the character! Pretend that 'A' contained a, 'B' contained b, and 'C' contained c. After substitution, the line would read

```
. matrix c = a'B'
```

which is not at all what was intended. To make your meaning clear, put a space after the backslash,

```
. matrix 'C' = 'A'\ 'B'
```

which would then be expanded to read

```
. matrix c = a\ b
```

❏

Matrix functions returning matrices

In addition to matrix operators, Stata has matrix functions, which allow expressions to be passed as arguments. The following matrix functions are provided:

matrix **A**=I(*dim*) defines **A** as the *dim* × *dim* identity matrix, where *dim* is a scalar expression and will be rounded to the nearest integer. For example, matrix **A**=I(3) defines **A** as the 3 × 3 identity matrix.

`matrix A=J(`*r*`,`*c*`,`*z*`)` defines **A** as an $r \times c$ matrix containing elements *z*. *r*, *c*, and *z* are scalar expressions with *r* and *c* rounded to the nearest integer. For example, `matrix A=J(2,3,0)` returns a 2×3 matrix containing 0 for each element.

`matrix L=cholesky(`*mexp*`)` performs Cholesky decomposition. An error is issued if the matrix expression *mexp* does not evaluate to a square, symmetric matrix. For example, `matrix L=cholesky(A)` produces the lower triangular (square root) matrix **L**, such that $\mathbf{LL}' = \mathbf{A}$. The row and column names of **L** are obtained from **A**.

`matrix B=invsym(`*mexp*`)`, if *mexp* evaluates to a square, symmetric, and positive-definite matrix, returns the inverse. If *mexp* does not evaluate to a positive-definite matrix, rows will be inverted until the diagonal terms are zero or negative; the rows and columns corresponding to these terms will be set to 0, producing a g2-inverse. The row names of **B** are obtained from the column names of *mexp*, and the column names of **B** are obtained from the row names of *mexp*.

`matrix B=inv(`*mexp*`)`, if *mexp* evaluates to a square but not necessarily symmetric or positive-definite matrix, returns the inverse. A singular matrix will result in an error. The row names of **B** are obtained from the column names of *mexp*, and the column names of **B** are obtained from the row names of *mexp*. `invsym()` should be used in preference to `inv()`, which is less accurate, whenever possible. (Also see [P] **matrix svd** for singular value decomposition.)

`matrix B=sweep(`*mexp*`,`*n*`)` applies the sweep operator to the *n*th row and column of the square matrix resulting from the matrix expression *mexp*. *n* is a scalar expression and will be rounded to the nearest integer. The names of **B** are obtained from *mexp*, except that the *n*th row and column names are interchanged. For **A**: $n \times n$, **B** = `sweep(A,k)` produces **B**: $n \times n$, defined as

$$B_{kk} = \frac{1}{A_{kk}}$$

$$B_{ik} = -\frac{A_{ik}}{A_{kk}}, \qquad i \neq k \qquad (kth\ column)$$

$$B_{kj} = \frac{A_{ij}}{A_{kk}}, \qquad j \neq k \qquad (jth\ row)$$

$$B_{ij} = A_{ij} - \frac{A_{ik}A_{kj}}{A_{kk}}, \qquad i \neq k, j \neq k$$

`matrix B=corr(`*mexp*`)`, where *mexp* evaluates to a covariance matrix, stores the corresponding correlation matrix in **B**. The row and column names are obtained from *mexp*.

`matrix B=diag(`*mexp*`)`, where *mexp* evaluates to a row or column vector ($1 \times c$ or $c \times 1$), creates **B**: $c \times c$ with diagonal elements from *mexp* and off-diagonal elements 0. The row and column names are obtained from the column names of *mexp* if *mexp* is a row vector or the row names if *mexp* is a column vector.

`matrix B=vec(`*mexp*`)`, where *mexp* evaluates to an $r \times c$ matrix, creates **B**: $rc \times 1$ containing the elements of *mexp* starting with the first column and proceeding column by column.

`matrix B=vecdiag(`*mexp*`)`, where *mexp* evaluates to a square $c \times c$ matrix, creates **B**: $1 \times c$ containing the diagonal elements from *mexp*. `vecdiag()` is the opposite of `diag()`. The row name is set to `r1`. The column names are obtained from the column names of *mexp*.

`matrix B=matuniform(`*r*`,`*c*`)` creates **B**: $r \times c$ containing uniformly distributed pseudorandom numbers on the interval $[0, 1]$.

`matrix B=hadamard(`*mexp*`,` *nexp*`)`, where *mexp* and *nexp* evaluate to $r \times c$ matrices, creates a matrix whose (i, j) element is *mexp*$[i, j] \cdot$ *nexp*$[i, j]$. If *mexp* and *nexp* do not evaluate to matrices of the same size, this function reports a conformability error.

nullmat($\mathbf{B}$) may only be used with the row-join (,) and column-join (\) operators, and informs Stata that $\mathbf{B}$ might not exist. If $\mathbf{B}$ does not exist, the row-join or column-join operator simply returns the other matrix-operator argument. An example of the use of nullmat() is given in [D] **functions**.

matrix $\mathbf{B}$=get(*systemname*) returns in $\mathbf{B}$ a copy of the Stata internal matrix *systemname*; see [P] **matrix get**. You can obtain the coefficient vector and variance–covariance matrix after an estimation command either with matrix get or by reference to e(b) and e(V).

▷ Example 3

The examples are, once again, artificial but informative.

```
. matrix myid = I(3)
. matrix list myid
symmetric myid[3,3]
      c1   c2   c3
r1     1
r2     0    1
r3     0    0    1
. matrix new = J(2,3,0)
. matrix list new
new[2,3]
      c1   c2   c3
r1     0    0    0
r2     0    0    0
. matrix A = (1,2\2,5)
. matrix Ainv = syminv(A)
. matrix list Ainv
symmetric Ainv[2,2]
      r1   r2
c1     5
c2    -2    1
. matrix L = cholesky(4*I(2) + A'*A)
. matrix list L
L[2,2]
              c1           c2
c1             3            0
c2             4    4.1231056
. matrix B = (1,5,9\2,1,7\3,5,1)
. matrix Binv = inv(B)
. matrix list Binv
Binv[3,3]
               r1           r2           r3
c1    -.27419355    .32258065    .20967742
c2     .15322581   -.20967742    .08870968
c3     .05645161    .08064516   -.07258065
. matrix C = sweep(B,1)
. matrix list C
C[3,3]
       r1   c2   c3
c1      1    5    9
r2     -2   -9  -11
r3     -3  -10  -26
. matrix C = sweep(C,1)
```

```
. matrix list C
C[3,3]
     c1  c2  c3
r1   1   5   9
r2   2   1   7
r3   3   5   1
. matrix Cov = (36.6598,-3596.48\-3596.48,604030)
. matrix R = corr(Cov)
. matrix list R
symmetric R[2,2]
           c1          c2
r1          1
r2  -.7642815           1
. matrix d = (1,2,3)
. matrix D = diag(d)
. matrix list D
symmetric D[3,3]
     c1  c2  c3
c1   1
c2   0   2
c3   0   0   3
. matrix e = vec(D)
. matrix list e
e[9,1]
        c1
c1:c1   1
c1:c2   0
c1:c3   0
c2:c1   0
c2:c2   2
c2:c3   0
c3:c1   0
c3:c2   0
c3:c3   3
. matrix f =vecdiag(D)
. matrix list f
f[1,3]
     c1  c2  c3
r1   1   2   3
. * matrix function arguments can be other matrix functions and expressions
. matrix G = diag(inv(B) * vecdiag(diag(d) + 4*sweep(B+J(3,3,10),2)'*I(3))')
. matrix list G
symmetric G[3,3]
            c1          c2          c3
c1  -3.2170088
c2           0  -7.686217
c3           0           0   2.3548387
. matrix U = matuniform(3,4)
. matrix list U
U[3,4]
           c1          c2          c3          c4
r1  .87169105   .46114288   .42167263   .89447457
r2  .05806615   .67594873   .71528048   .69906904
r3  .23226877   .09818778    .5948404   .35338737
. matrix H = hadamard(B,C)
```

```
. matrix list H
H[3,3]
      c1  c2  c3
r1     1  25  81
r2     4   1  49
r3     9  25   1
```

◁

Matrix functions returning scalars

In addition to the above functions used with `matrix define`, which can be described as matrix functions returning matrices, there are matrix functions that return mathematical scalars. The list of functions that follow should be viewed as a continuation of [U] **13.3 Functions**. If the functions listed below are used in a scalar context (for example, used with `display` or `generate`), then $\mathbf{A}$, $\mathbf{B}$, ... below stand for matrix names (possibly as a string literal or string variable name—details later). If the functions below are used in a matrix context (in `matrix define` for instance), then $\mathbf{A}$, $\mathbf{B}$, ... may also stand for matrix expressions.

`rowsof(`$\mathbf{A}$`)` and `colsof(`$\mathbf{A}$`)` return the number of rows or columns of $\mathbf{A}$.

`rownumb(`$\mathbf{A}$`,`*string*`)` and `colnumb(`$\mathbf{A}$`,`*string*`)` return the row or column number associated with the name specified by *string*. For instance, `rownumb(MYMAT,"price")` returns the row number (say, 3) in `MYMAT` that has the name `price` (subname `price` and equation name blank). `colnumb(MYMAT,"out2:price")` returns the column number associated with the name `out2:price` (subname `price` and equation name `out2`). If row or column name is not found, missing is returned.

`rownumb()` and `colnumb()` can also return the first row or column number associated with an equation name. For example, `colnumb(MYMAT,"out2:")` returns the first column number in `MYMAT` that has equation name `out2`. Missing is returned if the equation name `out2` is not found.

`trace(`$\mathbf{A}$`)` returns the sum of the diagonal elements of square matrix $\mathbf{A}$. If $\mathbf{A}$ is not square, missing is returned.

`det(`$\mathbf{A}$`)` returns the determinant of square matrix $\mathbf{A}$. The determinant is the volume of the $(p-1)$-dimensional manifold described by the matrix in p-dimensional space. If $\mathbf{A}$ is not square, missing is returned.

`diag0cnt(`$\mathbf{A}$`)` returns the number of zeros on the diagonal of the square matrix $\mathbf{A}$. If $\mathbf{A}$ is not square, missing is returned.

`issymmetric(`$\mathbf{A}$`)` returns 1 if the matrix is symmetric and 0 otherwise.

`matmissing(`$\mathbf{A}$`)` returns 1 if any elements of the matrix are missing and 0 otherwise.

`mreldif(`$\mathbf{A}$`,`$\mathbf{B}$`)` returns the relative difference of matrix $\mathbf{A}$ and $\mathbf{B}$. If $\mathbf{A}$ and $\mathbf{B}$ do not have the same dimensions, missing is returned. The matrix relative difference is defined as

$$\max_{i,j}\left(\frac{|\mathbf{A}[i,j]-\mathbf{B}[i,j]|}{|\mathbf{B}[i,j]|+1}\right)$$

`el(`$\mathbf{A}$`,`i`,`j`)` and $\mathbf{A}[i,j]$ return the (i,j) element of $\mathbf{A}$. Usually either construct may be used; `el(MYMAT,2,3)` and `MYMAT[2,3]` are equivalent, although `MYMAT[2,3]` is more readable. For the second construct, however, $\mathbf{A}$ must be a matrix name—it cannot be a string literal or string variable. The first construct allows $\mathbf{A}$ to be a matrix name, string literal, or string variable. For instance, assume that `mymat` (as opposed to `MYMAT`) is a string variable in the dataset containing matrix names. `mymat[2,3]` refers to the $(2, 3)$ element of the matrix named `mymat`, a matrix that probably does not exist, and so produces an error. `el(mymat,2,3)` refers to the data variable `mymat`; the contents of that variable will be taken to obtain the matrix name, and `el()` will then return the $(2, 3)$ element of that matrix. If that matrix does not exist, Stata will not issue an error; because you referred to it indirectly, the `el()` function will return missing.

In either construct, i and j may be any expression (an *exp*) evaluating to a real. `MYMAT[2,3+1]` returns the $(2, 4)$ element. In programs that loop, you might refer to `MYMAT['i','j'+1]`.

In a matrix context (such as `matrix define`), the first argument of `el()` may be a matrix expression. For instance, `matrix A = B*el(B-C,1,1)` is allowed, but `display el(B-C,1,1)` would be an error because `display` is in a scalar context.

The matrix functions returning scalars defined above can be used in any context that allows an expression—what is abbreviated *exp* in the syntax diagrams throughout this manual. For instance, `trace()` returns the (scalar) trace of a matrix. Say that you have a matrix called `MYX`. You could type

> . generate tr = trace(MYX)

although this would be a silly thing to do. It would force Stata to evaluate the trace of the matrix many times, once for each observation in the data, and it would then store that same result over and over again in the new data variable `tr`. But you could do it because, if you examine the syntax diagram for `generate` (see [D] **generate**), `generate` allows an *exp*.

If you just wanted to see the trace of `MYX`, you could type

> . display trace(MYX)

because the syntax diagram for `display` also allows an *exp*; see [P] **display**. You could do either of the following:

> . local tr = trace(MYX)
>
> . scalar tr = trace(MYX)

This is more useful because it will evaluate the trace only once and then store the result. In the first case, the result will be stored in a local macro (see [P] **macro**); in the second, it will be stored in a Stata scalar (see [P] **scalar**).

▷ Example 4

Storing the number as a scalar is better for two reasons: it is more accurate (scalars are stored in double precision), and it is faster (macros are stored as printable characters, and this conversion is a time-consuming operation). Not too much should be made of the accuracy issue; macros are stored with at least 13 digits, but it can sometimes make a difference.

In any case, let's demonstrate that both methods work by using the simple trace function:

> . matrix A = (1,6\8,4)
>
> . local tr = trace(A)
>
> . display 'tr'
> 5
>
> . scalar sctr = trace(A)
>
> . scalar list sctr
>   sctr =   5

◁

❏ Technical note

The use of a matrix function returning scalar with `generate` does not have to be silly because, instead of specifying a matrix name, you may specify a string variable in the dataset. If you do, in each observation the contents of the string variable will be taken as a matrix name, and the function will be applied to that matrix for that observation. If there is no such matrix, missing will be returned. Thus if your dataset contained

```
. list
```

	matname
1.	X1
2.	X2
3.	Z

you could type

```
. generate tr = trace(matname)
(1 missing value generated)
. list
```

	matname	tr
1.	X1	5
2.	X2	.
3.	Z	16

Evidently, we have no matrix called X2 stored. All the matrix functions returning scalars allow you to specify either a matrix name directly or a string variable that indirectly specifies the matrix name. When you indirectly specify the matrix and the matrix does not exist—as happened above—the function evaluates to missing. When you directly specify the matrix and it does not exist, you get an error:

```
. display trace(X2)
X2 not found
r(111);
```

This is true not only for `trace()` but also for every matrix function that returns a scalar described above.

❏

Subscripting and element-by-element definition

`matrix` $\mathbf{B}=\mathbf{A}[r_1,r_2]$, for range expressions r_1 and r_2 (defined below), extracts a submatrix from $\mathbf{A}$ and stores it in $\mathbf{B}$. Row and column names of $\mathbf{B}$ are obtained from the extracted rows and columns of $\mathbf{A}$. In what follows, assume that $\mathbf{A}$ is $a \times b$.

A range expression can be a literal number. For example, `matrix` $\mathbf{B}=\mathbf{A}[1,2]$ would return a 1×1 matrix containing $A_{1,2}$.

A range expression can be a number followed by two periods followed by another number, meaning the rows or columns from the first number to the second. For example, `matrix` $\mathbf{B}=\mathbf{A}[2..4,1..5]$ would return a 3×5 matrix containing the second through fourth rows and the first through fifth columns of $\mathbf{A}$.

A range expression can be a number followed by three periods, meaning all the remaining rows or columns from that number. For example, `matrix B=A[3,4...]` would return a $1 \times b - 3$ matrix (row vector) containing the fourth through last elements of the third row of **A**.

A range expression can be a quoted string, in which case it refers to the row or column with the specified name. For example, `matrix B=A["price","mpg"]` returns a 1×1 matrix containing the element whose row name is `price` and column name is `mpg`, which would be the same as `matrix B=A[2,3]` if the second row were named `price` and the third column `mpg`. `matrix B=A["price",1...]` would return the $1 \times b$ vector corresponding to the row named `price`. In either case, if there is no matrix row or column with the specified name, an error is issued, and the return code is set to 111. If the row or column names include both an equation name and a subname, the fully qualified name must be specified, as in `matrix B=A["eq1:price",1...]`.

A range expression can be a quoted string containing only an equation name, in which case it refers to all rows or columns with the specified equation name. For example, `matrix B=A["eq1:","eq1:"]` would return the submatrix of rows and columns that have equation names `eq1`.

A range expression containing a quoted string referring to an element (not to an entire equation) can be combined with the `..` and `...` syntaxes above: For example, `matrix B=A["price"...,"price"...]` would define **B** as the submatrix of **A** beginning with the rows and columns corresponding to `price`. `matrix B=A["price".."mpg","price".."mpg"]` would define **B** as the submatrix of **A** starting at rows and columns corresponding to `price` and continuing through the rows and columns corresponding to `mpg`.

A range expression can be mixed. For example, `matrix B=A[1.."price",2]` defines **B** as the column vector extracted from the second column of **A** containing the first element through the element corresponding to `price`.

Scalar expressions may be used in place of literal numbers. The resulting number will be rounded to the nearest integer. Subscripting with scalar expressions may be used in any expression context (such as `generate` or `replace`). Subscripting with row and column names may be used only in a matrix expression context. This is really not a constraint; see the `rownumb()` and `colnumb()` functions discussed previously in the section titled *Matrix functions returning scalars*.

`matrix A[r,c]=`*exp* changes the *r,c* element of **A** to contain the result of the evaluated scalar expression, as defined in [U] **13 Functions and expressions**, and as further defined in *Matrix functions returning scalars*. *r* and *c* may be scalar expressions and will be rounded to the nearest integer. The matrix **A** must already exist; the matrix function `J()` can be used to achieve this.

`matrix A[r,c]=`*mexp* places the matrix resulting from the *mexp* matrix expression into the already existing matrix **A**, with the upper-left corner of the *mexp* matrix located at the *r,c* element of **A**. If there is not enough room to place the *mexp* matrix at that location, a conformability error will be issued, and the return code will be set to 503. *r* and *c* may be scalar expressions and will be rounded to the nearest integer.

▷ Example 5

Continuing with our artificial but informative examples,

```
. matrix A = (1,2,3,4\5,6,7,8\9,10,11,12\13,14,15,16)
. matrix rownames A = mercury venus earth mars
. matrix colnames A = poor average good exc
```

```
. matrix list A
A[4,4]
           poor   average     good      exc
mercury       1         2        3        4
  venus       5         6        7        8
  earth       9        10       11       12
   mars      13        14       15       16
. matrix b = A[1,2..3]
. matrix list b
b[1,2]
         average     good
mercury       2        3
. matrix b = A[2...,1..3]
. matrix list b
b[3,3]
         poor   average     good
venus       5         6        7
earth       9        10       11
 mars      13        14       15
. matrix b = A["venus".."earth","average"...]
. matrix list b
b[2,3]
         average     good      exc
venus         6        7        8
earth        10       11       12
. matrix b = A["mars",2...]
. matrix list b
b[1,3]
       average     good      exc
mars      14        15       16
. matrix b = A[sqrt(9)+1..substr("xmars",2,4),2.8..2*2]  /* strange but valid */
. mat list b
b[1,2]
       good    exc
mars     15     16
. matrix rownames A = eq1:alpha eq1:beta eq2:alpha eq2:beta
. matrix colnames A = eq1:one eq1:two eq2:one eq2:two
. matrix list A
A[4,4]
            eq1:   eq1:   eq2:   eq2:
            one    two    one    two
eq1:alpha     1      2      3      4
 eq1:beta     5      6      7      8
eq2:alpha     9     10     11     12
 eq2:beta    13     14     15     16
. matrix b = A["eq1:","eq2:"]
. matrix list b
b[2,2]
            eq2:   eq2:
            one    two
eq1:alpha     3      4
 eq1:beta     7      8
. matrix A[3,2] = sqrt(9)
```

```
. matrix list A
A[4,4]
              eq1:   eq1:   eq2:   eq2:
              one    two    one    two
eq1:alpha       1      2      3      4
 eq1:beta       5      6      7      8
eq2:alpha       9      3     11     12
 eq2:beta      13     14     15     16
. matrix X = (-3,0\-1,-6)
. matrix A[1,3] = X
. matrix list A
A[4,4]
              eq1:   eq1:   eq2:   eq2:
              one    two    one    two
eq1:alpha       1      2     -3      0
 eq1:beta       5      6     -1     -6
eq2:alpha       9      3     11     12
 eq2:beta      13     14     15     16
```

◁

❏ Technical note

matrix $A[i,j]$=*exp* can be used to implement matrix formulas that perhaps Stata does not have built in. Let's pretend that Stata could not multiply matrices. We could still multiply matrices, and after some work, we could do so conveniently. Given two matrices, **A**: $a \times b$ and **B**: $b \times c$, the (i,j) element of $\mathbf{C} = \mathbf{AB}$, **C**: $a \times c$, is defined as

$$C_{ij} = \sum_{k=1}^{b} A_{ik} B_{kj}$$

Here is a Stata program to make that calculation:

```
program matmult                          // arguments A B C, creates C=A*B
        version 11
        args A B C                       // unload arguments into better names
        if colsof('A')!=rowsof('B') {    // check conformability
                error 503
        }
        local a = rowsof('A')            // obtain dimensioning information
        local b = colsof('A')            //    see Matrix functions returning
        local c = colsof('B')            //    scalars above
        matrix 'C' = J('a','c',0)        // create result containing 0s
        forvalues i = 1/'a' {
                forvalues 'j' = 1/'c' {
                        forvalues 'k' = 1/'b' {
                                matrix 'C'['i','j'] = 'C'['i','j'] + /*
                                */ 'A'['i','k']*'B'['k','j']
                        }
                }
        }
end
```

Now if in some other program, we needed to multiply matrix XXI by Xy to form result beta, we could type matmult XXI Xy beta and never use Stata's built-in method for multiplying matrices (matrix beta=XXI*Xy). If we typed the program matmult into a file named matmult.ado, we would not even have to bother to load matmult before using it—it would be loaded automatically; see [U] **17 Ado-files**.

❏

Name conflicts in expressions (namespaces)

See [P] **matrix** for a description of namespaces. A matrix might have the same name as a variable in the dataset, and if it does, Stata might appear confused when evaluating an expression (an *exp*). When the names conflict, Stata uses the rule that it always takes the data-variable interpretation. You can override this.

First, when working interactively, you can avoid the problem by simply naming your matrices differently from your variables.

Second, when writing programs, you can avoid name conflicts by obtaining names for matrices from `tempname`; see [P] **macro**.

Third, whether working interactively or writing programs, when using names that might conflict, you can use the `matrix()` pseudofunction to force Stata to take the matrix-name interpretation.

`matrix(`*name*`)` says that *name* is to be interpreted as a matrix name. For instance, consider the statement `local new=trace(xx)`. This might work and it might not. If `xx` is a matrix and there is no variable named `xx` in your dataset, it will work. If there is also a numeric variable named `xx` in your dataset, it will not work. Typing the statement will produce a type-mismatch error—Stata assumes that when you type `xx`, you are referring to the data variable `xx` because there is a data variable `xx`. Typing `local new=trace(matrix(xx))` will then produce the desired result. When writing programs using matrix names not obtained from `tempname`, you are strongly advised to state explicitly that all matrix names are indeed matrix names by using the `matrix()` function.

The only exception to this recommendation has to do with the construct $\mathbf{A}[i,j]$. The two subscripts indicate to Stata that $\mathbf{A}$ must be a matrix name and not an attempt to subscript a variable, so `matrix()` is not needed. This exception applies only to $\mathbf{A}[i,j]$; it does not apply to `el(`$\mathbf{A},i,j$`)`, which would be more safely written as `el(matrix(`$\mathbf{A}$`),`i,j`)`.

❑ Technical note

The `matrix()` and `scalar()` pseudofunctions (see [P] **scalar**) are really the same function, but you do not need to understand this fine point to program Stata successfully. Understanding this might, however, lead to producing more readable code. The formal definition is this:

`scalar(`*exp*`)` (and therefore `matrix(`*exp*`)`) evaluates *exp* but restricts Stata to interpreting all names in *exp* as scalar or matrix names. Scalars and matrices share the same namespace.

Therefore, because `scalar()` and `matrix()` are the same function, typing `trace(matrix(xx))` or `trace(scalar(xx))` would do the same thing, even though the second looks wrong. Because `scalar()` and `matrix()` allow an *exp*, you could also type `scalar(trace(xx))` and achieve the same result. `scalar()` evaluates the *exp* inside the parentheses: it merely restricts how names are interpreted, so now `trace(xx)` clearly means the trace of the matrix named `xx`.

How can you make your code more readable? Pretend that you wanted to calculate the trace plus the determinant of matrix `xx` and store it in the Stata scalar named `tpd` (no, there is no reason you would ever want to make such a silly calculation). You are writing a program and want to protect yourself from `xx` also existing in the dataset. One solution would be

```
scalar tpd = trace(matrix(xx)) + det(matrix(xx))
```

Knowing the full interpretation rule, however, you realize that you can shorten this to

```
scalar tpd = matrix(trace(xx) + det(xx))
```

and then, to make it more readable, you substitute `scalar()` for `matrix()`:

```
scalar tpd = scalar(trace(xx) + det(xx))
```

❑

Macro extended functions

The following macro extended functions (see [P] **macro**) are also defined:

rownames **A** and colnames **A** return a list of all the row or column subnames (with time-series operators if applicable) of **A**, separated by single blanks. The equation names, even if present, are not included.

roweq **A** and coleq **A** return the list of all row equation names or column equation names of **A**, separated by single blanks, and with each name appearing however many times it appears in the matrix.

rowfullnames **A** and colfullnames **A** return the list of all the row or column names, including equation names of **A**, separated by single blanks.

▷ Example 6

These functions are provided as macro functions and standard expression functions because Stata's expression evaluator works only with strings of no more than 244 characters, something not true of Stata's macro parser. A matrix with many rows or columns can produce an exceedingly long list of names.

In sophisticated programming situations, you sometimes want to process the matrices by row and column names rather than by row and column numbers. Assume that you are programming and have two matrices, xx and yy. You know that they contain the same column names, but they might be in a different order. You want to reorganize yy to be in the same order as xx. The following code fragment will create 'newyy' (a matrix name obtained from tempname) containing yy in the same order as xx:

```
tempname newyy newcol
local names : colfullnames(xx)
foreach name of local names {
        local j = colnumb(yy,"'name'")
        if 'j'>=. {
                display as error "column for 'name' not found"
                exit 111
        }
        matrix 'newcol' = yy[1...,'j']
        matrix 'newyy' = nullmat('newyy'),'newcol'
}
```

◁

References

Cox, N. J. 1999. dm69: Further new matrix commands. *Stata Technical Bulletin* 50: 5–9. Reprinted in *Stata Technical Bulletin Reprints*, vol. 9, pp. 29–34. College Station, TX: Stata Press.

——. 2000. dm79: Yet more new matrix commands. *Stata Technical Bulletin* 56: 4–8. Reprinted in *Stata Technical Bulletin Reprints*, vol. 10, pp. 17–23. College Station, TX: Stata Press.

Weesie, J. 1997. dm49: Some new matrix commands. *Stata Technical Bulletin* 39: 17–20. Reprinted in *Stata Technical Bulletin Reprints*, vol. 7, pp. 43–48. College Station, TX: Stata Press.

Also see

[P] **macro** — Macro definition and manipulation

[P] **matrix get** — Access system matrices

[P] **matrix utility** — List, rename, and drop matrices

[P] **scalar** — Scalar variables

[U] **13.3 Functions**

[U] **14 Matrix expressions**

[P] **matrix** — Introduction to matrix commands

Mata Reference Manual

Title

> **matrix dissimilarity** — Compute similarity or dissimilarity measures

Syntax

<u>matrix</u> <u>dis</u>similarity *matname* = [*varlist*] [*if*] [*in*] [, *options*]

options	description
measure	similarity or dissimilarity measure; default is L2 (Euclidean)
<u>observ</u>ations	compute similarities or dissimilarities between observations; the default
<u>var</u>iables	compute similarities or dissimilarities between variables
<u>names</u>(*varname*)	row/column names for *matname* (allowed with observations)
<u>allb</u>inary	check that all values are 0, 1, or missing
<u>proportions</u>	interpret values as proportions of binary values
dissim(*method*)	change similarity measure to dissimilarity measure

where *method* transforms similarities to dissimilarities by using

$$
\begin{array}{ll}
\text{oneminus} & d_{ij} = 1 - s_{ij} \\
\underline{\text{st}}\text{andard} & d_{ij} = \sqrt{s_{ii} + s_{jj} - 2s_{ij}}
\end{array}
$$

Description

matrix dissimilarity computes a similarity, dissimilarity, or distance matrix.

Options

measure specifies one of the similarity or dissimilarity measures allowed by Stata. The default is L2, Euclidean distance. Many similarity and dissimilarity measures are provided for continuous data and for binary data; see [MV] ***measure_option***.

observations and variables specify whether similarities or dissimilarities are computed between observations or variables. The default is observations.

names(*varname*) provides row and column names for *matname*. *varname* must be a string variable with a length of 32 or less. You will want to pick a *varname* that yields unique values for the row and column names. Uniqueness of values is not checked by matrix dissimilarity. names() is not allowed with the variables option. The default row and column names when the similarities or dissimilarities are computed between observations is obs#, where # is the observation number corresponding to that row or column.

allbinary checks that all values are 0, 1, or missing. Stata treats nonzero values as one (excluding missing values) when dealing with what are supposed to be binary data (including binary similarity *measure*s). allbinary causes matrix dissimilarity to exit with an error message if the values are not truly binary. allbinary is not allowed with proportions or the Gower *measure*.

proportions is for use with binary similarity *measure*s. It specifies that values be interpreted as proportions of binary values. The default action treats all nonzero values as one (excluding missing values). With proportions, the values are confirmed to be between zero and one, inclusive. See [MV] *measure_option* for a discussion of the use of proportions with binary *measure*s. proportions is not allowed with allbinary or the Gower *measure*.

dissim(*method*) specifies that similarity measures be transformed into dissimilarity measures. *method* may be oneminus or standard. oneminus transforms similarities to dissimilarities by using $d_{ij} = 1 - s_{ij}$ (Kaufman and Rousseeuw 1990, 21). standard uses $d_{ij} = \sqrt{s_{ii} + s_{jj} - 2s_{ij}}$ (Mardia, Kent, and Bibby 1979, 402). dissim() does nothing when the *measure* is already a dissimilarity or distance. See [MV] *measure_option* to see which *measure*s are similarities.

Remarks

Commands such as cluster singlelinkage, cluster completelinkage, and mds (see [MV] **cluster** and [MV] **mds**) have options allowing the user to select the similarity or dissimilarity measure to use for its computation. If you are developing a command that requires a similarity or dissimilarity matrix, the matrix dissimilarity command provides a convenient way to obtain it.

The similarity or dissimilarity between each observation (or variable if the variables option is specified) and the others is placed in *matname*. The element in the *i*th row and *j*th column gives either the similarity or dissimilarity between the *i*th and *j*th observation (or variable). Whether you get a similarity or a dissimilarity depends upon the requested *measure*; see [MV] *measure_option*.

If there are many observations (variables when the variables option is specified), you may need to increase the maximum matrix size; see [R] **matsize**. If the number of observations (or variables) is so large that storing the results in a matrix is not practical, you may wish to consider using the cluster measures command, which stores similarities or dissimilarities in variables; see [MV] **cluster programming utilities**.

When computing similarities or dissimilarities between observations, the default row and column names of *matname* are set to obs#, where # is the observation number. The names() option allows you to override this default. For similarities or dissimilarities between variables, the row and column names of *matname* are set to the appropriate variable names.

The order of the rows and columns corresponds with the order of your observations when you are computing similarities or dissimilarities between observations. Warning: If you reorder your data (e.g., using sort or gsort) after running matrix dissimilarity, the row and column ordering will no longer match your data.

Another use of matrix dissimilarity is in performing a cluster analysis on variables instead of observations. The cluster command performs a cluster analysis of the observations; see [MV] **cluster**. If you instead wish to cluster variables, you can use the variables option of matrix dissimilarity to obtain a dissimilarity matrix that can then be used with clustermat; see [MV] **clustermat** and example 2 below.

▷ Example 1

Example 1 of [MV] **cluster linkage** introduces data with four chemical laboratory measurements on 50 different samples of a particular plant. Let's find the Canberra distance between the measurements performed by lab technician Bill found among the first 25 observations of the labtech dataset.

```
. use http://www.stata-press.com/data/r11/labtech
. matrix dissim D = x1 x2 x3 x4 if labtech=="Bill" in 1/25, canberra
. matrix list D
symmetric D[6,6]
              obs7        obs18       obs20       obs22       obs23       obs25
 obs7            0
obs18    1.3100445           0
obs20    1.1134916    .87626565           0
obs22     1.452748    1.0363077   1.0621064           0
obs23    1.0380665    1.4952796    .81602718   1.6888123           0
obs25    1.4668898    1.5139834    1.4492336   1.0668425   1.1252514           0
```

By default, the row and column names of the matrix indicate the observations involved. The Canberra distance between the 23rd observation and the 18th observation is 1.4952796. See [MV] *measure_option* for a description of the Canberra distance.

◁

▷ Example 2

Example 2 of [MV] **cluster linkage** presents a dataset with 30 observations of 60 binary variables, a1, a2, ..., a30. In [MV] **cluster linkage**, the observations were clustered. Here we instead cluster the variables by computing the dissimilarity matrix by using `matrix dissimilarity` with the `variables` option followed by the `clustermat` command.

We use the `matching` option to obtain the simple matching similarity coefficient but then specify `dissim(oneminus)` to transform the similarities to dissimilarities by using the transformation $d_{ij} = 1 - s_{ij}$. The `allbinary` option checks that the variables really are binary (0/1) data.

```
. use http://www.stata-press.com/data/r11/homework
. matrix dissim Avars = a*, variables matching dissim(oneminus) allbinary
. matrix subA = Avars[1..5,1..5]
. matrix list subA
symmetric subA[5,5]
             a1          a2          a3          a4          a5
a1            0
a2           .4           0
a3           .4   .46666667           0
a4           .3          .3   .36666667           0
a5           .4          .4   .13333333          .3           0
```

We listed the first five rows and columns of the 60×60 matrix. The matrix row and column names correspond to the variable names.

To perform an average-linkage cluster analysis on the 60 variables, we supply the Avars matrix created by `matrix dissimilarity` to the `clustermat averagelinkage` command; see [MV] **cluster linkage**.

```
. clustermat averagelinkage Avars, clear
obs was 0, now 60
cluster name: _clus_1
. cluster generate g5 = groups(5)
```

```
. table g5
```

g5	Freq.
1	21
2	9
3	25
4	4
5	1

We generated a variable, g5, indicating the five-group cluster solution and then tabulated to show how many variables were clustered into each of the five groups. Group five has only one member.

```
. list g5 if g5==5
```

	g5
13.	5

The member corresponds to the 13th observation in the current dataset, which in turn corresponds to variable a13 from the original dataset. It appears that a13 is not like the other variables.

◁

▷ Example 3

matrix dissimilarity drops observations containing missing values, except when the Gower measure is specified. The computation of the Gower dissimilarity between 2 observations is based on the variables where the 2 observations both have nonmissing values.

We illustrate using a dataset with 6 observations and 4 variables where only 2 of the observations have complete data.

```
. use http://www.stata-press.com/data/r11/gower, clear
. list
```

	b1	b2	x1	x2
1.	0	1	.76	.75
2.	.	.	.	.
3.	1	0	.72	.88
4.	.	1	.4	.
5.	0	.	.	.14
6.	0	0	.55	.

```
. mat dissimilarity matL2 = b* x*, L2
. matlist matL2, format(%8.3f)
```

	obs1	obs3
obs1	0.000	
obs3	1.421	0.000

The resulting matrix is 2×2 and provides the dissimilarity between observations 1 and 3. All other observations contained at least one missing value.

However, with the `gower` measure we obtain a 6×6 matrix.

```
. matrix dissimilarity matgow = b1 b2 x1 x2, gower
. matlist matgow, format(%8.3f)
```

	obs1	obs2	obs3	obs4	obs5	obs6
obs1	0.000					
obs2	.	0.000				
obs3	0.572	.	0.000			
obs4	0.500	.	0.944	0.000		
obs5	0.412	.	1.000	.	0.000	
obs6	0.528	.	0.491	0.708	0.000	0.000

Because all the values for observation 2 are missing, the matrix contains missing values for the dissimilarity between observation 2 and the other observations. Notice the missing value in `matgow` for the dissimilarity between observations 4 and 5. There were no variables where observations 4 and 5 both had nonmissing values, and hence the Gower coefficient could not be computed.

◁

References

Kaufman, L., and P. J. Rousseeuw. 1990. *Finding Groups in Data: An Introduction to Cluster Analysis.* New York: Wiley.

Mardia, K. V., J. T. Kent, and J. M. Bibby. 1979. *Multivariate Analysis.* London: Academic Press.

Also see

[MV] **cluster** — Introduction to cluster-analysis commands

[MV] **clustermat** — Introduction to clustermat commands

[MV] **mdslong** — Multidimensional scaling of proximity data in long format

[MV] **cluster programming utilities** — Cluster-analysis programming utilities

[MV] *measure_option* — Option for similarity and dissimilarity measures

[P] **matrix** — Introduction to matrix commands

Title

Syntax

    matrix eigenvalues r c = A

where A is an $n \times n$ nonsymmetric, real matrix.

Menu

Data > Matrices, ado language > Eigenvalues and eigenvectors of symmetric matrices

Description

matrix eigenvalues returns the real part of the eigenvalues in the $1 \times n$ row vector r and the imaginary part of the eigenvalues in the $1 \times n$ row vector c. Thus the jth eigenvalue is $r[1,j] + i * c[1,j]$.

The eigenvalues are sorted by their moduli; $r[1,1] + i * c[1,1]$ has the largest modulus, and $r[1,n] + i * c[1,n]$ has the smallest modulus.

If you want the eigenvalues for a symmetric matrix, see [P] **matrix symeigen**.

Also see [M-5] **eigensystem( )** for alternative routines for obtaining eigenvalues and eigenvectors.

Remarks

Typing matrix eigenvalues r c = A for A $n \times n$ returns

$$r = (r_1, r_2, \ldots, r_n)$$
$$c = (c_1, c_2, \ldots, c_n)$$

where r_j is the real part and c_j the imaginary part of the jth eigenvalue. The eigenvalues are part of the solution to the problem

$$A x_j = \lambda_j x_j$$

and, in particular,

$$\lambda_j = r_j + i * c_j$$

The corresponding eigenvectors, x_j, are not saved by matrix eigenvalues. The returned r and c are ordered so that $|\lambda_1| \geq |\lambda_2| \geq \cdots \geq |\lambda_n|$, where $|\lambda_j| = \sqrt{r_j^2 + c_j^2}$.

▷ Example 1

In time-series analysis, researchers often use eigenvalues to verify the stability of the fitted model.

Suppose that we have fit a univariate time-series model and that the stability condition requires the moduli of all the eigenvalues of a "companion" matrix **A** to be less than 1. (See Hamilton [1994] for a discussion of these models and conditions.)

First, we form the companion matrix.

```
. matrix A = (0.66151492, .2551595, .35603325, -0.15403902, -.12734386)
. matrix A = A \ (I(4), J(4,1,0))
. mat list A

A[5,5]
            c1          c2          c3          c4          c5
r1    .66151492    .2551595   .35603325   -.15403902   -.12734386
r1            1           0           0           0           0
r2            0           1           0           0           0
r3            0           0           1           0           0
r4            0           0           0           1           0
```

Next we use `matrix eigenvalues` to obtain the eigenvalues, which we will then list:

```
. matrix eigenvalues re im = A
. mat list re

re[1,5]
            c1          c2          c3          c4          c5
real   .99121823   .66060006  -.29686008  -.29686008   -.3965832
. mat list im

im[1,5]
            c1          c2          c3          c4          c5
complex         0           0   .63423776  -.63423776           0
```

Finally, we compute and list the moduli, which are all less than 1, although the first is close:

```
. forvalues i = 1/5 {
  2.          di sqrt(re[1,`i']^2 + im[1,`i']^2)
  3. }
.99121823
.66060006
.70027384
.70027384
.3965832
```

◁

Methods and formulas

Stata's internal eigenvalue extraction routine for nonsymmetric matrices is based on the public domain LAPACK routine DGEEV. Anderson et al. (1999) provide an excellent introduction to these routines. Stata's internal routine also uses, with permission, **f2c** (©1990–1997 by AT&T, Lucent Technologies, and Bellcore).

References

Anderson, E., Z. Bai, C. Bischof, S. Blackford, J. Demmel, J. J. Dongarra, J. Du Croz, A. Greenbaum, S. Hammarling, A. McKenney, and D. Sorensen. 1999. *LAPACK Users' Guide.* 3rd ed. Philadelphia: Society for Industrial and Applied Mathematics.

Hamilton, J. D. 1994. *Time Series Analysis.* Princeton: Princeton University Press.

Also see

[P] **matrix symeigen** — Eigenvalues and eigenvectors of symmetric matrices

[U] **14 Matrix expressions**

[P] **matrix** — Introduction to matrix commands

[M-4] **matrix** — Matrix functions

Title

> **matrix get** — Access system matrices

Syntax

Obtain copy of internal Stata system matrix

> <u>matr</u>ix [<u>def</u>ine] *matname* = get(*systemname*)

Post matrix as internal **Rr** *matrix*

> mat_put_rr *matname*

where *systemname* is

_b	coefficients after any estimation command
VCE	covariance matrix of estimators after any estimation command
Rr	constraint matrix after test
Cns	constraint matrix after any estimation command

Description

The get() matrix function obtains a copy of an internal Stata system matrix. Some system matrices can also be obtained more easily by directly referring to the returned result after a command. In particular, the coefficient vector can be referred to as e(b), the variance–covariance matrix of estimators as e(V), and the constraints matrix as e(Cns) after an estimation command.

mat_put_rr is a programmer's command that posts *matname* as the internal **Rr** matrix. *matname* must have one more than the number of columns in the e(b) or e(V) matrices. The extra column contains the *r* vector, and the earlier columns contain the **R** matrix for the Wald test

$$Rb = r$$

The matrix ... get(Rr) command provides a way to obtain the current **Rr** system matrix.

Remarks

get() obtains copies of matrices containing coefficients and the covariance matrix of the estimators after estimation commands (such as regress and probit) and obtains copies of matrices left behind by other Stata commands. The other side of get() is ereturn post, which allows ado-file estimation commands to post results to Stata's internal areas; see [P] **ereturn**.

▷ Example 1

After any model fitting command, the coefficients are available in _b and the variance–covariance matrix of the estimators in VCE.

```
. use http://www.stata-press.com/data/r11/auto
(1978 Automobile Data)
. regress price weight mpg
  (output omitted )
```

Here we can directly use e(b) and e(V) to obtain the matrices:

```
. matrix list e(b)
e(b)[1,3]
        weight         mpg       _cons
y1   1.7465592  -49.512221  1946.0687
. matrix list e(V)
symmetric e(V)[3,3]
              weight         mpg       _cons
weight    .41133468
   mpg    44.601659    7422.863
 _cons  -2191.9032  -292759.82   12938766
```

We can also use the matrix get() function to obtain these matrices:

```
. matrix b = get(_b)
. matrix V = get(VCE)
. matrix list b
b[1,3]
        weight         mpg       _cons
y1   1.7465592  -49.512221  1946.0687
. matrix list V
symmetric V[3,3]
              weight         mpg       _cons
weight    .41133468
   mpg    44.601659    7422.863
 _cons  -2191.9032  -292759.82   12938766
```

The columns of b and both dimensions of V are properly labeled.

◁

▷ Example 2

After test, the restriction matrix is available in Rr. Having just estimated a regression of price on weight and mpg, we will run a test and then get the restriction matrix:

```
. test weight=1, notest
 ( 1)   weight = 1
. test mpg=40, accum
 ( 1)   weight = 1
 ( 2)   mpg = 40
       F(  2,    71) =    6.29
            Prob > F =    0.0030
. matrix rxtr=get(Rr)
```

```
. matrix list rxtr
rxtr[2,4]
     c1  c2  c3  c4
r1   1   0   0   1
r2   0   1   0  40
```

◁

Also see

[U] **13.5 Accessing coefficients and standard errors**

[U] **14 Matrix expressions**

[P] **matrix** — Introduction to matrix commands

Title

> **matrix mkmat** — Convert variables to matrix and vice versa

Syntax

Create matrix from variables

mkmat *varlist* [*if*] [*in*] [, <u>matr</u>ix(*matname*) <u>nomiss</u>ing <u>rown</u>ames(*varname*)

<u>roweq</u>(*varname*) <u>rowpre</u>fix(*string*) obs <u>nchar</u>(*#*)]

Create variables from matrix

svmat [*type*] **A** [, <u>n</u>ames(col | eqcol | matcol | *string*)]

Rename rows and columns of matrix

matname **A** *namelist* [, <u>r</u>ows(*range*) <u>c</u>olumns(*range*) <u>e</u>xplicit]

where **A** is the name of an existing matrix, *type* is a storage type for the new variables, and *namelist* is one of 1) a varlist, i.e., names of existing variables possibly abbreviated; 2) _cons and the names of existing variables possibly abbreviated; or 3) arbitrary names when the explicit option is specified.

Menu

mkmat

Data > Matrices, ado language > Convert variables to matrix

svmat

Data > Matrices, ado language > Convert matrix to variables

Description

mkmat stores the variables listed in *varlist* in column vectors of the same name, that is, $N \times 1$ matrices, where $N = \_N$, the number of observations in the dataset. Optionally, they can be stored as an $N \times k$ matrix, where k is the number of variables in *varlist*. The variable names are used as column names. By default, the rows are named r1, r2, ...

svmat takes a matrix and stores its columns as new variables. It is the reverse of the mkmat command, which creates a matrix from existing variables.

matname renames the rows and columns of a matrix. matname differs from the matrix rownames and matrix colnames commands in that matname expands varlist abbreviations and allows a restricted range for the rows or columns. See [P] **matrix rownames**.

Options

matrix(*matname*) requests that the vectors be combined in a matrix instead of creating the column vectors.

nomissing specifies that observations with missing values in any of the variables be excluded ("listwise deletion").

rownames(*varname*) and roweq(*varname*) specify that the row names and row equations of the created matrix or vectors be taken from *varname*. *varname* should be a string variable or an integer positive-valued numeric variable. (Value labels are ignored; use decode if you want to use value labels.) Within the names, spaces and periods are replaced by an underscore (_).

rowprefix(*string*) specifies that the string *string* be prefixed to the row names of the created matrix or column vectors. In the prefix, spaces and periods are replaced by an underscore (_). If rownames() is not specified, rowprefix() defaults to r, and to nothing otherwise.

obs specifies that the observation numbers be used as row names. This option may not be combined with rownames().

nchar(#) specifies that row names be truncated to # characters, $1 \leq \# \leq 32$. The default is nchar(32).

names(col | eqcol | matcol | *string*) specifies how the new variables are to be named.
names(col) uses the column names of the matrix to name the variables.
names(eqcol) uses the equation names prefixed to the column names.
names(matcol) uses the matrix name prefixed to the column names.
names(*string*) names the variables *string*1, *string*2, ..., *string*n, where *string* is a user-specified *string* and *n* is the number of columns of the matrix.
If names() is not specified, the variables are named **A**1, **A**2, ..., **A**n, where **A** is the name of the matrix.

rows(*range*) and columns(*range*) specify the rows and columns of the matrix to rename. The number of rows or columns specified must be equal to the number of names in *namelist*. If both rows() and columns() are given, the specified rows are named *namelist*, and the specified columns are also named *namelist*. The range must be given in one of the following forms:

rows(.)	renames all the rows
rows(2..8)	renames rows 2–8
rows(3)	renames only row 3
rows(4...)	renames row 4 to the last row

If neither rows() nor columns() is given, rows(.) columns(.) is the default. That is, the matrix must be square, and both the rows and the columns are named *namelist*.

explicit suppresses the expansion of varlist abbreviations and omits the verification that the names are those of existing variables. That is, the names in *namelist* are used explicitly and can be any valid row or column names.

Remarks

Remarks are presented under the following headings:

> *mkmat*
> *svmat*

mkmat

Although cross-products of variables can be loaded into a matrix with the `matrix accum` command, programmers may sometimes find it more convenient to work with the variables in their datasets as vectors instead of as cross-products. `mkmat` allows the user a simple way to load specific variables into matrices in Stata's memory.

▷ Example 1

`mkmat` uses the variable name to name the single column in the vector. This feature guarantees that the variable name will be carried along in any additional matrix calculations. This feature is also useful when vectors are combined in a general matrix.

```
. use http://www.stata-press.com/data/r11/test

. describe
Contains data from http://www.stata-press.com/data/r11/test.dta
  obs:            10
  vars:            3                          13 Apr 2009 12:50
  size:          160 (99.9% of memory free)
```

variable name	storage type	display format	value label	variable label
x	float	%9.0g		
y	float	%9.0g		
z	float	%9.0g		

```
Sorted by:
. list
```

	x	y	z
1.	1	10	2
2.	2	9	4
3.	3	8	3
4.	4	7	5
5.	5	6	7
6.	6	5	6
7.	7	4	8
8.	8	3	10
9.	9	2	1
10.	10	1	9

```
. mkmat x y z, matrix(xyzmat)

. matrix list xyzmat
xyzmat[10,3]
       x   y   z
 r1    1  10   2
 r2    2   9   4
 r3    3   8   3
 r4    4   7   5
 r5    5   6   7
 r6    6   5   6
 r7    7   4   8
 r8    8   3  10
 r9    9   2   1
r10   10   1   9
```

If the variables contain missing values, so will the corresponding matrix or matrices. Many matrix commands, such as the matrix inversion functions `inv()` and `invsym()`, do not allow missing values in matrices. If you specify the `nomissing` option, `mkmat` will exclude observations with missing values so that subsequent matrix computations will not be hampered by missing values. Listwise deletion parallels missing-value handling in most Stata commands.

◁

❑ Technical note

`mkmat` provides a useful addition to Stata's matrix commands, but it will work only with small datasets.

Stata limits matrices to no more than matsize × matsize, which means a maximum of 800×800 for Stata/IC and $11,000 \times 11,000$ for Stata/SE and Stata/MP. By limiting Stata's matrix capabilities to matsize × matsize, has not Stata's matrix language itself been limited to datasets no larger than matsize? It would certainly appear so; in the simple matrix calculation for regression coefficients $(\mathbf{X}'\mathbf{X})^{-1}\mathbf{X}'\mathbf{y}$, $\mathbf{X}$ is an $n \times k$ matrix (n being the number of observations and k being the number of variables), and given the matsize constraint, n must be less than 800 (or up to 11,000 in Stata/MP and Stata/SE).

Our answer is as follows: yes, $\mathbf{X}$ is limited in the way stated, but $\mathbf{X}'\mathbf{X}$ is a mere $k \times k$ matrix, and, similarly, $\mathbf{X}'\mathbf{y}$ is only $k \times 1$. Both of these matrices are well within Stata's matrix-handling capabilities, and the `matrix accum` command (see [P] **matrix accum**) can directly create both of them.

Moreover, even if Stata could hold the $n \times k$ matrix $\mathbf{X}$, it would still be more efficient to use `matrix accum` to form $\mathbf{X}'\mathbf{X}$. $\mathbf{X}'\mathbf{X}$, interpreted literally, says to load a copy of the dataset, transpose it, load a second copy of the dataset, and then form the matrix product. Thus two copies of the dataset occupy memory in addition to the original copy Stata already had available (and from which `matrix accum` could directly form the result with no additional memory use). For small n, the inefficiency is not important, but for large n, the inefficiency could make the calculation infeasible. For instance, with $n = 12,000$ and $k = 6$, the additional memory use is 1,125 kilobytes.

More generally, matrices in statistical applications tend to have dimensions $k \times k$, $n \times k$, and $n \times n$, with k small and n large. Terms dealing with the data are of the generic form $\mathbf{X}'_{k_1 \times n} \mathbf{W}_{n \times n} \mathbf{Z}_{n \times k_2}$. ($\mathbf{X}'\mathbf{X}$ fits the generic form with $\mathbf{X} = \mathbf{X}$, $\mathbf{W} = \mathbf{I}$, and $\mathbf{Z} = \mathbf{X}$.) Matrix programming languages cannot deal with the deceptively simple calculation $\mathbf{X}'\mathbf{W}\mathbf{Z}$ because of the staggering size of the $\mathbf{W}$ matrix. For $n = 12,000$, storing $\mathbf{W}$ requires a little more than a gigabyte of memory. In statistical formulas, however, $\mathbf{W}$ is given by formula and, in fact, never needs to be stored in its entirety. Exploitation of this fact is all that is needed to resurrect the use of a matrix programming language in statistical applications. Matrix programming languages may be inefficient because of copious memory use, but in statistical applications, the inefficiency is minor for matrices of size $k \times k$ or smaller. Our design of the various `matrix accum` commands allows calculating terms of the form $\mathbf{X}'\mathbf{W}\mathbf{Z}$, and this one feature is all that is necessary to allow efficient and robust use of matrix languages.

Programs for creating data matrices, such as that offered by `mkmat`, are useful for pedagogical purposes and for a specific application where Stata's matsize constraint is not binding, it seems so natural. On the other hand, it is important that general tools not be implemented by forming data matrices because such tools will be drastically limited in dataset size. Coding the problem in terms of the various `matrix accum` commands (see [P] **matrix accum**) is admittedly more tedious, but by abolishing data matrices from your programs, you will produce tools suitable for use on large datasets.

❑

svmat

▷ Example 2

Let's get the vector of coefficients from a regression and use `svmat` to save the vector as a new variable, save the dataset, load the dataset back into memory, use `mkmat` to create a vector from the variable, and finally, use `matname` to rename the columns of the row vector.

```
. use http://www.stata-press.com/data/r11/auto
(1978 Automobile Data)
. quietly regress mpg weight gear_ratio foreign
. matrix b = e(b)
. matrix list b
b[1,4]
          weight   gear_ratio      foreign        _cons
y1  -.00613903    1.4571134   -2.2216815    36.101353
. matrix c = b'
. svmat double c, name(bvector)
. list bvector1 in 1/5
```

	bvector1
1.	-.00613903
2.	1.4571134
3.	-2.2216815
4.	36.101353
5.	.

```
. save example
file example.dta saved
. use example
. mkmat bvector1 if bvector1< .
. matrix list bvector1
bvector1[4,1]
        bvector1
r1  -.00613903
r2    1.4571134
r3   -2.2216815
r4    36.101353
. matrix d = bvector1'
. matname d wei gear for _cons, c(.)
. matrix list d
d[1,4]
              weight   gear_ratio      foreign        _cons
bvector1  -.00613903    1.4571134   -2.2216815    36.101353
```

◁

Methods and formulas

`mkmat`, `svmat`, and `matname` are implemented as ado-files.

Acknowledgment

mkmat was written by Ken Heinecke of Kenwood Capital Management, Minneapolis, MN.

References

Gould, W. W. 1994. ip6.1: Data and matrices. *Stata Technical Bulletin* 20: 10. Reprinted in *Stata Technical Bulletin Reprints*, vol. 4, pp. 70–71. College Station, TX: Stata Press.

Heinecke, K. 1994. ip6: Storing variables in vectors and matrices. *Stata Technical Bulletin* 20: 8–9. Reprinted in *Stata Technical Bulletin Reprints*, vol. 4, pp. 68–70. College Station, TX: Stata Press.

Sribney, W. M. 1995. ip6.2: Storing matrices as variables. *Stata Technical Bulletin* 24: 9–10. Reprinted in *Stata Technical Bulletin Reprints*, vol. 4, pp. 71–73. College Station, TX: Stata Press.

Also see

[P] **matrix accum** — Form cross-product matrices

[U] **14 Matrix expressions**

[P] **matrix** — Introduction to matrix commands

[M-4] **stata** — Stata interface functions

Title

matrix rownames — Name rows and columns

Syntax

Reset row names of matrix

> matrix <u>rown</u>ames **A** = *names*

Reset column names of matrix

> matrix <u>coln</u>ames **A** = *names*

Reset row names and interpret simple names as equation names

> matrix <u>rowe</u>q **A** = *names*

Reset column names and interpret simple names as equation names

> matrix <u>coleq</u> **A** = *names*

where *name* can be

- a simple name;
- a colon follow by a simple name;
- an equation name followed by a colon; or
- an equation name, a colon, and a simple name.

and a simple name may be augmented with time-series operators and factor-variable specifications.

Description

matrix rownames and colnames reset the row and column names of an already existing matrix.

matrix roweq and coleq also reset the row and column names of an already existing matrix, but if a simple name (a name without a colon) is specified, it is interpreted as an equation name.

In either case, the part of the name not specified is left unchanged.

Remarks

See [U] **14.2 Row and column names** for a description of the row and column names bordering a matrix.

286

▷ Example 1

In general, the names bordering matrices are set correctly by Stata because of the tracking of the matrix algebra, and you will not need to reset them. Nevertheless, imagine that you have formed $\mathbf{X}'\mathbf{X}$ in the matrix named XX and that it corresponds to the underlying variables price, weight, and mpg:

```
. matrix list XX

symmetric XX[3,3]
           c1          c2          c3
r1   3.448e+09
r2   1.468e+09   7.188e+08
r3     9132716     4493720       36008
```

You did not form this matrix with matrix accum because, had you done so, the rows and columns would already be correctly named. However you formed it, you now want to reset the names:

```
. matrix rownames XX = price weight mpg

. matrix colnames XX = price weight mpg

. matrix list XX

symmetric XX[3,3]
             price      weight         mpg
 price   3.448e+09
weight   1.468e+09   7.188e+08
   mpg     9132716     4493720       36008
```

◁

▷ Example 2

We now demonstrate setting the equation names and names with time-series operators.

```
. matrix list AA

symmetric AA[4,4]
           c1           c2           c3           c4
r1    .2967663
r2    .03682017    .57644416
r3   -.87052852    .32713601    20.274957
r4    -1.572579   -.63830843   -12.150097    26.099582

. matrix rownames AA = length L3D2.length mpg L.mpg

. matrix colnames AA = length L3D2.length mpg L.mpg

. matrix roweq AA = eq1 eq1 eq2 eq2

. matrix coleq AA = eq1 eq1 eq2 eq2

. matrix list AA

symmetric AA[4,4]
                        eq1:         eq1:         eq2:         eq2:
                                     L3D2.                     L.
                      length       length          mpg          mpg
      eq1:length    .2967663
 eq1:L3D2.length    .03682017    .57644416
        eq2:mpg   -.87052852    .32713601    20.274957
      eq2:L.mpg    -1.572579   -.63830843   -12.150097    26.099582
```

Factor variables and interactions are much like time-series–operated variables, we specify each level variable.

```
. mat rownames AA = 0b.foreign 1.foreign 0.foreign#c.mpg 1.foreign#c.mpg
. mat colnames AA = 0b.foreign 1.foreign 0.foreign#c.mpg 1.foreign#c.mpg
```

As in factor-variable varlists, we can combine any time-series lead and lag operators with factor variables.

```
. mat rownames XX = 0bL2.foreign 1L2.foreign 0L3.foreign#cL3.mpg
> 1L3.foreign#cL3.mpg
. mat colnames XX = 0bL2.foreign 1L2.foreign 0L3.foreign#cL3.mpg
> 1L3.foreign#cL3.mpg
```

◁

❏ Technical note

`matrix rownames` and `colnames` sometimes behave in surprising ways:

1. If your list of names includes no colons—does not mention the equation names—whatever equation names are in place are left in place; they are not changed.

2. If your list of names has every name ending in a colon—so that it mentions only the equation names and not the subnames—whatever subnames are in place are left in place; they are not changed.

3. If your list of names has fewer names than are required to label all the rows or columns, the last name in the list is replicated. (If you specify too many names, you will get the conformability error message, and no names will be changed.)

4. `matrix rownames` and `matrix colnames` that are not interactions are limited to 32 characters, exclusive of time-series and factor-variable operators. Each component of an interaction is limited to 32 characters, exclusive of operators.

These surprises have their uses, but if you make a mistake, the result really may surprise you. For instance, rule 3, by itself, is just odd. Combined with rule 2, however, rule 3 allows you to set all the equation names in a matrix easily. If you type 'matrix rownames XX = myeq:', all the equation names in the row are reset while the subnames are left unchanged:

```
. matrix rownames XX = myeq:
. matrix list XX
symmetric XX[3,3]
                    price      weight        mpg
 myeq:price   3.448e+09
myeq:weight   1.468e+09   7.188e+08
   myeq:mpg     9132716     4493720       36008
```

Setting equation names is often done before forming a partitioned matrix so that, when the components are assembled, each has the correct equation name.

Thus to review, to get the result above, we could have typed

```
. matrix rownames XX = myeq:price myeq:weight myeq:mpg
```

or

```
. matrix rownames XX = price weight mpg
. matrix rownames XX = myeq:
```

or even

```
. matrix rownames XX = myeq:
. matrix rownames XX = price weight mpg
```

All would have resulted in the same outcome. The real surprise comes, however, when you make a mistake:

```
. matrix rownames XX = myeq:
. matrix rownames XX = price weight
. matrix list XX
symmetric XX[3,3]
                  price      weight         mpg
 myeq:price   3.448e+09
myeq:weight   1.468e+09   7.188e+08
myeq:weight    9132716     4493720       36008
```

Our mistake above is that we listed only two names for the subnames of the rows of XX and matrix rownames and then labeled both of the last rows with the subname weight.

❑

❑ Technical note

The equation name _: by itself is special; it means the null equation name. For instance, as of the last technical note, we were left with

```
. matrix list XX
symmetric XX[3,3]
                  price      weight         mpg
 myeq:price   3.448e+09
myeq:weight   1.468e+09   7.188e+08
myeq:weight    9132716     4493720       36008
```

Let's fix it:

```
. matrix rownames XX = price weight mpg
. matrix rownames XX = _:
. matrix list XX
symmetric XX[3,3]
               price      weight         mpg
 price     3.448e+09
weight     1.468e+09   7.188e+08
   mpg      9132716     4493720       36008
```

❑

❑ Technical note

matrix roweq and matrix coleq are really the same commands as matrix rownames and matrix colnames. They differ in only one respect: if a specified name does not contain a colon, matrix roweq and matrix coleq interpret that name as if it did end in a colon.

matrix rownames, matrix colnames, matrix roweq, and matrix coleq are often used in conjunction with the rowfullnames, colfullnames, rownames, colnames, roweq, and coleq extended macro functions introduced in [P] **matrix define**. The rownames and colnames extended macro functions return only the name, including any time-series or factor-variable operators, but not the equation name.

```
. matrix list AA
symmetric AA[4,4]
                           eq1:           eq1:          eq2:          eq2:
                                          L3D2.                       L.
                          length         length          mpg          mpg
      eq1:length        .2967663
  eq1:L3D2.length       .03682017      .57644416
        eq2:mpg        -.87052852      .32713601     20.274957
      eq2:L.mpg         -1.572579     -.63830843    -12.150097     26.099582
. local rsubs : rownames AA
. display "The row subnames of AA are -- 'rsubs' --"
The row subnames of AA are -- length L3D2.length mpg L.mpg --
```

Similarly, the `roweq` extended macro function returns only the equation names without the trailing colon:

```
. local reqs : roweq AA
. display "The row equations of AA are -- 'reqs' --"
The row equations of AA are -- eq1 eq1 eq2 eq2 --
```

Now consider the problem that you have two matrices named A and B that have the same number of rows. A is correctly labeled and includes equation names. You want to copy the complete names of A to B. You might be tempted to type

```
. local names : rownames A
. matrix rownames B = 'names'
```

This is not adequate. You will have copied the names but not the equation names. To copy both parts of the complete names, you can type

```
. local subs : rownames A
. local eqs : roweq A
. matrix rownames B = 'subs'
. matrix roweq B = 'eqs'
```

This method can be used even when there might not be equation names. The equation name _ is special; not only does setting an equation to that name remove the equation name, but when there is no equation name, the `roweq` and `coleq` extended macro functions return that name.

A better way to copy the names is to use the `rowfullnames` and `colfullnames` extended macro functions (see [P] **matrix define** and [P] **macro**). You can more compactly type

```
. local rname : rowfullnames A
. matrix rownames B = 'rname'
```

❏

Also see

[P] **macro** — Macro definition and manipulation

[P] **matrix define** — Matrix definition, operators, and functions

[U] **14 Matrix expressions**

[P] **matrix** — Introduction to matrix commands

Title

> **matrix score** — Score data from coefficient vectors

Syntax

<u>mat</u>rix <u>score</u> [*type*] *newvar* = **b** [*if*] [*in*]

    [, <u>eq</u>uation(# #│*eqname*) <u>m</u>issval(#) replace forcezero]

where **b** is a $1 \times p$ matrix.

Description

matrix score creates $newvar_j = \mathbf{x}_j \mathbf{b}'$ (**b** being a row vector), where $\mathbf{x}_j$ is the row vector of values of the variables specified by the column names of **b**. The name _cons is treated as a variable equal to 1.

Options

equation(# #│*eqname*) specifies the equation—by either number or name—for selecting coefficients from **b** to use in scoring. See [U] **14.2 Row and column names** and [P] **matrix rownames** for more on equation labels with matrices.

missval(#) specifies the value to be assumed if any values are missing from the variables referred to by the coefficient vector. By default, this value is taken to be missing (.), and any missing value among the variables produces a missing score.

replace specifies that *newvar* already exists. Here observations not included by if *exp* and in range are left unchanged; that is, they are not changed to missing. Be warned that replace does not promote the storage type of the existing variable; if the variable was stored as an int, the calculated scores would be truncated to integers when stored.

forcezero specifies that, should a variable described by the column names of **b** not exist, the calculation treat the missing variable as if it did exist and was equal to zero for all observations. It contributes nothing to the summation. By default, a missing variable would produce an error message.

Remarks

Scoring refers to forming linear combinations of variables in the data with respect to a coefficient vector. For instance, let's create and then consider the vector coefs:

```
. use http://www.stata-press.com/data/r11/auto
(1978 Automobile Data)
. quietly regress price weight mpg
. matrix coefs = e(b)
. matrix list coefs

coefs[1,3]
        weight         mpg       _cons
y1   1.7465592   -49.512221   1946.0687
```

Scoring the data with this vector would create a new variable equal to the linear combination

$$1.7465592 \, \text{weight} - 49.512221 \, \text{mpg} + 1946.0687$$

The vector is interpreted as coefficients; the corresponding names of the variables are obtained from the column names (row names if `coefs` were a column vector). To form this linear combination, we type

```
. matrix score lc = coefs

. summarize lc
```

Variable	Obs	Mean	Std. Dev.	Min	Max
lc	74	6165.257	1597.606	3406.46	9805.269

If the coefficient vector has equation names, `matrix score` with the `eq()` option selects the appropriate coefficients for scoring. `eq(#1)` is assumed if no `eq()` option is specified.

```
. quietly sureg (price weight mpg) (displacement weight)

. matrix coefs = e(b)

. matrix list coefs

coefs[1,5]
            price:      price:      price:   displacement:   displacement:
           weight         mpg       _cons          weight           _cons
y1      1.7358275   -51.298248   2016.5101       .10574552      -121.99702
. matrix score lcnoeq = coefs

. matrix score lca = coefs , eq(price)

. matrix score lc1 = coefs , eq(#1)

. matrix score lcb = coefs , eq(displacement)

. matrix score lc2 = coefs , eq(#2)

. summarize lcnoeq lca lc1 lcb lc2
```

Variable	Obs	Mean	Std. Dev.	Min	Max
lcnoeq	74	6165.257	1598.264	3396.859	9802.336
lca	74	6165.257	1598.264	3396.859	9802.336
lc1	74	6165.257	1598.264	3396.859	9802.336
lcb	74	197.2973	82.18474	64.1151	389.8113
lc2	74	197.2973	82.18474	64.1151	389.8113

❑ Technical note

If the same equation name is scattered in different sections of the coefficient vector, the results may not be what you expect.

```
. matrix list bad

bad[1,5]
            price:      price:   displacement:      price:   displacement:
           weight         mpg          weight       _cons           _cons
y1      1.7358275   -51.298248       .10574552   2016.5101      -121.99702
. matrix score badnoeq = bad

. matrix score bada = bad , eq(price)

. matrix score bad1 = bad , eq(#1)

. matrix score badb = bad , eq(displacement)

. matrix score bad2 = bad , eq(#2)

. matrix score bad3 = bad , eq(#3)
```

```
. matrix score bad4 = bad , eq(#4)

. summarize bad*
```

Variable	Obs	Mean	Std. Dev.	Min	Max
badnoeq	74	4148.747	1598.264	1380.349	7785.826
bada	74	4148.747	1598.264	1380.349	7785.826
bad1	74	4148.747	1598.264	1380.349	7785.826
badb	74	319.2943	82.18474	186.1121	511.8083
bad2	74	319.2943	82.18474	186.1121	511.8083
bad3	74	2016.51	0	2016.51	2016.51
bad4	74	-121.997	0	-121.997	-121.997

Coefficient vectors created by Stata estimation commands will have equation names together.

❏

Also see

[U] **14 Matrix expressions**

[P] **matrix** — Introduction to matrix commands

Title

> **matrix svd** — Singular value decomposition

Syntax

> <u>matr</u>ix svd U w V = A

where **U**, **w**, and **V** are matrix names (the matrices may exist or not) and **A** is the name of an existing $m \times n$ matrix, $m \geq n$.

Menu

Data > Matrices, ado language > Singular value decomposition

Description

matrix svd produces the singular value decomposition (SVD) of **A**.

Also see [M-5] **svd( )** for alternative routines for obtaining the singular value decomposition.

Remarks

The singular value decomposition of $m \times n$ matrix **A**, $m \geq n$, is defined as

$$\mathbf{A} = \mathbf{U}\operatorname{diag}(\mathbf{w})\mathbf{V}'$$

U: $m \times n$, **w**: $1 \times n$, diag(**w**): $n \times n$, and **V**: $n \times n$, where **U** is column orthogonal ($\mathbf{U}'\mathbf{U} = \mathbf{I}$ if $m = n$), all the elements of **w** are positive or zero, and $\mathbf{V}'\mathbf{V} = \mathbf{I}$.

Singular value decomposition can be used to obtain a g2-inverse of **A** ($\mathbf{A}^*$: $n \times m$, such that $\mathbf{A}\mathbf{A}^*\mathbf{A} = \mathbf{A}$ and $\mathbf{A}^*\mathbf{A}\mathbf{A}^* = \mathbf{A}^*$—the first two Moore–Penrose conditions) via $\mathbf{A}^* = \mathbf{V}\{\operatorname{diag}(1/w_j)\}\mathbf{U}'$, where $1/w_j$ refers to individually taking the reciprocal of the elements of **w** and substituting 0 if $w_j = 0$ or is small. If **A** is square and of full rank, $\mathbf{A}^* = \mathbf{A}^{-1}$.

▷ Example 1

Singular value decomposition is used to obtain accurate inverses of nearly singular matrices and to obtain g2-inverses of matrices that are singular, to construct orthonormal bases, and to develop approximation matrices. Our example will prove that matrix svd works:

```
. matrix A = (1,2,9\2,7,5\2,4,18)

. matrix svd U w V = A

. matrix list U

U[3,3]
            c1          c2          c3
r1    .42313293    .89442719   -.1447706
r2     .3237169   -6.016e-17    .94615399
r3    .84626585    -.4472136   -.2895412

. matrix list w

w[1,3]
           c1          c2          c3
r1   21.832726   2.612e-16   5.5975071
```

```
. matrix list V

V[3,3]
             c1           c2           c3
c1    .12655765    .96974658     .2087456
c2    .29759672   -.23786237    .92458514
c3    .94626601   -.05489132   -.31869671

. matrix newA = U*diag(w)*V'

. matrix list newA

newA[3,3]
     c1  c2  c3
r1    1   2   9
r2    2   7   5
r3    2   4  18
```

As claimed, **newA** is equal to our original **A**.

The g2-inverse of **A** is computed below. The second element of **w** is small, so we decide to set the corresponding element of $\mathrm{diag}(1/w_j)$ to zero. We then show that the resulting **Ainv** matrix has the properties of a g2-inverse for **A**.

```
. matrix Winv = J(3,3,0)

. matrix Winv[1,1] = 1/w[1,1]

. matrix Winv[3,3] = 1/w[1,3]

. matrix Ainv = V*Winv*U'

. matrix list Ainv

Ainv[3,3]
             r1           r2           r3
c1    -.0029461    .03716103    -.0058922
c2    -.0181453    .16069635   -.03629059
c3     .02658185   -.0398393    .05316371

. matrix AAiA = A*Ainv*A

. matrix list AAiA

AAiA[3,3]
     c1  c2  c3
r1    1   2   9
r2    2   7   5
r3    2   4  18

. matrix AiAAi = Ainv*A*Ainv

. matrix list AiAAi

AiAAi[3,3]
             r1           r2           r3
c1    -.0029461    .03716103    -.0058922
c2    -.0181453    .16069635   -.03629059
c3     .02658185   -.0398393    .05316371
```

◁

Methods and formulas

Stewart (1993) surveys the contributions of five mathematicians—Beltrami, Jordan, Sylvester, Schmidt, and Weyl—who established the existence of the singular value decomposition and developed its theory.

Reference

Stewart, G. W. 1993. On the early history of the singular value decomposition. *SIAM Review* 35: 551–566.

Also see

[P] **matrix define** — Matrix definition, operators, and functions

[U] **14 Matrix expressions**

[P] **matrix** — Introduction to matrix commands

[M-4] **matrix** — Matrix functions

[M-5] **svd( )** — Singular value decomposition

Title

matrix symeigen — Eigenvalues and eigenvectors of symmetric matrices

Syntax

matrix symeigen $\mathbf{X}$ v = $\mathbf{A}$

where $\mathbf{A}$ is an $n \times n$ symmetric matrix.

Menu

Data > Matrices, ado language > Eigenvalues and eigenvectors of symmetric matrices

Description

matrix symeigen returns the eigenvectors in the columns of $\mathbf{X}$: $n \times n$ and the corresponding eigenvalues in $\mathbf{v}$: $1 \times n$. The eigenvalues are sorted: $\mathbf{v}[1,1]$ contains the largest eigenvalue (and $\mathbf{X}[1\ldots,1]$ its corresponding eigenvector), and $\mathbf{v}[1,n]$ contains the smallest eigenvalue (and $\mathbf{X}[1\ldots,n]$ its corresponding eigenvector).

If you want the eigenvalues for a nonsymmetric matrix, see [P] **matrix eigenvalues**.

Also see [M-5] **eigensystem( )** for other routines for obtaining eigenvalues and eigenvectors.

Remarks

Typing matrix symeigen $\mathbf{X}$ v = $\mathbf{A}$ for $\mathbf{A}$: $n \times n$ returns

$$\mathbf{v} = \left(\lambda_1, \lambda_2, \ldots, \lambda_n\right)$$
$$\mathbf{X} = \left(\mathbf{x}_1, \mathbf{x}_2, \ldots, \mathbf{x}_n\right)$$

where $\lambda_1 \geq \lambda_2 \geq \ldots \geq \lambda_n$. Each $\mathbf{x}_i$ and λ_i is a solution to

$$\mathbf{A}\mathbf{x}_i = \lambda_i \mathbf{x}_i$$

or, more compactly,

$$\mathbf{A}\mathbf{X} = \mathbf{X} \operatorname{diag}(\mathbf{v})$$

> Example 1

Eigenvalues and eigenvectors have many uses. We will demonstrate that symeigen returns matrices meeting the definition:

```
. use http://www.stata-press.com/data/r11/auto
(1978 Automobile Data)
. matrix accum A = weight mpg length, noconstant deviation
(obs=74)
```

```
. matrix list A

symmetric A[3,3]
              weight         mpg        length
weight      44094178
   mpg    -264948.11    2443.4595
length    1195077.3    -7483.5135    36192.662

. matrix symeigen X lambda = A

. matrix list lambda

lambda[1,3]
            e1           e2           e3
r1    44128163    3830.4869    820.73955

. matrix list X

X[3,3]
              e1           e2           e3
weight    .99961482   -.02756261    .00324179
   mpg   -.00600667    -.1008305    .99488549
length    .02709477    .99452175    .10095722

. matrix AX = A*X

. matrix XLambda = X*diag(lambda)

. matrix list AX

AX[3,3]
              e1           e2           e3
weight    44111166    -105.57823    2.6606641
   mpg    -265063.5   -386.22991    816.54187
length    1195642.6    3809.5025    82.859585

. matrix list XLambda

XLambda[3,3]
              e1           e2           e3
weight    44111166    -105.57823    2.6606641
   mpg    -265063.5   -386.22991    816.54187
length    1195642.6    3809.5025    82.859585
```

◁

Methods and formulas

Stata's internal eigenvalue and eigenvector extraction routines are translations of the public domain EISPACK routines, Smith et al. (1976), which are in turn based on Wilkinson and Reinsch (1971). EISPACK was developed under contract for the Office of Scientific and Technical Information, U.S. Department of Energy, by Argonne National Laboratory and supported by funds provided by the Nuclear Regulatory Commission. Stata's use of these routines is by permission of the National Energy Software Center of the Argonne National Laboratory. A brief but excellent introduction to the techniques used by these routines can be found in Press et al. (2007, 563–599).

References

Press, W. H., S. A. Teukolsky, W. T. Vetterling, and B. P. Flannery. 2007. *Numerical Recipes in C: The Art of Scientific Computing.* 3rd ed. Cambridge: Cambridge University Press.

Smith, B. T., J. M. Boyle, J. J. Dongarra, B. S. Garbow, Y. Ikebe, V. C. Klema, and C. B. Moler. 1976. *Matrix Eigensystem Routines–EISPACK Guide.* 2nd ed. Berlin: Springer.

Wilkinson, J. H., and C. Reinsch. 1971. *Handbook for Automatic Computation, Vol. 2: Linear Algebra.* New York: Springer.

Also see

[P] **matrix eigenvalues** — Eigenvalues of nonsymmetric matrices

[U] **14 Matrix expressions**

[P] **matrix** — Introduction to matrix commands

[M-4] **matrix** — Matrix functions

Title

matrix utility — List, rename, and drop matrices

Syntax

List matrix names

> matrix dir

List contents of matrix

> matrix list *mname* [, noblank nohalf noheader nonames format(%*fmt*)
>
> title(*string*) nodotz]

Rename matrix

> matrix rename *oldname newname*

Drop matrix

> matrix drop { _all | *mnames* }

Menu

matrix list

Data > Matrices, ado language > List contents of matrix

matrix rename

Data > Matrices, ado language > Rename matrix

matrix drop

Data > Matrices, ado language > Drop matrices

Description

matrix dir lists the names of currently existing matrices. matrix list lists the contents of a matrix. matrix rename changes the name of a matrix. matrix drop eliminates a matrix.

Options

noblank suppresses printing a blank line before printing the matrix. This is useful in programs.

nohalf specifies that, even if the matrix is symmetric, the full matrix be printed. The default is to print only the lower triangle in such cases.

300

noheader suppresses the display of the matrix name and dimension before the matrix itself. This is useful in programs.

nonames suppresses the display of the bordering names around the matrix.

format(%*fmt*) specifies the format to be used to display the individual elements of the matrix. The default is format(%10.0g).

title(*string*) adds the specified title *string* to the header displayed before the matrix itself. If noheader is specified, title() does nothing because displaying the header is suppressed.

nodotz specifies that .z missing values be displayed as blanks.

Remarks

> Example 1

In the example below, matrix list normally displays only the lower half of symmetric matrices. nohalf prevents this.

```
. mat b = (2, 5, 4\ 5, 8, 6\ 4, 6, 3)
. mat a = (1, 2\ 2, 4)
. matrix dir
            a[2,2]
            b[3,3]
. matrix rename a z
. matrix dir
            z[2,2]
            b[3,3]
. matrix list b
symmetric b[3,3]
       c1   c2   c3
r1     2
r2     5    8
r3     4    6    3
. matrix list b, nohalf
symmetric b[3,3]
       c1   c2   c3
r1     2    5    4
r2     5    8    6
r3     4    6    3
. matrix drop b
. matrix dir
            z[2,2]
. matrix drop _all
. matrix dir
```

◁

❑ Technical note

When writing programs and using matrix names obtained through tempname (see [P] **macro**), it is not necessary to explicitly drop matrices; the matrices are removed automatically at the conclusion of the program.

```
. program example
  1.         tempname a
  2.         matrix 'a' = (1,2\3,4)              // this is temporary
  3.         matrix b = (5,6\7,8)               // and this permanent
  4.         display "The temporary matrix a contains"
  5.         matrix list 'a', noheader
  6. end

. example
The temporary matrix a contains
     c1  c2
r1   1   2
r2   3   4
. matrix dir
          b[2,2]
```

Nevertheless, dropping matrices with temporary names in programs when they are no longer needed is recommended, unless the program is about to exit (when they will be dropped anyway). Matrices consume memory; dropping them frees memory.

❏

Also see

[P] **matlist** — Display a matrix and control its format

[U] **14 Matrix expressions**

[P] **matrix** — Introduction to matrix commands

Title

more — Pause until key is pressed

Syntax

<u>more</u>

Description

more causes Stata to display —more— and pause until any key is pressed if more is set on and does nothing if more is set off.

The current value of set more is stored in c(more); see [P] **creturn**.

See [R] **more** for information on set more on and set more off.

Remarks

Ado-file programmers need take no special action to have —more— conditions arise when the screen is full. Stata handles that automatically.

If, however, you wish to force a —more— condition early, you can include the more command in your program. The syntax of more is

more

more takes no arguments.

Also see

[P] **creturn** — Return c-class values

[P] **sleep** — Pause for a specified time

[R] **query** — Display system parameters

[U] **7 –more– conditions**

Title

nopreserve option — nopreserve option

Syntax

stata_command ... [, ... `nopreserve` ...]

Description

Some Stata commands have a `nopreserve` option. This option is for use by programmers when *stata_command* is used as a subroutine of another command.

Option

`nopreserve` specifies that *stata_command* need not bother to `preserve` the data in memory. The usual situation is that *stata_command* is being used as a subroutine by another program, the data in memory have been preserved by the caller, and the caller will not need to access the data again before the data are restored from the caller's preserved copy.

Remarks

Some commands change the data in memory in the process of performing their task even though the command officially does not change the data in memory. Such commands achieve this by using `preserve` to make a temporary copy of the data on disk, which is later restored to memory.

Even some commands whose entire purpose is to make a modification to the data in memory sometimes make temporary copies of the data just in case the user should press *Break* while the changes to the data are still being completed.

This is done using `preserve`; see [P] **preserve**.

Assume `alpha` and `beta` are each implemented using `preserve`. Assume that `alpha` uses `beta` as a subroutine. If `alpha` itself does not intend to use the data after calling `beta`, then `beta` preserving and restoring the data is unnecessary because `alpha` already has preserved the data from which memory will be restored. Then `alpha` should specify the `nopreserve` option when calling `beta`.

Also see

[P] **preserve** — Preserve and restore data

Title

numlist — Parse numeric lists

Syntax

numlist "*numlist*" [, <u>asc</u>ending <u>desc</u>ending <u>integer</u> <u>miss</u>ingokay min(*#*) max(*#*)

<u>r</u>ange(*operator #* [*operator #*]) sort]

where *numlist* consists of one or more *numlist_elements* shown below

and where *operator* is   < | <= | > | >=

There is no space between *operator* and *#*; for example,

    range(>=0)
    range(>0 <=50)

numlist_element	Example	Expands to	Definition
#	3.82	3.82	a number
.	.	.	a missing value
$\#_1/\#_2$	4/6 2.3/5.7	4 5 6 2.3 3.3 4.3 5.3	starting at $\#_1$, increment by 1 to $\#_2$
$\#_1(\#_2)\#_3$	2(3)10 4.8(2.1)9.9	2 5 8 4.8 6.9 9	starting at $\#_1$, increment by $\#_2$ to $\#_3$
$\#_1[\#_2]\#_3$	2[3]10 4.8[2.1]9.9	2 5 8 4.8 6.9 9	starting at $\#_1$, increment by $\#_2$ to $\#_3$
$\#_1 \#_2 : \#_3$	5 7 : 13 1.1 2.4 : 5.8	5 7 9 11 13 1.1 2.4 3.7 5	starting at $\#_1$, increment by $(\#_2 - \#_1)$ to $\#_3$
$\#_1 \#_2$ to $\#_3$	5 7 to 13 1.1 2.4 to 5.8	same	same

Description

The numlist command expands the numeric list supplied as a string argument and performs error checking based on the options specified. Any numeric sequence operators in the *numlist* string are evaluated, and the expanded list of numbers is returned in r(numlist). See [U] **11.1.8 numlist** for a discussion of numeric lists.

305

Options

ascending indicates that the user must give the numeric list in ascending order without repeated values. This is different from the sort option.

descending indicates that the numeric list must be given in descending order without repeated values.

integer specifies that the user may give only integer values in the numeric list.

missingokay indicates that missing values are allowed in the numeric list. By default, missing values are not allowed.

min(*#*) specifies the minimum number of elements allowed in the numeric list. The default is min(1). If you want to allow empty numeric lists, specify min(0).

max(*#*) specifies the maximum number of elements allowed in the numeric list. The default is max(1600), which is the largest allowed maximum.

range(*operator* # [*operator* #]) specifies the acceptable range for the values in the numeric list. The *operator*s are < (less than), <= (less than or equal to), > (greater than), and >= (greater than or equal to). No space is allowed between the *operator* and the #.

sort specifies that the returned numeric list be sorted. This is different from the ascending option, which places the responsibility for providing a sorted list on the user who will not be allowed to enter a nonsorted list. sort, on the other hand, puts no restriction on the user and takes care of sorting the list. Repeated values are also allowed with sort.

Remarks

Programmers rarely use the numlist command because syntax also expands numeric lists, and it handles the rest of the parsing problem, too, at least if the command being parsed follows standard syntax. numlist is used for expanding numeric lists when what is being parsed does not follow standard syntax.

▷ Example 1

We demonstrate the numlist command interactively.

```
. numlist "5.3 1.0234 3 6:18 -2.0033 5.3/7.3"

. display "'r(numlist)'"
5.3 1.0234 3 6 9 12 15 18 -2.0033 5.3 6.3 7.3

. numlist "5.3 1.0234 3 6:18 -2.0033 5.3/7.3", integer
invalid numlist has noninteger elements
r(126);

. numlist "1 5 8/12 15", integer descending
invalid numlist has elements out of order
r(124);

. numlist "1 5 8/12 15", integer ascending

. display "'r(numlist)'"
1 5 8 9 10 11 12 15
```

```
. numlist "100 1 5 8/12 15", integer ascending
invalid numlist has elements out of order
r(124);
. numlist "100 1 5 8/12 15", integer sort
. display "`r(numlist)'"
1 5 8 9 10 11 12 15 100
. numlist "3 5 . 28 -3(2)5"
invalid numlist has missing values
r(127);
. numlist "3 5 . 28 -3(2)5", missingokay min(3) max(25)
. display "`r(numlist)'"
3 5 . 28 -3 -1 1 3 5
. numlist "28 36", min(3) max(6)
invalid numlist has too few elements
r(122);
. numlist "28 36 -3 5 2.8 7 32 -8", min(3) max(6)
invalid numlist has too many elements
r(123);
. numlist "3/6 -4 -1 to 5", range(>=1)
invalid numlist has elements outside of allowed range
r(125);
. numlist "3/6", range(>=0 <30)
. display "`r(numlist)'"
3 4 5 6
```

◁

Saved results

numlist saves the following in r():

Macros
  r(numlist)   expanded numeric list

Also see

[P] **syntax** — Parse Stata syntax

[U] **11.1.8 numlist**

Title

pause — Program debugging command

Syntax

pause { on | off | [*message*] }

Description

If pause is on, the pause [*message*] command displays *message* and temporarily suspends execution of the program, returning control to the keyboard. Execution of keyboard commands continues until you type end or q, at which time execution of the program resumes. Typing BREAK in pause mode (as opposed to pressing the *Break* key) also resumes program execution, but the break signal is sent to the calling program.

If pause is off, pause does nothing.

Pause is off by default. Type pause on to turn pause on. Type pause off to turn it back off.

Remarks

pause assists in debugging Stata programs. The line pause or pause *message* is placed in the program where problems are suspected (more than one pause may be placed in a program). For instance, you have a program that is not working properly. A piece of this program reads

```
gen 'tmp'=exp('1')/'2'
summarize 'tmp'
local mean=r(mean)
```

You think that the error may be in the creation of 'tmp'. You change the program to read

```
gen 'tmp'=exp('1')/'2'
pause Just created tmp          /* this line is new */
summarize 'tmp'
local mean=r(mean)
```

Let's pretend that your program is named myprog; interactively, you now type

```
. myprog
(output from your program appears)
```

That is, pause does nothing because pause is off, so pauses in your program are ignored. If you turn pause on,

```
. pause on

. myprog
(any output myprog creates up to the pause appears)
pause:  Just created tmp
-> . describe
  (output omitted)
-> . list
  (output omitted)
-> . end
execution resumes...
(remaining output from myprog appears)
```

308

The "->" is called the pause-mode prompt. You can give any Stata command. You can examine variables and, if you wish, even change them. If while in pause mode, you wish to terminate execution of your program, you type BREAK (in capitals):

```
. myprog
(any output myprog creates up to the pause appears)
pause:  Just created tmp
-> . list
  (output omitted )
-> . BREAK
sending Break to calling program...
--Break--
r(1);

. _
```

The results are the same as if you pressed *Break* while your program was executing. If you press the *Break* key in pause mode (as opposed to typing BREAK), however, it means only that the execution of the command you have just given interactively is to be interrupted.

Notes:

- You may put many pauses in your programs.

- By default, pause is off, so the pauses will not do anything. Even so, you should remove the pauses after your program is debugged because each execution of a do-nothing pause will slow your program slightly.

- pause is implemented as an ado-file; this means that the definitions of local macros in your program are unavailable to you. To see the value of local macros, display them in the pause message; for instance,

```
                pause Just created tmp, i='i'
```

When the line is executed, you will see something like

```
pause:  Just created tmp, i=1
-> . _
```

- Remember, temporary variables (e.g., tempvar tmp ... gen 'tmp'=...) are assigned real names, such as __00424, by Stata; see [P] **macro**. Thus, in pause mode, you want to examine __00424 and not tmp. Generally, you can determine the real name of your temporary variables from describe's output, but in the example above, it would have been better if pause had been invoked with

```
                pause Just created tmp, called 'tmp', i='i'
```

When the line was executed, you would have seen something like

```
pause:  Just created tmp, called __00424, i=1
-> . _
```

- When giving commands that include double quotes, you may occasionally see the error message "type mismatch", but then the command will work properly:

```
pause:  Just created tmp, called __00424, i=1
-> . list if __00424=="male"
type mismatch
(output from request appears as if nothing is wrong)
-> . _
```

Methods and formulas

pause is implemented as an ado-file.

Reference

Becketti, S. 1993. ip4: Program debugging command. *Stata Technical Bulletin* 13: 13–14. Reprinted in *Stata Technical Bulletin Reprints*, vol. 3, pp. 57–58. College Station, TX: Stata Press.

Also see

[P] **program** — Define and manipulate programs

[P] **more** — Pause until key is pressed

[P] **trace** — Debug Stata programs

[U] **18 Programming Stata**

Title

> **plugin** — Load a plugin

Syntax

program *handle*, plugin [using(*filespec*)]

Description

In addition to using ado-files and Mata, you can add new commands to Stata by using the C language by following a set of programming conventions and dynamically linking your compiled library into Stata. The program command with the plugin option finds plugins and loads (dynamically links) them into Stata.

Options

plugin specifies that plugins be found and loaded into Stata.

using(*filespec*) specifies a file, *filespec*, containing the plugin. If you do not specify using(), program assumes that the file is named *handle*.plugin and can be found along the ado-path (see [U] **17.5 Where does Stata look for ado-files?**).

Remarks

Plugins are most useful for methods that require the greatest possible speed and involve heavy looping, recursion, or other computationally demanding approaches. They may also be useful if you have a solution that is already programmed in C.

For complete documentation on plugin programming and loading compiled programs into Stata, see http://www.stata.com/plugins/.

Also see

[P] **program** — Define and manipulate programs

Mata Reference Manual

Title

> **postfile** — Save results in Stata dataset

Syntax

Declare variable names and filename of dataset where results will be stored

postfile *postname* *newvarlist* using *filename* [, <u>e</u>very(*#*) replace]

Add new observation to declared dataset

post *postname* (*exp*) (*exp*) ... (*exp*)

Declare end to posting of observations

postclose *postname*

List all open postfiles

postutil dir

Close all open postfiles

postutil clear

Description

These commands are utilities to assist Stata programmers in performing Monte Carlo–type experiments.

postfile declares the variable names and the filename of a (new) Stata dataset where results will be stored.

post adds a new observation to the declared dataset.

postclose declares an end to the posting of observations. After postclose, the new dataset contains the posted results and may be loaded with use; see [D] **use**.

postutil dir lists all open postfiles. postutil clear closes all open postfiles.

All five commands manipulate the new dataset without disturbing the data in memory.

If *filename* is specified without an extension, .dta is assumed.

Options

every(*#*) specifies that results be written to disk every #th call to post. post temporarily holds results in memory and periodically opens the Stata dataset being built to append the stored results. every() should typically not be specified, because you are unlikely to choose a value for # that is as efficient as the number post chooses on its own, which is a function of the number of results being written and their storage type.

replace indicates that the file specified may already exist, and if it does, that postfile may erase the file and create a new one.

Remarks

The typical use of the `post` commands is

```
tempname memhold
tempfile results
...
postfile 'memhold' ... using "'results'"
...
while ... {
        ...
        post 'memhold' ...
        ...
}
postclose 'memhold'
...
use "'results'", clear
...
```

Two names are specified with `postfile`: *postname* is a name assigned to internal memory buffers, and *filename* is the name of the file to be created. Subsequent `post`s and the `postclose` are followed by *postname* so that Stata will know to what file they refer.

In our sample, we obtain both names from Stata's temporary name facility (see [P] **macro**), although, in some programming situations, you may wish to substitute a hard-coded *filename*. We recommend that *postname* always be obtained from `tempname`. This ensures that your program can be nested within any other program and ensures that the memory used by `post` is freed if anything goes wrong. Using a temporary filename, too, ensures that the file will be erased if the user presses *Break*. Sometimes, however, you may wish to leave the file of incomplete results behind. That is allowed, but remember that the file is not fully up to date if `postclose` has not been executed. `post` buffers results in memory and only periodically updates the file.

Because `postfile` accepts a *newvarlist*, storage types may be interspersed, so you could have

```
postfile 'memhold' a b str20 c double(d e f) using "'results'"
```

▷ Example 1

We wish to write a program to collect means and variances from 10,000 randomly constructed 100-observation samples of lognormal data and store the results in `results.dta`. Suppose that we are evaluating the coverage of the 95%, *t*-based confidence interval when applied to lognormal data. As background, we can obtain a 100-observation lognormal sample by typing

```
drop _all
set obs 100
gen z = exp(rnormal())
```

We can obtain the mean and standard deviation by typing

```
summarize z
```

Moreover, `summarize` stores the sample mean in `r(mean)` and variance in `r(Var)`. It is those two values we wish to collect. Our program is

```
program lnsim
        version 11
        tempname sim
        postfile 'sim' mean var using results, replace
        quietly {
                forvalues i = 1/10000 {
                        drop _all
                        set obs 100
                        gen z = exp(rnormal())
                        summarize z
                        post 'sim' (r(mean)) (r(Var))
                }
        }
        postclose 'sim'
end
```

The postfile command begins the accumulation of results. 'sim' is the name assigned to the internal memory buffers where results will be held; mean and var are the names to be given to the two variables that will contain the information we collect; and variables will be stored in the file named results.dta. Because two variable names were specified on the postfile line, two expressions must be specified following post. Here the expressions are simply r(mean) and r(Var). If we had wanted, however, to save the mean divided by the standard deviation and the standard deviation, we could have typed

```
post 'sim' (r(mean)/r(sd)) (r(sd))
```

Finally, postclose 'sim' concluded the simulation. The dataset results.dta is now complete.

```
. lnsim
. use results, clear
. describe
Contains data from results.dta
  obs:        10,000
  vars:            2                          26 Mar 2009 09:31
  size:      120,000 (88.6% of memory free)
```

variable name	storage type	display format	value label	variable label
mean	float	%9.0g		
var	float	%9.0g		

```
Sorted by:
. summarize
```

Variable	Obs	Mean	Std. Dev.	Min	Max
mean	10000	1.648316	.2186988	1.041816	3.308971
var	10000	4.757646	6.235164	.6765768	350.761

◁

References

Gould, W. W. 1994. ssi6: Routines to speed Monte Carlo experiments. *Stata Technical Bulletin* 20: 18–22. Reprinted in *Stata Technical Bulletin Reprints*, vol. 4, pp. 202–207. College Station, TX: Stata Press.

Van Kerm, P. 2007. Stata tip 54: Post your results. *Stata Journal* 7: 587–589.

Also see

[R] **bootstrap** — Bootstrap sampling and estimation

[R] **simulate** — Monte Carlo simulations

Title

> **_predict** — Obtain predictions, residuals, etc., after estimation programming command

Syntax

After regress

> _predict [*type*] *newvar* [*if*] [*in*] [, xb stdp stdf stdr <u>h</u>at <u>c</u>ooksd
>
> <u>resid</u>uals <u>rsta</u>ndard <u>rstu</u>dent <u>noof</u>fset <u>nolab</u>el]

After single-equation (SE) estimators

> _predict [*type*] *newvar* [*if*] [*in*] [, xb stdp <u>noof</u>fset <u>nolab</u>el]

After multiple-equation (ME) estimators

> _predict [*type*] *newvar* [*if*] [*in*] [, xb stdp stddp <u>noof</u>fset <u>nolab</u>el
>
> <u>e</u>quation(*eqno* [, *eqno*])]

Description

_predict is for use by programmers as a subroutine for implementing the predict command for use after estimation; see [R] **predict**.

Options

xb calculates the linear prediction from the fitted model. That is, all models can be thought of as estimating a set of parameters $b_1, b_2, \ldots, b_k$, and the linear prediction is $\widehat{y}_j = b_1 x_{1j} + b_2 x_{2j} + \cdots + b_k x_{kj}$, often written in matrix notation as $\widehat{y}_j = x_j b$. For linear regression, the values $\widehat{y}_j$ are called the predicted values, or for out-of-sample predictions, the forecast. For logit and probit, for example, $\widehat{y}_j$ is called the logit or probit index.

It is important to understand that the $x_{1j}, x_{2j}, \ldots, x_{kj}$ used in the calculation are obtained from the data currently in memory and do not have to correspond to the data on the independent variables used in fitting the model (obtaining the $b_1, b_2, \ldots, b_k$).

stdp calculates the standard error of the prediction after any estimation command. Here the prediction is understood to mean the same thing as the "index", namely, $x_j b$. The statistic produced by stdp can be thought of as the standard error of the predicted expected value, or mean index, for the observation's covariate pattern. This is also commonly referred to as the standard error of the fitted value.

stdf calculates the standard error of the forecast, which is the standard error of the point prediction for 1 observation. It is commonly referred to as the standard error of the future or forecast value. By construction, the standard errors produced by stdf are always larger than those produced by stdp; see *Methods and formulas* in [R] **predict**.

stdr calculates the standard error of the residuals.

hat (or `leverage`) calculates the diagonal elements of the projection hat matrix.

`cooksd` calculates the Cook's D influence statistic (Cook 1977).

`residuals` calculates the residuals.

`rstandard` calculates the standardized residuals.

`rstudent` calculates the studentized (jackknifed) residuals.

`nooffset` may be combined with most statistics and specifies that the calculation be made, ignoring any offset or exposure variable specified when the model was fit.

This option is available, even if not documented, for `predict` after a specific command. If neither the `offset`(*varname*) option nor the `exposure`(*varname*) option was specified when the model was fit, specifying `nooffset` does nothing.

`nolabel` prevents `_predict` from labeling the newly created variable.

`stddp` is allowed only after you have previously fit a multiple-equation model. The standard error of the difference in linear predictions $(\mathbf{x}_{1j}\mathbf{b} - \mathbf{x}_{2j}\mathbf{b})$ between equations 1 and 2 is calculated. Use the `equation()` option to get the standard error of the difference between other equations.

`equation`(*eqno*[, *eqno*]) is relevant only when you have previously fit a multiple-equation model. It specifies the equation to which you are referring.

`equation()` is typically filled in with one *eqno*—it would be filled in that way with options `xb` and `stdp`, for instance. `equation(#1)` would mean that the calculation is to be made for the first equation, `equation(#2)` would mean the second, and so on. You could also refer to the equations by their names: `equation(income)` would refer to the equation named `income` and `equation(hours)` to the equation named `hours`.

If you do not specify `equation()`, the results are the same as if you specified `equation(#1)`.

Other statistics refer to between-equation concepts; `stddp` is an example. You might then specify `equation(#1,#2)` or `equation(income,hours)`. When two equations must be specified, `equation()` is required.

Methods and formulas

See *Methods and formulas* in [R] **predict** and [R] **regress**.

Reference

Cook, R. D. 1977. Detection of influential observation in linear regression. *Technometrics* 19: 15–18.

Also see

[R] **predict** — Obtain predictions, residuals, etc., after estimation

[U] **20 Estimation and postestimation commands**

Title

> **preserve** — Preserve and restore data

Syntax

Preserve data

> preserve [, <u>ch</u>anged]

Restore data

> restore [, not <u>pre</u>serve]

Description

preserve preserves the data, guaranteeing that data will be restored after program termination.

restore forces a restore of the data now.

Options

changed instructs preserve to preserve only the flag indicating that the data have changed because the last save. Use of this option is strongly discouraged, as explained in the technical note below.

not instructs restore to cancel the previous preserve.

preserve instructs restore to restore the data now, but not to cancel the restoration of the data again at program conclusion. If preserve is not specified, the scheduled restoration at program conclusion is canceled.

Remarks

preserve and restore deal with the programming problem where the user's data must be changed to achieve the desired result but, when the program concludes, the programmer wishes to undo the damage done to the data. When preserve is issued, the user's data are preserved. The data in memory remain unchanged. When the program or do-file concludes, the user's data are automatically restored.

After a preserve, the programmer can also instruct Stata to restore the data now with the restore command. This is useful when the programmer needs the original data back and knows that no more damage will be done to the data. restore, preserve can be used when the programmer needs the data back but plans further damage. restore, not can be used when the programmer wishes to cancel the previous preserve and to have the data currently in memory returned to the user.

▷ Example 1

preserve is usually used by itself and is used early in the program. Say that a programmer is writing a program to report some statistic, but the statistic cannot be calculated without changing the user's data. Here changing does not mean merely adding a variable or two; that could be done with temporary variables as described in [P] **macro**. Changing means that the data really must be changed: observations might be discarded, the contents of existing variables changed, and the like. Although the programmer could just ignore the destruction of the user's data, the programmer might actually want to use the program herself and knows that she will become exceedingly irritated when she uses it without remembering to first save her data. The programmer wishes to write a programmatically correct, or PC, command. Doing so is not difficult:

```
program myprog
        (code for interpreting—parsing—the user's request)
        preserve
        (code that destroys the data)
        (code that makes the calculation)
        (code that reports the result)
end
```

To preserve the data, preserve must make a copy of it on disk. Therefore, our programmer smartly performs all the parsing and setup, where errors are likely, before the preserve. Once she gets to the point in the code where the damage must be done, however, she preserves the data. After that, she forgets the problem. Stata handles restoring the user's data, even if the user presses *Break* in the middle of the program.

◁

▷ Example 2

Now let's consider a program that must destroy the user's data but needs the data back again, and, once the data are recovered, will do no more damage. The outline is

```
program myprog
        (code for interpreting—parsing—the user's request)
        preserve
        (code that destroys the data)
        (code that makes the first part of the calculation)
        restore
        (code that makes the second part of the calculation)
        (code that reports the result)
end
```

Although there are other ways the programmer could have arranged to save the data and get the data back [snapshot (see [D] **snapshot**) or save and use with temporary files as described in [P] **macro** come to mind], this method is better because should the user press *Break* after the data are damaged but before the data are restored, Stata will handle restoring the data.

◁

▷ Example 3

This time the program must destroy the user's data, bring the data back and destroy the data again, and finally report its calculation. The outline is

```
program myprog
        (code for interpreting — parsing — the user's request)
        preserve
        (code that destroys the data)
        (code that makes the first part of the calculation)
        restore, preserve
        (code that makes the second part of the calculation)
        (code that reports the result)
end
```

The programmer could also have coded a `restore` on one line and a `preserve` on the next. It would have the same result but would be inefficient, because Stata would then rewrite the data to disk. `restore, preserve` tells Stata to reload the data but to leave the copy on disk for ultimate restoration.

◁

> Example 4

A programmer is writing a program that intends to change the user's data in memory — the damage the programmer is about to do is not damage at all. Nevertheless, if the user pressed *Break* while the programmer was in the midst of the machinations, what would be left in memory would be useless. The programmatically correct outline is

```
program myprog
        (code for interpreting — parsing — the user's request)
        preserve
        (code that reforms the data)
        restore, not
end
```

Before undertaking the reformation, the programmer smartly preserves the data. When everything is complete, the programmer cancels the restoration by typing `restore, not`.

◁

❑ Technical note

`preserve, changed` is best avoided, although it is very fast. `preserve, changed` does not preserve the data; it merely records whether the data have changed since the data were last saved (as mentioned by `describe` and as checked by `exit` and `use` when the user does not also say `clear`) and restores the flag at the conclusion of the program. The programmer must ensure that the data really have not changed.

As long as the programs use temporary variables, as created by `tempvar` (see [P] **macro**), the changed-since-last-saved flag would not be changed anyway — Stata can track such temporary changes to the data that it will, itself, be able to undo. In fact, we cannot think of one use for `preserve, changed`, and included it only to preserve the happiness of our more imaginative users.

❑

Also see

[P] **nopreserve option** — nopreserve option

[D] **snapshot** — Save and restore data snapshots

[P] **macro** — Macro definition and manipulation

Title

---
program — Define and manipulate programs

Syntax

Define program

> program [define] *program_name* [, [nclass|rclass|eclass|sclass]
>
>   byable(recall[, noheader]|onecall) properties(*namelist*) sortpreserve
>
>   plugin]

List names of programs stored in memory

> program dir

Eliminate program from memory

> program drop {*program_name* [*program_name* [...]] | _all | _allado}

List contents of program

> program list [*program_name* [*program_name* [...]] | _all]

Description

program define defines and manipulates programs. define is required if *program_name* is any of the words define, dir, drop, list, or plugin.

program dir lists the names of all the programs stored in memory.

program list lists the contents of the named program or programs. program list _all lists the contents of all programs stored in memory.

program drop eliminates the named program or programs from memory. program drop _all eliminates all programs stored in memory. program drop _allado eliminates all programs stored in memory that were loaded from ado-files. See [U] **17 Ado-files** for an explanation of ado-files.

See [U] **18 Programming Stata** for a description of programs. The remarks below address only the use of the program dir, program drop, and program list commands.

See [P] **trace** for information on debugging programs.

See the *Subject table of contents*, which immediately follows the *Table of contents*, for a subject summary of the programming commands.

Options

nclass states that the program being defined does not return results in r(), e(), or s(), and is the default.

rclass states that the program being defined returns results in r(). This is done using the return command; see [P] **return**. If the program is not explicitly declared to be rclass, it may not change or replace results in r().

eclass states that the program being defined returns results in e() or modifies already existing results in e(). This is done using the ereturn command; see [P] **return** and [P] **ereturn**. If the program is not explicitly declared to be eclass, it may not replace or change results in e().

sclass states that the program being defined returns results in s(). This is done using the sreturn command; see [P] **return**. If the program is not explicitly declared to be sclass, it may not change or replace results in s(), but it still may clear s() by using sreturn clear; see [P] **return**.

byable(recall[, noheader] | onecall) specifies that the program allow Stata's by *varlist*: prefix. There are two styles for writing byable programs: byable(recall) and byable(onecall). The writing of byable programs is discussed in [P] **byable**.

properties(*namelist*) states that *program_name* has the specified properties. *namelist* may contain up to 80 characters, including separating spaces. See [P] **program properties**.

sortpreserve states that the program changes the sort order of the data and that Stata is to restore the original order when the program concludes; see [P] **sortpreserve**.

plugin specifies that a plugin (a specially compiled C program) be dynamically loaded and that the plugin define the new command; see [P] **plugin**.

Remarks

The program dir command lists the names of all the programs stored in memory. program list lists contents of the program or programs.

> ## Example 1

When you start Stata, there are no programs stored in memory. If you type program dir, Stata displays an empty list:

```
. program dir

.
```

Later during the session, you might see

```
. program dir
 (output omitted )
    ado       756  _pred_se
    ado       644  logit_p.GenScores
    ado       306  logit_p.GetRhs
    ado      5294  logit_p
    ado       339  predict
 (output omitted )
    ado       559  logit.Replay
    ado      4169  logit.Estimate
    ado       827  logit
    ado       238  webuse.Query
    ado       588  webuse.Set
    ado       266  webuse.GetDefault
    ado       686  webuse
    ---------
          114306
```

The `ado` in front indicates that the program was automatically loaded and thus can be automatically dropped should memory become scarce; see [U] **17 Ado-files**. The number is the size, in bytes, of the program. The total amount of memory occupied by programs is 114,306 bytes. Notice the `logit_p.GetRhs` and `logit_p.GenScores` entries. These programs are defined in the `logit_p.ado` file and were loaded when `logit_p` was loaded.

Let's now create two of our own programs with `program`:

```
. program rng
  1. args n a b
  2. if "'b'"=="" {
  3.     display "You must type three arguments: n a b"
  4.     exit
  5. }
  6. drop _all
  7. set obs 'n'
  8. generate x = (_n-1)/(_N-1)*('b'-'a')+'a'
  9. end

. program smooth
  1. args v1 v2
  2. confirm variable 'v1'
  3. confirm new variable 'v2'
  4. generate 'v2' = cond(_n==1|_n==_N,'v1',('v1'[_n-1]+'v1'+'v1'[_n+1])/3)
  5. end
```

After you type `program`, lines are collected until you type a line with the word `end`. For our purposes, it does not matter what these programs do. If we were now to type `program dir`, we would see

```
. program dir
              286    smooth
              319    rng
  (output omitted )
   ado        756    _pred_se
   ado        644    logit_p.GenScores
   ado        306    logit_p.GetRhs
   ado       5294    logit_p
   ado        339    predict
  (output omitted )
   ado        559    logit.Replay
   ado       4169    logit.Estimate
   ado        827    logit
   ado        238    webuse.Query
   ado        588    webuse.Set
   ado        266    webuse.GetDefault
   ado        686    webuse
           ────────
            114911
```

We can list a program by using the `program list` command:

```
. program list smooth
smooth:
  1. args v1 v2
  2. confirm variable 'v1'
  3. confirm new variable 'v2'
  4. generate 'v2' = cond(_n==1|_n==_N,'v1',('v1'[_n-1]+'v1'+'v1'[_n+1])/3)
```

If we do not specify the program that we want listed, `program list` lists all the programs stored in memory.

The `program drop` command eliminates programs from memory. Typing `program drop` *program_name* eliminates *program_name* from memory. Typing `program drop _all` eliminates all programs from memory.

```
. program drop smooth
. program dir
            319  rng
  (output omitted )
   ado     756  _pred_se
   ado     644  logit_p.GenScores
   ado     306  logit_p.GetRhs
   ado    5294  logit_p
   ado     339  predict
  (output omitted )
   ado     559  logit.Replay
   ado    4169  logit.Estimate
   ado     827  logit
   ado     238  webuse.Query
   ado     588  webuse.Set
   ado     266  webuse.GetDefault
   ado     686  webuse
          _____
         114625
. program drop _all
. program dir
.
```

◁

Also see

[P] **byable** — Make programs byable

[P] **discard** — Drop automatically loaded programs

[D] **clear** — Clear memory

[P] **sortpreserve** — Sort within programs

[P] **trace** — Debug Stata programs

[R] **query** — Display system parameters

[U] **18 Programming Stata**

Title

Description

User-defined programs can have properties associated with them. Some of Stata's prefix commands—such as `svy` and `stepwise`—use these properties for command validation. You can associate program properties with programs by using the `properties()` option of `program`.

> program [define] *command* [, properties(*namelist*) ...]
>> // *body of the program*
>
> end

You can retrieve program properties of *command* by using the `properties` extended macro function.

> global *mname* : properties *command*
>
> local *lclname* : properties *command*

Option

`properties(`*namelist*`)` states that *command* has the specified properties. *namelist* may contain up to 80 characters, including separating spaces.

Remarks

Remarks are presented under the following headings:

> *Introduction*
> *Writing programs for use with nestreg and stepwise*
> *Writing programs for use with svy*
> *Writing programs for use with mi*
> *Properties for survival-analysis commands*
> *Properties for exponentiating coefficients*
> *Putting it all together*
> *Checking for program properties*

Introduction

Properties provide a way for a program to indicate to other programs that certain features have been implemented. Suppose that you want to use `stepwise` with the `lr` option so that likelihood-ratio tests are performed in the model-selection process. To do that, `stepwise` must know that the estimation command you are using in conjunction with it is a maximum likelihood estimator. If a command declares itself to have the `swml` property, `stepwise` knows that the command can be used with likelihood-ratio tests.

The next few sections discuss properties that are checked by some of Stata's prefix commands and how to make your own programs work with those prefix commands.

Writing programs for use with nestreg and stepwise

Some of Stata's estimation commands can be used with the nestreg and stepwise prefix commands; see [R] **nestreg** and [R] **stepwise**. For example, the syntax diagram for the regress command could be presented as

$$\big[\, \texttt{nestreg, } \ldots : \big]\ \underline{\texttt{regress}} \ \ldots$$

or

$$\big[\, \texttt{stepwise, } \ldots : \big]\ \underline{\texttt{regress}} \ \ldots$$

In general, the syntax for these prefix commands is

$$\textit{prefix\_command}\ \big[\, ,\ \textit{prefix\_options}\, \big]\ :\ \textit{command depvar (varlist)}\ \big[\, \textit{(varlist)}\ \ldots \big]$$
$$\big[\, \textit{if}\, \big]\ \big[\, \textit{in}\, \big]\ \big[\, ,\ \textit{options}\, \big]$$

where *prefix_command* is either nestreg or stepwise.

You must follow some additional programming requirements to write programs (ado-files) that can be used with the nestreg and stepwise prefix commands. Some theoretical requirements must be satisfied to justify using nestreg or stepwise with a given command.

- *command* must be eclass and accept the standard estimation syntax; see [P] **program**, [P] **syntax**, and [P] **mark**.

  $$\textit{command varlist}\ \big[\, \textit{if}\, \big]\ \big[\, \textit{in}\, \big]\ \big[\, \textit{weight}\, \big]\ \big[\, ,\ \textit{options}\, \big]$$

- *command* must save the model coefficients and ancillary parameters in e(b) and the estimation sample size in e(N), and it must identify the estimation subsample in e(sample); see [P] **ereturn**.

- For the likelihood-ratio test, *command* must have property swml. For example, the program definition for poisson appears as

  ```
  program poisson, ... properties(... swml ...)
  ```

  command must also save the log-likelihood value in e(ll) and the model degrees of freedom in e(df_m).

- For the Wald test, *command* must have property sw if it does not already have property swml. For example, the program definition for qreg appears as

  ```
  program qreg, ... properties(... sw ...)
  ```

  command must also save the variance estimates for the coefficients and ancillary parameters in e(V); see [R] **test**.

Writing programs for use with svy

Some of Stata's estimation commands can be used with the svy prefix; see [SVY] **svy**. For example, the syntax diagram for the regress command could be presented as

$$\big[\, \texttt{svy, } \ldots : \big]\ \underline{\texttt{regress}} \ \ldots$$

In general, the syntax for the svy prefix is

$$\texttt{svy}\ \big[\, ,\ \textit{svy\_options}\, \big]\ :\ \textit{command varlist}\ \big[\, \textit{if}\, \big]\ \big[\, \textit{in}\, \big]\ \big[\, ,\ \textit{options}\, \big]$$

You must follow some additional programming requirements to write programs (ado-files) that can be used with the svy prefix. The extra requirements imposed by the svy prefix command are from the three variance-estimation methods that it uses: vce(brr), vce(jackknife), and vce(linearized). Each of these variance-estimation methods has theoretical requirements that must be satisfied to justify using them with a given command.

- *command* must be eclass and allow iweights and accept the standard estimation syntax; see [P] **program**, [P] **syntax**, and [P] **mark**.

    command varlist $\left[\,if\,\right]$ $\left[\,in\,\right]$ $\left[\,weight\,\right]$ $\left[\,,\ options\,\right]$

- *command* must save the model coefficients and ancillary parameters in e(b) and the estimation sample size in e(N), and it must identify the estimation subsample in e(sample); see [P] **ereturn**.

- svy's vce(brr) requires that *command* have svyb as a property. For example, the program definition for regress appears as

    program regress, ... properties(... svyb ...)

- vce(jackknife) requires that *command* have svyj as a property.

- vce(linearized) has the following requirements:

  a. *command* must have svyr as a property.

  b. predict after *command* must be able to generate scores with the following syntax:

    predict $\left[\,type\,\right]$ *stub** $\left[\,if\,\right]$ $\left[\,in\,\right]$, <u>sc</u>ores

    This syntax implies that estimation results with k equations will cause predict to generate k new equation-level score variables. These new equation-level score variables are *stub*1 for the first equation, *stub*2 for the second equation, ..., and *stubk* for the last equation. Actually svy does not strictly require that these new variables be named this way, but this is a good convention to follow.

    The equation-level score variables generated by predict must be of the form that can be used to estimate the variance by using Taylor linearization (otherwise known as the delta method); see [SVY] **variance estimation**.

  c. *command* must save the model-based variance estimator for the coefficients and ancillary parameters in e(V); see [SVY] **variance estimation**.

Writing programs for use with mi

Stata's mi suite of commands provides multiple imputation to provide better estimates of parameters and their standard errors in the presence of missing values; see [MI] **intro**. Estimation commands intended for use with the mi estimate prefix must have property mi, indicating that the command meets the following requirements:

- The command is eclass.

- The command saves its name in e(cmd).

- The command saves the model coefficients and ancillary parameters in e(b), saves the corresponding variance matrix in e(V), saves the estimation sample size in e(N), and identifies the estimation subsample in e(sample).

- If the command employs a small-sample adjustment for tests of coefficients and reports of confidence intervals, the command saves the numerator (residual) degrees of freedom in e(df_r).

- Because mi estimate uses its own routines to display the output, to ensure that results display well the command also saves its title in e(title). mi estimate also uses macros e(vcetype) or e(vce) to label the within-imputation variance, but those macros are usually set automatically by other Stata routines.

Properties for survival-analysis commands

Stata's st suite of commands have the st program property, indicating that they have the following characteristics:

- The command should only be run on data that have been previously stset.

- No dependent variable is specified when calling that command. All variables in *varlist* are regressors. The "dependent" variable is time or failure, handled by stset.

- Weights are not specified with the command but instead obtained from stset.

- If robust or replication-based standard errors are requested, the default level of clustering is according to the ID variable that was stset, if any.

Properties for exponentiating coefficients

Stata has several prefix commands—such as bootstrap, jackknife, and svy—that use alternative variance-estimation techniques for existing commands. These prefix commands behave like conventional estimation commands when reporting and saving estimation results. Given the appropriate program properties, these prefix commands can also report exponentiated coefficients. In fact, the property names for the various shortcuts for the eform() option are the same as the option names:

option/property	Description
hr	hazard ratio
nohr	coefficient instead of hazard ratio
shr	subhazard ratio
noshr	coefficient instead of subhazard ratio
irr	incidence-rate ratio
or	odds ratio
rrr	relative-risk ratio

For example, the program definition for logit looks something like the following:

```
program logit, ... properties(... or ...)
```

Putting it all together

logit can report odds ratios, works with svy, and works with stepwise. The program definition for logit reads

> program logit, ... properties(or svyb svyj svyr swml) ...

Checking for program properties

You can use the properties extended macro function to check the properties associated with a program; see [P] **macro**. For example, the following macro retrieves and displays the program properties for logit.

```
. local logitprops : properties logit
. di "`logitprops'"
or svyb svyj svyr swml
```

Also see

[R] **nestreg** — Nested model statistics

[R] **stepwise** — Stepwise estimation

[SVY] **svy** — The survey prefix command

[U] **20 Estimation and postestimation commands**

[P] **program** — Define and manipulate programs

Title

quietly — Quietly and noisily perform Stata command

Syntax

Perform command but suppress terminal output

> quietly $\begin{bmatrix} : \end{bmatrix}$ *command*

Perform command and ensure terminal output

> noisily $\begin{bmatrix} : \end{bmatrix}$ *command*

Specify type of output to display

> set output { proc | inform | error }

Description

quietly suppresses all terminal output for the duration of *command*.

noisily turns back on terminal output, if appropriate, for the duration of *command*. It is useful only in programs.

set output specifies the output to be displayed.

Remarks

Remarks are presented under the following headings:

> *quietly used interactively*
> *quietly used in programs*
> *Note for programmers*

quietly used interactively

▷ Example 1

quietly is useful when you are using Stata interactively and want to temporarily suppress the terminal output. For instance, to estimate a regression of mpg on the variables weight, foreign, and headroom and to suppress the terminal output, type

```
. use http://www.stata-press.com/data/r11/auto
(1978 Automobile Data)
. quietly regress mpg weight foreign headroom
. _
```

Admittedly, it is unlikely that you would ever want to do this in real life.

◁

quietly used in programs

❏ Technical note

quietly is often used in programs. Say that you have the following program to run a regression of y on x, calculate the residuals, and then list the outliers, which are defined as points with residuals below the 5th percentile or above the 95th percentile:

```
program myprog
        regress '1' '2'
        predict resid, resid
        sort resid
        summarize resid, detail
        list '1' '2' resid if resid< r(p5) | resid> r(p95)
        drop resid
end
```

Although the program will work, it will also fill the screen with the regression output, any notes that predict feels obligated to mention, and the detailed output from summarize. A better version of this program might read

```
program myprog
        quietly regress '1' '2'
        quietly predict resid, resid
        quietly sort resid
        quietly summarize resid, detail
        list '1' '2' resid if resid< r(p5) | resid> r(p95)
        drop resid
end
```

You can also combine quietly with { }:

```
program myprog
        quietly {
                regress '1' '2'
                predict resid, resid
                sort resid
                summarize resid, detail
        }
        list '1' '2' resid if resid< r(p5) | resid> r(p95)
        drop resid
end
```

❏

❏ Technical note

noisily is the antonym of quietly, and it too can be used in programs and do-files. In fact, that is its only real use. We could recode our example program to read as follows:

```
program myprog
        quietly {
                regress '1' '2'
                predict resid, resid
                sort resid
                summarize resid, detail
                noisily list '1' '2' resid if resid< r(p5) | resid> r(p95)
                drop resid
        }
end
```

Here we have not improved readability.

❏

❏ Technical note

noisily is not really the antonym of quietly. If the user types quietly myprog yvar xvar, the output will be suppressed because that is what the user wants. Here a noisily inside myprog will not display the output—noisily means noisily only if the program was allowed to be noisy when it was invoked.

❏

❏ Technical note

If you think you understand all this, take the following test. Is there any difference between quietly do *filename* and run *filename*? How about noisily run *filename* and do *filename*? What would happen if you typed quietly noisily summarize *myvar*? If you typed noisily quietly summarize *myvar*?

When you are ready, we will tell you the answers.

quietly do *filename* is equivalent to run *filename*. Typing run is easier, however.

noisily run *filename* is not at all the same as do *filename*. run produces no output, and no matter how noisily you run run, it is still quiet.

Typing quietly noisily summarize *myvar* is the same as typing summarize myvar. Think of it as quietly {noisily summarize *myvar*}. It is the inside noisily that takes precedence.

Typing noisily quietly summarize *myvar* is the same as typing quietly summarize *myvar*—it does nothing but burn computer time. Again it is the inside term, quietly this time, that takes precedence.

❏

❏ Technical note

set output proc means that all output, including procedure (command) output, is displayed. inform suppresses procedure output but displays informative messages and error messages. error suppresses all output except error messages. In practice, set output is seldom used.

❏

Note for programmers

If you write a program or ado-file, say, mycmd, there is nothing special you need to do so that your command can be prefixed with quietly. That said, c-class value c(noisily) (see [P] **creturn**) will return 0 if output is being suppressed and 1 otherwise. Thus your program might read

```
program mycmd
    ...
    display ...
    display ...
    ...
end
```

or

```
program mycmd
   ...
   if c(noisily) {
      display ...
      display ...
   }
   ...
end
```

The first style is preferred. If the user executes `quietly mycmd`, the output from `display` itself, along with the output of all other commands, will be automatically suppressed.

If the program must work substantially to produce what is being displayed, however, and the only reason for doing that work is because of the display, then the second style is preferred. In such cases, you can include the extra work within the block of code executed only when `c(noisily)` is true and thus make your program execute more quickly when it is invoked `quietly`.

Also see

[P] **capture** — Capture return code

[U] **18 Programming Stata**

Title

_return — Preserve saved results

Syntax

Save contents of r()

    _return hold *name*

Restore contents of r() from name

    _return restore *name* [, hold]

Drop specified _return name

    _return drop {*name* | _all}

List names currently saved by _return

    _return dir

Description

_return saves and restores the contents of r().

_return hold saves under *name* the contents of r() and clears r(). If *name* is a name obtained from *tempname*, *name* will be dropped automatically at the program's conclusion, if it is not automatically or explicitly dropped before that.

_return restore restores from *name* the contents of r() and, unless option hold is specified, drops *name*.

_return drop removes from memory (drops) *name* or, if _all is specified, all _return names currently saved.

_return dir lists the names currently saved by _return.

Option

hold, specified with _return restore, specifies that results continue to be held so that they can be _return restored later, as well. If the option is not specified, the specified results are restored and *name* is dropped.

Remarks

_return is rarely necessary. Most programs open with

```
program example
        version 11
        syntax ...
        marksample touse
        if '"'exp'"' != "" {
                touse e
                qui gen double 'e' = 'exp' if 'touse'
        }
        ... (code to calculate final results)...
end
```

In the program above, no commands are given that change the contents of r() until all parsing is complete and the if *exp* and =*exp* are evaluated. Thus the user can type

```
. summarize myvar
. example ... if myvar>r(mean) ...
```

and the results will be as the user expects.

Some programs, however, have nonstandard and complicated syntax, and in the process of deciphering that syntax, other r-class commands might be run before the user-specified expressions are evaluated. Consider a command that reads

```
program example2
        version 11
        ... (commands that parse)...
        ... (r()  might be reset at this stage)...
        ... commands that evaluate user-specified expressions...
        tempvar touse
        mark 'touse' 'if'
        tempvar v1 v2
        gen double 'v1' = 'exp1' if 'touse'
                                // 'exp1' specified by user
        gen double 'v2' = 'exp2' if 'touse'
                                // 'exp2' specified by user
        ... (code to calculate final results)...
end
```

Here it would be a disaster if the user typed

```
. summarize myvar
. example2 ... if myvar>r(mean) ...
```

because r(mean) would not mean what the user expected it to mean, which is the mean of myvar. The solution to this problem is to code the following:

```
program example2
        version 11
                                        // save r()
        tempname myr
        _return hold 'myr'
        ... (commands that parse)...
        ... (r()  might be reset at this stage)...
        ... commands that evaluate user-specified expressions...
```

```
                                // restore r()
               _return restore 'myr'

               tempvar touse
               mark 'touse' 'if'
               tempvar v1 v2
               gen double 'v1' = 'exp1' if 'touse'
                                // 'exp1' specified by user
               gen double 'v2' = 'exp2' if 'touse'
                                // 'exp2' specified by user
               . . .(code to calculate final results). . .
         end
```

In the above example, we save the contents of r() in 'myr' and then later bring them back.

Saved results

_return restore resaves in r() what was saved in r() when _return hold was executed.

Also see

[P] **return** — Return saved results

Title

---

return — Return saved results

Syntax

Return results stored in r()

   <u>ret</u>urn clear

   <u>ret</u>urn <u>sca</u>lar *name* = *exp*

   <u>ret</u>urn <u>loc</u>al *name* = *exp*

   <u>ret</u>urn <u>loc</u>al *name* $\begin{bmatrix} " \end{bmatrix}$ *string* $\begin{bmatrix} " \end{bmatrix}$

   <u>ret</u>urn <u>mat</u>rix *name* $\begin{bmatrix} = \end{bmatrix}$ *matname* $\begin{bmatrix} , & \text{copy} \end{bmatrix}$

   <u>ret</u>urn add

Return results stored in e()

   <u>eret</u>urn clear

   <u>eret</u>urn post $\begin{bmatrix} \mathbf{b} & \begin{bmatrix} \mathbf{V} & \begin{bmatrix} \mathbf{Cns} \end{bmatrix} \end{bmatrix} \end{bmatrix}$ $\begin{bmatrix} weight \end{bmatrix}$ $\begin{bmatrix} , & \underline{\text{dep}}\text{name}(string) & \underline{\text{obs}}(\#) & \underline{\text{dof}}(\#) \end{bmatrix}$

      <u>e</u>sample(*varname*) <u>prop</u>erties(*string*) $\Big]$

   <u>eret</u>urn <u>sca</u>lar *name* = *exp*

   <u>eret</u>urn <u>loc</u>al *name* = *exp*

   <u>eret</u>urn <u>loc</u>al *name* $\begin{bmatrix} " \end{bmatrix}$ *string* $\begin{bmatrix} " \end{bmatrix}$

   <u>eret</u>urn <u>mat</u>rix *name* $\begin{bmatrix} = \end{bmatrix}$ *matname* $\begin{bmatrix} , & \text{copy} \end{bmatrix}$

   <u>eret</u>urn repost $\begin{bmatrix} \mathbf{b} = \mathbf{b} \end{bmatrix}$ $\begin{bmatrix} \mathbf{V} = \mathbf{V} \end{bmatrix}$ $\begin{bmatrix} \mathbf{Cns} = \mathbf{Cns} \end{bmatrix}$ $\begin{bmatrix} weight \end{bmatrix}$ $\begin{bmatrix} , & \underline{\text{e}}\text{sample}(varname) \end{bmatrix}$

      <u>prop</u>erties(*string*) <u>ren</u>ame $\Big]$

Return results stored in s()

   <u>sret</u>urn clear

   <u>sret</u>urn <u>loc</u>al *name* = *exp*

   <u>sret</u>urn <u>loc</u>al *name* $\begin{bmatrix} " \end{bmatrix}$ *string* $\begin{bmatrix} " \end{bmatrix}$

where **b**, **V**, and **Cns** are *matnames*, which is the name of an existing matrix.

fweights, aweights, iweights, and pweights are allowed; see [U] **11.1.6 weight**.

337

Description

Results of calculations are saved by many Stata commands so that they can be easily accessed and substituted into subsequent commands. This entry summarizes for programmers how to save results. If your interest is in using previously saved results, see [R] **saved results**.

return saves results in r().

ereturn saves results in e().

sreturn saves results in s().

Stata also has the values of system parameters and certain constants such as pi stored in c(). Because these values may be referred to but not assigned, the c-class is discussed in a different entry; see [P] **creturn**.

Options

copy specified with return matrix or ereturn matrix indicates that the matrix is to be copied; that is, the original matrix should be left in place. The default is to "steal" or "rename" the existing matrix, which is fast and conserves memory.

depname(*string*) is for use with ereturn post. It supplies the name of the dependent variable to appear in the estimation output. The name specified need not be the name of an existing variable.

obs(#) is for use with ereturn post. It specifies the number of observations on which the estimation was performed. This number is stored in e(N), and obs() is provided simply for convenience. Results are no different from those for ereturn post followed by ereturn scalar N = #.

dof(#) is for use with ereturn post. It specifies the number of denominator degrees of freedom to be used with t and F statistics and so is used in calculating significance levels and confidence intervals. The number specified is saved in e(df_r), and dof() is provided simply for convenience. Results are no different from those for ereturn post followed by ereturn scalar df_r = #.

esample(*varname*) is for use with ereturn post and ereturn repost. It specifies the name of a 0/1 variable that is to become the e(sample) function. *varname* must contain 0 and 1 values only, with 1 indicating that the observation is in the estimation subsample. ereturn post and ereturn repost will be able to execute a little more quickly if *varname* is stored as a byte variable.

varname is dropped from the dataset, or more correctly, it is stolen and stashed in a secret place.

properties(*string*) specified with ereturn post or ereturn repost sets the e(properties) macro. By default, e(properties) is set to b V if properties() is not specified.

rename is for use with the b = b syntax of ereturn repost. All numeric estimation results remain unchanged, but the labels of **b** are substituted for the variable and equation names of the already posted results.

Remarks

Remarks are presented under the following headings:

Introduction
Saving results in r()
Saving results in e()
Saving results in s()
Recommended names for saved results

Introduction

This entry summarizes information that is presented in greater detail in other parts of the Stata documentation. Most particularly, we recommend that you read [U] **18 Programming Stata**. The commands listed above are used by programmers to save results, which are accessed by others using r(), e(), and s(); see [R] **saved results**.

The commands listed above may be used only in programs—see [U] **18 Programming Stata** and [P] **program**—and then only when the program is declared explicitly as being rclass, eclass, or sclass:

```
program ..., rclass
        ...
        return ...
        ...
end

program ..., eclass
        ...
        ereturn ...
        ...
end

program ..., sclass
        ...
        sreturn ...
        ...
end
```

Saving results in r()

• The program must be declared explicitly to be r-class: program ... , rclass.

• Distinguish between r() (returned results) and return() (results being assembled that will be returned). The program you write actually stores results in return(). Then when your program completes, whatever is in return() is copied to r(). Thus the program you write can consume r() results from other programs, and there is no conflict.

• return clear clears the return() class. This command is seldom used because return() starts out empty when your program begins. return clear is for those instances when you have started assembling results and all is going well, but given the problem at hand, you need to start all over again.

• return scalar *name* = *exp* evaluates *exp* and stores the result in the scalar return(*name*). *exp* must evaluate to a numeric result or missing. If your code has previously stored something in return(*name*), whether a scalar, matrix, or whatever else, the previous value is discarded and this result replaces it.

- return local *name* = *exp* evaluates *exp* and stores the result in the macro return(*name*). *exp* may evaluate to a numeric or string result. If your code has previously stored something in return(*name*), whether a scalar, matrix, or whatever else, the previous value is discarded and this result replaces it.

  Be careful with this syntax: do not code

  ```
  return local name = 'mymacro'
  ```

  because that will copy just the first 244 characters of '*mymacro*'. Instead, code

  ```
  return local name '"'mymacro'"'
  ```

- return local *name string* copies *string* to macro return(*name*). If your code has previously stored something in return(*name*), whether a scalar, matrix, or whatever else, the previous value is discarded and this result replaces it.

  If you do not enclose *string* in double quotes, multiple blanks in *string* are compressed into single blanks.

- return matrix *name matname* destructively copies matname into matrix return(*name*), meaning that *matname* is erased (*matname* is renamed return(*name*)). If your code has previously stored something in return(*name*), whether a scalar, matrix, or whatever else, the previous value is discarded and this result replaces it.

- return add copies everything new in r() into return(). Say that your program performed a summarize. return add lets you add everything just returned by summarize to the to-be-returned results of your program. If your program had already set return(N), summarize's r(N) would not replace the previously set result. The remaining r() results set by summarize would be copied.

Saving results in e()

For detailed guidance on saving in e(), see [P] **ereturn**. What follows is a summary.

- The program must be declared explicitly to be e-class: program ... , eclass.

- The e-class is cleared whenever an ereturn post is executed. The e-class is a static, single-level class, meaning that results are posted to the class the instant that they are stored.

- ereturn clear clears e(). This is a rarely used command.

- ereturn post is how you must begin saving results in e(). Because ereturn post clears e(), anything saved in e() prior to the ereturn post is lost.

  ereturn post saves matrix (vector, really) e(b), matrices e(V) and e(Cns), weight-related macros e(wtype) and e(wexp), and function e(sample). The most common syntax is

  ```
  ereturn post 'b' 'V', esample('touse') ...
  ```

  where 'b' is a row vector containing the parameter estimates, 'V' is a symmetric matrix containing the variance estimates, and 'touse' is a 0/1 variable recording 1 in observations that appear in the estimation subsample.

  The result of this command will be that 'b', 'V', and 'touse' all disappear. In fact, ereturn post examines what you specify and, if it is satisfied with them, renames them e(b), e(V), and e(sample).

  For more advanced usage that also posts constraint and weight information, see [P] **ereturn**.

In terms of `ereturn post`'s other options,

a. We recommend that you specify `depname(`*string*`)` if there is one dependent variable name that you want to appear on the output. Whether you specify `depname()` or not, remember later to define macro `e(depvar)` to contain the names of the dependent variables.

b. Specify `obs(#)`, or remember later to define scalar `e(N)` to contain the number of observations.

c. Few models require specifying `dof(#)`, or, if that is not done, remembering to later define scalar `e(df_r)`. This all has to do with substituting t and F statistics on the basis of # (denominator) degrees of freedom for asymptotic z and χ^2 statistics in the estimation output.

- `ereturn scalar` *name* = *exp* evaluates *exp* and stores the result in the scalar `e(`*name*`)`. *exp* must evaluate to a numeric result or missing. If your code has previously stored something in `e(`*name*`)`, whether that be a scalar, matrix, or whatever else, the previous value is discarded and this result replaces it.

- `ereturn local` *name* = *exp* evaluates *exp* and stores the result in the macro `e(`*name*`)`. *exp* may evaluate to a numeric or string result. If your code has previously stored something in `e(`*name*`)`, whether that be a scalar, matrix, or whatever else, the previous value is discarded and this result replaces it.

Be careful with this syntax: do not code

> `ereturn local` *name* = `'`*mymacro*`'`

because that will copy just the first 244 characters of `'`*mymacro*`'`. Instead, code

> `ereturn local` *name* `'"'`*mymacro*`'"'`

- `ereturn local` *name* *string* copies *string* to macro `e(`*name*`)`. If your code has previously stored something in `e(`*name*`)`, whether a scalar, matrix, or whatever else, the previous value is discarded and this result replaces it.

If you do not enclose *string* in double quotes, multiple blanks in *string* are compressed into single blanks.

- `ereturn matrix` *name* = *matname* destructively copies `matname` into matrix `e(`*name*`)`, meaning that *matname* is erased. At least, that is what happens if you do not specify the `copy` option. What actually occurs is that *matname* is renamed `e(`*name*`)`. If your code has previously stored something in `e(`*name*`)`, whether a scalar, matrix, or whatever else, the previous value is discarded and this result replaces it, with two exceptions:

`ereturn matrix` cannot be used to save in `e(b)` or `e(V)`. The only way to post matrices to these special names is to use `ereturn post` and `ereturn repost` so that various tests can be run on them before they are made official. Other Stata commands use `e(b)` and `e(V)` and expect to see a valid estimation result. If `e(b)` is $1 \times k$, they expect `e(V)` to be $k \times k$. They expect that the names of rows and columns will be the same so that the ith column of `e(b)` corresponds to the ith row and column of `e(V)`. They expect `e(V)` to be symmetric. They expect `e(V)` to have positive or zero elements along its diagonal, and so on. `ereturn post` and `ereturn repost` check these assumptions.

- `ereturn repost` allows changing `e(b)`, `e(V)`, `e(Cns)`, `e(wtype)`, `e(wexp)`, `e(properties)`, and `e(sample)` without clearing the estimation results and starting all over again. As with `ereturn post`, specified matrices and variables disappear after reposting because they are renamed `e(b)`, `e(V)`, `e(Cns)`, or `e(sample)` as appropriate.

- Programmers posting estimation results should remember to save
  a. Macro e(cmd), containing the name of the estimation command. Make this the last thing you save in e().
  b. Macro e(cmdline), containing the command the user typed.
  c. Macro e(depvar), containing the names of the dependent variables.
  d. Scalar e(N), containing the number of observations.
  e. Scalar e(df_m), containing the model degrees of freedom.
  f. Scalar e(df_r), containing the denominator degrees of freedom if estimates are nonasymptotic; otherwise, do not define this result.
  g. Scalar e(ll), containing the log-likelihood value, if relevant.
  h. Scalar e(ll_0), containing the log-likelihood value for the constant-only model, if relevant.
  i. Scalar e(chi2), containing the χ^2 test of the model against the constant-only model, if relevant.
  j. Macro e(chi2type), containing LR, Wald, or other, depending on how e(chi2) was obtained.
  k. Scalar e(r2), containing the value of the R^2 if it is calculated.
  l. Scalar e(r2_p), containing the value of the pseudo-R^2 if it is calculated.
  m. Macro e(vce), containing the name of the *vcetype* that was specified in the vce() option; see [R] *vce_option*.
  n. Macro e(vcetype), containing the text to appear above standard errors in estimation output, typically Robust, or it is undefined.
  o. Macro e(clustvar), containing the name of the cluster variable, if any.
  p. Scalar e(N_clust), containing the number of clusters.
  q. Scalar e(rank), containing the rank of e(V).
  r. Macro e(predict), containing the name of the command that predict is to use; if this is blank, predict uses the default _predict.
  s. Macro e(estat_cmd), containing the name of an estat handler program if you wish to customize the behavior of estat.
  t. Macro e(properties), containing properties of the estimation command, typically b V, indicating that the command produces a legitimate coefficient vector and VCE matrix.

Saving results in s()

- The program must be declared explicitly to be s-class: program ... , sclass.

- The s-class is not cleared automatically. It is a static, single-level class. Results are posted to s() the instant they are saved.

- sreturn clear clears s(). We recommend that you use this command near the top of s-class routines. sreturn clear may be used in non–s-class programs, too.

- The s-class provides macros only and is intended for returning results of subroutines that parse input. At the parsing step, it is important that the r-class not be changed or cleared because some of what still awaits being parsed might refer to r(), and the user expects those results to substitute according to what was in r() when he or she typed the command.

- sreturn local *name* = *exp* evaluates *exp* and stores the result in the macro s(*name*). *exp* may evaluate to a numeric or string result. If your code has previously stored something else in s(*name*), the previous value is discarded and this result replaces it.

Be careful with this syntax: do not code

> sreturn local *name* = `'mymacro'`

because that will copy just the first 244 characters of `'mymacro'`. Instead, code

> sreturn local *name* `'"'mymacro'"'`

- sreturn local *name string* copies *string* to macro s(*name*). If your code has previously stored something else in s(*name*), the previous value is discarded and this result replaces it.

  If you do not enclose *string* in double quotes, multiple blanks in *string* are compressed into single blanks.

Recommended names for saved results

Users will appreciate it if you use predictable names for your saved results. We use these rules:

- Mathematical and statistical concepts such as number of observations and degrees of freedom are given short mathematical-style names. Subscripting is indicated with '_'. Names are to proceed from the general to the specific. If N means number of observations, N_1 might be the number of observations in the first group.

  Suffixes are to be avoided where possible. For instance, a χ^2 statistic would be recorded in a variable starting with chi2. If, in the context of the command, a statement about "the χ^2 statistic" would be understood as referring to this statistic, then the name would be chi2. If it required further modification, such as χ^2 for the comparison test, then the name might be chi2_c.

  Common prefixes are

N	number of observations
df	degrees of freedom
k	count of parameters
n	generic count
lb and ub	lower and upper bound of confidence interval
chi2	χ^2 statistic
t	t statistic
F	F statistic
p	significance
p and pr	probability
ll	log likelihood
D	deviance
r2	R^2

- Programming concepts, such as lists of variable names, are given English-style names. Names should proceed from the specific to the general. The name of the dependent variable is depvar, not vardep.

  Some examples are

depvar	dependent variable names
eqnames	equation names
model	name of model fit
xvar	x variable
title	title used

- Popular usage takes precedence over the rules. For example:

  a. mss is model sum of squares, even though, per the first rule of this section, it ought to be ss_m.

  b. mean is used as the prefix to record means.

  c. Var is used as the prefix to mean variance.

  d. The returned results from most Stata commands follow this rule.

Also see

[P] **creturn** — Return c-class values

[P] **ereturn** — Post the estimation results

[P] **_estimates** — Manage estimation results

[P] **_return** — Preserve saved results

[R] **saved results** — Saved results

[U] **18 Programming Stata**

[U] **18.10 Saving results**

Title

_rmcoll — Remove collinear variables

Syntax

Identify variables to be omitted because of collinearity

    _rmcoll *varlist* [*if*] [*in*] [*weight*] [, noconstant collinear expand forcedrop]

Identify independent variables to be omitted because of collinearity

    _rmdcoll *depvar indepvars* [*if*] [*in*] [*weight*] [, noconstant collinear expand

        forcedrop normcoll]

fweights, aweights, iweights, and pweights are allowed; see [U] **11.1.6 weight**.

Description

    _rmcoll returns in r(varlist) an updated version of *varlist* that is specific to the sample identified by if, in, and any missing values in *varlist*. _rmcoll flags variables that are to be omitted because of collinearity. If *varlist* contains factor variables, then _rmcoll also enumerates the levels of factor variables, identifies the base levels of factor variables, and identifies empty cells in interactions.

    The following message is displayed for each variable that _rmcoll flags as omitted because of collinearity:

        note: _____ omitted because of collinearity

The following message is displayed for each empty cell of an interaction that _rmcoll encounters:

        note: _____ identifies no observations in the sample

    ml users: it is not necessary to call _rmcoll because ml flags collinear variables for you, assuming that you do not specify ml model's collinear option. Even so, ml programmers sometimes use _rmcoll because they need the sample-specific set of variables, and in such cases, they specify ml model's collinear option so that ml does not waste time looking for collinearity again.

    _rmdcoll performs the same task as _rmcoll and checks that *depvar* is not collinear with the variables in *indepvars*. If *depvar* is collinear with any of the variables in *indepvars*, then _rmdcoll reports the following message with the 459 error code:

        _____ collinear with _____

Options

noconstant specifies that, in looking for collinearity, an intercept not be included. That is, a variable that contains the same nonzero value in every observation should not be considered collinear.

collinear specifies that collinear variables not be flagged.

expand specifies that the expanded, level-specific variables be posted to r(varlist). This option will have an effect only if there are factor variables in the variable list.

345

forcedrop specifies that collinear variables be dropped from the variable list instead of being flagged. This option is not allowed when the variable list already contains flagged variables, factor variables, or interactions.

normcoll specifies that collinear variables have already been flagged in *indepvars*. Otherwise, _rmcoll is called first to flag any such collinearity.

Remarks

_rmcoll and _rmdcoll are typically used when writing estimation commands.

_rmcoll is used if the programmer wants to flag the collinear variables from the independent variables.

_rmdcoll is used if the programmer wants to detect collinearity of the dependent variable with the independent variables.

▷ Example 1: Flagging variables because of collinearity

Let's load auto.dta and add a variable called tt that is collinear with variables turn and trunk. The easiest way to do this is to generate tt as the sum of turn and trunk.

```
. use http://www.stata-press.com/data/r11/auto
(1978 Automobile Data)
. generate tt = turn + trunk
```

Now we can use _rmcoll to identify that we have a collinearity and flag a variable because of it.

```
. _rmcoll turn trunk tt
note: tt omitted because of collinearity
. display r(varlist)
turn trunk o.tt
```

_rmcoll reported that tt was being flagged because of collinearity and attached the omit operator to tt resulting in "o.tt" being returned in r(varlist).

◁

▷ Example 2: Factor variables

_rmcoll works with factor variables. Let's pass rep78 as a factor variable to _rmcoll.

```
. _rmcoll i.rep78
. display r(varlist)
i(1 2 3 4 5)b1.rep78
```

The updated variable list now contains the enumerated levels of rep78 and identifies its base level. Use the expand option if you want to be able to loop over the level-specific, individual variables in r(varlist).

```
. _rmcoll i.rep78, expand
. display r(varlist)
1b.rep78 2.rep78 3.rep78 4.rep78 5.rep78
```

◁

▷ Example 3: Interactions

_rmcoll works with interactions and reports when it encounters empty cells. An empty cell is a combination of factor levels that does not occur in the dataset. Let's use the table command with factor variables rep78 and foreign to see that there are two empty cells:

```
. table rep78 foreign
```

Repair Record 1978	Car type Domestic	Foreign
1	2	
2	8	
3	27	3
4	9	9
5	2	9

Now let's pass the interaction of factor variables rep78 and foreign to _rmcoll.

```
. _rmcoll rep78#foreign
note: 1.rep78#1.foreign identifies no observations in the sample
note: 2.rep78#1.foreign identifies no observations in the sample
. display r(varlist)
i(1 2 3 4 5)b1o(1 1 2).rep78#i(0 1)b0o(0 1 1).foreign
```

◁

▷ Example 4: Coding fragment for standard variables

A code fragment for a program that uses _rmcoll might read

```
...
syntax varlist [fweight iweight] ... [, noCONStant ... ]
marksample touse
if "'weight'" != "" {
        tempvar w
        quietly gen double 'w' = 'exp' if 'touse'
        local wgt ['weight'='w']
}
else    local wgt /* is nothing */
gettoken depvar xvars : varlist
_rmcoll 'xvars' 'wgt' if 'touse', 'constant'
local xvars 'r(varlist)'
...
```

In this code fragment, varlist contains one dependent variable and zero or more independent variables. The dependent variable is split off and stored in the local macro depvar. Then the remaining variables are passed through _rmcoll, and the resulting updated independent variable list is stored in the local macro xvars.

◁

▷ Example 5: Coding fragment for factor variables and time-series operators

Here we modified the above code fragment to allow for factor variables and time-series operators.

```
. . .
syntax varlist(fv ts) [fweight iweight] ... [, noCONStant ... ]
marksample touse
if "`weight'" != "" {
        tempvar w
        quietly gen double `w' = `exp' if `touse'
        local wgt [`weight'=`w']
}
else   local wgt /* is nothing */
gettoken depvar xvars : varlist
_rmcoll `xvars' `wgt' if `touse', expand `constant'
local xvars `r(varlist)'
. . .
```

The `varlist` argument in the `syntax` command contains the `fv` specifier to allow factor variables and the `ts` specifier to allow time-series operators. We also added the `expand` option in case the remaining code needs to loop over the level-specific, individual variables in the `xvars` macro.

◁

Saved results

_rmcoll and _rmdcoll save the following in `r()`:

Scalars
    r(omitted)   number of omitted variables in r(varlist)

Macros
    r(varlist)   the flagged and expanded variable list

Also see

[R] **ml** — Maximum likelihood estimation

[U] **18 Programming Stata**

Title

> **rmsg** — Return messages

Syntax

set $\underline{r}$msg { on | off } [, $\underline{perman}$ently]

Description

set rmsg determines whether the return message is to be displayed at the completion of each command. The initial setting is off. The return message shows how long the command took to execute and what time it completed execution.

Option

$\underline{perman}$ently specifies that, in addition to making the change right now, the rmsg setting be remembered and become the default setting when you invoke Stata.

Remarks

See [U] **8 Error messages and return codes** for a description of return messages and for use of this command.

Also see

[P] **timer** — Time sections of code by recording and reporting time spent

[P] **error** — Display generic error message and exit

[R] **query** — Display system parameters

[U] **8 Error messages and return codes**

Title

_robust — Robust variance estimates

Syntax

_robust *varlist* [*if*] [*in*] [*weight*] [, <u>var</u>iance(*matname*) minus(*#*)

<u>stra</u>ta(*varname*) psu(*varname*) <u>cl</u>uster(*varname*) fpc(*varname*)

<u>sub</u>pop(*varname*) vsrs(*matname*) <u>srs</u>subpop <u>zero</u>weight]

_robust works with models that have all types of varlists, including those with factor variables and times-series operators; see [U] **11.4.3 Factor variables** and [U] **11.4.4 Time-series varlists**.

pweights, aweights, fweights, and iweights are allowed; see [U] **11.1.6 weight**.

Description

_robust helps implement estimation commands and is rarely used. That is because other commands are implemented in terms of it and are easier and more convenient to use. For instance, if all you want to do is make your estimation command allow the vce(robust) and vce(cluster *clustvar*) options, see [R] **ml**. If you want to make your estimation command work with survey data, it is easier to make your command work with the svy prefix—see [P] **program properties**—rather than to use _robust.

If you really want to understand what ml and svy are doing, however, this is the section for you. Or, if you have an estimation problem that does not fit with the ml or svy framework, then _robust may be able to help.

_robust is a programmer's command that computes a robust variance estimator based on a varlist of equation-level scores and a covariance matrix. It produces estimators for ordinary data (each observation independent), clustered data (data not independent within groups, but independent across groups), and complex survey data from one stage of stratified cluster sampling.

The robust variance estimator goes by many names: Huber/White/sandwich are typically used in the context of robustness against heteroskedasticity. Survey statisticians often refer to this variance calculation as a first-order Taylor-series linearization method. Despite the different names, the estimator is the same.

The equation-level score variables (*varlist*) consist of one variable for single-equation models or multiple variables for multiple-equation models, one variable for each equation. The "covariance" matrix before adjustment is either posted using ereturn post (see [P] **ereturn**) or specified with the variance(*matname*) option. In the former case, _robust replaces the covariance in the post with the robust covariance matrix. In the latter case, the matrix *matname* is overwritten with the robust covariance matrix. Note: The robust covariance formula is $\mathbf{V} = \mathbf{DMD}$, where $\mathbf{D}$ is what we are calling the "covariance" matrix before adjustment; this is not always a true covariance. See *Remarks* below.

Before reading this section, you should be familiar with [U] **20.16 Obtaining robust variance estimates** and the *Methods and formulas* section of [R] **regress**. We assume that you have already programmed an estimator in Stata and now wish to have it compute robust variance estimates. If you have not yet programmed your estimator, see [U] **18 Programming Stata**, [R] **ml**, and [P] **ereturn**.

If you wish to program an estimator for survey data, then you should write the estimator for nonsurvey data first and then use the instructions in [P] **program properties** (making programs svyable) to get your estimation command to work properly with the svy prefix. See [SVY] **variance estimation** for a discussion of variance estimation for survey data.

Options

variance(*matname*) specifies a matrix containing the unadjusted "covariance" matrix, i.e., the D in $V = DMD$. The matrix must have its rows and columns labeled with the appropriate corresponding variable names, i.e., the names of the x's in $\mathbf{x}\beta$. If there are multiple equations, the matrix must have equation names; see [P] **matrix rownames**. The D matrix is overwritten with the robust covariance matrix V. If variance() is not specified, Stata assumes that D has been posted using ereturn post; _robust will then automatically post the robust covariance matrix V and replace D.

minus(#) specifies $k = \#$ for the multiplier $n/(n - k)$ of the robust variance estimator. Stata's maximum likelihood commands use $k = 1$, and so does the svy prefix. regress, vce(robust) uses, by default, this multiplier with k equal to the number of explanatory variables in the model, including the constant. The default is $k = 1$. See *Methods and formulas* for details.

strata(*varname*) specifies the name of a variable (numeric or string) that contains stratum identifiers.

psu(*varname*) specifies the name of a variable (numeric or string) that contains identifiers for the primary sampling unit (PSU). psu() and cluster() are synonyms; they both specify the same thing.

cluster(*varname*) is a synonym for psu().

fpc(*varname*) requests a finite population correction for the variance estimates. If the variable specified has values less than or equal to 1, it is interpreted as a stratum sampling rate $f_h = n_h/N_h$, where n_h is the number of PSUs sampled from stratum h and N_h is the total number of PSUs in the population belonging to stratum h. If the variable specified has values greater than 1, it is interpreted as containing N_h.

subpop(*varname*) specifies that estimates be computed for the single subpopulation defined by the observations for which *varname* $\neq 0$ (and is not missing). This option would typically be used only with survey data; see [SVY] **subpopulation estimation**.

vsrs(*matname*) creates a matrix containing $\widehat{V}_{\mathrm{srswor}}$, an estimate of the variance that would have been observed had the data been collected using simple random sampling without replacement. This is used to compute design effects for survey data; see [SVY] **estat** for details.

srssubpop can be specified only if vsrs() and subpop() are specified. srssubpop requests that the estimate of simple-random-sampling variance, vsrs(), be computed assuming sampling within a subpopulation. If srssubpop is not specified, it is computed assuming sampling from the entire population.

zeroweight specifies whether observations with weights equal to zero should be omitted from the computation. This option does not apply to frequency weights; observations with zero frequency weights are always omitted. If zeroweight is specified, observations with zero weights are included in the computation. If zeroweight is not specified (the default), observations with zero weights are omitted. Including the observations with zero weights affects the computation in that it may change the counts of PSUs (clusters) per stratum. Stata's svy prefix command includes observations with zero weights; all other commands exclude them. This option is typically used only with survey data.

Remarks

Remarks are presented under the following headings:

    Introduction
    Clustered data
    Survey data
    Controlling the header display
    Maximum likelihood estimators
    Multiple-equation estimators

Introduction

This section explains the formulas behind the robust variance estimator and how to use _robust through an informal development with some simple examples. For an alternative discussion, see [U] **20.16 Obtaining robust variance estimates**. See the references cited at the end of this entry for more formal expositions.

First, consider ordinary least-squares regression. The estimator for the coefficients is

$$\widehat{\beta} = (\mathbf{X'X})^{-1}\mathbf{X'y}$$

where $\mathbf{y}$ is an $n \times 1$ vector representing the dependent variable and $\mathbf{X}$ is an $n \times k$ matrix of covariates.

Because everything is considered conditional on $\mathbf{X}$, $(\mathbf{X'X})^{-1}$ can be regarded as a constant matrix. Hence, the variance of $\widehat{\beta}$ is

$$V(\widehat{\beta}) = (\mathbf{X'X})^{-1} V(\mathbf{X'y}) (\mathbf{X'X})^{-1}$$

What is the variance of $\mathbf{X'y}$, a $k \times 1$ vector? Look at its first element; it is

$$\mathbf{X}_1'\mathbf{y} = x_{11}y_1 + x_{21}y_2 + \cdots + x_{n1}y_n$$

where $\mathbf{X}_1$ is the first column of $\mathbf{X}$. Because $\mathbf{X}$ is treated as a constant, you can write the variance as

$$V(\mathbf{X}_1'\mathbf{y}) = x_{11}^2 V(y_1) + x_{21}^2 V(y_2) + \cdots + x_{n1}^2 V(y_n)$$

The only assumption made here is that the y_j are independent.

The obvious estimate for $V(y_j)$ is $\widehat{e}_j^2$, the square of the residual $\widehat{e}_j = y_j - \mathbf{x}_j\widehat{\beta}$, where $\mathbf{x}_j$ is the jth row of $\mathbf{X}$. You must estimate the off-diagonal terms of the covariance matrix for $\mathbf{X'y}$, as well. Working this out, you have

$$\widehat{V}(\mathbf{X'y}) = \sum_{j=1}^{n} \widehat{e}_j^2 \, \mathbf{x}_j'\mathbf{x}_j$$

$\mathbf{x}_j$ is defined as a row vector so that $\mathbf{x}_j'\mathbf{x}_j$ is a $k \times k$ matrix.

You have just derived the robust variance estimator for linear regression coefficient estimates for independent observations:

$$\widehat{V}(\widehat{\beta}) = (\mathbf{X'X})^{-1} \left(\sum_{j=1}^{n} \widehat{e}_j^2 \, \mathbf{x}_j'\mathbf{x}_j \right) (\mathbf{X'X})^{-1}$$

You can see why it is called the sandwich estimator.

❑ Technical note

The only detail not discussed is the multiplier. You will see later that survey statisticians like to view the center of the sandwich as a variance estimator for totals. They use a multiplier of $n/(n-1)$, just as $1/(n-1)$ is used for the variance estimator of a mean. However, for survey data, n is no longer the total number of observations but is the number of clusters in a stratum. See *Methods and formulas* at the end of this entry.

Linear regression is, however, special. Assuming homoskedasticity and normality, you can derive the expectation of $\hat{e}_j^2$ for finite n. This is discussed in [R] **regress**. Under the assumptions of homoskedasticity and normality, $n/(n-k)$ is a better multiplier than $n/(n-1)$.

If you specify the minus(#) option, _robust will use $n/(n-\#)$ as the multiplier. regress, vce(robust) also gives two other options for the multiplier: hc2 and hc3. Because these multipliers are special to linear regression, _robust does not compute them.

❑

▷ Example 1

Before we show how _robust is used, let's compute the robust variance estimator "by hand" for linear regression for the case in which observations are independent (i.e., no clusters).

We need to compute $\mathbf{D} = (\mathbf{X}'\mathbf{X})^{-1}$ and the residuals $\hat{e}_j$. regress with the mse1 option will allow us to compute both easily; see [R] **regress**.

```
. use http://www.stata-press.com/data/r11/_robust
(1978 Automobile Data -- modified)

. regress mpg weight gear_ratio foreign, mse1
(output omitted )

. matrix D = e(V)

. predict double e, residual
```

We can write the center of the sandwich as

$$\mathbf{M} = \sum_{j=1}^{n} \hat{e}_j^2 \mathbf{x}_j' \mathbf{x}_j = \mathbf{X}'\mathbf{W}\mathbf{X}$$

where $\mathbf{W}$ is a diagonal matrix with $\hat{e}_j^2$ on the diagonal. matrix accum with iweights can be used to calculate this (see [P] **matrix accum**):

```
. matrix accum M = weight gear_ratio foreign [iweight=e^2]
(obs=813.7814109)
```

We now assemble the sandwich. To match regress, vce(robust), we use a multiplier of $n/(n-k)$.

```
. matrix V = 74/70 * D*M*D

. matrix list V

symmetric V[4,4]
                weight  gear_ratio     foreign       _cons
    weight    3.788e-07
gear_ratio    .00039798   1.9711317
   foreign    .00008463   -.55488334   1.4266939
     _cons   -.00236851   -6.9153285   1.2149035   27.536291
```

The result is the same as that from `regress, vce(robust)`:

```
. regress mpg weight gear_ratio foreign, vce(robust)
(output omitted)
. matrix Vreg = e(V)
. matrix list Vreg
symmetric Vreg[4,4]
                    weight   gear_ratio      foreign        _cons
    weight       3.788e-07
gear_ratio       .00039798    1.9711317
   foreign       .00008463   -.55488334    1.4266939
     _cons      -.00236851   -6.9153285    1.2149035    27.536291
```

If we use _robust, the initial steps are the same. We still need **D**, the "bread" of the sandwich, and the residuals. The residuals e are the varlist for _robust. **D** is passed via the `variance()` option (abbreviation `v()`). **D** is overwritten and contains the robust variance estimate.

```
. drop e
. regress mpg weight gear_ratio foreign, mse1
(output omitted)
. matrix D = e(V)
. predict double e, residual
. _robust e, v(D) minus(4)
. matrix list D
symmetric D[4,4]
                    weight   gear_ratio      foreign        _cons
    weight       3.788e-07
gear_ratio       .00039798    1.9711317
   foreign       .00008463   -.55488334    1.4266939
     _cons      -.00236851   -6.9153285    1.2149035    27.536291
```

Rather than specifying the `variance()` option, we can use `ereturn post` to post **D** and the point estimates. _robust alters the post, substituting the robust variance estimates.

```
. drop e
. regress mpg weight gear_ratio foreign, mse1
(output omitted)
. matrix D = e(V)
. matrix b = e(b)
. local n = e(N)
. local k = colsof(D)
. local dof = `n' - `k'
. predict double e, residual
. ereturn post b D, dof(`dof')
. _robust e, minus(`k')
. ereturn display
```

	Coef.	Robust Std. Err.	t	P>|t|	[95% Conf.	Interval]
weight	-.006139	.0006155	-9.97	0.000	-.0073666	-.0049115
gear_ratio	1.457113	1.40397	1.04	0.303	-1.343016	4.257243
foreign	-2.221682	1.194443	-1.86	0.067	-4.603923	.1605598
_cons	36.10135	5.247503	6.88	0.000	25.63554	46.56717

Again what we did matches `regress, vce(robust)`:

```
. regress mpg weight gear_ratio foreign, vce(robust)
Linear regression                               Number of obs =       74
                                                F(  3,    70) =    48.30
                                                Prob > F      =   0.0000
                                                R-squared     =   0.6670
                                                Root MSE      =   3.4096
```

mpg	Coef.	Robust Std. Err.	t	P>|t|	[95% Conf. Interval]	
weight	-.006139	.0006155	-9.97	0.000	-.0073666	-.0049115
gear_ratio	1.457113	1.40397	1.04	0.303	-1.343016	4.257243
foreign	-2.221682	1.194443	-1.86	0.067	-4.603923	.1605598
_cons	36.10135	5.247503	6.88	0.000	25.63554	46.56717

◁

❏ Technical note

Note the simple ways in which _robust was called. When we used the `variance()` option, we called it by typing

```
. _robust e, v(D) minus(4)
```

As we described, _robust computed

$$\widehat{V}(\widehat{\beta}) = \mathbf{D}\left(\frac{n}{n-k}\sum_{j=1}^{n}\widehat{e}_j^2\mathbf{x}_j'\mathbf{x}_j\right)\mathbf{D}$$

We passed $\mathbf{D}$ to _robust by using the `v(D)` option and specified $\widehat{e}_j$ as the variable e. So how did _robust know what variables to use for $\mathbf{x}_j$? It got them from the row and column names of the matrix D. Recall how we generated D initially:

```
. regress mpg weight gear_ratio foreign, mse1
(output omitted)
. matrix D = e(V)
. matrix list D
symmetric D[4,4]
                weight  gear_ratio     foreign        _cons
   weight    5.436e-08
gear_ratio   .00006295   .20434146
   foreign   .00001032  -.08016692    .1311889
     _cons  -.00035697    -.782292   .17154326    3.3988878
```

Stata's estimation commands and the `ml` commands produce matrices with appropriately labeled rows and columns. If that is how we generate our $\mathbf{D}$, this will be taken care of automatically. But if we generate $\mathbf{D}$ in another manner, we must be sure to label it appropriately; see [P] **matrix rownames**.

When _robust is used after `ereturn post`, it gets the variable names from the row and column names of the posted matrices. So again, the matrices must be labeled appropriately.

Let us make another rather obvious comment. _robust uses the variables from the row and column names of the $\mathbf{D}$ matrix at the time _robust is called. It is the programmer's responsibility to ensure that the data in these variables have not changed and that _robust selects the appropriate observations for the computation, using an `if` restriction if necessary (for instance, `if e(sample)`).

❏

Clustered data

▷ Example 2

To get robust variance estimates for clustered data or for complex survey data, simply use the cluster(), strata(), etc., options when you call _robust.

The first steps are the same as before. For clustered data, the number of degrees of freedom of the t statistic is the number of clusters minus one (we will discuss this later).

```
. drop e
. quietly regress mpg weight gear_ratio foreign, mse1
. gen byte samp = e(sample)
. matrix D = e(V)
. matrix b = e(b)
. predict double e, residual
. local k = colsof(D)
. tabulate rep78
```

Repair Record 1978	Freq.	Percent	Cum.
1	2	2.90	2.90
2	8	11.59	14.49
3	30	43.48	57.97
4	18	26.09	84.06
5	11	15.94	100.00
Total	69	100.00	

```
. local nclust = r(r)
. di 'nclust'
5
. local dof = 'nclust' - 1
. ereturn post b D, dof('dof') esample(samp)
. _robust e, minus('k') cluster(rep78)
. ereturn display
```
                                    (Std. Err. adjusted for 5 clusters in rep78)

	Coef.	Robust Std. Err.	t	P>|t|	[95% Conf. Interval]
weight	-.006139	.0008399	-7.31	0.002	-.008471	-.0038071
gear_ratio	1.457113	1.801311	0.81	0.464	-3.544129	6.458355
foreign	-2.221682	.8144207	-2.73	0.053	-4.482876	.0395129
_cons	36.10135	3.39887	10.62	0.000	26.66458	45.53813

What you get is, of course, the same as regress, vce(cluster rep78). Wait a minute. It is not the same!

```
. regress mpg weight gear_ratio foreign, vce(cluster rep78)
```

```
Linear regression                               Number of obs =       69
                                                F( 3,      4) =    78.61
                                                Prob > F      =   0.0005
                                                R-squared     =   0.6631
                                                Root MSE      =   3.4827
```

(Std. Err. adjusted for 5 clusters in rep78)

mpg	Coef.	Robust Std. Err.	t	P>|t|	[95% Conf. Interval]	
weight	-.005893	.0008214	-7.17	0.002	-.0081735	-.0036126
gear_ratio	1.904503	2.18322	0.87	0.432	-4.157088	7.966093
foreign	-2.149017	1.20489	-1.78	0.149	-5.49433	1.196295
_cons	34.09959	4.215275	8.09	0.001	22.39611	45.80307

Not even the point estimates are the same. This is the classic programmer's mistake of not using the same sample for the initial regress, mse1 call as done with _robust. The cluster variable rep78 is missing for 5 observations. _robust omitted these observations, but regress, mse1 did not.

_robust is best used only in programs for just this reason. So, you can write a program and use marksample and markout (see [P] **mark**) to determine the sample in advance of running regress and _robust.

```
──────────────────────────────────── begin  myreg.ado ────────────
program myreg, eclass sortpreserve
        version 11
        syntax varlist [if] [in] [, CLuster(varname) ]
        marksample touse
        markout 'touse' 'cluster', strok

        tempvar e count
        tempname D b

        quietly {
                regress 'varlist' if 'touse', mse1
                matrix 'D' = e(V)
                matrix 'b' = e(b)
                local n = e(N)
                local k = colsof('D')
                predict double 'e' if 'touse', residual

                if "'cluster'"!="" {
                        sort 'touse' 'cluster'
                        by 'touse' 'cluster': gen byte 'count' = 1 if _n==1 & 'touse'
                        summarize 'count', meanonly
                        local nclust = r(sum)
                        local dof = 'nclust' - 1
                        local clopt "cluster('cluster')"
                }
                else   local dof = 'n' - 'k'

                ereturn post 'b' 'D', dof('dof') esample('touse')

                _robust 'e' if e(sample), minus('k') 'clopt'
        }
        ereturn display
end
────────────────────────────────────── end  myreg.ado ────────────
```

Running this program produces the same results as regress, vce(cluster *clustvar*).

```
. myreg mpg weight gear_ratio foreign, cluster(rep78)
                                (Std. Err. adjusted for 5 clusters in rep78)
```

	Coef.	Robust Std. Err.	t	P>|t|	[95% Conf.	Interval]
weight	-.005893	.0008214	-7.17	0.002	-.0081735	-.0036126
gear_ratio	1.904503	2.18322	0.87	0.432	-4.157088	7.966093
foreign	-2.149017	1.20489	-1.78	0.149	-5.49433	1.196295
_cons	34.09959	4.215275	8.09	0.001	22.39611	45.80307

◁

Survey data

▷ Example 3

We will now modify our myreg command so that it handles complex survey data. Our new version will allow pweights and iweights, stratification, and clustering.

```
                                                       begin  myreg.ado
program myreg, eclass
        version 11
        syntax varlist [if] [in] [pweight iweight] [, /*
                */ STRata(varname) CLuster(varname) ]
        marksample touse, zeroweight
        markout 'touse' 'cluster' 'strata', strok
        if "'weight'"!="" {
                tempvar w
                quietly gen double 'w' 'exp' if 'touse'
                local iwexp "[iw='w']"
                if "'weight'" == "pweight" {
                        capture assert 'w' >= 0 if 'touse'
                        if c(rc) error 402
                }
        }
        if "'cluster'"!="" {
                local clopt "cluster('cluster')"
        }
        if "'strata'"!="" {
                local stopt "strata('strata')"
        }
        tempvar e
        tempname D b
        quietly {
                regress 'varlist' 'iwexp' if 'touse', mse1
                matrix 'D' = e(V)
                matrix 'b' = e(b)
                predict double 'e' if 'touse', residual
                _robust 'e' 'iwexp' if 'touse', v('D') 'clopt' 'stopt' zeroweight
                local dof = r(N_clust) - r(N_strata)
                local depn : word 1 of 'varlist'
                ereturn post 'b' 'D', depn('depn') dof('dof') esample('touse')
        }
        di
        ereturn display
end
                                                         end  myreg.ado
```

Note the following details about our version of `myreg` for survey data:

- We called _robust before we posted the matrices with `ereturn post`, whereas in our previous version of `myreg`, we called `ereturn post` and then _robust. Here we called _robust first so that we could use its `r(N_strata)`, containing the number of strata, and `r(N_clust)`, containing the number of clusters; see *Saved results* at the end of this entry. We did this so that we could pass the correct degrees of freedom (= number of clusters − number of strata) to `ereturn post`.

  This works even if the `strata()` and `cluster()` options are not specified: `r(N_strata)` = 1 if `strata()` is not specified (there truly is one stratum); and `r(N_clust)` = number of observations if `cluster()` is not specified (each observation is a cluster).

- The call to _robust was made with `iweights`, whether `myreg` was called with `pweights` or `iweights`. Computationally, _robust treats `pweights` and `iweights` the same. The only difference is that it puts out an error message if it encounters a negative `pweight`, whereas negative `iweights` are allowed. As good programmers, we put out the error message early before any time-consuming computations are done.

- We used the `zeroweight` option with the `marksample` command so that zero weights would not be excluded from the sample. We gave the `zeroweight` option with _robust so that it, too, would not exclude zero weights.

  Observations with zero weights affect results only by their effect (if any) on the counts of the clusters. Setting some weights temporarily to zero will, for example, produce subpopulation estimates. If subpopulation estimates are desired, however, it would be better to implement _robust's `subpop()` option and restrict the call to `regress, mse1` to this subpopulation.

- Stata's `svyset` accepts a *psu* variable rather than having a `cluster()` option. This is only a matter of style. They are synonyms, as far as _robust is concerned.

Our program gives the same results as `svy: regress`. For our example, we add a `strata` variable and a `psu` variable to the `auto` dataset.

```
. use http://www.stata-press.com/data/r11/auto, clear
(1978 Automobile Data)
. set seed 1
. gen strata = int(3*runiform()) + 1
. gen psu = int(5*runiform()) + 1
. myreg mpg weight gear_ratio foreign [pw=displ], strata(strata) cluster(psu)
```

mpg	Coef.	Std. Err.	t	P>|t|	[95% Conf. Interval]	
weight	-.0057248	.0004125	-13.88	0.000	-.0066237	-.004826
gear_ratio	.7775839	1.326424	0.59	0.569	-2.112447	3.667614
foreign	-1.86776	1.381047	-1.35	0.201	-4.876802	1.141282
_cons	36.64061	4.032525	9.09	0.000	27.85449	45.42673

```
. svyset psu [pw=displ], strata(strata)
      pweight: displacement
          VCE: linearized
  Single unit: missing
     Strata 1: strata
         SU 1: psu
        FPC 1: <zero>
```

```
. svy: regress mpg weight gear_ratio foreign
(running regress on estimation sample)
Survey: Linear regression
Number of strata   =        3           Number of obs     =        74
Number of PSUs     =       15           Population size   =     14600
                                        Design df         =        12
                                        F(   3,      10)  =     64.73
                                        Prob > F          =    0.0000
                                        R-squared         =    0.6900
```

mpg	Coef.	Linearized Std. Err.	t	P>|t|	[95% Conf. Interval]	
weight	-.0057248	.0004125	-13.88	0.000	-.0066237	-.004826
gear_ratio	.7775839	1.326424	0.59	0.569	-2.112447	3.667614
foreign	-1.86776	1.381047	-1.35	0.201	-4.876802	1.141282
_cons	36.64061	4.032525	9.09	0.000	27.85449	45.42673

◁

Controlling the header display

> Example 4

Let's compare the output for our survey version of myreg with the earlier version that handled only clustering. The header for the earlier version was

```
                            (Std. Err. adjusted for 5 clusters in rep78)
```

	Coef.	Robust Std. Err.	t	P>|t|	[95% Conf. Interval]	

The header for the survey version lacked the word "Robust" above "Std. Err.", and it lacked the banner "(Std. Err. adjusted for # clusters in *varname*)".

Both of these headers were produced by ereturn display, and programmers can control what it produces. The word above "Std. Err." is controlled by setting e(vcetype). The banner "(Std. Err. adjusted for # clusters in *varname*)" is controlled by setting e(clustvar) to the cluster variable name. These can be set using the ereturn local command; see [P] **ereturn**.

When _robust is called after ereturn post (as it was in the earlier version that produced the above header), it automatically sets these macros. To not display the banner, the code should read

```
        ereturn post ...
        _robust ...
        ereturn local clustvar ""
```

We can also change the phrase displayed above "Std. Err." by resetting e(vcetype). To display nothing there, reset e(vcetype) to empty—ereturn local vcetype "".

For our survey version of myreg, we called _robust before calling ereturn post. Here _robust does not set these macros. Trying to do so would be futile because ereturn post clears all previous estimation results, including all e() macros, but you can set them yourself after calling ereturn post. We make this addition to our survey version of myreg:

```
        _robust ...
        ereturn post ...
        ereturn local vcetype "Design-based"
```

The output is

```
. myreg mpg weight gear_ratio foreign [pw=displ], strata(strata) cluster(psu)
```

mpg	Coef.	Design-based Std. Err.	t	P>|t|	[95% Conf. Interval]
weight	-.0057248	.0004125	-13.88	0.000	-.0066237	-.004826
gear_ratio	.7775839	1.326424	0.59	0.569	-2.112447	3.667614
foreign	-1.86776	1.381047	-1.35	0.201	-4.876802	1.141282
_cons	36.64061	4.032525	9.09	0.000	27.85449	45.42673

◁

Maximum likelihood estimators

Maximum likelihood estimators are basically no different from linear regression when it comes to the use of _robust. We will first do a little statistics and then give a simple example.

We can write our maximum-likelihood estimation equation as

$$\mathbf{G}(\beta) = \sum_{j=1}^{n} \mathbf{S}(\beta; y_j, \mathbf{x}_j) = \mathbf{0}$$

where $\mathbf{S}(\beta; y_j, \mathbf{x}_j) = \partial \ln L_j / \partial \beta$ is the score and $\ln L_j$ is the log likelihood for the jth observation. Here β represents all the parameters in the model, including any auxiliary parameters. We will discuss how to use _robust when there are auxiliary parameters or multiple equations in the next section. But for now, all the theory works out fine for any set of parameters.

Using a first-order Taylor-series expansion (i.e., the delta method), we can write the variance of $\mathbf{G}(\beta)$ as

$$\widehat{V}\{\mathbf{G}(\beta)\}\big|_{\beta=\widehat{\beta}} = \left.\frac{\partial \mathbf{G}(\beta)}{\partial \beta}\right|_{\beta=\widehat{\beta}} \widehat{V}(\widehat{\beta}) \left.\frac{\partial \mathbf{G}(\beta)}{\partial \beta\prime}\right|_{\beta=\widehat{\beta}}$$

Solving for $\widehat{V}(\widehat{\beta})$ gives

$$\widehat{V}(\widehat{\beta}) = \left[\left\{\frac{\partial \mathbf{G}(\beta)}{\partial \beta}\right\}^{-1} \widehat{V}\{\mathbf{G}(\beta)\} \left\{\frac{\partial \mathbf{G}(\beta)}{\partial \beta\prime}\right\}^{-1}\right]\Bigg|_{\beta=\widehat{\beta}}$$

but

$$\mathbf{H} = \frac{\partial \mathbf{G}(\beta)}{\partial \beta}$$

is the Hessian (matrix of second derivatives) of the log likelihood. Thus we can write

$$\widehat{V}(\widehat{\beta}) = \mathbf{D}\,\widehat{V}\{\mathbf{G}(\beta)\}\big|_{\beta=\widehat{\beta}}\mathbf{D}$$

where $\mathbf{D} = -\mathbf{H}^{-1}$ is the traditional covariance estimate.

Now $\mathbf{G}(\beta)$ is simply a sum, and we can estimate its variance just as we would the sum of any other variable—it is n^2 times the standard estimator of the variance of a mean:

$$\frac{n}{n-1}\sum_{j=1}^{n}(z_j - \bar{z})^2$$

But here, the scores $\mathbf{u}_j = \mathbf{S}(\hat{\beta}; y_j, \mathbf{x}_j)$ are (row) vectors. Their sum, and thus their mean, is zero. So, we have

$$\widehat{V}\{\mathbf{G}(\beta)\}\big|_{\beta=\hat{\beta}} = \frac{n}{n-1}\sum_{j=1}^{n}\mathbf{u}_j'\mathbf{u}_j$$

Thus our robust variance estimator is

$$\widehat{V}(\hat{\beta}) = \mathbf{D}\left(\frac{n}{n-1}\sum_{j=1}^{n}\mathbf{u}_j'\mathbf{u}_j\right)\mathbf{D}$$

so we see that the robust variance estimator is just the delta method combined with a simple estimator for totals!

The above estimator for the variance of the total (the center of the sandwich) is appropriate only when observations are independent. For clustered data and complex survey data, this estimator is replaced by one appropriate for the independent units of the data. Clusters (or PSUs) are independent, so we can sum the scores within a cluster to create a "superobservation" and then use the standard formula for a total on these independent superobservations. Our robust variance estimator thus becomes

$$\widehat{V}(\hat{\beta}) = \mathbf{D}\left\{\frac{n_c}{n_c-1}\sum_{i=1}^{n_c}\left(\sum_{j\in C_i}\mathbf{u}_j\right)'\left(\sum_{j\in C_i}\mathbf{u}_j\right)\right\}\mathbf{D}$$

where C_i contains the indices of the observations belonging to the ith cluster for $i = 1, 2, \ldots, n_c$, with n_c the total number of clusters.

See [SVY] **variance estimation** for the variance estimator for a total that is appropriate for complex survey data. Our development here has been heuristic. We have, for instance, purposefully omitted sampling weights from our discussion; see [SVY] **variance estimation** for a better treatment.

See Gould, Pitblado, and Sribney (2006) for a discussion of maximum likelihood and of Stata's `ml` command.

❑ Technical note

It is easy to see where the appropriate degrees of freedom for the robust variance estimator come from: the center of the sandwich is n^2 times the standard estimator of the variance for the mean of n observations. A mean divided by its standard error has exactly a Student's t distribution with $n - 1$ degrees of freedom for normal i.i.d. variables but also has approximately this distribution under many other conditions. Thus a point estimate divided by the square root of its robust variance estimate is approximately distributed as a Student's t with $n - 1$ degrees of freedom.

More importantly, this also applies to clusters, where each cluster is considered a "superobservation". Here the degrees of freedom is $n_c - 1$, where n_c is the number of clusters (superobservations). If there are only a few clusters, confidence intervals using t statistics can become quite large. It is just like estimating a mean with only a few observations.

When there are strata, the degrees of freedom is $n_c - L$, where L is the number of strata; see [SVY] **variance estimation** for details.

Not all of Stata's maximum likelihood estimators that produce robust variance estimators for clustered data use t statistics. Obviously, this matters only when the number of clusters is small. Users who want to be rigorous in handling clustered data should use the `svy` prefix, which always uses t statistics and adjusted Wald tests (see [R] **test**). Programmers who want to impose similar rigor should do likewise.

❑

We have not yet given any details about the functional form of our scores $\mathbf{u}_j = \partial \ln L_j / \partial \beta$. The log likelihood $\ln L_j$ is a function of $\mathbf{x}_j \beta$ (the "index"). Logistic regression, probit regression, and Poisson regression are examples. There are no auxiliary parameters, and there is only one equation.

We can then write $\mathbf{u}_j = \widehat{s}_j \mathbf{x}_j$, where

$$\widehat{s}_j = \left. \frac{\partial \ln L_j}{\partial (\mathbf{x}_j \beta)} \right|_{\beta = \widehat{\beta}}$$

We refer to s_j as the equation-level score. Our formula for the robust estimator when observations are independent becomes

$$\widehat{V}(\widehat{\beta}) = \mathbf{D} \left(\frac{n}{n-1} \sum_{j=1}^{n} \widehat{s}_j^2 \, \mathbf{x}_j' \mathbf{x}_j \right) \mathbf{D}$$

This is precisely the formula that we used for linear regression, with $\widehat{e}_j$ replaced by $\widehat{s}_j$ and $k = 1$ in the multiplier.

Before we discuss auxiliary parameters, let's show how to implement _robust for single-equation models.

▷ Example 5

The robust variance implementation for single-equation maximum-likelihood estimators with no auxiliary parameters is almost the same as it is for linear regression. The only differences are that $\mathbf{D}$ is now the traditional covariance matrix (the negative of the inverse of the matrix of second derivatives) and that the variable passed to _robust is the equation-level score $\widehat{s}_j$ rather than the residuals $\widehat{e}_j$.

Let's alter our last `myreg` program for survey data to make a program that does logistic regression for survey data. We have to change only a few lines of the program.

(Continued on next page)

```
────────────────────────────────────────────── begin  mylogit.ado ──────────
     program mylogit, eclass
             version 11
             syntax varlist [if] [in] [pweight] [, /*
                     */ STRata(varname) CLuster(varname) ]
             marksample touse, zeroweight
             markout 'touse' 'strata' 'cluster', strok
             if "'weight'"!="" {
                     tempvar w
                     quietly gen double 'w' 'exp' if 'touse'
                     local iwexp "[iw='w']"
                     capture assert 'w' >= 0 if 'touse'
                     if c(rc) error 402
             }
             if "'cluster'"!="" {
                     local clopt "cluster('cluster')"
             }
             if "'strata'"!="" {
                     local stopt "strata('strata')"
             }
             tempvar s
             tempname D b
             quietly {
                     logit 'varlist' 'iwexp' if 'touse'
                     matrix 'D' = e(V)
                     matrix 'b' = e(b)
                     predict double 's' if e(sample), score
                     _robust 's' 'iwexp' if e(sample), v('D') 'clopt' 'stopt' zeroweight
                     local dof =  r(N_clust) - r(N_strata)
                     local depn : word 1 of 'varlist'
                     replace 'touse' = e(sample)
                     ereturn post 'b' 'D', depn('depn') dof('dof') esample('touse')
                     ereturn local vcetype "Design-based"
             }
             di
             ereturn display
     end
────────────────────────────────────────────── end  mylogit.ado ──────────
```

Note the following about our program:

- We use the score option of predict after logit to obtain the equation-level scores. If predict does not have a score option, then we must generate the equation-level score variable some other way.

- logit is a unique command in that it will sometimes drop observations for reasons other than missing values (e.g., when success or failure is predicted perfectly), so our 'touse' variable may not represent the true estimation sample. That is why we used the if e(sample) condition with the predict and _robust commands. Then, to provide ereturn post with an appropriate esample() option, we set the 'touse' variable equal to the e(sample) from the logit command and then use this 'touse' variable in the esample() option.

Our `mylogit` program gives the same results as `svy: logit`:

```
. mylogit foreign mpg weight gear_ratio [pw=displ], strata(strata) cluster(psu)
```

foreign	Coef.	Design-based Std. Err.	t	P>|t|	[95% Conf. Interval]	
mpg	-.3489011	.1032582	-3.38	0.005	-.5738813	-.1239209
weight	-.0040789	.0008986	-4.54	0.001	-.0060368	-.0021209
gear_ratio	6.324169	1.332611	4.75	0.000	3.420659	9.227679
_cons	-2.189748	6.077171	-0.36	0.725	-15.43077	11.05127

```
. svyset psu [pw=displ], strata(strata)
      pweight: displacement
          VCE: linearized
  Single unit: missing
     Strata 1: strata
         SU 1: psu
        FPC 1: <zero>
. svy: logit foreign mpg weight gear_ratio
(running logit on estimation sample)

Survey: Logistic regression

Number of strata   =          3          Number of obs    =          74
Number of PSUs     =         15          Population size  =       14600
                                         Design df        =          12
                                         F(   3,     10)  =       16.60
                                         Prob > F         =      0.0003
```

foreign	Coef.	Linearized Std. Err.	t	P>|t|	[95% Conf. Interval]	
mpg	-.3489011	.1032582	-3.38	0.005	-.5738813	-.1239209
weight	-.0040789	.0008986	-4.54	0.001	-.0060368	-.0021209
gear_ratio	6.324169	1.332611	4.75	0.000	3.420659	9.227679
_cons	-2.189748	6.077171	-0.36	0.725	-15.43077	11.05127

◁

❑ Technical note

The theory developed here applies to full-information maximum-likelihood estimators. Conditional likelihoods, such as conditional (fixed-effects) logistic regression (`clogit`) and Cox regression (`stcox`), use variants on this theme. The `vce(robust)` option on `stcox` uses a similar, but not identical, formula; see [ST] **stcox** and Lin and Wei (1989) for details.

On the other hand, the theory developed here applies not only to maximum likelihood estimators but also to general estimating equations:

$$\mathbf{G}(\beta) = \sum_{j=1}^{n} \mathbf{g}(\beta; y_j, \mathbf{x}_j) = \mathbf{0}$$

See Binder (1983) for a formal development of the theory.

Programmers: You are responsible for the theory behind your implementation.

❑

Multiple-equation estimators

The theory for auxiliary parameters and multiple-equation models is no different from that described earlier. For independent observations, just as before, the robust variance estimator is

$$\widehat{V}(\widehat{\beta}) = \mathbf{D}\left(\frac{n}{n-1}\sum_{j=1}^{n}\mathbf{u}_j'\mathbf{u}_j\right)\mathbf{D}$$

where $\mathbf{u}_j = \partial\ln L_j/\partial\beta$ is the score (row) vector and $\mathbf{D}$ is the traditional covariance estimate (the negative of the inverse of the matrix of second derivatives).

With auxiliary parameters and multiple equations, β can be viewed as the vector of all the parameters in the model. Without loss of generality, you can write the log likelihood as

$$\ln L_j = \ln L_j(\mathbf{x}_j^{(1)}\beta^{(1)}, \mathbf{x}_j^{(2)}\beta^{(2)}, \ldots, \mathbf{x}_j^{(p)}\beta^{(p)})$$

An auxiliary parameter is regarded as $\mathbf{x}_j^{(i)}\beta^{(i)}$ with $\mathbf{x}_j \equiv 1$ and $\beta^{(i)}$ a scalar. The score vector becomes

$$\mathbf{u}_j = (\, s_j^{(1)}\mathbf{x}_j^{(1)} \quad s_j^{(2)}\mathbf{x}_j^{(2)} \quad \cdots \quad s_j^{(p)}\mathbf{x}_j^{(p)} \,)$$

where $s_j^{(i)} = \partial\ln L_j/\partial(\mathbf{x}_j\beta^{(i)})$ is the equation-level score for the ith equation.

This notation has been introduced so that it is clear how to call _robust. You use

. _robust $s_j^{(1)}\ s_j^{(2)}\ \cdots\ s_j^{(p)}$, *options*

where $s_j^{(1)}$, etc., are variables that contain the equation-level score values. The $\mathbf{D}$ matrix that you pass to _robust or post with ereturn post must be labeled with exactly p equation names.

_robust takes the first equation-level score variable, $s_j^{(1)}$, and matches it to the first equation on the $\mathbf{D}$ matrix to determine $\mathbf{x}_j^{(1)}$, takes the second equation-level score variable and matches it to the second equation, etc. Some examples will make this perfectly clear.

▷ Example 6

Here is what a matrix with equation names looks like:

```
. gen cat = rep78 - 3
(5 missing values generated)

. replace cat = 2 if cat < 0
(10 real changes made)

. mlogit cat price foreign, base(0)
(output omitted )

. matrix D = e(V)

. matrix list D
symmetric D[6,6]
                     1:          1:          1:          2:          2:          2:
                  price     foreign       _cons       price     foreign       _cons
  1:price     1.240e-08
1:foreign    -1.401e-06     .593554
  1:_cons    -.00007592   -.13992997   .61347545
  2:price     4.265e-09   -5.366e-07   -.00002693   1.207e-08
2:foreign    -1.590e-06    .37202357   -.02774147   -3.184e-06    .56833685
  2:_cons     -.0000265    -.0343682    .20468675   -.00007108    -.1027108    .54017838
```

The call to __robust would then be

```
. _robust s1 s2, v(D)
```

where s1 and s2 are the equation-level score variables for equation 1 and equation 2, respectively.

Covariance matrices from models with auxiliary parameters look just like multiple-equation matrices:

```
. matrix list D
symmetric D[5,5]
                       eq1:        eq1:        eq1:       eq1:      sigma:
                    weight  gear_ratio     foreign      _cons       _cons
   eq1:weight   5.978e-07
eq1:gear_ratio    .00069222   2.2471526
 eq1:foreign     .00011344  -.88159935   1.4426905
    eq1:_cons   -.00392566  -8.6029018   1.8864693   37.377729
  sigma:_cons    6.157e-14  -1.448e-10   3.579e-12  -9.902e-09   .07430437
```

The second equation consists of the auxiliary parameter only. The call to __robust would be the same as before:

```
. _robust s1 s2, v(D)
```

◁

▷ Example 7

We will now give an example using ml and __robust to produce an estimation command that has vce(robust) and vce(cluster *clustvar*) options. You can actually accomplish all of this easily by using ml without using the __robust command because ml has robust and cluster() options. We will pretend that these two options are unavailable to illustrate the use of __robust.

To keep the example simple, we will do linear regression as a maximum likelihood estimator. Here the log likelihood is

$$\ln L_j = -\frac{1}{2}\left\{\left(\frac{y_j - \mathbf{x}_j\boldsymbol{\beta}}{\sigma}\right)^2 + \ln\left(2\pi\sigma^2\right)\right\}$$

There is an auxiliary parameter, σ, and thus we have two equation-level scores:

$$\frac{\partial \ln L_j}{\partial (\mathbf{x}_j\boldsymbol{\beta})} = \frac{y_j - \mathbf{x}_j\boldsymbol{\beta}}{\sigma^2}$$

$$\frac{\partial \ln L_j}{\partial \sigma} = \frac{1}{\sigma}\left\{\left(\frac{y_j - \mathbf{x}_j\boldsymbol{\beta}}{\sigma}\right)^2 - 1\right\}$$

Here are programs to compute this estimator. We have two ado-files: mymle.ado and likereg.ado. The first ado-file contains two programs, mymle and Scores. mymle is the main program, and Scores is a subprogram that computes the equation-level scores after we compute the maximum likelihood solution. Because Scores is called only by mymle, we can nest it in the mymle.ado file; see [U] **17 Ado-files**.

```
─────────────────────────────────────────────────── begin mymle.ado ─────────
program mymle, eclass
        version 11
        local options "Level(cilevel)"
        if replay() {
                if "`e(cmd)'"!="mymle" {
                        error 301
                }
                syntax [, `options']
                ml display, level(`level')
                exit
        }
        syntax varlist [if] [in] [, /*
                */ `options' Robust CLuster(varname) * ]
/* Determine estimation sample. */
        marksample touse

        if "`cluster'"!="" {
                markout `touse' `cluster', strok
                local clopt "cluster(`cluster')"
        }
/* Get starting values. */
        tokenize `varlist'
        local depn "`1'"
        macro shift

        quietly summarize `depn' if `touse'
        local cons = r(mean)
        local sigma = r(sd)
/* Do ml. */
        ml model lf likereg (`depn'=`*') /sigma if `touse', /*
                */ init(/eq1=`cons' /sigma=`sigma')  max /*
                */ title("MLE linear regression") `options'

        if "`robust'"!="" | "`cluster'"!="" {
                tempvar s1 s2
                Scores `depn' `s1' `s2'
                _robust `s1' `s2' if `touse', `clopt'
        }
        ereturn local cmd "mymle"
        ml display, level(`level')
end

program Scores
        version 11
        args depn s1 s2

        quietly {
                predict double `s1'
                gen double `s2' = (((`depn' - `s1')/[sigma][_cons])^2 - 1) /*
                */                 /[sigma][_cons]
                replace `s1' = (`depn' - `s1')/([sigma][_cons]^2)
        }
end
─────────────────────────────────────────────────────── end mymle.ado ─────────
```

Our `likereg` program computes the likelihood. Because it is called by Stata's `ml` commands, we cannot nest it in the other file.

```
──────────────────────────────────────────── begin likereg.ado ────────────
. type likereg.do
program likereg
        version 11
        args lf xb s
        qui replace 'lf' = -0.5*((($ML_y1 - 'xb')/'s')^2 + log(2*_pi*'s'^2))
end
──────────────────────────────────────────── end likereg.ado ────────────
```

Note the following:

- Our command `mymle` will produce robust variance estimates if either the `robust` or the `cluster()` option is specified. Otherwise, it will display the traditional estimates.

- We used the `lf` method with `ml`; see [R] **ml**. We could have used the d1 or d2 methods. Because we would probably include code to compute the first derivatives analytically for the `vce(robust)` option, there is no point in using d0. (However, we could compute the first derivatives numerically and pass these to `_robust`.)

- Our `Scores` program uses `predict` to compute the index $x_j\beta$. Because we had already posted the results using `ml`, `predict` is available to us. By default, `predict` computes the index for the first equation.

- Again because we had already posted the results by using `ml`, we can use `[sigma][_cons]` to get the value of σ; see [U] **13.5 Accessing coefficients and standard errors** for the syntax used to access coefficients from multiple-equation models.

- `ml` calls `ereturn post`, so when we call `_robust`, it alters the posted covariance matrix, replacing it with the robust covariance matrix. `_robust` also sets `e(vcetype)`, and if the `cluster()` option is specified, it sets `e(clustvar)` as well.

- We let `ml` produce z statistics, even when we specified the `cluster()` option. If the number of clusters is small, it would be better to use t statistics. To do this, we could specify the `dof()` option on the `ml` command, but we would have to compute the number of clusters in advance. We could also get the number of clusters from `_robust`'s `r(N_clust)` and then repost the matrices by using `ereturn repost`.

(Continued on next page)

If we run our command with the `cluster()` option, we get

```
. mymle mpg weight gear_ratio foreign, cluster(rep78)
initial:       log likelihood =  -219.4845
rescale:       log likelihood =  -219.4845
rescale eq:    log likelihood =  -219.4845
Iteration 0:   log likelihood =  -219.4845  (not concave)
Iteration 1:   log likelihood = -207.02829  (not concave)
Iteration 2:   log likelihood = -202.61339
Iteration 3:   log likelihood = -189.82343
Iteration 4:   log likelihood =  -181.9475
Iteration 5:   log likelihood = -181.94473
Iteration 6:   log likelihood = -181.94473

MLE linear regression                          Number of obs   =         69
                                               Wald chi2(3)    =     135.82
Log likelihood = -181.94473                    Prob > chi2     =     0.0000

                               (Std. Err. adjusted for 5 clusters in rep78)
```

mpg	Coef.	Robust Std. Err.	z	P>|z|	[95% Conf. Interval]	
eq1						
weight	-.005893	.000803	-7.34	0.000	-.0074669	-.0043191
gear_ratio	1.904503	2.134518	0.89	0.372	-2.279075	6.08808
foreign	-2.149017	1.178012	-1.82	0.068	-4.457879	.1598441
_cons	34.09959	4.121243	8.27	0.000	26.02211	42.17708
sigma						
_cons	3.380223	.8840543	3.82	0.000	1.647508	5.112937

These results are similar to the earlier results that we got with our first `myreg` program and `regress, cluster`.

Our likelihood is not globally concave. Linear regression is not globally concave in β and σ. `ml`'s `lf` convergence routine encountered a little trouble in the beginning but had no problem coming to the right solution.

◁

Saved results

`_robust` saves the following in `r()`:

Scalars

`r(N)`	number of observations
`r(N_strata)`	number of strata
`r(N_clust)`	number of clusters (PSUs)
`r(sum_w)`	sum of weights
`r(N_subpop)`	number of observations for subpopulation (`subpop()` only)
`r(sum_wsub)`	sum of weights for subpopulation (`subpop()` only)

`r(N_strata)` and `r(N_clust)` are always set. If the `strata()` option is not specified, then `r(N_strata) = 1` (there truly is one stratum). If neither the `cluster()` nor the `psu()` option is specified, then `r(N_clust)` equals the number of observations (each observation is a PSU).

When _robust alters the post of `ereturn post`, it also saves the following in e():

> Macros
> e(vcetype)   Robust
> e(clustvar)   name of cluster (PSU) variable

e(vcetype) controls the phrase that `ereturn display` displays above "Std. Err."; e(vcetype) can be set to another phrase (or to empty for no phrase). e(clustvar) displays the banner "(Std. Err. adjusted for # clusters in *varname*)", or it can be set to empty (ereturn local clustvar "").

Methods and formulas

We give the formulas here for complex survey data from one stage of stratified cluster sampling, as this is the most general case.

Our parameter estimates, $\widehat{\beta}$, are the solution to the estimating equation

$$\mathbf{G}(\beta) = \sum_{h=1}^{L} \sum_{i=1}^{n_h} \sum_{j=1}^{m_{hi}} w_{hij} \mathbf{S}(\beta; y_{hij}, \mathbf{x}_{hij}) = \mathbf{0}$$

where (h, i, j) index the observations: $h = 1, \ldots, L$ are the strata; $i = 1, \ldots, n_h$ are the sampled PSUs (clusters) in stratum h; and $j = 1, \ldots, m_{hi}$ are the sampled observations in PSU (h, i). The outcome variable is represented by y_{hij}; the explanatory variables are $\mathbf{x}_{hij}$ (a row vector); and w_{hij} are the weights.

If no weights are specified, $w_{hij} = 1$. If the weights are `aweights`, they are first normalized to sum to the total number of observations in the sample: $n = \sum_{h=1}^{L} \sum_{i=1}^{n_h} m_{hi}$. If the weights are `fweights`, the formulas below do not apply; `fweights` are treated in such a way to give the same results as unweighted observations duplicated the appropriate number of times.

For maximum likelihood estimators, $\mathbf{S}(\beta; y_{hij}, \mathbf{x}_{hij}) = \partial \ln L_j / \partial \beta$ is the score vector, where $\ln L_j$ is the log likelihood. For survey data, this is not a true likelihood, but a "pseudolikelihood"; see [SVY] **survey**.

Let

$$\mathbf{D} = -\left. \frac{\partial \mathbf{G}(\beta)}{\partial \beta} \right|_{\beta = \widehat{\beta}}^{-1}$$

For maximum likelihood estimators, $\mathbf{D}$ is the traditional covariance estimate—the negative of the inverse of the Hessian. In the following, the sign of $\mathbf{D}$ does not matter.

The robust covariance estimate calculated by _robust is

$$\widehat{V}(\widehat{\beta}) = \mathbf{DMD}$$

where $\mathbf{M}$ is computed as follows. Let $\mathbf{u}_{hij} = \mathbf{S}(\beta; y_{hij}, \mathbf{x}_{hij})$ be a row vector of scores for the (h, i, j) observation. Let

$$\mathbf{u}_{hi\bullet} = \sum_{j=1}^{m_{hi}} w_{hij} \mathbf{u}_{hij} \quad \text{and} \quad \overline{\mathbf{u}}_{h\bullet\bullet} = \frac{1}{n_h} \sum_{i=1}^{n_h} \mathbf{u}_{hi\bullet}$$

$\mathbf{M}$ is given by

$$\mathbf{M} = \frac{n-1}{n-k} \sum_{h=1}^{L} (1 - f_h) \frac{n_h}{n_h - 1} \sum_{i=1}^{n_h} (\mathbf{u}_{hi\bullet} - \overline{\mathbf{u}}_{h\bullet\bullet})'(\mathbf{u}_{hi\bullet} - \overline{\mathbf{u}}_{h\bullet\bullet})$$

where k is the value given in the minus() option. By default, $k = 1$, and the term $(n-1)/(n-k)$ vanishes. Stata's regress, vce(robust) and regress, vce(cluster *clustvar*) commands use k equal to the number of explanatory variables in the model, including the constant (Fuller et al. 1986). The svy prefix uses $k = 1$.

The specification $k = 0$ is handled differently. If minus(0) is specified, $(n-1)/(n-k)$ and $n_h/(n_h - 1)$ are both replaced by 1.

The factor $(1 - f_h)$ is the finite population correction. If the fpc() option is not specified, $f_h = 0$ is used. If fpc() is specified and the variable is greater than or equal to n_h, it is assumed to contain the values of N_h, and f_h is given by $f_h = n_h/N_h$, where N_h is the total number of PSUs in the population belonging to the hth stratum. If the fpc() variable is less than or equal to 1, it is assumed to contain the values of f_h. See [SVY] **variance estimation** for details.

For the vsrs() option and the computation of $\widehat{V}_{\mathrm{srswor}}$, the subpop() option, and the srssubpop option, see [SVY] **estat** and [SVY] **subpopulation estimation**.

References

Binder, D. A. 1983. On the variances of asymptotically normal estimators from complex surveys. *International Statistical Review* 51: 279–292.

Fuller, W. A. 1975. Regression analysis for sample survey. *Sankhyā, Series C* 37: 117–132.

Fuller, W. A., W. Kennedy Jr., D. Schnell, G. Sullivan, and H. J. Park. 1986. *PC CARP.* Software package. Ames, IA: Statistical Laboratory, Iowa State University.

Gail, M. H., W. Y. Tan, and S. Piantadosi. 1988. Tests for no treatment effect in randomized clinical trials. *Biometrika* 75: 57–64.

Gould, W. W., J. Pitblado, and W. M. Sribney. 2006. *Maximum Likelihood Estimation with Stata.* 3rd ed. College Station, TX: Stata Press.

Huber, P. J. 1967. The behavior of maximum likelihood estimates under nonstandard conditions. In Vol. 1 of *Proceedings of the Fifth Berkeley Symposium on Mathematical Statistics and Probability,* 221–233. Berkeley: University of California Press.

Kent, J. T. 1982. Robust properties of likelihood ratio tests. *Biometrika* 69: 19–27.

Kish, L., and M. R. Frankel. 1974. Inference from complex samples. *Journal of the Royal Statistical Society, Series B* 36: 1–37.

Lin, D. Y., and L. J. Wei. 1989. The robust inference for the Cox proportional hazards model. *Journal of the American Statistical Association* 84: 1074–1078.

MacKinnon, J. G., and H. White. 1985. Some heteroskedasticity-consistent covariance matrix estimators with improved finite sample properties. *Journal of Econometrics* 29: 305–325.

Rogers, W. H. 1993. sg17: Regression standard errors in clustered samples. *Stata Technical Bulletin* 13: 19–23. Reprinted in *Stata Technical Bulletin Reprints,* vol. 3, pp. 88–94. College Station, TX: Stata Press.

Royall, R. M. 1986. Model robust confidence intervals using maximum likelihood estimators. *International Statistical Review* 54: 221–226.

White, H. 1980. A heteroskedasticity-consistent covariance matrix estimator and a direct test for heteroskedasticity. *Econometrica* 48: 817–838.

——. 1982. Maximum likelihood estimation of misspecified models. *Econometrica* 50: 1–25.

Also see

[P] **ereturn** — Post the estimation results

[R] **ml** — Maximum likelihood estimation

[R] **regress** — Linear regression

[SVY] **variance estimation** — Variance estimation for survey data

[U] **18 Programming Stata**

[U] **20.16 Obtaining robust variance estimates**

[U] **26 Overview of Stata estimation commands**

Title

scalar — Scalar variables

Syntax

Define scalar variable

scalar [define] *scalar_name* = *exp*

List contents of scalars

scalar {dir|list} [_all | *scalar_names*]

Drop specified scalars from memory

scalar drop { _all | *scalar_names* }

Description

scalar define defines the contents of the scalar variable *scalar_name*. The expression may be either a numeric or a string expression.

scalar dir and scalar list both list the contents of scalars.

scalar drop eliminates scalars from memory.

Remarks

Stata scalar variables are different from variables in the dataset. Variables in the dataset are columns of observations in your data. Stata scalars are named entities that store single numbers or strings, which may include missing values. For instance,

```
. scalar a = 2
. display a + 2
4
. scalar b = a + 3
. display b
5
. scalar root2 = sqrt(2)
. display %18.0g root2
 1.414213562373095
. scalar im = sqrt(-1)
. display im
.
. scalar s = "hello"
. display s
hello
```

374

`scalar list` can be used to display the contents of macros (as can `display` for reasons that will be explained below), and `scalar drop` can be used to eliminate scalars from memory:

```
. scalar list
          s = hello
         im =         .
      root2 =   1.4142136
          b =           5
          a =           2
. scalar list a b
          a =           2
          b =           5
. scalar drop a b
. scalar list
          s = hello
         im =         .
      root2 =   1.4142136
. scalar drop _all
. scalar list
.
```

Although scalars can be used interactively, their real use is in programs. Stata has macros and scalars, and deciding when to use which can be confusing.

▷ Example 1

Let's examine a problem where either macros or numeric scalars could be used in the solution. There will be occasions in your programs where you need something that we will describe as a mathematical scalar—one number. For instance, let's assume that you are writing a program and need the mean of some variable for use in a subsequent calculation. You can obtain the mean after `summarize` from `r(mean)` (see *Saved results* in [R] **summarize**), but you must obtain it immediately because the numbers stored in `r()` are reset almost every time you give a statistical command.

Let's complicate the problem: to make some calculation, you need to calculate the difference in the means of two variables, which we will call `var1` and `var2`. One solution to your problem is to use macros:

```
summarize var1, meanonly
local mean1 = r(mean)
summarize var2, meanonly
local mean2 =  r(mean)
local diff = 'mean1' - 'mean2'
```

Subsequently, you use `'diff'` in your calculation. Let's understand how this works. You `summarize var1, meanonly`; including the `meanonly` option suppresses the output from the `summarize` command and the calculation of the variance. You then save the contents of `r(mean)`—the just-calculated mean—in the local macro `mean1`. You then `summarize var2`, again suppressing the output, and store that just-saved result in the local macro `mean2`. Finally, you create another local macro called `diff`, which contains the difference. In making this calculation, you must put the `mean1` and `mean2` local macro names in single quotes because you want the contents of the macros. If the mean of `var1` is 3 and the mean of `var2` is 2, you want the numbers 3 and 2 substituted into the formula for `diff` to produce 1. If you omitted the single quotes, Stata would think that you are referring to the difference—not of the contents of macros named `mean1` and `mean2`—but of two variables named `mean1` and `mean2`. Those variables probably do not exist, so Stata would then produce an error message. In any case, you put the names in the single quotes.

Now let's consider the solution using Stata scalars:

```
summarize var1, meanonly
scalar m1 = r(mean)
summarize var2, meanonly
scalar m2 = r(mean)
scalar df = m1 - m2
```

The program fragments are similar, although this time we did not put the names of the scalars used in calculating the difference—which we called df this time—in single quotes. Stata scalars are allowed only in expressions—they are a kind of variable—and Stata knows that you want the contents of those variables.

So, which solution is better? There is certainly nothing to recommend one over the other in terms of program length—both programs have the same number of lines and, in fact, there is a one-to-one correspondence between what each line does. Nevertheless, the scalar-based solution is better, and here is why:

Macros are printable representations of things. When we said local mean1 = r(mean), Stata took the contents of r(mean), converted them into a printable form from its internal (and highly accurate) binary representation, and stored that string of characters in the macro mean1. When we created mean2, Stata did the same thing again. Then when we said local diff = 'mean1' - 'mean2', Stata first substituted the contents of the macros mean1 and mean2—which are really strings—into the command. If the means of the two variables are 3 and 2, the printable string representations stored in mean1 and mean2 are "3" and "2". After substitution, Stata processed the command local diff = 3 - 2, converting the 3 and 2 back into internal binary representation to take the difference, producing the number 1, which it then converted into the printable representation "1", which it finally stored in the macro diff.

All of this conversion from binary to printable representation and back again is a lot of work for Stata. Moreover, although there are no accuracy issues with numbers like 3 and 2, if the first number had been $3.67108239891 \times 10^{-8}$, there would have been. When converting to printable form, Stata produces representations containing up to 17 digits and, if necessary, uses scientific notation. The first number would have become 3.6710823989e-08, and the last digit would have been lost. In computer scientific notation, 17 printable positions provides you with at least 13 significant digits. This is a lot, but not as many as Stata carries internally.

Now let's trace the execution of the solution by using scalars. scalar m1 = r(mean) quickly copied the binary representation stored in r(mean) into the scalar m1. Similarly, executing scalar m2 = r(mean) did the same thing, although it saved it in m2. Finally, scalar df = m1 - m2 took the two binary representations, subtracted them, and copied the result to the scalar df. This produces a more accurate result.

◁

Naming scalars

Scalars can have the same names as variables in the data and Stata will not become confused. You, however, may. Consider the following Stata command:

```
. generate newvar = alpha*beta
```

What does it mean? It certainly means to create a new data variable named newvar, but what will be in newvar? There are four possibilities:

• Take the data variable alpha and the data variable beta, and multiply the corresponding observations together.

• Take the scalar alpha and the data variable beta, and multiply each observation of beta by alpha.

- Take the data variable `alpha` and the scalar `beta`, and multiply each observation of `alpha` by `beta`.

- Take the scalar `alpha` and the scalar `beta`, multiply them together, and store the result repeatedly into `newvar`.

How Stata decides among these four possibilities is the topic of this section.

Stata's first rule is that if there is only one `alpha` (a data variable or a scalar) and one `beta` (a data variable or a scalar), Stata selects the one feasible solution and does it. If, however, there is more than one `alpha` or more than one `beta`, Stata always selects the data-variable interpretation in preference to the scalar.

Assume that you have a data variable called `alpha` and a scalar called `beta`:

```
. list
```

```
        alpha
    1.      1
    2.      3
    3.      5
```

```
. scalar list
         beta =              3
. gen newvar = alpha*beta
. list
```

```
        alpha   newvar
    1.      1        3
    2.      3        9
    3.      5       15
```

The result was to take the data variable `alpha` and multiply it by the scalar `beta`. Now let's start again, but this time, assume that you have a data variable called `alpha` and both a data variable and a scalar called `beta`:

```
. scalar list
         beta =              3
. list
```

```
        alpha    beta
    1.      1       2
    2.      3       3
    3.      5       4
```

```
. gen newvar = alpha*beta
. list
```

```
        alpha    beta   newvar
    1.      1       2        2
    2.      3       3        9
    3.      5       4       20
```

The result is to multiply the data variables, ignoring the scalar beta. In situations like this, you can force Stata to use the scalar by specifying scalar(beta) rather than merely beta:

```
. gen newvar2 = alpha*scalar(beta)
. list
```

	alpha	beta	newvar	newvar2
1.	1	2	2	3
2.	3	3	9	9
3.	5	4	20	15

The scalar() pseudofunction, placed around a name, says that the name is to be interpreted as the name of a scalar, even if a data variable by the same name exists. You can use scalar() around all your scalar names if you wish; there need not be a name conflict. Obviously, it will be easiest if you give your data and scalars different names.

❑ Technical note

The advice to name scalars and data variables differently may work interactively, but in programming situations, you cannot know whether the name you have chosen for a scalar conflicts with the data variables because the data are typically provided by the user and could have any names whatsoever.

One solution—and not a good one—is to place the scalar() pseudofunction around the names of all your scalars when you use them. A much better solution is to obtain the names for your scalars from Stata's tempname facility; see [P] **macro**. There are other advantages as well. Let's go back to calculating the sum of the means of variables var1 and var2. Our original draft looked like

```
summarize var1, meanonly
scalar m1 = r(mean)
summarize var2, meanonly
scalar m2 = r(mean)
scalar df = m1 - m2
```

A well-written draft would look like

```
tempname m1 m2 df
summarize var1, meanonly
scalar `m1' = r(mean)
summarize var2, meanonly
scalar `m2' = r(mean)
scalar `df' = `m1' - `m2'
```

We first declared the names of our temporary scalars. Actually, tempname creates three new local macros named m1, m2, and df, and places in those macros names that Stata makes up, names that are guaranteed to be different from the data. (m1, for your information, probably contains something like __000001.) When we use the temporary names, we put single quotes around them—m1 is not the name we want; we want the name that is stored in the local macro named m1.

That is, if we type

```
scalar m1 = r(mean)
```

then we create a scalar named m1. After tempname m1 m2 df, if we type

```
scalar `m1' = r(mean)
```

then we create a scalar named with whatever name happens to be stored in m1. It is Stata's responsibility to make sure that name is valid and unique, and Stata did that when we issued the tempname command. As programmers, we never need to know what is really stored in the macro m1; all we need to do is put single quotes around the name whenever we use it.

There is a second advantage to naming scalars with names obtained from `tempname`. Stata knows that they are temporary—when our program concludes, all temporary scalars will be automatically dropped from memory. And, if our program calls another program, that program will not accidentally use one of our scalars, even if the programmer happened to use the same name. Consider

```
program myprog
        ( lines omitted )
        tempname m1
        scalar 'm1' = something
        mysub
        ( lines omitted )
end
program mysub
        ( lines omitted )
        tempname m1
        scalar 'm1' = something else
        ( lines omitted )
end
```

Both `myprog` and `mysub` refer to a scalar, `'m1'`; `myprog` defines `'m1'` and then calls `mysub`, and `mysub` then defines `'m1'` differently. When `myprog` regains control, however, `'m1'` is just as it was before `myprog` called `mysub`!

It is unchanged because the scalar is not named `m1`: it is named something returned by `tempname`—a guaranteed unique name—and that name is stored in the local macro `m1`. When `mysub` is executed, Stata safely hides all local macros, so the local macro `m1` in `mysub` has no relation to the local macro `m1` in `myprog`. `mysub` now puts a temporary name in its local macro `m1`—a different name because `tempname` always returns unique names—and `mysub` now uses that different name. When `mysub` completes, Stata discards the temporary scalars and macros and restores the definitions of the old temporary macros, and `myprog` is off and running again.

Even if `mysub` had been poorly written in the sense of not obtaining its temporary names from `tempname`, `myprog` would have no difficulty. The use of `tempname` by `myprog` is sufficient to guarantee that no other program can harm it. For instance, pretend `mysub` looked like

```
program mysub
        ( lines omitted )
        scalar m1 = something else
        ( lines omitted )
end
```

`mysub` is now directly using a scalar named `m1`. That will not interfere with `myprog`, however, because `myprog` has no scalar named `m1`. Its scalar is named `'m1'`, a name obtained from `tempname`.

❑

❑ Technical note

One result of the above is that scalars are not automatically shared between programs. The scalar `'m1'` in `myprog` is different from either of the scalars `m1` or `'m1'` in `mysub`. What if `mysub` needs `myprog`'s `'m1'`?

One solution is not to use `tempname`: you could write `myprog` to use the scalar `m1` and `mysub` to use the scalar `m1`. Both will be accessing the same scalar. This, however, is not recommended.

A better solution is to pass 'm1' as an argument. For instance,

```
program myprog
        ( lines omitted )
        tempname m1
        scalar 'm1' = something
        mysub 'm1'
        ( lines omitted )
end
program mysub
        args m1
        ( lines omitted )
        commands using 'm1'
        ( lines omitted )
end
```

We passed the name of the scalar given to us by `tempname`—'m1'—as the first argument to `mysub`. `mysub` picked up its first argument and stored that in its own local macro by the same name—m1. Actually, `mysub` could have stored the name in any macro name of its choosing; the line reading `args m1` could read `args m2`, as long as we changed the rest of `mysub` to use the name 'm2' wherever it uses the name 'm1'.

❑

Reference

Kolev, G. I. 2006. Stata tip 31: Scalar or variable? The problem of ambiguous names. *Stata Journal* 6: 279–280.

Also see

[P] **matrix** — Introduction to matrix commands

[P] **macro** — Macro definition and manipulation

[U] **18.3 Macros**

[U] **18.7.2 Temporary scalars and matrices**

Title

> **serset** — Create and manipulate sersets

Syntax

Create new serset from data in memory

  serset <u>cr</u>eate *varlist* [*if*] [*in*] [, <u>omitanym</u>iss <u>omitallm</u>iss

  <u>omitdupm</u>iss <u>omitn</u>othing sort(*varlist*)]

Create serset of cross medians

  serset create_xmedians svn_y svn_x [svn_w] [, bands(#) xmin(#) xmax(#)

  logx logy]

Create serset of interpolated points from cubic spline interpolation

  serset create_cspline svn_y svn_x [, n(#)]

Make previously created serset the current serset

  serset [set] $\#_s$

Change order of observations in current serset

  serset sort [*svn* [*svn* [...]]]

Return summary statistics about current serset

  serset <u>su</u>mmarize *svn* [, <u>d</u>etail]

Return in r() information about current serset

  serset

Load serset into memory

  serset use [, clear]

Change ID of current serset

  serset reset_id $\#_s$

Eliminate specified sersets from memory

  serset drop [*numlist* | _all]

Eliminate all sersets from memory

  serset clear

Describe existing sersets

```
serset dir
```

The `file` command is also extended to allow

Write serset into file

```
file sersetwrite handle
```

Read serset from file

```
file sersetread handle
```

The following extended macro functions are also available:

Extended function	Returns from the *current serset*
: serset id	ID
: serset k	number of variables
: serset N	number of observations
: serset varnum *svn*	*svnum* of *svn*
: serset type *svn*	storage type of *svn*
: serset format *svn*	display format of *svn*
: serset varnames	list of *svns*
: serset min *svn*	minimum of *svn*
: serset max *svn*	maximum of *svn*

Extended macro functions have the syntax
```
          local macname : ...
```
The *current serset* is the most recently created or the most recently set by the `serset set` command.

In the above syntax diagrams,

$\#_s$ refers to a serset number, $0 \leq \#_s \leq 1,999$.

varlist refers to the usual Stata varlist, that is, a list of variables that appear in the current dataset, not the current serset.

svn refers to a variable in a serset. The variable may be referred to by either its name (e.g., `mpg` or `l.gnp`) or its number (e.g., 1 or 5); which is used makes no difference.

svnum refers to a variable number in a serset.

Description

`serset` creates and manipulates sersets.

`file sersetwrite` writes and `file sersetread` reads sersets into files.

The extended macro function `:serset` reports information about the current serset.

Options for serset create

omitanymiss, omitallmiss, omitdupmiss, and omitnothing specify how observations with missing values are to be treated.

omitanymiss is the default. Observations in which any of the numeric variables contain missing are omitted from the serset being created.

omitallmiss specifies that only observations in which all the numeric variables contain missing be omitted.

omitdupmiss specifies that only duplicate observations in which all the numeric variables contain missing be omitted. Observations omitted will be a function of the sort order of the original data.

omitnothing specifies that no observations be omitted (other than those excluded by if *exp* and in *range*).

sort(*varlist*) specifies that the serset being created is to be sorted by the specified variables. The result is no different from, after serset creation, using the serset sort command, but total execution time is a little faster. The sort order of the data in memory is unaffected by this option.

Options for serset create_xmedians

bands(*#*) specifies the number of divisions along the x scale in which cross medians are to be calculated; the default is bands(200). bands() may be specified to be between 3 and 200.

Let m and M specify the minimum and maximum value of x. If the scale is divided into n bands (i.e., bands(*n*) is specified), the first band is m to $m + (M - m)/n$, the second $m + (M - m)/n$ to $m + 2 * (M - m)/n$, ..., and the nth $m + (n - 1) * (M - m)/n$ to $m + n * (M - m)/n = m + M - m = M$.

xmin(*#*) and xmax(*#*) specify the minimum and maximum values of the x variable to be used in the bands calculation—m and M in the formulas above. The actual minimum and maximum are used if these options are not specified. Also, if xmin() is specified with a number that is greater than the actual minimum, the actual minimum is used, and if xmax() is specified with a number that is less than the actual maximum, the actual maximum is used.

logx and logy specify that cross medians be created using a "log" scale. The exponential of the median of the log of the values is calculated in each band.

Option for serset create_cspline

n(*#*) specifies the number of points to be evaluated between each pair of x values, which are treated as the knots. The default is n(5), and n() may be between 1 and 300.

Option for serset summarize

detail specifies additional statistics, including skewness, kurtosis, the four smallest and four largest values, and various percentiles. This option is identical to the detail option of summarize.

Option for serset use

`clear` permits the serset to be loaded, even if there is a dataset already in memory and even if that dataset has changed since it was last saved.

Remarks

Remarks are presented under the following headings:

Introduction
serset create
serset create_xmedians
serset create_cspline
serset set
serset sort
serset summarize
serset
serset use
serset reset_id
serset drop
serset clear
serset dir
file sersetwrite and file sersetread

Introduction

Sersets are used in implementing Stata's graphics capabilities. When you make a graph, the data for the graph are extracted into a serset and then, at the lowest levels of Stata's graphics implementation, are graphed from there.

Sersets are like datasets: they contain observations on one or more variables. Each serset is assigned a number, and in your program, you use that number when referring to a serset. Thus multiple sersets can reside simultaneously in memory. (Sersets are, in fact, stored in a combination of memory and temporary disk files, so accessing their contents is slower than accessing the data in memory. Sersets, however, are fast enough to keep up with graphics operations.)

serset create

`serset create` creates a new serset from the data in memory. For instance,

    . serset create mpg weight

creates a new serset containing variables mpg and weight. When using the serset later, you can refer to these variables by their names, mpg and weight, or by their numbers, 1 and 2.

`serset create` also returns the following in r():

r(N)	the number of observations placed into the serset
r(k)	the number of variables placed into the serset
r(id)	the number assigned to the serset

r(N) and r(k) are just for your information; by far the most important returned result is r(id). You will need to use this number in subsequent commands to refer to this serset.

`serset create` also sets the current serset to the one just created. Commands that use sersets always use the current serset. If, in later commands, the current serset is not the one desired, you can set the desired one by using `serset set`, described below.

serset create_xmedians

serset create_xmedians creates a new serset based on the currently set serset. The basic syntax is

serset create_xmedians svn_y svn_x $[svn_w]$ $[, \ldots]$

The new serset will contain cross medians. Put that aside. In the serset create_xmedians command, you specify two or three variables to be recorded in the current serset. The result is to create a new serset containing two variables (svn_y and svn_x) and a different number of observations. As with serset create, the result will also be to save the following in r():

r(id)   the number assigned to the serset
r(k)   the number of variables in the serset
r(N)   the number of observations in the serset

The newly created serset will become the current serset.

In actual use, you might code

```
serset create 'yvar' 'xvar' 'zvar'
local base = r(id)
...
serset set 'base'
serset create_xmedians 'yvar' 'xvar'
local cross = r(id)
...
```

serset create_xmedians obtains data from the original serset and calculates the median values of svn_y and the median values of svn_x for bands of svn_x values. The result is a new dataset of n observations (one for each band) containing median y and median x values, where the variables have the same name as the original variables. These results are stored in the newly created serset. If a third variable is specified, svn_w, the medians are calculated with weights.

serset create_cspline

serset create_cspline works in the same way as serset create_xmedians: it takes one serset and creates another serset from it, leaving the first unchanged. Thus, as with all serset creation commands, returned in r() is

r(id)   the number assigned to the serset
r(k)   the number of variables in the serset
r(N)   the number of observations in the serset

and the newly created serset will become the current serset.

serset create_cspline performs cubic spline interpolation, and here the new serset will contain the interpolated points. The original serset should contain the knots through which the cubic spline is to pass. serset create_cspline also has the n(#) option, which specifies how many points are to be interpolated, so the resulting dataset will have $N + (N - 1) * n()$ observations, where N is the number of observations in the original dataset. A typical use of serset create_cspline would be

```
serset create 'yvar' 'xvar'
local base = r(id)
. . .
serset set 'base'
serset create_xmedians 'yvar' 'xvar'
local cross = r(id)
. . .
serset set 'cross'
serset create_cspline 'yvar' 'xvar'
. . .
```

Here the spline is placed not through the original data but through cross medians of the data.

serset set

serset set is used to make a previously created serset the current serset. You may omit the set. Typing

```
serset 5
```

is equivalent to typing

```
serset set 5
```

You would never actually know ahead of time the number of a serset that you needed to code. Instead, when you created the serset, you would have recorded the identity of the serset created, say, in a local macro, by typing

```
local id = r(id)
```

and then later, you would make that serset the current serset by coding

```
serset set 'id'
```

serset sort

serset sort changes the order of the observations of the current serset. For instance,

```
serset create mpg weight
local id = r(id)
serset sort weight mpg
```

would place the observations of the serset in ascending order of variable weight and, within equal values of weight, in ascending order of variable mpg.

If no variables are specified after serset sort, serset sort does nothing. That is not considered an error.

serset summarize

serset summarize returns summary statistics about a variable in the current serset. It does not display output or in any way change the current serset.

Returned in r() is exactly what the summarize command returns in r().

serset

serset typed without arguments produces no output but returns in r() information about the current serset:

r(id)	the number assigned to the current serset
r(k)	the number of variables in the current serset
r(N)	the number of observations in the current serset

If no serset is in use, r(id) is set to -1, and r(k) and r(N) are left undefined; no error message is produced.

serset use

serset use loads a serset into memory. That is, it copies the current serset into the current data. The serset is left unchanged.

serset reset_id

serset reset_id is a rarely used command. Its syntax is

> serset reset_id $\#_s$

serset reset_id changes the ID of the current serset—its number—to the number specified, if that is possible. If not, it produces the error message "series $\#_s$ in use"; r(111).

Either way, the same serset continues to be the current serset (i.e., the number of the current serset changes if the command is successful).

serset drop

serset drop eliminates (erases) the specified sersets from memory. For instance,

> serset drop 5

would eliminate serset 5, and

> serset drop 5/9

would eliminate sersets 5–9. Using serset drop to drop a serset that does not exist is not an error; it does nothing.

Typing serset drop _all would drop all existing sersets.

Be careful not to drop sersets that are not yours: Stata's graphics system creates and holds onto sersets frequently, and, if you drop one of its sersets that are in use, the graph on the screen will eventually "fall apart", and Stata will produce error messages (Stata will not crash). The graphics system will itself drop sersets when it is through with them.

The discard command also drops all existing sersets. This, however, is safe because discard also closes any open graphs.

serset clear

serset clear is a synonym for serset drop _all.

serset dir

serset dir displays a description of all existing sersets.

file sersetwrite and file sersetread

file sersetwrite and file sersetread are extensions to the file command; see [P] **file**. These extensions write and read sersets into files. The files may be opened text or binary, but, either way, what is written into the file will be in a binary format.

file sersetwrite writes the current serset. A code fragment might read

```
serset create ...
local base = r(id)
...
tempname hdl
file open 'hdl' using "'filename'", write ...
...
serset set 'base'
file sersetwrite 'hdl'
...
file close 'hdl'
```

file sersetread reads a serset from a file, creating a new serset in memory. file sersetread returns in r(id) the serset ID of the newly created serset. A code fragment might read

```
tempname hdl
file open 'hdl' using "'filename'", read ...
...
file sersetread 'hdl'
local new = r(id)
...
file close 'hdl'
```

See [P] **file** for more information on the file command.

Saved results

serset create, serset create_xmedians, serset create_cspline, serset set, and serset save the following in r():

> Scalars
> > r(id)   the serset ID
> > r(k)   the number of variables in the serset
> > r(N)   the number of observations in the serset

serset summarize returns in r() the same results as returned by the summarize command.

serset use returns in macro r(varnames) the names of the variables in the newly created dataset.

file sersetread returns in scalar r(id) the serset ID, which is the identification number assigned to the serset.

Also see

[P] **class** — Class programming

[P] **file** — Read and write ASCII text and binary files

Title

> **signestimationsample** — Determine whether the estimation sample has changed

Syntax

```
signestimationsample varlist
```

```
checkestimationsample
```

Description

signestimationsample and checkestimationsample are easy-to-use interfaces into datasignature for use with estimation commands; see [D] **datasignature**.

signestimationsample obtains a data signature for the estimation sample and stores it in e().

checkestimationsample obtains a data signature and compares it with that stored by signestimationsample and, if they are different, reports "data have changed since estimation"; r(459).

If you just want to know whether any of the data in memory have changed since they were last saved, see [D] **describe**. Examine saved result r(changed) after describe; it will be 0 if the data have not changed and 1 otherwise.

Remarks

Remarks are presented under the following headings:

> Using signestimationsample and checkestimationsample
> Signing
> Checking
> Handling of weights
> Do not sign unnecessarily

Using signestimationsample and checkestimationsample

Estimators often come as a suite of commands: the estimation command itself (say, myest) and postestimation commands such as predict, estat, or even myest_stats. The calculations made by the postestimation commands are sometimes appropriate for use with any set of data values—not just the data used for estimation—and sometimes not. For example, predicted values can be calculated with any set of explanatory variables, whereas scores are valid only if calculated using the original data.

Postestimation calculations that are valid only when made using the estimation sample are the exception, but when they arise, signestimationsample and checkestimationsample provide the solution. The process is as follows:

1. At the time of estimation, sign the estimation sample (save the data's signature in e()).

2. At the time of use, obtain the signature of the data in memory and compare it with the original stored previously.

Signing

To sign the estimation sample, include in your estimation command the following line after e(sample) is set (that is, after `ereturn post`):

```
. signestimationsample 'varlist'
```

'varlist' should contain all variables used in estimation, string and numeric, used directly or indirectly, so you may in fact code

```
. signestimationsample 'lhsvar' 'rhsvars' 'clustervar'
```

or something similar. If you are implementing a time-series estimator, do not forget to include the time variable:

```
. quietly tsset
. signestimationsample 'r(timevar)' 'lhsvar' 'rhsvars' 'othervars'
```

The time variable may be among the 'rhsvars', but it does not matter if time is specified twice.

If you are implementing an xt estimator, do not forget to include the panel variable and the optional time variable:

```
. quietly xtset
. signestimationsample 'r(panelvar)' 'r(timevar)' 'lhsvar' 'rhsvars' 'clustervar'
```

In any case, specify all relevant variables and don't worry about duplicates. signestimation-sample produces no output, but behind the scenes, it adds two new results to e():

- e(datasignature)—the signature formed by the variables specified in the observations for which e(sample) = 1
- e(datasignaturevars)—the names of the variables used in forming the signature

Checking

Now that the signature is stored, include the following line in the appropriate place in your postestimation command:

```
. checkestimationsample
```

checkestimationsample will compare e(datasignature) with a newly obtained signature based on e(datasignaturevars) and e(sample). If the data have not changed, the results will match, and checkestimationsample will silently return. Otherwise, it will issue the error message "data have changed since estimation"; r(459).

Handling of weights

When you code

```
. signestimationsample 'lhsvar' 'rhsvars' 'clustervar'
```

and

```
. checkestimationsample
```

weights are handled automatically.

That is, when you signestimationsample, the command looks for e(wexp) and automatically includes any weighting variables in the calculation of the checksum. checkestimationsample does the same thing.

Do not sign unnecessarily

signestimationsample and checkestimationsample are excellent solutions for restricting postestimation calculations to the estimation sample. However, most statistics do not need to be so restricted. If none of your postestimation commands need to checkestimationsample, do not bother to signestimationsample.

Calculation of the checksum requires time. It's not much, but neither is it zero. On a 2.8-GHz computer, calculating the checksum over 100 variables and 50,000 observations requires about a quarter of a second.

Saved results

signestimationsample saves the following in e():

> Macros
>   e(datasignaturevars)   variables used in calculation of checksum
>   e(datasignature)   the checksum

The format of the stored signature is that produced by datasignature, fast nonames; see [D] **datasignature**.

Methods and formulas

signestimationsample and checkestimationsample are implemented as ado-files.

Also see

[D] **datasignature** — Determine whether data have changed

[D] **describe** — Describe data in memory or in file

Title

sleep — Pause for a specified time

Syntax

sleep #

where # is the number of milliseconds (1,000 ms = 1 second).

Description

sleep tells Stata to pause for # ms before continuing with the next command.

Remarks

Use sleep when you want Stata to wait for some amount of time before executing the next command.

```
. sleep 10000
```

pauses Stata for 10 seconds.

Title

> **smcl** — Stata Markup and Control Language

Description

SMCL, which stands for Stata Markup and Control Language and is pronounced "smickle", is Stata's output language. SMCL directives, such as "{it:...}" in

```
You can output {it:italics} using SMCL
```

affect how output appears:

> You can output *italics* using SMCL

All Stata output is processed by SMCL: help files, statistical results, and even the output of `display` in the programs you write.

Remarks

Remarks are presented under the following headings:

> *Introduction*
> *SMCL modes*
> *Command summary—general syntax*
> *Help file preprocessor directive for substituting repeated material*
> *Formatting directives for use in line and paragraph modes*
> *Link directives for use in line and paragraph modes*
> *Formatting directives for use in line mode*
> *Formatting directives for use in paragraph mode*
> *Directive for entering the as-is mode*
> *Directive for entering the Stata 6 help mode*
> *Inserting values from constant and current-value class*
> *Displaying characters using ASCII code*
> *Advice on using display*
> *Advice on formatting help files*

Introduction

You will use SMCL mainly in the programs you compose and in the help files you write to document them, although you can use it in any context. Everything Stata displays on the screen is processed by SMCL. You can even use some of SMCL's features to change how text appears in graphs; see [G] **text**.

Your first encounter with SMCL was probably in the Stata session logs created by the `log using` command. By default, Stata creates logs in SMCL format and gives them the file suffix `.smcl`. The file suffix does not matter; that the output is in SMCL format does. Files containing SMCL can be redisplayed in their original rendition, and SMCL output can be translated to other formats through the `translate` command; see [R] **translate**.

SMCL is mostly just ASCII text, for instance,

```
. display "this is SMCL"
this is SMCL
```

but that text can contain SMCL directives, which are enclosed in braces. Try the following:

```
. display "{title:this is SMCL, too}"
this is SMCL, too
```

The "{title:...}" directive told SMCL to output what followed the colon in title format. Exactly how the title format appears on your screen—or on paper if you print it—will vary, but SMCL will ensure that it always appears as a recognizable title.

Now try this:

```
. display "now we will try {help summarize:clicking}"
now we will try clicking
```

The word *clicking* will appear as a link—probably in some shade of blue. Click on the word. This will bring up Stata's Viewer and show you the help for the summarize command. The SMCL {help:...} directive is an example of a *link*. The directive {help summarize:clicking} displayed the word *clicking* and arranged things so that when the user clicked on the highlighted word, help for summarize appeared.

Here is another example of a link:

```
. display "You can also run Stata commands by {stata summarize mpg:clicking}"
You can also run Stata commands by clicking
```

Click on the word, and this time the result will be exactly as if you had typed the command summarize mpg into Stata. If you have the automobile data loaded, you will see the summary statistics for the variable mpg.

Simply put, you can use SMCL to make your output look better and to add links.

SMCL modes

SMCL is always in one of four modes:

1. SMCL line mode
2. SMCL paragraph mode
3. As-is mode
4. Stata 6 help mode

Modes 1 and 2 are nearly alike—in these two modes, SMCL directives are understood, and the modes differ only in how they treat blanks and carriage returns. In paragraph mode—so called because it is useful for formatting text into paragraphs—SMCL joins one line to the next and splits lines to form output with lines that are of nearly equal length. In line mode, SMCL shows the line much as you entered it. For instance, in line mode, the input text

```
Variable name          mean          standard error
```

(which might appear in a help file) would be spaced in the output exactly as you entered it. In paragraph mode, the above would be output as "Variable name mean standard error", meaning that it would all run together. On the other hand, the text

```
The two main uses of SMCL are in the programs you compose and in the help files
you write to document them, although SMCL may be used in any context.
Everything Stata displays on the screen is processed by SMCL.
```

would display as a nicely formatted paragraph in paragraph mode.

In mode 3, as-is mode, SMCL directives are not interpreted. {title:...}, for instance, has no special meaning—it is just the characters open brace, t, i, and so on. If {title:...} appeared in SMCL input text,

```
{title:My Title}
```

it would be displayed exactly as it appears: {title:My Title}. In as-is mode, SMCL just displays text as it was entered. As-is mode is useful only for those wishing to document how SMCL works because, with as-is mode, they can show examples of what SMCL input looks like.

Mode 4, Stata 6 help mode, is included for backward compatibility and should be avoided. Before Stata 7, Stata's help files had special encoding that allowed some words to be highlighted and allowed the creation of links to other help files. However, it did not have the features of SMCL, and, moreover, it could be used only in help files. In Stata 6 help mode, SMCL recreates this old environment so that old help files continue to display correctly, even if they have not been updated.

Those are the four modes, and the most important of them are the first two, the SMCL modes, and the single most important mode is SMCL line mode—mode 1. Line mode is the mother of all modes in that SMCL continually returns to it, and you can get to the other modes only from line mode. For instance, to enter paragraph mode, you use the {p} directive, and you use it from line mode, although you typically do not think of that. Paragraphs end when SMCL encounters a blank line, and SMCL then returns to line mode. Consider the following lines appearing in some help file:

```
{p}
The two main uses of SMCL are in the programs you compose and the
help files you write to document them, although SMCL may be used in any context.
Everything Stata displays on the screen is processed by SMCL.
{p}
Your first encounter with SMCL was probably the Stata session
...
```

Between the paragraphs above, SMCL returned to line mode because it encountered a blank line. SMCL stayed in paragraph mode as long as the paragraph continued without a blank line, but once the paragraph ended, SMCL returned to line mode. There are ways of ending paragraphs other than using blank lines, but they are the most common. Regardless of how paragraphs end, SMCL returns to line mode.

In another part of our help file, we might have

```
{p}
SMCL, which stands for Stata Markup and Control Language
and is pronounced "smickle", is Stata's output language.
SMCL directives, for example, the {c -(}it:...{c )-} in the following,
        One can output {it:italics} using SMCL
{p} affects how output appears:  ...
```

Between the paragraphs, SMCL entered line mode (again, because SMCL encountered a blank line), so the "One can output..." part will appear as you have spaced it, namely, indented. It will appear that way because SMCL is in line mode.

The other two modes are invoked using the {asis} and {s6hlp} directives and do not end with blank lines. They continue until you enter the {smcl} directive, and here {smcl} must be followed by a carriage return. You may put a carriage return at the end of {asis} or the {s6hlp} directives—it will make no difference—but to return to SMCL line mode, you must put a carriage return directly after the {smcl} directive.

To summarize, when dealing with SMCL, begin by assuming that you are in line mode; you almost certainly will be. If you wish to enter a paragraph, you will use the {p} directive, but once the paragraph ends, you will be back in line mode and ready to start another paragraph. If you want to enter as-is mode, perhaps to include a piece of ASCII text output, use the {asis} directive, and at the end of the piece, use the {smcl}(carriage return) directive to return to line mode. To include a piece of an old Stata 6 help file, use the {s6hlp} directive to enter Stata 6 help mode, and, at its conclusion, use {smcl}(carriage return) to return to line mode.

Command summary—general syntax

Pretend that {xyz} is a SMCL directive, although it is not. {xyz} might have any of the following syntaxes:

Syntax 1: {xyz}

Syntax 2: {xyz:*text*}

Syntax 3: {xyz *args*}

Syntax 4: {xyz *args*:*text*}

Syntax 1 means "do whatever it is that {xyz} does". Syntax 2 means "do whatever it is that {xyz} does, do it on the text *text*, and then stop doing it". Syntax 3 means "do whatever it is that {xyz} does, as modified by *args*". Finally, syntax 4 means "do whatever it is that {xyz} does, as modified by *args*, do it on the text *text*, and then stop doing it".

Not every SMCL directive has all four syntaxes, and which syntaxes are allowed is made clear in the descriptions below.

In syntaxes 3 and 4, *text* may contain other SMCL directives, so the following is valid:

```
{center:The use of {ul:SMCL} in help files}
```

The *text* of one SMCL directive may itself contain other SMCL directives. However, not only must the braces match, but they must match on the same physical (input) line. Typing

```
{center:The use of {ul:SMCL} in help files}
```

is correct, but

```
{center:The use of {ul:SMCL} in
help files}
```

is an error. When SMCL encounters an error, it simply displays the text in the output it does not understand, so the result of making the error above would be to display

```
{center:The use of SMCL in
help files}
```

SMCL understood {ul:...} but not {center:...} because the braces did not match on the input line, so it displayed only that part. If you see SMCL directives in your output, you have made an error.

Help file preprocessor directive for substituting repeated material

INCLUDE help *arg* follows syntax 3.

INCLUDE specifies that SMCL substitute the contents of a file named *arg*.ihlp. This is useful when you need to include the same text multiple times. This substitution is performed only when the file is viewed using help.

Example:

We have several commands that accept the replace option. Instead of typing the description under *Options* of each help file, we create the file replace.ihlp, which contains something like the following:

```
{* 01apr2005}{...}
{phang}
{opt replace} overwrite existing {it:filename}{p_end}
```

To include the text in our help file, we type

```
INCLUDE help replace
```

Formatting directives for use in line and paragraph modes

{sf}, {it}, and {bf} follow syntaxes 1 and 2.

These directives specify how the font is to appear. {sf} indicates standard face, {it} italic face, and {bf} boldface.

Used in syntax 1, these directives switch to the font face specified, and that rendition will continue to be used until another one of the directives is given.

Used in syntax 2, they display *text* in the specified way and then switch the font face back to whatever it was previously.

Examples:
```
the value of {it}varlist {sf}may be specified ...
the value of {it:varlist} may be specified ...
```

{input}, {error}, {result}, and {text} follow syntaxes 1 and 2.

These directives specify how the text should be rendered: in the style that indicates user input, an error, a calculated result, or the text around calculated results.

These styles are often rendered as color. In the Results window, on a white background, Stata by default shows input in black and bold, error messages in red, calculated results in black and bold, and text in black. However, the relationship between the real colors and {input}, {error}, {result}, and {text} may not be the default (the user could reset it), and, in fact, these renditions may not be shown in color at all. The user might have set {result}, for instance, to show in yellow, or in highlight, or in something else. However the styles are rendered, SMCL tries to distinguish among {input}, {error}, {result}, and {text}.

Examples:
```
{text}the variable mpg has mean {result:21.3} in the sample.
{text}mpg      {c |} {result}21.3
{text}mpg      {c |} {result:21.3}
{error:variable not found}
```

{inp}, {err}, {res}, and {txt} follow syntaxes 1 and 2.

These four commands are synonyms for {input}, {error}, {result}, and {text}.

Examples:
{txt}the variable mpg has mean {res:21.3} in the sample.
{txt}mpg   {c |} {res}21.3
{txt}mpg   {c |} {res:21.3}
{err:variable not found}

{cmd} follows syntaxes 1 and 2.

{cmd} is similar to the "color" styles and is the recommended way to show Stata commands in help files. Do not confuse {cmd} with {inp}. {inp} is the way commands actually typed are shown, and {cmd} is the recommended way to show commands you might type. We recommend that you present help files in terms of {txt} and use {cmd} to show commands; use any of {sf}, {it}, or {bf} in a help file, but we recommend that you not use any of the "colors" {inp}, {err}, or {res}, except where you are showing actual Stata output.

Example:
When using the {cmd:summarize} command, specify ...

{cmdab:*text1*:*text2*} follows a variation on syntax 2 (note the double colons).

{cmdab} is the recommended way to show minimum abbreviations for Stata commands and options in help files; *text1* represents the minimum abbreviation, and *text2* represents the rest of the text. When the entire command or option name is the minimum abbreviation, you may omit *text2* along with the extra colon. {cmdab:*text*} is then equivalent to {cmd:*text*}; it makes no difference which you use.

Examples:
{cmdab:su:mmarize} [{it:varlist}] [{it:weight}] [{cmdab:if} {it:exp}]
the option {cmdab:ef:orm}{cmd:({it:varname})} ...

{opt *option*}, {opt *option*(*arg*)}, {opt *option*(*a*,*b*)}, and {opt *option*(*a*|*b*)} follow syntax 3; alternatives to using {cmd}.

{opt *option1*:*option2*}, {opt *option1*:*option2*(*arg*)}, {opt *option1*:*option2*(*a*,*b*)}, and {opt *option1*:*option2*(*a*|*b*)} follow syntaxes 3 and 4; alternatives to using {cmdab}.

{opt} is the recommended way to show options. {opt} allows you to easily include arguments.

SMCL directive ...	is equivalent to typing ...
{opt *option*}	{cmd:*option*}
{opt *option*(*arg*)}	{cmd:*option*(}{it:*arg*}{cmd:)}
{opt *option*(*a*,*b*)}	{cmd:*option*(}{it:*a*}{cmd:,}{it:*b*}{cmd:)}
{opt *option*(*a*|*b*)}	{cmd:*option*(}{it:*a*}|{it:*b*}{cmd:)}
{opt *option1*:*option2*}	{cmd:*option1*:*option2*}
{opt *option1*:*option2*(*arg*)}	{cmd:*option1*:*option2*(}{it:*arg*}{cmd:)}
{opt *option1*:*option2*(*a*,*b*)}	{cmd:*option1*:*option2*(}{it:*a*}{cmd:,}{it:*b*}{cmd:)}
{opt *option1*:*option2*(*a*|*b*)}	{cmd:*option1*:*option2*(}{it:*a*}|{it:*b*}{cmd:)}

option1 represents the minimum abbreviation, and *option2* represents the rest of the text.

a,*b* and *a*|*b* may have any number of elements. Available elements that are displayed in {cmd} style are ,, =, :, *, %, and (). Several elements are displayed in plain text style: |, { }, and [].

Also, {opth *option*(*arg*)} is equivalent to {opt}, except that *arg* is displayed as a link to help; see *Link directives for use in line and paragraph modes* for more details.

Examples:
```
{opt replace}
{opt bseunit(varname)}
{opt f:ormat}
{opt sep:arator(#)}
```

{hilite} and {hi} follow syntaxes 1 and 2.

    {hilite} and {hi} are synonyms. {hilite} is the recommended way to highlight (draw attention to) something in help files. You might highlight, for example, a reference to a manual, the *Stata Journal*, or a book.

Examples:
```
see {hilite:[R] anova} for more details.
see {hi:[R] anova} for more details.
```

{ul} follows syntaxes 2 and 3.

    {ul on} starts underlining mode. {ul off} ends it. {ul:*text*} underlines *text*.

Examples:
```
You can {ul on}underline{ul off} this way or
you can {ul:underline} this way
```

{*} follows syntaxes 2 and 4.

    {*} indicates a comment. What follows it (inside the braces) is ignored.

Examples:
```
{* this text will be ignored}
{*:as will this}
```

{hline} follows syntaxes 1 and 3.

    {hline} (syntax 1) draws a horizontal line the rest of the way across the page. {hline #} (syntax 3) draws a horizontal line of # characters. {hline} (either syntax) is generally used in line mode.

Examples:
```
{hline}
{hline 20}
```

{.-} follows syntax 1.

    {.-} is a synonym for {hline} (syntax 1).

Example:
```
{.-}
```

{dup #:*text*} follows syntax 4.

    {dup} repeats *text* # times.

Examples:
```
{dup 20:A}
{dup 20:ABC}
```

{char *code*} and {c *code*} are synonyms and follow syntax 3.

These directives display the specified characters that otherwise might be difficult to type on your keyboard. See *Displaying characters using ASCII code* below.

Examples:
```
C{c o'}rdoba es una joya arquitect{c o'}nica.
{c S|}57.20
The ASCII character 206 in the current font is {c 206}
The ASCII character 5a (hex) is {c 0x5a}
{c -(} is open brace and {c )-} is close brace
```

{reset} follows syntax 1.

{reset} is equivalent to coding {txt}{sf}.

Example:
```
{reset}
```

Link directives for use in line and paragraph modes

All the link commands share the feature that when syntax 4 is allowed,

Syntax 4: {xyz *args*:*text*}

then syntax 3 is also allowed,

Syntax 3: {xyz *args*}

and if you specify syntax 3, Stata treats it as if you specified syntax 4, inserting a colon and then repeating the argument. For instance, {help} is defined below as allowing syntaxes 3 and 4. Thus the directive

```
{help summarize}
```

is equivalent to the directive

```
{help summarize:summarize}
```

Coding {help summarize} or {help summarize:summarize} both display the word *summarize*, and if the user clicks on that, the action of help summarize is taken. Thus you might code

```
See help for {help summarize} for more information.
```

This would display "See help for **summarize** for more information" and make the word *summarize* a link. To make the words describing the action different from the action, use syntax 4,

```
You can also {help summarize:examine the summary statistics} if you wish.
```

which results in "You can also **examine the summary statistics** if you wish."

The link directives, which may be used in either line mode or paragraph mode, are the following:

{help *args*[:*text*]} follows syntaxes 3 and 4.

{help} displays *args* as a link to help *args*; see [R] **help**. If you also specify the optional :*text*, *text* is displayed instead of *args*, but you are still directed to the help file for *args*.

Examples:
```
{help epitab}
{help summarize:the mean}
```

{helpb *args*[:*text*]} follows syntaxes 3 and 4.

> {helpb} is equivalent to {help}, except that *args* or *text* is displayed in boldface.

> *Examples:*
> {helpb summarize}
> {helpb generate}

{manhelp *args1 args2*[:*text*]} follows syntaxes 3 and 4.

> {manhelp} displays [*args2*] *args1* as a link to help *args1*; thus our first example below would display [R] summarize as a link to help summarize. Specifying the optional :*text* displays *text* instead of *args1*, but you are still directed to the help file for *args1*.

> *Examples:*
> {manhelp summarize R}
> {manhelp weight U:14 Language syntax}
> {manhelp graph_twoway G:graph twoway}

{manhelpi *args1 args2*[:*text*]} follows syntaxes 3 and 4.

> {manhelpi} is equivalent to {manhelp}, except that *args* or *text* is displayed in italics.

> *Examples:*
> {manhelpi twoway_options G}
> {manhelpi mata M:Mata Reference Manual}

{help *args*##*markername*[|*viewername*] [:*text*]} and {marker *markername*} follow syntax 3.

> They let the user jump to a specific location within a file, not just to the top of the file. {help *args*##*markername*} displays *args*##*markername* as a link that will jump to the location marked by {marker *markername*}. Specifying the optional |*viewername* will display the results of {marker *markername*} in a new Viewer window named *viewername*; _new is a valid *viewername* that assigns a unique name for the new Viewer. Specifying the optional :*text* displays *text* instead of *args*##*markername*. *args* represents the name of the file where the {marker} is located. If *args* contains spaces, be sure to specify it within quotes.

> We document the directive as {help ... }; however, view, news, net, ado, and update may be used in place of help, although you would probably want to use only help or view.

> *Examples:*
> > {pstd}You can change the style of the text using the {cmd}
> > directive; see {help example##cmd} below.
> >
> > You can underline a word or phrase with the {ul} directive;
> > see {help example##ul:below}.
> >
> > {marker cmd}{...}
> > {phang}{cmd} follows syntaxes 1 and 2.{break}
> > {cmd} is another style not unlike the ...
> >
> > {marker ul}{...}
> > {phang}{ul} follows syntaxes 2 and 3.{break}
> > {ul on} starts underlining mode. {ul} ...

{help_d:*text*} follows syntax 2.

> {help_d} displays *text* as a link that will display a help dialog box from which the user may obtain interactive help on any Stata command.

> *Example:*
> ... using the {help_d:help system} ...

{newvar[:*args*]} follows syntaxes 1 and 2.

{newvar} displays *newvar* as a link to help newvar. If you also specify the optional :*args*, Stata concatenates *args* to *newvar* to display *newvarargs*.

Examples:
{newvar}
{newvar:2}

{var[:*args*]} and {varname[:*args*]} follow syntaxes 1 and 2.

{var} and {varname} display *varname* as a link to help varname. If you also specify the optional :*args*, Stata concatenates *args* to *varname* to display *varnameargs*.

Examples:
{var}
{var:1}
{varname}
{varname:2}

{vars[:*args*]} and {varlist[:*args*]} follow syntaxes 1 and 2.

{vars} and {varlist} display *varlist* as a link to help varlist. If you also specify the optional :*args*, Stata concatenates *args* to *varlist* to product *varlistargs*.

Examples:
{vars}
{vars:1}
{varlist}
{varlist:2}

{depvar[:*args*]} follows syntaxes 1 and 2.

{depvar} displays *depvar* as a link to help depvar. If you also specify the optional :*args*, Stata concatenates *args* to *depvar* to display *depvarargs*.

Examples:
{depvar}
{depvar:1}

{depvars[:*args*]} and {depvarlist[:*args*]} follow syntaxes 1 and 2.

{depvars} and {depvarlist} display *depvarlist* as a link to help depvarlist. If you also specify the optional :*args*, Stata concatenates *args* to *depvarlist* to display *depvarlistargs*.

Examples:
{depvars}
{depvars:1}
{depvarlist}
{depvarlist:2}

{indepvars[:*args*]} follows syntaxes 1 and 2.

{indepvars} displays *indepvars* as a link to help varlist. If you also specify the optional :*args*, Stata concatenates *args* to *indepvars* to display *indepvarsargs*.

Examples:
{indepvars}
{indepvars:1}

{ifin} follows syntax 1.

    {ifin} displays [*if*] and [*in*], where *if* is a link to the help for the if qualifier and *in* is a link to the help for the in qualifier.

    Example:
    {ifin}

{weight} follows syntax 1.

    {weight} displays [*weight*], where *weight* is a link to the help for the *weight* specification.

    Example:
    {weight}

{dtype} follows syntax 1.

    {dtype} displays [*type*], where *type* is a link to help data types.

    Example:
    {dtype}

{search *args*[:*text*]} follows syntaxes 3 and 4.

    {search} displays *text* as a link that will display the results of search on *args*; see [R] **search**.

    Examples:
    {search anova:click here} for the latest information on ANOVA
    Various programs are available for {search anova}

{search_d:*text*} follows syntax 2.

    {search_d} displays *text* as a link that will display a *Keyword Search* dialog box from which the user can obtain interactive help by entering keywords of choice.

    Example:
    ... using the {search_d:search system} ...

{dialog *args*[:*text*]} follows syntaxes 3 and 4.

    {dialog} displays *text* as a link that will launch the dialog box for *args*. *args* must contain the name of the dialog box and may optionally contain , message(*string*), where *string* is the message to be passed to the dialog box.

    Example:
    ... open the {dialog regress:regress dialog box} ...

{browse *args*[:*text*]} follows syntaxes 3 and 4.

    {browse} displays *text* as a link that will launch the user's browser pointing at *args*. Because *args* is typically a URL containing a colon, *args* usually must be specified within quotes.

    Example:
    ... you can {browse "http://www.stata.com":visit the Stata web site} ...

{view *args*[:*text*]} follows syntaxes 3 and 4.

    {view} displays *text* as a link that will present in the Viewer the filename *args*. If *args* is a URL, be sure to specify it within quotes. {view} is seldom used in a SMCL file (such as a help file) because you will seldom know of a fixed location for the file unless it is a URL. {view} is sometimes used from programs because the program knows the location of the file it created.

    {view} can also be used with {marker}; see {help *args*##*markername*[|*viewername*][:*text*]} and {marker *markername*}, earlier in this section.

Examples:
see {view "http://www.stata.com/man/readme.smcl"}
display '"{view "'newfile'":click here} to view the file created"'

{view_d:*text*} follows syntax 2.

{view_d} displays *text* as a link that will display the *Choose File to View* dialog box in which the user may type the name of a file or a URL to be displayed in the Viewer.

Example:
{view_d:Click here} to view your current log

{manpage *args*[:*text*]} follows syntaxes 3 and 4.

{manpage} displays *text* as a link that will launch the user's PDF viewer pointing at *args. args* are a Stata manual (such as R or SVY) and a page number. The page number is optional. If the page number is not specified, the PDF viewer will open to the first page of the file.

Example:
The formulas are given on {manpage R 342:page 342 of [R] manual}.

{mansection *args*[:*text*]} follows syntaxes 3 and 4.

{mansection} displays *text* as a link that will launch the user's PDF viewer pointing at *args. args* are a Stata manual (such as R or SVY) and a named destination within that manual (such as predict or regress postestimation). The named destination is optional. If the named destination is not specified, the PDF viewer will open to the first page of the file.

Example:
See {mansection R clogitpostestimation:[R] clogit postestimation}.

{manlink *man entry*} and {manlinki *man entry*} follow syntax 3.

{manlink} and {manlinki} display *man* and *entry* using the {mansection} directive as a link that will launch the user's PDF viewer pointing at that manual entry. *man* is a Stata manual (such as R or SVY) and *entry* is the name of an entry within that manual (such as predict or regress postestimation). The named destination should be written as it appears in the title of the manual entry.

SMCL directive ...	is equivalent to typing ...
{manlink *man entry*}	{bf:{mansection *man entry_ns*:[*man*] *entry*}}
{manlinki *man entry*}	{bf:{mansection *man entry_ns*:[*man*] {it:*entry*}}}

entry_ns is *entry* with the following characters removed: space, left and right quotes (' and '), #, $, ~, {, }, [, and].

{news:*text*} follows syntax 2.

{news} displays *text* as a link that will display in the Viewer the latest news from http://www.stata.com.

{news} can also be used with {marker}; see {help *args*##*markername*[|*viewername*][:*text*]} and {marker *markername*} earlier in this section.

Example:
For the latest NetCourse offerings, see the {news:news}.

{net *args*[:*text*]} follows syntaxes 3 and 4.

{net} displays *args* as a link that will display in the Viewer the results of net *args*; see [R] **net**. Specifying the optional :*text*, displays *text* instead of *args*. For security reasons, net get and net install cannot be executed in this way. Instead, use {net describe ...} to show the page, and from there, the user can click on the appropriate links to install the materials. Whenever *args* contains a colon, as it does when *args* is a URL, be sure to enclose *args* within quotes.

{net cd .:*text*} displays *text* as a link that will display the contents of the current net location.

{net} can also be used with {marker}; see {help *args*##*markername*[|*viewername*] [:*text*]} and {marker *markername*}, earlier in this section.

Examples:
```
programs are available from {net "from http://www.stata.com":Stata}
Nicholas Cox has written a series of matrix commands which you can obtain
by {net "describe http://www.stata.com/stb/stb56/dm79":clicking here}.
```

{net_d:*text*} follows syntax 2.

{net_d} displays *text* as a link that will display a *Keyword Search* dialog box from which the user can search the Internet for additions to Stata.

Example:
```
To search the Internet for the latest additions to Stata available,
{net_d:click here}.
```

{netfrom_d:*text*} follows syntax 2.

{netfrom_d} displays *text* as a link that will display a *Choose Download Site* dialog box into which the user may enter a URL and then see the contents of the site. This directive is seldom used.

Example:
```
If you already know the URL, {netfrom_d:click here}.
```

{ado *args*[:*text*]} follows syntaxes 3 and 4.

{ado} displays *text* as a link that will display in the Viewer the results of ado *args*; see [R] **net**. For security reasons, ado uninstall cannot be executed in this way. Instead, use {ado describe ...} to show the package, and from there, the user can click to uninstall (delete) the material.

{ado} can also be used with {marker}; see {help *args*##*markername*[|*viewername*] [:*text*]} and {marker *markername*}, earlier in this section.

Example:
```
You can see the user-written packages you have installed (and uninstall
any that you wish) by {ado dir:clicking here}.
```

{ado_d:*text*} follows syntax 2.

{ado_d} displays *text* as a link that will display a *Search Installed Programs* dialog box from which the user can search for user-written routines previously installed (and uninstall them if desired).

Example:
```
You can search the user-written ado-files you have installed
by {ado_d:clicking here}.
```

{update *args*[:*text*]} follows syntaxes 3 and 4.

{update} displays *text* as a link that will display in the Viewer the results of update *args*; see [R] **update**. If *args* contains a URL, be careful to place the *args* in quotes.

args can be omitted because the update command is valid without arguments. {update:*text*} is really the best way to use the {update} directive because it allows the user to choose whether and from where to update their Stata.

{update} can also be used with {marker}; see {help *args##markername*[| *viewername*] [: *text*]} and {marker *markername*}, earlier in this section.

Examples:
Check whether your Stata is {update:up to date}.
Check whether your Stata is {update "from http://www.stata.com":up to date}.

{update_d:*text*} follows syntax 2.

{update_d} displays *text* as a link that will display a *Choose Official Update Site* dialog box into which the user may type a source (typically http://www.stata.com, but perhaps a local CD drive) from which to install official updates to Stata.

Example:
If you are installing from CD or some other source,
{update_d:click here}.

{back:*text*} follows syntax 2.

{back} displays *text* as a link that will take an action equivalent to pressing the Viewer's **Back** button.

Example:
{back:go back to the previous page}

{clearmore:*text*} follows syntax 2.

{clearmore} displays *text* as a link that will take an action equivalent to pressing Stata's **Clear –more– Condition** button. {clearmore} is of little use to anyone but the developers of Stata.

Example:
{clearmore:{hline 2}more{hline 2}}

{stata *args*[:*text*]} follows syntaxes 3 and 4.

{stata} displays *text* as a link that will execute the Stata command *args* in the Results window. Stata will first ask before executing a command that is displayed in a web browser. If *args* (the Stata command) contains a colon, remember to enclose the command in quotes.

Example:
... {stata summarize mpg:to obtain the mean of mpg}...

Remember, like all SMCL directives, {stata} can be used in programs as well as files. Thus you could code

display "... {stata summarize mpg:to obtain the mean of mpg}... "

or, if you were in the midst of outputting a table,

di "{stata summarize mpg:mpg}   {c |}" ...

However, it is more likely that, rather than being hardcoded, the variable name would be in a macro, say, 'vn':

di "{stata summarize 'vn':'vn'}   {c |}" ...

Here you probably would not know how many blanks to put after the variable name because it could be of any length. Thus you might code

di "{ralign 12:{stata summ 'vn':'vn'}} {c |}" ...

thus allocating 12 spaces for the variable name, which would be followed by a blank and the vertical bar. Then you would want to allow for a 'vn' longer than 12 characters:

```
local vna = abbrev('vn',12)
di "{ralign 12:{stata summ 'vn':'vna'}} {c |}" ...
```

There you have a line that will output a part of a table, with the linked variable name on the left and with the result of clicking on the variable name being to summ 'vn'. Of course, you could make the action whatever else you wanted.

{matacmd *args*[:*text*]} follows syntaxes 3 and 4.

{matacmd} works the same as {stata}, except that it submits a command to Mata. If Mata is not already active, the command will be prefixed with mata to allow Stata to execute it.

Formatting directives for use in line mode

{title:*text*}(carriage return) follows syntax 2.

{title:*text*} displays *text* as a title. {title:...} should be followed by a carriage return and, usually, by one more blank line so that the title is offset from what follows. (In help files, we precede titles by two blank lines and follow them by one.)

Example:
```
{title:Command summary -- general syntax}

{p}
Pretend that {cmd:{c -({xyz}c )-}} is a SMCL directive, although ...
```

{center:*text*} and {centre:*text*} follow syntax 2.
{center #:*text*} and {centre #:*text*} follow syntax 4.

{center:*text*} and {centre:*text*} are synonyms; they center the text on the line. {center:*text*} should usually be followed by a carriage return; otherwise, any text that follows it will appear on the same line. With syntax 4, the directives center the text in a field of width #.

Examples:
```
{center:This text will be centered}
{center:This text will be centered} and this will follow it
{center 60:This text will be centered within a width of 60 columns}
```

{rcenter:*text*} and {rcentre:*text*} follow syntax 2.
{rcenter #:*text*} and {rcentre #:*text*} follow syntax 4.

{rcenter:*text*} and {rcentre:*text*} are synonyms. {rcenter} is equivalent to {center}, except that *text* is displayed one space to the right when there are unequal spaces left and right. {rcenter:*text*} should be followed by a carriage return; otherwise, any text that follows it will appear on the same line. With syntax 4, the directives center the text in a field of width #.

Example:
```
{rcenter:this is shifted right one character}
```

{right:*text*} follows syntax 2.

{right} displays *text* with its last character aligned on the right margin. {right:*text*} should be followed by a carriage return.

Examples:
```
{right:this is right-aligned}
{right:this is shifted left one character }
```

{lalign #:*text*} and {ralign #:*text*} follow syntax 4.

    {lalign} left-aligns *text* in a field # characters wide, and {ralign} right-aligns *text* in a field # characters wide.

    Example:
    {lalign 12:mpg}{ralign 15:21.2973}

{dlgtab [# [#]]:*text*} follows syntaxes 2 and 4.

    {dlgtab} displays *text* as a dialog tab. The first # specifies how many characters to indent the dialog tab from the left-hand side, and the second # specifies how much to indent from the right-hand side. The default is {dlgtab 4 2:*text*}.

    Examples:
    {dlgtab:Model}
    {dlgtab 8 2:Model}

{...} follows syntax 1.

    {...} specifies that the next carriage return be treated as a blank.

    Example:
    Sometimes you need to type a long line and, while {...}
    that is fine with SMCL, some word processors balk. {...}
    In line mode, the above will appear as one long line to SMCL.

{col #} follows syntax 3.

    {col #} skips forward to column #. If you are already at or beyond that column in the output, then {col #} does nothing.

    Example:
    mpg{col 20}21.3{col 30}5.79

{space #} follows syntax 3.

    {space} is equivalent to typing # blank characters.

    Example:
    20.5{space 20}17.5

{tab} follows syntax 1.

    {tab} has the same effect as typing a tab character. Tab stops are set every eight spaces.

    Examples:
    {tab}This begins one tab stop in
    {tab}{tab}This begins two tab stops in

    Note: SMCL also understands tab characters and treats them the same as the {tab} command, so you may include tabs in your files.

Formatting directives for use in paragraph mode

{p} follows syntax 3. The full syntax is {p # # # #}.

    {p # # # #} enters paragraph mode. The first # specifies how many characters to indent the first line; the second #, how much to indent the second and subsequent lines; the third #, how much to bring in the right margin on all lines; and the fourth # is the total width for the paragraph. Numbers, if not specified, default to zero, so typing {p} without numbers is equivalent to typing {p 0 0 0 0}, {p #} is equivalent to {p # 0 0 0}, and so on. A zero for the fourth # means use the default paragraph width; see set linesize in [R] **log**. {p} (with or without numbers) may be followed by a carriage return or not; it makes no difference.

Paragraph mode ends when a blank line is encountered, the {p_end} directive is encountered, or {smcl}(carriage return) is encountered.

Examples:
{p}
{p 4}
{p 0 4}
{p 8 8 8 60}

Note concerning paragraph mode: In paragraph mode, you can have either one space or two spaces at the end of sentences, following the characters '.', '?', '!', and ':'. In the output, SMCL puts two spaces after each of those characters if you put two or more spaces after them in your input, or if you put a carriage return; SMCL puts one space if you put one space. Thus

```
{p}
Dr. Smith was near panic.  He could not reproduce the result.
Now he wished he had read about logging output in Stata.
```

will display as

```
Dr. Smith was near panic.  He could not reproduce the result.  Now he wished he
had read about logging output in Stata.
```

Several shortcut directives have also been added for commonly used paragraph mode settings:

SMCL directive ...	is equivalent to typing ...
{pstd}	{p 4 4 2}
{psee}	{p 4 13 2}
{phang}	{p 4 8 2}
{pmore}	{p 8 8 2}
{pin}	{p 8 8 2}
{phang2}	{p 8 12 2}
{pmore2}	{p 12 12 2}
{pin2}	{p 12 12 2}
{phang3}	{p 12 16 2}
{pmore3}	{p 16 16 2}
{pin3}	{p 16 16 2}

{p_end} follows syntax 1.

{p_end} is a way of ending a paragraph without having a blank line between paragraphs. {p_end} may be followed by a carriage return or not; it will make no difference in the output.

Example:
{p_end}

{p2colset # # # #} follows syntax 3.
{p2col [# # # #] : [*first_column_text*] } [*second_column_text*] follows syntaxes 2 and 4.
{p2line [# #]} follows syntaxes 1 and 3.
{p2colreset} follows syntax 1.

{p2colset} sets column spacing for a two-column table. The first # specifies the beginning position of the first column, the second # specifies the placement of the second column, the third # specifies the placement for subsequent lines of the second column, and the last # specifies the number to indent from the right-hand side for the second column.

{p2col} specifies the rows that make up the two-column table. Specifying the optional numbers redefines the numbers specified in {p2colset} for this row only. If the *first_column_text* or the *second_column_text* is not specified, the respective column is left blank.

{p2line} draws a dashed line for use with a two-column table. The first # specifies the left indentation, and the second # specifies the right indentation. If no numbers are specified, the defaults are based on the numbers provided in {p2colset}.

{p2colreset} restores the {p2col} default values.

Examples:
{p2colset 9 26 27 2}{...}
{p2col:{keyword}}rules{p_end}
{p2line}
{p2col:{opt nonm:issing}}all nonmissing values not changed by the
rules{p_end}
{p2col 7 26 27 2:* {opt m:issing}}all missing values not changed by
the rules{p_end}
{p2line}
{p2colreset}{...}

{synoptset [#] [tabbed|notes]} follows syntaxes 1 and 3.
{synopthdr: [*first_column_header*]} follows syntaxes 1 and 2.
{syntab:*text*} follows syntax 2.
{synopt: [*first_column_text*]} [*second_column_text*] follows syntax 2.
{p2coldent: [*first_column_text*] } [*second_column_text*] follows syntax 2.
{synoptline} follows syntax 1.

{synoptset} sets standard column spacing for a two-column table used to document options in syntax diagrams. # specifies the width of the first column; the width defaults to 20 if # is not specified. The optional argument tabbed specifies that the table will contain headings or "tabs" for sets of options. The optional argument notes specifies that some of the table entries will have footnotes and results in a larger indentation of the first column than the tabbed argument implies.

{synopthdr} displays a standard header for a syntax-diagram-option table. *first_column_header* is used to title the first column in the header; if *first_column_header* is not specified, the default title "*options*" is displayed. The second column is always titled "description".

{syntab} displays *text* positioned as a subheading or "tab" in a syntax-diagram-option table.

{synopt} specifies the rows that make up the two-column table; it is equivalent to {p2col} (see above).

{p2coldent} is the same as {synopt}, except the *first_column_text* is displayed with the standard indentation (which may be negative). The *second_column_text* is displayed in paragraph mode and ends when a blank line, {p_end}, or a carriage return is encountered. The location of the columns is determined by a prior {synoptset} or {p2colset} directive.

{synoptline} draws a horizontal line that extends to the boundaries of the previous {synoptset} or, less often, {p2colset} directive.

Examples:
{synoptset 21 tabbed}{...}
{synopthdr}
{synoptline}
{syntab:Model}
{p2coldent:* {opth a:bsorb(varname)}}categorical variable to be absorbed{p_end}
{synopt:{opt clear}}reminder that untransposed data will be lost if not previously
saved{p_end}
{synoptline}
{p2colreset}{...}

{bind:*text*} follows syntax 2.

> {bind:...} keeps *text* together on a line, even if that makes one line of the paragraph unusually short. {bind:...} can also be used to insert one or more real spaces into the paragraph if you specify *text* as one or more spaces.
>
> *Example:*
> Commonly, bind is used {bind:to keep words together} on a line.

{break} follows syntax 1.

> {break} forces a line break without ending the paragraph.
>
> *Example:*
> {p 4 8 4}
> {it:Example:}{break}
> Commonly, ...

Directive for entering the as-is mode

{asis} follows syntax 1.

> {asis} begins as-is mode, which continues until {smcl}(carriage return) is encountered. {asis} may be followed by a carriage return or not; it makes no difference, but {smcl} must be immediately followed by a carriage return. {smcl} returns SMCL to line mode. No other SMCL commands are interpreted in as-is mode.

Directive for entering the Stata 6 help mode

{s6hlp} follows syntax 1.

> {s6hlp} begins Stata 6 help mode, which continues until {smcl}(carriage return) is encountered. {s6hlp} may be followed by a carriage return or not; it makes no difference, but {smcl} must be immediately followed by a carriage return. {smcl} returns SMCL to line mode. No other SMCL commands are interpreted in Stata 6 help mode. In this mode, text surrounded by ^carets^ is highlighted, and there are some other features that are not documented here. The purpose of Stata 6 help mode is to properly display old help files.

Inserting values from constant and current-value class

The {ccl} directive outputs the value contained in a constant and current-value class (c()) object. For instance, {ccl pi} provides the value of the constant pi (3.14159...) contained in c(pi). See [P] **creturn** for a list of all the available c() objects.

Displaying characters using ASCII code

The {char} directive—synonym {c}—allows you to output any ASCII character. For instance, {c 106} is equivalent to typing the letter j because ASCII code 106 is defined as the letter j.

You can get to all the ASCII characters by typing {c #}, where # is between 1 and 255. Or, if you prefer, you can type {c 0x#}, where # is a hexadecimal number between 1 and ff. Thus {c 0x6a} is also j because the hexadecimal number 6a is equal to the decimal number 106.

Also, so that you do not have to remember the ASCII numbers, {c} provides special codes for characters that are, for one reason or another, difficult to type. These include

{c S|}	$ (dollar sign)
{c 'g}	' (open single quote)
{c -(}	{ (left curly brace)
{c)-}	} (right curly brace)

{c S\|} and {c 'g} are included not because they are difficult to type or cause SMCL any problems but because in Stata display statements, they can be difficult to display, since they are Stata's macro substitution characters and tend to be interpreted by Stata. For instance,

```
. display "shown in $US"
shown in
```

drops the $US part because Stata interpreted $US as a macro, and the global macro was undefined. A way around this problem is to code

```
. display "shown in {c S|}US"
shown in $US
```

{c -(} and {c)-} are included because { and } are used to enclose SMCL directives. Although { and } have special meaning to SMCL, SMCL usually displays the two characters correctly when they do not have a special meaning. SMCL follows the rule that, when it does not understand what it thinks ought to be a directive, it shows what it did not understand in unmodified form. Thus

```
. display "among the alternatives {1, 2, 4, 7}"
among the alternatives {1, 2, 4, 7}
```

works, but

```
. display "in the set {result}"
in the set
```

does not because SMCL interpreted {result} as a SMCL directive to set the output style (color) to that for results. The way to code the above is to type

```
. display "in the set {c -(}result{c )-}"
in the set {result}
```

SMCL also provides the following line-drawing characters:

{c -}	–	a wide dash character
{c |}	|	a tall | character
{c +}	┼	a wide dash on top of a tall |
{c TT}	⊤	a top T
{c BT}	⊥	a bottom T
{c LT}	├	a left T
{c RT}	┤	a right T
{c TLC}	┌	a top-left corner
{c TRC}	┐	a top-right corner
{c BRC}	┘	a bottom-right corner
{c BLC}	└	a bottom-left corner

{hline} constructs the line by using the {c -} character. The above are not really ASCII; they are instructions to SMCL to draw lines. The "characters" are, however, one character wide and one character tall, so you can use them as characters in your output. The result is that Stata output that appears on your screen can look like

```
. summarize mpg weight
    Variable │     Obs        Mean    Std. Dev.        Min        Max
        mpg │      74     21.2973     5.785503         12         41
     weight │      74    3019.459     777.1936        1760       4840
```

but, if the result is translated into straight ASCII, it will look like

```
. summarize mpg weight
    Variable |     Obs        Mean    Std. Dev.        Min        Max
-------------+-------------------------------------------------------
        mpg |      74     21.2973     5.785503         12         41
     weight |      74    3019.459     777.1936        1760       4840
```

because SMCL will be forced to restrict itself to the ASCII characters.

Finally, SMCL provides the following Western European characters:

{c a'}	á	{c e'}	é	{c i'}	í	{c o'}	ó	{c u'}	ú
{c A'}	Á	{c E'}	É	{c I'}	Í	{c O'}	Ó	{c U'}	Ú
{c a'g}	à	{c e'g}	è	{c i'g}	ì	{c o'g}	ò	{c u'g}	ù
{c A'g}	À	{c E'g}	È	{c I'g}	Ì	{c O'g}	Ò	{c U'g}	Ù
{c a^}	â	{c e^}	ê	{c i^}	î	{c o^}	ô	{c u^}	û
{c A^}	Â	{c E^}	Ê	{c I^}	Î	{c O^}	Ô	{c U^}	Û
{c a~}	ã					{c o~}	õ		
{c A~}	Ã					{c O~}	Õ		
{c a:}	ä	{c e:}	ë	{c i:}	ï	{c o:}	ö	{c u:}	ü
{c A:}	Ä	{c E:}	Ë	{c I:}	Ï	{c O:}	Ö	{c U:}	Ü
{c ae}	æ	{c c,}	ç	{c n~}	ñ	{c o/}	ø	{c y'}	ý
{c AE}	Æ	{c C,}	Ç	{c N~}	Ñ	{c O/}	Ø	{c Y'}	Ý
{c y:}	ÿ	{c ss}	ß	{c r?}	¿	{c r!}	¡		
{c L-}	£	{c Y=}	(yen)	{c E=}	€				

SMCL uses ISO-8859-1 (Latin1) to render the above characters. For instance, {c e'} is equivalent to {c 0xe9}, if you care to look it up. {c 0xe9} will display as é if you are using an ISO-8859-1 (Latin1)–compatible font. Most are.

For the Mac, however, Stata uses the Mac encoding in which, for instance, {c e'} is equivalent to {c 8e}. This should work for Mac users, unless they are using an ISO-8859-1 (Latin1)–encoded font. To find out, run the following experiment:

```
. display "{c e'}"
é
```

Do you see é as we do? If not, and you are on a Mac, type

```
. set charset latin1
```

and try the experiment again. If that solves the problem, you will want to include that line in your profile.do. You can set the encoding back to Mac style by typing set charset mac. set charset typed without an argument will display the current setting. (set charset works on all platforms but is really useful only on the Mac.)

Advice on using display

Do not think twice; you can just use SMCL directives in your `display` statements, and they will work. What we are really talking about, however, is programming, and there are two things to know.

First, remember how `display` lets you display results `as text`, `as result`, `as input`, and `as error`, with the abbreviations `as txt`, `as res`, `as inp`, and `as err`. For instance, a program might contain the lines

```
program ...
        ...
        quietly summarize 'varname'
        display as txt "the mean of 'varname' is " as res r(mean)
        ...
end
```

Results would be the same if you coded the `display` statement

```
display "{txt}the mean of 'varname' is {res}" r(mean)
```

That is, the `display` directive `as txt` just sends {txt} to SMCL, the display directive `as res` just sends {res} to SMCL, and so on.

However, `as err` does not just send {err}. `as err` also tells Stata that what is about to be displayed is an error message so that, if output is being suppressed, Stata knows to display this message anyway. For example,

```
display as err "varname undefined"
```

is the right way to issue the error message "varname undefined".

```
display "{err}varname undefined"
```

would not work as well; if the program's output were suppressed, the error message would not be displayed because Stata would not know to stop suppressing output. You could code

```
display as err "{err}varname undefined"
```

but that is redundant. `display`'s `as error` directive both tells Stata that this is an error message and sends the {err} directive to SMCL. The last part makes output appear in the form of error messages, probably in red. The first part is what guarantees that the error message appears, even if output is being suppressed.

If you think about this, you will now realize that you could code

```
display as err "{txt}varname undefined"
```

to produce an error message that would appear as ordinary text (meaning that it would probably be in black) and yet still display in all cases. Please do not do this. By convention, all error messages should be displayed in SMCL's {err} (default red) rendition.

The second thing to know is how Stata sets the state of SMCL the instant before `display` displays its output. When you use `display` interactively—when you use it at the keyboard or in a do-file—Stata sets SMCL in line mode, font face {sf}, and style {res}. For instance, if you type

```
. display 2+2
4
```

the 4 will appear in {sf}{res}, meaning in standard font face and in result style, which probably means in black and bold. On the other hand, consider the following:

```
. program demonstrate_display
  1. display 2+2
  2. end
. demonstrate_display
4
```

Here the 4 will appear in {sf}{inp}, meaning that the result is probably also shown in black and bold. However, if your preferences are set to display input differently than results, the output from the program will be different from the interactive output.

When display is executed from inside a program, no changes are made to SMCL. SMCL is just left in the mode it happens to be in, and here it happened to be in line mode {sf}{inp} because that was the mode it was in after the user typed the command demonstrate_display.

This is an important feature of display because it means that, in your programs, one display can pick up where the last left off. Perhaps you have four or five displays in a row that produce the text to appear in a paragraph. The first display might begin paragraph mode, and the rest of the displays finish it off, with the last display displaying a blank line to end paragraph mode. Here it is of great importance that SMCL stay in the mode you left it in between displays.

That leaves only the question of what mode SMCL is in when your program begins. You should assume that SMCL is in line mode but make no assumptions about the style (color) {txt}, {res}, {err}, or {inp}. Within a program, all display commands should be coded as

        display as ... ...

or

        display "*one of* {txt}, {res}, {err}, *or* {inp} ..." ...

although you may violate this rule if you really intend one display to pick up where another left off. For example,

```
        display as text "{p}"
        display "This display violates the rule, but that is all right"
        display "because it is setting a paragraph, and we want all"
        display "these displays to be treated as a whole."
        display "We did follow the rule with the first display in the"
        display "sequence."
        display
        display "Now we are back in line mode because of the blank line"
```

You could even code

```
program example2
        display as text "{p}"
        display "Below we will call a subroutine to contribute a sentence"
        display "to this paragraph being constructed by example2:"
        example2_subroutine
        display "The text that example2_subroutine contributed became"
        display "part of this single paragraph.  Now we will end the paragraph."
        display
end

program example2_subroutine
        display "This sentence is being displayed by"
        display "example2_subroutine."
end
```

The result of running this would be

```
. example2
Below we will call a subroutine to contribute a sentence to this paragraph
being constructed by example2: This sentence is being displayed by
example2_subroutine.  The text that example2_subroutine contributed became
part of this single paragraph.  Now we will end the paragraph.
```

Advice on formatting help files

Help files are just files named *filename*.sthlp that Stata displays when the user types "help *filename*". The first line of a help file should read

```
{smcl}
```

Because help files may exist in an old format, before displaying a help file Stata issues a {s6hlp} directive to SMCL before displaying the text, thus putting SMCL in Stata 6 help mode. The {smcl} at the top of your help file returns SMCL to line mode. Old help files do not have that, and because SMCL faithfully reproduces the old Stata 6 help file formatting commands, they display correctly, too.

After that, it is a matter of style. To see examples of our style, type

. viewsource assert.sthlp	(simple example with a couple of options)
. viewsource centile.sthlp	(example with an options table)
. viewsource regress.sthlp	(example of an estimation command)
. viewsource regress_postestimation.sthlp	(example of a postestimation entry)

We recommend opening a second Viewer window (one way is to right-click within an existing Viewer and select "Open New Viewer") to look at the help file and the raw source file side by side.

Also see

[P] **display** — Display strings and values of scalar expressions

[R] **log** — Echo copy of session to file

Title

> **sortpreserve** — Sort within programs

Description

This entry discusses the use of `sort` (see [D] **sort**) within programs.

Remarks

Remarks are presented under the following headings:

Introduction
sortpreserve
The cost of sortpreserve
How sortpreserve works
Use of sortpreserve with preserve
Use of sortpreserve with subroutines that use sortpreserve

Introduction

Properly written programs do one of three things:

1. Report results
2. Add new variables to the dataset
3. Modify the data in memory

However, you do not want to get carried away with the idea. A properly written program might, for instance, report results and yet still have an option to add a new variable to the dataset, but a properly written program would not do all three. The user should be able to obtain reports over and over again by simply retyping the command, and if a command both reports results and modifies the data, that will not be possible.

Properly written programs of the first two types should also not change the sort order of the data. If the data are sorted on `mpg` and `foreign` before the command is given, and all the command does is report results, the data should still be sorted on `mpg` and `foreign` at the conclusion of the command. Yet the command might find it necessary to `sort` the data to obtain the results it calculates.

This entry deals with how to easily satisfy both needs.

sortpreserve

You may include `sort` commands inside your programs and leave the user's data in the original order when your program concludes by specifying the `sortpreserve` option on the `program` definition line:

```
program whatever, sortpreserve
      . . .
end
```

That is all there is to it. `sortpreserve` tells Stata when it starts your program to first record the information about how the data are currently sorted and then later use that information to restore the order to what it previously was. Stata will do this no matter how your program ends, whether as you expected, with an error, or because the user pressed the *Break* key.

The cost of sortpreserve

There is a cost to sortpreserve, so you do not want to specify the option when it is not needed, but the cost is not much. sortpreserve will consume a little computer time in restoring the sort order at the conclusion of your program. Rather than talking about this time in seconds or milliseconds, which can vary according to the computer you use, let's define our unit of time as the time to execute:

```
. generate long x = _n
```

Pretend that you added that command to your program, just as we have typed it, without using temporary variables. You could then make careful timings of your program to find out just how much extra time your program would take to execute. It would not be much. Let's call that amount of time one *genlong* unit. Then

- sortpreserve, if it has to restore the order because your program has changed it, takes 2 *genlong* units.

- sortpreserve, if it does not need to change the order because your program has not changed it yet, takes one-half a *genlong* unit.

The above results are based on empirical timings using 100,000 and 1,000,000 observations.

How sortpreserve works

sortpreserve works by adding a temporary variable to the dataset before your program starts, and if you are curious about the name of that variable, it is recorded in the macro '_sortindex'. Sometimes you will want to know that name. It is important that the variable '_sortindex' still exist at the conclusion of your program. If your program concludes with something like

```
keep 'id' 'varlist'
```

you must change that line to read

```
keep 'id' 'varlist' '_sortindex'
```

If you fail to do that, Stata will report the error message "could not restore sort order because variables were dropped". Actually, even that little change may be insufficient because the dataset in its original form might have been sorted on something other than 'id' and 'varlist'. What you really need to do is add, early in your program and before you change the sort order,

```
local sortvars : sort
```

and then change the keep statement to read

```
keep 'id' 'varlist' 'sortvars' '_sortindex'
```

This discussion concerns only the use of the keep command. Few programs would even include a keep statement because we are skirting the edge of what is a properly written program.

sortpreserve is intended for use in programs that report results or add new variables to the dataset, not programs that modify the data in memory. Including keep at the end of your program really makes it a class 3 program, and then the idea of preserving the sort order makes no sense anyway.

Use of sortpreserve with preserve

sortpreserve may be used with preserve (see [P] **preserve** for a description of preserve). We can imagine a complicated program that re-sorts the data, and then, under certain conditions, discovers it has to do real damage to the data to calculate its results, and so then preserves the data to boot:

```
program ..., sortpreserve
        ...
        sort ...
        ...
        if ... {
                preserve
                ...
        }
        ...
end
```

The above program will work. When the program ends, Stata will first restore any preserved data and then reestablish the sort of the original dataset.

Use of sortpreserve with subroutines that use sortpreserve

Programs that use sortpreserve may call other programs that use sortpreserve, and this can be a good way to speed up code. Consider a calculation where you need the data first sorted by 'i' 'j', then by 'j' 'i', and finally by 'i' 'j' again. You might code

```
program ..., sortpreserve
        ...
        sort 'i' 'j'
        ...
        sort 'j' 'i'
        ...
        sort 'i' 'j'
        ...
end
```

but executing

```
program ..., sortpreserve
        ...
        sort 'i' 'j'
        mysubcalculation 'i' 'j' ...
        ...
end
program mysubcalculation, sortpreserve
        args i j ...
        sort 'j' 'i'
        ...
end
```

will be faster.

Also see

[P] **byable** — Make programs byable

[P] **program** — Define and manipulate programs

Title

> **syntax** — Parse Stata syntax

Syntax

Parse Stata syntax positionally

> args *macroname1* [*macroname2* [*macroname3* ...]]

Parse syntax according to a standard syntax grammar

> syntax *description_of_syntax*

Description

There are two ways that a Stata program can interpret what the user types:

1. positionally, meaning first argument, second argument, and so on, or

2. according to a grammar, such as standard Stata syntax.

args does the first. The first argument is assigned to *macroname1*, the second to *macroname2*, and so on. In the program, you later refer to the contents of the macros by enclosing their names in single quotes: '*macroname1*', '*macroname2*', ...:

```
program myprog
        version 11
        args varname dof beta
        (the rest of the program would be coded in terms of 'varname', 'dof', and 'beta')
        ...
end
```

syntax does the second. You specify the new command's syntax on the syntax command; for instance, you might code

```
program myprog
        version 11
        syntax varlist [if] [in] [, DOF(integer 50) Beta(real 1.0)]
        (the rest of the program would be coded in terms of 'varlist', 'if', 'in', 'dof', and 'beta')
        ...
end
```

syntax examines what the user typed and attempts to match it to the syntax diagram. If it does not match, an error message is issued and the program is stopped (a nonzero return code is returned). If it does match, the individual components are stored in particular local macros where you can subsequently access them. In the example above, the result would be to define the local macros 'varlist', 'if', 'in', 'dof', and 'beta'.

For an introduction to Stata programming, see [U] **18 Programming Stata** and especially [U] **18.4 Program arguments**.

Standard Stata syntax is

> *cmd* [*varlist* | *namelist* | *anything*]
>
> [*if*]
>
> [*in*]
>
> [<u>using</u> *filename*]
>
> [= *exp*]
>
> [*weight*]
>
> [, *options*]

Each of these building blocks, such as *varlist*, *namelist*, and if, is outlined below.

Syntax, continued

The *description_of_syntax* allowed by syntax includes

---

description_of_varlist:

type	*nothing*
or	
optionally type	[
then type one of	varlist varname newvarlist newvarname
optionally type	(*varlist_specifiers*)
type	] (if you typed [at the start)

varlist_specifiers are default=none min=# max=# <u>numeric</u> <u>string</u> fv ts
<u>generate</u>   (newvarlist and newvarname only)

Examples: syntax varlist ...
syntax [varlist] ...
syntax varlist(min=2) ...
syntax varlist(max=4) ...
syntax varlist(min=2 max=4 numeric) ...
syntax varlist(default=none) ...

syntax newvarlist(max=1) ...

syntax varname ...
syntax [varname] ...

If you type nothing, the command does not allow a varlist.

Typing [and] means that the varlist is optional.

default= specifies how the varlist is to be filled in when the varlist is optional and the user does not specify it. The default is to fill it in with all the variables. If default=none is specified, it is left empty.

min= and max= specify the minimum and maximum number of variables that may be specified. Typing varname is equivalent to typing varlist(max=1).

numeric and string restrict the specified varlist to consist of entirely numeric or entirely string variables.

fv allows the varlist to contain factor variables.

ts allows the varlist to contain time-series operators.

generate specifies, for newvarlist or newvarname, that the new variables be created and filled in with missing values.

After the syntax command, the resulting varlist is returned in 'varlist'. If there are new variables (you coded newvarname or newvarlist), the macro 'typlist' is also defined, containing the storage type of each new variable, listed one after the other.

description_of_namelist:

type	*nothing*
or	
optionally type	[
then type one of	namelist name
optionally type	(*namelist_specifiers*)
type	] (if you typed [at the start)

namelist_specifiers are   name=*name*   id="*text*"   local
min=#   (namelist only) max=#   (namelist only)

Examples:
```
syntax namelist ...
syntax [namelist] ...
syntax name(id="equation name") ...
syntax [namelist(id="equation name")] ...
syntax namelist(name=eqlist id="equation list")...
syntax [name(name=eqname id="equation name")] ...
syntax namelist(min=2 max=2) ...
```

namelist is an alternative to varlist; it relaxes the restriction that the names the user specifies be of variables. name is a shorthand for namelist(max=1).

namelist is for use when you want the command to have the nearly standard syntax of command name followed by a list of names (not necessarily variable names), followed by if, in, *options*, etc. For instance, perhaps the command is to be followed by a list of variable-label names.

If you type nothing, the command does not allow a namelist. Typing [and] means that the namelist is optional. After the syntax command, the resulting namelist is returned in 'namelist' unless name=*name* is specified, in which case the result is returned in '*name*'.

id= specifies the name of namelist and is used in error messages. The default is id=namelist. If namelist were required and id= was not specified, and the user typed "mycmd if..." (omitting the namelist), the error message would be "namelist required". If you specified id="equation name", the error message would be "equation name required".

name= specifies the name of the local macro to receive the namelist; not specifying the option is equivalent to specifying name=namelist.

local specifies that the names that the user specifies satisfy the naming convention for local macro names. If this option is not specified, standard naming convention is used (names may begin with a letter or underscore, may thereafter also include numbers, and must not be longer than 32 characters). If the user specifies an invalid name, an error message will be issued. If local is specified, specified names are allowed to begin with numbers but may not be longer than 31 characters.

description_of_anything:

type	*nothing*
or	
optionally type	[
type	anything
optionally type	(*anything_specifiers*)
type	] (if you typed [at the start)

anything_specifiers are name=*name*   id="*text*"   equalok
everything

Examples:
```
syntax anything ...
syntax [anything] ...
syntax anything(id="equation name") ...
syntax [anything(id="equation name")] ...
syntax anything(name=eqlist id="equation list") ...
syntax [anything(name=eqlist id="equation list")] ...
syntax anything(equalok) ...
syntax anything(everything) ...
syntax [anything(name=0 id=clist equalok)] ...
```

anything is for use when you want the command to have the nearly standard syntax of command name followed by something followed by if, in, *options*, etc. For instance, perhaps the command is to be followed by an expression or expressions or a list of numbers.

If you type nothing, the command does not allow an "anything". Typing [and] means the "anything" is optional. After the syntax command, the resulting "anything list" is returned in 'anything' unless name=*name* is specified, in which case the result is returned in 'name'.

id= specifies the name of "anything" and is used only in error messages. For instance, if anything were required and id= was not specified, and the user typed "mycmd if..." (omitting the "anything"), the error message would be "something required". If you specified id="expression list", the error message would be "expression list required".

name= specifies the name of the local macro to receive the "anything"; not specifying the option is equivalent to specifying name=anything.

equalok specifies that = is not to be treated as part of =*exp* in subsequent standard syntax but instead as part of the anything.

everything specifies that if, in, and using are not to be treated as part of standard syntax but instead as part of the anything.

varlist, varname, namelist, name, and anything are alternatives; you may specify at most one.

description_of_if:

type	*nothing*
or	
optionally type	[
type	if
optionally type	/
type	] (if you typed [at the start)

Examples:
```
syntax ... if ...
syntax ... [if] ...
syntax ... [if/] ...
syntax ... if/ ...
```

If you type nothing, the command does not allow an if *exp*.

Typing [and] means that the if *exp* varlist is optional.

After the syntax command, the resulting if *exp* is returned in 'if'. The macro contains if followed by the expression, unless you specified /, in which case the macro contains just the expression.

description_of_in:

type	*nothing*
or	
optionally type	[
type	in
optionally type	/
type	] (if you typed [at the start)

Examples:	syntax ... in ...
	syntax ... [in] ...
	syntax ... [in/] ...
	syntax ... in/ ...

If you type nothing, the command does not allow an in *range*.

Typing [and] means that the in *range* is optional.

After the syntax command, the resulting in *range* is returned in 'in'. The macro contains in followed by the range, unless you specified /, in which case the macro contains just the range.

description_of_using:

type	*nothing*
or	
optionally type	[
type	using
optionally type	/
type	] (if you typed [at the start)

Examples:	syntax ... using ...
	syntax ... [using] ...
	syntax ... [using/] ...
	syntax ... using/ ...

If you type nothing, the command does not allow using *filename*.

Typing [and] means that the using *filename* is optional.

After the syntax command, the resulting filename is returned in 'using'. The macro contains using followed by the filename in quotes, unless you specified /, in which case the macro contains just the filename without quotes.

description_of_=exp:

type	*nothing*
or	
optionally type	[
type	=
optionally type	/
type	exp
type	] (if you typed [at the start)

Examples:	syntax ... =exp ...
	syntax ... [=exp] ...
	syntax ... [=/exp] ...
	syntax ... =/exp ...

If you type nothing, the command does not allow an =*exp*.

Typing [and] means that the =*exp* is optional.

After the syntax command, the resulting expression is returned in 'exp'. The macro contains =, a space, and the expression, unless you specified /, in which case the macro contains just the expression.

description_of_weights:

type	*nothing*
or	
type	[
type any of	<u>f</u>weight <u>aw</u>eight <u>p</u>weight <u>iw</u>eight
optionally type	/
type	]

Examples: syntax ... [fweight] ...
             syntax ... [fweight pweight] ...
             syntax ... [pweight fweight] ...
             syntax ... [fweight pweight iweight/] ...

If you type nothing, the command does not allow weights. A command may not allow both a weight and =*exp*.

You must type [and]; they are not optional. Weights are always optional.

The first weight specified is the default weight type.

After the syntax command, the resulting weight and expression are returned in 'weight' and 'exp'. 'weight' contains the weight type or nothing if no weights were specified. 'exp' contains =, a space, and the expression, unless you specified /, in which case the macro contains just the expression.

description_of_options:

type	*nothing*	
or		
type	[,	
type	*option_descriptors*	(these options will be optional)
optionally type	*	
type	]	
or		
type	,	
type	*option_descriptors*	(these options will be required)
optionally type	[	
optionally type	*option_descriptors*	(these options will be optional)
optionally type	*	
optionally type	]	

Examples: syntax ... [, MYopt Thisopt]
             syntax ..., MYopt Thisopt
             syntax ..., MYopt [Thisopt]
             syntax ... [, MYopt Thisopt *]

If you type nothing, the command does not allow options.

The brackets distinguish optional from required options. All options can be optional, all options can be required, or some can be optional and others be required.

After the syntax command, options are returned to you in local macros based on the first 31 letters of each option's name. If you also specify *, any remaining options are collected and placed, one after the other, in 'options'. If you do not specify *, an error is returned if the user specifies any options that you do not list.

option_descriptors include the following; they are documented below.

> *optionally_on*
> *optionally_off*
> *optional_integer_value*
> *optional_real_value*
> *optional_confidence_interval*
> *optional_numlist*
> *optional_varlist*
> *optional_namelist*
> *optional_string*
> *optional_passthru*

option_descriptor optionally_on:

type	OPname	(capitalization indicates minimal abbreviation)

Examples:

```
syntax ..., ... replace ...
syntax ..., ... REPLACE ...
syntax ..., ... detail ...
syntax ..., ... Detail ...
syntax ..., ... CONStant ...
```

The result of the option is returned in a macro name formed by the first 31 letters of the option's name. Thus option `replace` is returned in local macro 'replace'; option `detail`, in local macro 'detail'; and option constant, in local macro 'constant'.

The macro contains nothing if not specified, or else it contains the macro's name, fully spelled out.

Warning: Be careful if the first two letters of the option's name are no, such as the option called `notice`. You must capitalize at least the N in such cases.

option_descriptor optionally_off:

type	no	
type	OPname	(capitalization indicates minimal abbreviation)

Examples:

```
syntax ..., ... noreplace ...
syntax ..., ... noREPLACE ...
syntax ..., ... nodetail ...
syntax ..., ... noDetail ...
syntax ..., ... noCONStant ...
```

The result of the option is returned in a macro name formed by the first 31 letters of the option's name, excluding the no. Thus option `noreplace` is returned in local macro 'replace'; option `nodetail`, in local macro 'detail'; and option `noconstant`, in local macro 'constant'.

The macro contains nothing if not specified, or else it contains the macro's name, fully spelled out, with a no prefixed. That is, in the `noREPLACE` example above, macro 'replace' contains nothing, or it contains `noreplace`.

option_descriptor optional_integer_value:

type	OPname	(capitalization indicates minimal abbreviation)
type	(integer	
type	# (unless the option is required)	(the default integer value)
type	)	

Examples:

```
syntax ..., ... Count(integer 3) ...
syntax ..., ... SEQuence(integer 1) ...
syntax ..., ... dof(integer -1) ...
```

The result of the option is returned in a macro name formed by the first 31 letters of the option's name.

The macro contains the integer specified by the user, or else it contains the default value.

option_descriptor optional_real_value:

type	OPname	(capitalization indicates minimal abbreviation)
type	(real	
type	# (unless the option is required)	(the default value)
type	)	

Examples:

```
syntax ..., ... Mean(real 2.5) ...
syntax ..., ... SD(real -1) ...
```

The result of the option is returned in a macro name formed by the first 31 letters of the option's name.

The macro contains the real number specified by the user, or else it contains the default value.

option_descriptor optional_confidence_interval:

type	*OPname*	(capitalization indicates minimal abbreviation)
type	(`cilevel`)	

Example: syntax ..., ... Level(cilevel) ...

The result of the option is returned in a macro name formed by the first 31 letters of the option's name.

If the user specifies a valid level for a confidence interval, the macro contains that value; see [R] **level**. If the user specifies an invalid level, an error message is issued, and the return code is 198.

If the user does not type this option, the macro contains the default level obtained from `c(level)`.

---

option_descriptor optional_numlist:

type	*OPname*	(capitalization indicates minimal abbreviation)
type	(numlist	
type	<u>asc</u>ending or <u>desc</u>ending or *nothing*	
optionally type	<u>int</u>eger	
optionally type	<u>miss</u>ingokay	
optionally type	min=#	
optionally type	max=#	
optionally type	># or >=# or *nothing*	
optionally type	<# or <=# or *nothing*	
optionally type	sort	
type	)	

Examples: syntax ..., ... VALues(numlist) ...
syntax ..., ... VALues(numlist max=10 sort) ...
syntax ..., ... TIME(numlist >0) ...
syntax ..., ... FREQuency(numlist >0 integer) ...
syntax ..., ... OCCur(numlist missingokay >=0 <1e+9) ...

The result of the option is returned in a macro name formed by the first 31 letters of the option's name.

The macro contains the values specified by the user, but listed out, one after the other. For instance, the user might specify `time(1(1)4,10)` so that the local macro 'time' would contain "1 2 3 4 10".

min and max specify the minimum and maximum number of elements that may be in the list.

<, <=, >, and >= specify the range of elements allowed in the list.

integer indicates that the user may specify integer values only.

missingokay indicates that the user may specify missing values as list elements.

ascending specifies that the user must give the list in ascending order without repeated values. descending specifies that the user must give the list in descending order without repeated values.

sort specifies that the list be sorted before being returned. Distinguish this from modifier ascending, which states that the user must type the list in ascending order. sort says that the user may type the list in any order but it is to be returned in ascending order. ascending states that the list may have no repeated elements. sort places no such restriction on the list.

option_descriptor optional_varlist:

type	OPname	(capitalization indicates minimal abbreviation)
type	(varlist or (varname	
optionally type	<u>numeric</u> or <u>string</u>	
optionally type	min=#	
optionally type	max=#	
optionally type	fv	
optionally type	ts	
type	)	

Examples:
```
syntax ..., ... ROW(varname) ...
syntax ..., ... BY(varlist) ...
syntax ..., ... Counts(varname numeric) ...
syntax ..., ... TItlevar(varname string) ...
syntax ..., ... Sizes(varlist numeric min=2 max=10) ...
```

The result of the option is returned in a macro name formed by the first 31 letters of the option's name.

The macro contains the names specified by the user, listed one after the other.

min indicates the minimum number of variables to be specified if the option is given. min=1 is the default.

max indicates the maximum number of variables that may be specified if the option is given. max=800 is the default for varlist (you may set it to be larger), and max=1 is the default for varname.

numeric specifies that the variable list must consist entirely of numeric variables; string specifies string variables.

fv specifies that the variable list may contain factor variables.

ts specifies that the variable list may contain time-series operators.

---

option_descriptor optional_namelist:

type	OPname	(capitalization indicates minimal abbreviation)
type	(namelist or (name	
optionally type	min=#	
optionally type	max=#	
optionally type	local	
type	)	

Examples:
```
syntax ..., ... GENerate(name) ...
syntax ..., ... MATrix(name) ...
syntax ..., ... REsults(namelist min=2 max=10) ...
```

The result of the option is returned in a macro name formed by the first 31 letters of the option's name.

The macro contains the variables specified by the user, listed one after the other.

Do not confuse namelist with varlist. varlist is the appropriate way to specify an option that is to receive the names of existing variables. namelist is the appropriate way to collect names of other things—such as matrices—and namelist is sometimes used to obtain the name of a new variable to be created. It is then your responsibility to verify that the name specified does not already exist as a Stata variable.

min indicates the minimum number of names to be specified if the option is given. min=1 is the default.

max indicates the maximum number of names that may be specified if the option is given. The default is max=1 for name. For namelist, the default is the maximum number of variables allowed in Stata.

local specifies that the names the user specifies are to satisfy the naming convention for local macro names.

---

option_descriptor optional_string:

type	*OPname*	(capitalization indicates minimal abbreviation)
type	(<u>string</u>	
optionally type	asis	
type	)	

Examples:
```
syntax ..., ... Title(string) ...
syntax ..., ... XTRAvars(string) ...
syntax ..., ... SAVing(string asis) ...
```

The result of the option is returned in a macro name formed by the first 31 letters of the option's name.

The macro contains the string specified by the user, or else it contains nothing.

asis specifies that the option's arguments be returned just as the user typed them, with quotes (if specified) and with any leading and trailing blanks. asis should be specified if the option's arguments might contain suboptions or expressions that contain quoted strings. If you specify asis, be sure to use compound double quotes when referring to the macro.

---

option_descriptor optional_passthru:

type	*OPname*	(capitalization indicates minimal abbreviation)
type	(passthru)	

Examples:
```
syntax ..., ... Title(passthru) ...
syntax ..., ... SAVing(passthru) ...
```

The result of the option is returned in a macro name formed by the first 31 letters of the option's name.

The macro contains the full option—unabbreviated option name, parentheses, and argument—as specified by the user, or else it contains nothing. For instance, if the user typed ti("My Title"), the macro would contain title("My Title").

Remarks

Remarks are presented under the following headings:

Introduction
The args command
The syntax command

Introduction

Stata is programmable, making it possible to implement new commands. This is done with the program definition statement:

```
program newcmd
        ...
end
```

The first duty of the program is to parse the arguments that it receives.

Programmers use positional argument passing for subroutines and for some new commands with exceedingly simple syntax. It is so easy to program. If program myprog is to receive a variable name (call it varname) and two numeric arguments (call them dof and beta), all they need to code is

```
program myprog
        args varname dof beta
        (the rest of the program would be coded in terms of 'varname', 'dof', and 'beta')
        ...
end
```

The disadvantage of this is from the caller's side, because problems would occur if the caller got the arguments in the wrong order or did not spell out the variable name, etc.

The alternative is to use standard Stata syntax. `syntax` makes it easy to make new command `myprog` have the syntax

> `myprog` *varname* $\big[$, <u>d</u>of(*#*) <u>b</u>eta(*#*) $\big]$

and even to have defaults for `dof()` and `beta()`:

```
program myprog
        syntax varlist(max=1) [, Dof(integer 50) Beta(real 1.0)]
        (the rest of the program would be coded in terms of 'varlist', 'dof', and 'beta')
        . . .
end
```

The args command

`args` splits what the user typed into words and places the first word in the first macro specified; the second, in the second macro specified; and so on:

```
program myprog
        args arg1 arg2 arg3 . . .
        do computations using local macros 'arg1', 'arg2', 'arg3', . . .
end
```

`args` never produces an error. If the user specified more arguments than the macros specified, the extra arguments are ignored. If the user specified fewer arguments, the extra macros are set to contain `""`.

A better version of this program would read

```
program myprog
        version 11                                  ← new
        args arg1 arg2 arg3 . . .
        do computations using local macros 'arg1', 'arg2', 'arg3', . . .
end
```

Placing `version 11` as the first line of the program ensures that the command will continue to work with future versions of Stata; see [U] **16.1.1 Version** and [P] **version**. We will include the `version` line from now on.

▷ Example 1

The following command displays the three arguments it receives:

```
. program argdisp
  1.          version 11
  2.          args first second third
  3.          display "1st argument = 'first'"
  4.          display "2nd argument = 'second'"
  5.          display "3rd argument = 'third'"
  6. end
. argdisp cat dog mouse
1st argument = cat
2nd argument = dog
3rd argument = mouse
. argdisp 3.456 2+5-12 X*3+cat
1st argument = 3.456
2nd argument = 2+5-12
3rd argument = X*3+cat
```

Arguments are defined by the spaces that separate them. "X∗3+cat" is one argument, but if we had typed "X∗3 + cat", that would have been three arguments.

If the user specifies fewer arguments than expected by args, the additional local macros are set as empty. By the same token, if the user specifies too many, they are ignored:

```
. argdisp cat dog
1st argument = cat
2nd argument = dog
3rd argument =
. argdisp cat dog mouse cow
1st argument = cat
2nd argument = dog
3rd argument = mouse
```
◁

❏ Technical note

When a program is invoked, exactly what the user typed is stored in the macro '0'. Also the first word of that is stored in '1'; the second, in '2'; and so on. args merely copies the '1', '2', ... macros. Coding

```
args arg1 arg2 arg3
```

is no different from coding

```
local arg1 '"'1'"'
local arg2 '"'2'"'
local arg3 '"'3'"'
```
❏

The syntax command

syntax is easy to use. syntax parses standard Stata syntax, which is

command varlist if *exp* in *range* [*weight*] using *filename, options*

Actually, standard syntax is a little more complicated than that because you can substitute other things for *varlist*. In any case, the basic idea is that you code a syntax command describing which parts of standard Stata syntax you expect to see. For instance, you might code

```
syntax varlist if in, title(string) adjust(real 1)
```

or

```
syntax [varlist] [if] [in] [, title(string) adjust(real 1)]
```

In the first example, you are saying that everything is required. In the second, everything is optional. You can make some elements required and others optional:

```
syntax varlist [if] [in], adjust(real) [title(string)]
```

or

```
syntax varlist [if] [in] [, adjust(real 1) title(string)]
```

or many other possibilities. Square brackets denote that something is optional. Put them around what you wish.

You code what you expect the user to type. syntax then compares that with what the user actually did type, and, if there is a mismatch, syntax issues an error message. Otherwise, syntax processes what the user typed and stores the pieces, split into categories, in macros. These macros are named the same as the syntactical piece:

The varlist specified	will go into	'varlist'
The if *exp*	will go into	'if'
The in *range*	will go into	'in'
The adjust() option's contents	will go into	'adjust'
The title() option's contents	will go into	'title'

Go back to the section *Syntax, continued*; where each element is stored is explicitly stated. When a piece is not specified by the user, the corresponding macro is cleared.

▷ Example 2

The following program simply displays the pieces:

```
. program myprog
1. version 11
2. syntax varlist [if] [in] [, adjust(real 1) title(string)]
3. display "varlist contains |'varlist'|"
4. display "     if contains |'if'|"
5. display "     in contains |'in'|"
6. display " adjust contains |'adjust'|"
7. display "  title contains |'title'|"
8. end
. myprog
varlist required
r(100);
```

Well, that should not surprise us; we said that the varlist was required in the syntax command, so when we tried myprog without explicitly specifying a varlist, Stata complained.

```
. myprog mpg weight
varlist contains |mpg weight|
     if contains ||
     in contains ||
 adjust contains |1|
  title contains ||
. myprog mpg weight if foreign
varlist contains |mpg weight|
     if contains |if foreign|
     in contains ||
 adjust contains |1|
  title contains ||
. myprog mpg weight in 1/20
varlist contains |mpg weight|
     if contains ||
     in contains |in 1/20|
 adjust contains |1|
  title contains ||
. myprog mpg weight in 1/20 if foreign
varlist contains |mpg weight|
     if contains |if foreign|
     in contains |in 1/20|
 adjust contains |1|
  title contains ||
```

```
. myprog mpg weight in 1/20 if foreign, title("My Results")
varlist contains |mpg weight|
      if contains |if foreign|
      in contains |in 1/20|
  adjust contains |1|
   title contains |My Results|
. myprog mpg weight in 1/20 if foreign, title("My Results") adjust(2.5)
varlist contains |mpg weight|
      if contains |if foreign|
      in contains |in 1/20|
  adjust contains |2.5|
   title contains |My Results|
```

That is all there is to it.

◁

▷ Example 3

After completing the last example, it would not be difficult to actually make myprog do something. For lack of a better example, we will change myprog to display the mean of each variable, with said mean multiplied by adjust():

```
program myprog
        version 11
        syntax varlist [if] [in] [, adjust(real 1) title(string)]
        display
        if "`title'" != "" {
                display "`title':"
        }
        foreach var of local varlist {
                quietly summarize `var' `if' `in'
                display %9s "`var'" "   " %9.0g r(mean)*`adjust'
        }
end

. myprog mpg weight
      mpg     21.2973
   weight    3019.459
. myprog mpg weight if foreign==1
      mpg    24.77273
   weight    2315.909
. myprog mpg weight if foreign==1, title("My title")
My title:
      mpg    24.77273
   weight    2315.909
. myprog mpg weight if foreign==1, title("My title") adjust(2)
My title:
      mpg    49.54545
   weight    4631.818
```

◁

❑ Technical note

myprog is hardly deserving of any further work, given what little it does, but let's illustrate two ideas that use it.

First, we will learn about the `marksample` command; see [P] **mark**. A common mistake is to use one sample in one part of the program and a different sample in another part. The solution is to create at the outset a variable that contains 1 if the observation is to be used and 0 otherwise. `marksample` will do this correctly because `marksample` knows what `syntax` has just parsed:

```
program myprog
        version 11
        syntax varlist [if] [in] [, adjust(real 1) title(string)]
        marksample touse                                ← new
        display
        if "`title'" != "" {
                display "`title':"
        }
        foreach var of local varlist {
                quietly summarize `var' if `touse'      ← changed
                display %9s "`var'" "  " %9.0g r(mean)*`adjust'
        }
end
```

Second, we will modify our program so that what is done with each variable is done by a subroutine. Pretend here that we are doing something more involved than calculating and displaying a mean.

We want to make this modification to show you the proper use of the `args` command. Passing arguments by position to subroutines is convenient, and there is no chance of error due to arguments being out of order (assuming that we wrote our program properly):

```
program myprog
        version 11
        syntax varlist [if] [in] [, adjust(real 1) title(string)]
        marksample touse
        display
        if "`title'" != "" {
                display "`title':"
        }
        foreach var of local varlist {
                doavar `touse' `var' `adjust'
        }
end
program doavar
        version 11
        args touse name value
        qui summarize `name' if `touse'
        display %9s "`name'" "  " %9.0g r(mean)*`value'
end
```

Also see

[P] **mark** — Mark observations for inclusion

[P] **numlist** — Parse numeric lists

[P] **program** — Define and manipulate programs

[P] **gettoken** — Low-level parsing

[P] **tokenize** — Divide strings into tokens

[P] **unab** — Unabbreviate variable list

[TS] **tsrevar** — Time-series operator programming command

[U] **11 Language syntax**

[U] **16.1.1 Version**

[U] **18 Programming Stata**

[U] **18.3.1 Local macros**

[U] **18.3.5 Double quotes**

Title

sysdir — Query and set system directories

Syntax

List Stata's system directories

sysdir [ḻist]

Reset Stata's system directories

sysdir set *codeword* ["]*path*["]

Display path of PERSONAL directory and list files in it

personal [dir]

Display ado-file path

adopath

Add directory to end of ado-path

adopath + *path_or_codeword*

Add directory to beginning of ado-path

adopath ++ *path_or_codeword*

Remove directory from ado-path

adopath - {*path_or_codeword* | #}

Set maximum memory ado-files may consume

set ḁdosize # [, ṟermanently] $10 \le \# \le 10000$

where *path* must be enclosed in double quotes if it contains blanks or other special characters and *codeword* is { STATA | UPDATES | BASE | SITE | PLUS | PERSONAL | OLDPLACE }.

Description

sysdir lists Stata's system directories.

sysdir set changes the path to Stata's system directories.

personal displays the path of the PERSONAL directory. personal dir gives a directory listing of the files contained in the PERSONAL directory.

adopath displays the ado-file path stored in the global macro S_ADO.

adopath + adds a new directory or moves an existing directory to the end of the search path stored in the global macro S_ADO.

adopath ++ adds a new directory or moves an existing directory to the beginning of the search path stored in the global macro S_ADO.

adopath - removes a directory from the search path stored in the global macro S_ADO.

set adosize sets the maximum amount of memory in kilobytes that automatically loaded do-files may consume. The default is set adosize 1000. To view the current setting, type display c(adosize).

These commands have to do with technical aspects of Stata's implementation. Except for sysdir list, you should never have to use them.

Option

permanently specifies that, in addition to making the change right now, the adosize setting be remembered and become the default setting when you invoke Stata.

Remarks

Remarks are presented under the following headings:

> *Introduction*
> *sysdir*
> *adopath*
> *set adosize*

Introduction

In various parts of the Stata documentation, you will read that "Stata searches along the ado-path" for such-and-such. When we say that, what we really mean is "Stata searches along the path stored in the global macro $S_ADO". Equivalently, we could say "searches along the path stored in c(adopath)" because c(adopath) = $S_ADO. These are just two different ways of saying the same thing. If you wanted to change the path, however, you would change the $S_ADO because there is no way to change c(adopath).

Do not, however, directly change $S_ADO. Even if you have good reason to change it, you will find it easier to change it via the adopath command.

If you were to look inside $S_ADO (and we will), you would discover that it does not actually contain directory names—although it could—but contains codewords that stand for directory names. The sysdir command will show you the meaning of the codewords and allow you to change them.

sysdir

Stata expects to find various parts of itself in various directories (folders). Rather than describing these directories as C:\Program Files\Stata11\ado\base or /usr/local/stata/ado, these places are referred to by codewords. Here are the definitions of the codewords on a particular Windows computer:

```
. sysdir
     STATA:  C:\Program Files\Stata11\
   UPDATES:  C:\Program Files\Stata11\ado\updates\
      BASE:  C:\Program Files\Stata11\ado\base\
      SITE:  C:\Program Files\Stata11\ado\site\
      PLUS:  C:\ado\plus\
  PERSONAL:  C:\ado\personal\
  OLDPLACE:  C:\ado\
```

Even if you use Stata for Windows, when you type sysdir, you might see different directories listed.

The sysdir command allows you to obtain the correspondence between codeword and actual directory, and it allows you to change the mapping. Each directory serves a particular purpose:

STATA refers to the directory where the Stata executable is to be found.

UPDATES is where the updates to the official ado-files that were shipped with Stata are installed. The update command places files in this directory; see [R] **update**.

BASE is where the original official ado-files that were shipped with Stata are installed. This directory was written when Stata was installed, and thereafter the contents are never changed.

SITE is relevant only on networked computers. It is where administrators may place ado-files for sitewide use on networked computers. No Stata command writes to this directory, but administrators may move files into the directory or obtain ado-files by using net and choose to install them into this directory; see [R] **net**.

PLUS is relevant on all systems. It is where ado-files written by other people that you obtain using the net command are installed; by default, net installs files to this directory; see [R] **net**.

PERSONAL is where you are to copy ado-files that you write and that you wish to use regardless of your current directory when you use Stata. (The alternative is to put ado-files in your current directory, and then they will be available only when you are in that directory.)

OLDPLACE is included for backward compatibility. Stata 5 users used to put ado-files here, both the personal ones and the ones written by others. Nowadays, they are supposed to put their personal files in PERSONAL and the ones written by others in PLUS.

Do not change the definitions of UPDATES or BASE, You may want to change the definitions of SITE, PERSONAL, PLUS, or especially OLDPLACE. For instance, if you want to change the definition of OLDPLACE to d:\ado, type

```
. sysdir set OLDPLACE "d:\ado"
```

Resetting a system directory affects only the current session; the next time you enter Stata, the system directories will be set back to being as they originally were. If you want to reset a system directory permanently, place the sysdir set command in your profile.do; see [GSW] **C.3 Executing commands every time Stata is started**, [GSM] **C.1 Executing commands every time Stata is started**, or [GSU] **C.1 Executing commands every time Stata is started**.

adopath

adopath displays and resets the contents of the global macro $S_ADO, the path over which Stata searches for ado-files. The default search path is

```
. adopath
  [1]  (UPDATES)    "C:\Program Files\Stata11\ado\updates"
  [2]  (BASE)       "C:\Program Files\Stata11\ado\base"
  [3]  (SITE)       "C:\Program Files\Stata11\ado\site"
  [4]               "."
  [5]  (PERSONAL)   "C:\ado\personal"
  [6]  (PLUS)       "C:\ado\plus"
  [7]  (OLDPLACE)   "C:\ado"
```

Focus on the codewords on the left. `adopath` mentions the actual directories, but if you changed the meaning of a codeword by using `sysdir`, that change would affect `adopath`.

The above states that, when Stata looks for an ado-file, first it looks in UPDATES. If the ado-file is found, then that copy is used. If it is not found, then Stata next looks in BASE, and if it is found there, then that copy is used. And so the process continues. At the fourth step, Stata looks in the current directory (for which there is no codeword).

`adopath` merely presents the information in $S_ADO in a more readable form:

```
. display "$S_ADO"
UPDATES;BASE;SITE;.;PERSONAL;PLUS;OLDPLACE
```

`adopath` can also change the contents of the path. In general, you should not do this unless you are sure of what you are doing because many features of Stata will stop working if you change the path incorrectly. At worst, however, you might have to exit and reenter Stata, so you cannot do any permanent damage. Moreover, it is safe to add to the end of the path.

The path may include actual directory names, such as `C:\myprogs`, or codewords, such as PERSONAL, PLUS, and OLDPLACE. To add `C:\myprogs` to the end of the path, type

```
. adopath + C:\myprogs
  [1]  (UPDATES)    "C:\Program Files\Stata11\ado\updates"
  [2]  (BASE)       "C:\Program Files\Stata11\ado\base"
  [3]  (SITE)       "C:\Program Files\Stata11\ado\site"
  [4]               "."
  [5]  (PERSONAL)   "C:\ado\personal"
  [6]  (PLUS)       "C:\ado\plus"
  [7]  (OLDPLACE)   "C:\ado"
  [8]               "C:\myprogs"
```

If later you want to remove `C:\myprogs` from the ado-path, you could type `adopath - C:\myprogs`, but easier is

```
. adopath - 8
  [1]  (UPDATES)    "C:\Program Files\Stata11\ado\updates"
  [2]  (BASE)       "C:\Program Files\Stata11\ado\base"
  [3]  (SITE)       "C:\Program Files\Stata11\ado\site"
  [4]               "."
  [5]  (PERSONAL)   "C:\ado\personal"
  [6]  (PLUS)       "C:\ado\plus"
  [7]  (OLDPLACE)   "C:\ado"
```

When followed by a number, 'adopath -' removes that element from the path. If you cannot remember what the numbers are, you can first type `adopath` without arguments.

❑ Technical note

`adopath ++` *path* works like `adopath +` *path*, except that it adds to the beginning rather than to the end of the path. Our recommendation is that you not do this. When looking for *name*.ado, Stata loads the first file it encounters as it searches along the path. If you did not like our implementation of the command `ci`, for instance, even if you wrote your own and stored it in `ci.ado`, Stata would continue to use the one in the Stata directory because that is the directory listed earlier in the path. To force Stata to use yours rather than ours, you would have to put at the front of the path the name of the directory where your ado-file resides.

You should not, however, name any of your ado-files the same as we have named ours. If you add to the front of the path, you assume exclusive responsibility for the Stata commands working as documented in this manual.

❏

set adosize

Stata keeps track of the ado-commands you use and discards from memory commands that have not been used recently. Stata discards old commands to keep the amount of memory consumed by such commands less than adosize. The default value of 1,000 means the total amount of memory consumed by ado-commands is not to exceed 1,000 KB. When an ado-command has been discarded, Stata will have to reload the command the next time you use it.

You can increase adosize. Typing set adosize 1550 would allow up to 1,550 KB to be allocated to ado-commands. This would improve performance slightly if you happened to use one of the not-recently-used commands, but at the cost of some memory no longer being available for your dataset. In practice, there is little reason to increase adosize.

adosize must be between 10 and 10,000.

Methods and formulas

personal and adopath are implemented as ado-files.

Also see

[R] **net** — Install and manage user-written additions from the Internet

[R] **query** — Display system parameters

[R] **update** — Update Stata

[U] **17.5 Where does Stata look for ado-files?**

Title

tabdisp — Display tables

Syntax

tabdisp *rowvar* [*colvar* [*supercolvar*]] [*if*] [*in*], <u>c</u>ellvar(*varnames*)

[by(*superrowvars*) <u>f</u>ormat(%*fmt*) <u>cen</u>ter <u>l</u>eft <u>con</u>cise <u>m</u>issing <u>t</u>otals

dotz <u>cell</u>width(#) <u>csep</u>width(#) <u>scsep</u>width(#) <u>stubw</u>idth(#)]

by is allowed; see [D] **by**.

rowvar, *colvar*, and *supercolvar* may be numeric or string variables. Rows, columns, supercolumns, and superrows are thus defined as

				supercol 1		supercol 2	
				col 1	col 2	col 1	col 2
row 1	.			row 1	.	.	.	.
row 2	.			row 2	.	.	.	.

				supercol 1		supercol 2	
				col 1	col 2	col 1	col 2
	col 1	col 2	superrow 1:				
			row 1	.	.	.	.
row 1	.	.	row 2	.	.	.	.
row 2	.	.	superrow 2:				
			row 1	.	.	.	.
			row 2	.	.	.	.

Description

tabdisp displays data in a table. tabdisp calculates no statistics and is intended for use by programmers.

For the corresponding command that calculates statistics and displays them in a table, see [R] **table**.

Although tabdisp is intended for programming applications, it can be used interactively for listing data.

Options

cellvar(*varnames*) is required; it specifies the numeric or string variables containing the values to be displayed in the table's cells. Up to five variable names may be specified.

by(*superrowvars*) specifies numeric or string variables to be treated as superrows. Up to four variables may be specified.

format(%*fmt*) specifies the display format for presenting numbers in the table's cells. format(%9.0g) is the default; format(%9.2f) is a popular alternative. The width of the format you specify does not matter, except that %*fmt* must be valid. The width of the cells is chosen by tabdisp to be what it thinks looks best. The cellwidth() option allows you to override tabdisp's choice.

center specifies that results be centered in the table's cells. The default is to right-align results. For centering to work well, you typically need to specify a display format as well. center format(%9.2f) is popular.

left specifies that column labels be left-aligned. The default is to right-align column labels to distinguish them from supercolumn labels, which are left-aligned. If you specify left, both column and supercolumn labels are left-aligned.

concise specifies that rows with all missing entries not be displayed.

missing specifies that, in cells containing missing values, the missing value (., .a, .b, ..., or .z) be displayed. The default is that cells with missing values are left blank.

totals specifies that observations where *rowvar*, *colvar*, *supercolvar*, or *superrowvars* contain the system missing value (.) be interpreted as containing the corresponding totals of cellvar(), and that the table be labeled accordingly. If the dotz option is also specified, observations where the stub variables contain .z will be thus interpreted.

dotz specifies that the roles of missing values . and .z be interchanged in labeling the stubs of the table. By default, if any of *rowvar*, *colvar*, *supercolvar*, and *superrowvars* contains missing (., .a, .b, ..., or .z), then "." is placed last in the ordering. dotz specifies that .z be placed last. Also, if option totals is specified, .z values rather than "." values will be labeled "Total".

cellwidth(#) specifies the width of the cell in units of digit widths; 10 means the space occupied by 10 digits, which is 0123456789. The default cellwidth() is not a fixed number but rather a number chosen by tabdisp to spread the table out while presenting a reasonable number of columns across the page.

csepwidth(#) specifies the separation between columns in units of digit widths. The default is not a fixed number but rather a number chosen by tabdisp according to what it thinks looks best.

scsepwidth(#) specifies the separation between supercolumns in units of digit widths. The default is not a fixed number but rather a number chosen by tabdisp according to what it thinks looks best.

stubwidth(#) specifies the width, in units of digit widths, to be allocated to the left stub of the table. The default is not a fixed number but rather a number chosen by tabdisp according to what it thinks looks best.

Remarks

Remarks are presented under the following headings:

> *Limits*
> *Introduction*
> *Treatment of string variables*
> *Treatment of missing values*

Limits

Up to four variables may be specified in the by() option, so with the three row, column, and supercolumn variables, seven-way tables may be displayed.

Up to five variables may be displayed in each cell of the table.

The sum of the number of rows, columns, supercolumns, and superrows is called the number of margins. A table may contain up to 3,000 margins. Thus a one-way table may contain 3,000 rows. A two-way table could contain 2,998 rows and 2 columns, 2,997 rows and 3 columns, ..., 1,500 rows and 1,500 columns, ..., or 2 rows and 2,998 columns. A three-way table is similarly limited by the sum of the number of rows, columns, and supercolumns. An $r \times c \times d$ table is feasible if $r + c + d \leq 3,000$. The limit is set in terms of the sum of the rows, columns, supercolumns, and superrows—not, as you might expect, their product.

Introduction

If you have not read [R] **table**, please do so. tabdisp is what table uses to display the tables.

tabdisp calculates nothing. tabdisp instead displays the data in memory. In this, think of tabdisp as an alternative to list. Consider the following little dataset:

```
. use http://www.stata-press.com/data/r11/tabdxmpl1
. list
```

	a	b	c
1.	0	1	15
2.	0	2	26
3.	0	3	11
4.	1	1	14
5.	1	2	12
6.	1	3	7

We can use tabdisp to list it:

```
. tabdisp a b, cell(c)
```

		b	
a	1	2	3
0	15	26	11
1	14	12	7

tabdisp is merely an alternative way to list the data. It is when the data in memory are statistics by category that tabdisp becomes really useful. table provides one prepackaging of that idea.

Unlike list, tabdisp is unaffected by the order of the data. Here are the same data in a different order:

```
. use http://www.stata-press.com/data/r11/tabdxmpl2
. list
```

	a	b	c
1.	1	3	7
2.	0	3	11
3.	1	2	12
4.	1	1	14
5.	0	1	15
6.	0	2	26

and yet the output of `tabdisp` is unaffected.

```
. tabdisp a b, cell(c)
```

		b		
a	1	2	3	
0	15	26	11
1	14	12	7

Nor does `tabdisp` care if one of the cells is missing in the data.

```
. drop in 6
(1 observation deleted)
. tabdisp a b, cell(c)
```

		b		
a	1	2	3	
0	15		11
1	14	12	7

On the other hand, `tabdisp` assumes that each value combination of the row, column, superrow, and supercolumn variables occurs only once. If that is not so, `tabdisp` displays the earliest occurring value:

```
. input
            a          b          c
6. 0 1 99
7. end
. list
```

	a	b	c
1.	1	3	7
2.	0	3	11
3.	1	2	12
4.	1	1	14
5.	0	1	15
6.	0	1	99

```
. tabdisp a b, cell(c)
```

a	b 1	2	3
0	15		11
1	14	12	7

Thus our previous claim that `tabdisp` was unaffected by sort order has this one exception.

Finally, `tabdisp` uses variable and value labels when they are defined:

```
. label var a "Sex"
. label define sex 0 male 1 female
. label values a sex
. label var b "Treatment Group"
. label def tg 1 "controls" 2 "low dose" 3 "high dose"
. label values b tg
. tabdisp a b, cell(c)
```

Sex	Treatment Group controls	low dose	high dose
male	15		11
female	14	12	7

There are two things you can do with `tabdisp`.

You can use it to list data, but be certain that you have a unique identifier. In the automobile dataset, the variable `make` is unique:

```
. use http://www.stata-press.com/data/r11/auto, clear
(1978 Automobile Data)
. list make mpg weight displ rep78
```

	make	mpg	weight	displa~t	rep78
1.	AMC Concord	22	2,930	121	3
2.	AMC Pacer	17	3,350	258	3
3.	AMC Spirit	22	2,640	121	.
	(output omitted)				
74.	Volvo 260	17	3,170	163	5

```
. tabdisp make, cell(mpg weight displ rep78)
```

Make and Model	Mileage (mpg)	Weight (lbs.)	displacement	rep78
AMC Concord	22	2,930	121	3
AMC Pacer	17	3,350	258	3
AMC Spirit	22	2,640	121	
(output omitted)				
Volvo 260	17	3,170	163	5

Mostly, however, `tabdisp` is intended for use when you have a dataset of statistics that you want to display:

```
. collapse (mean) mpg, by(foreign rep78)
. list
```

	rep78	foreign	mpg
1.	1	Domestic	21
2.	2	Domestic	19.125
3.	3	Domestic	19
4.	4	Domestic	18.4444
5.	5	Domestic	32
6.	.	Domestic	23.25
7.	3	Foreign	23.3333
8.	4	Foreign	24.8889
9.	5	Foreign	26.3333
10.	.	Foreign	14

```
. tabdisp foreign rep78, cell(mpg)
```

Car type						

Car type	1	2	Repair Record 1978 3	4	5	.
Domestic	21	19.125	19	18.4444	32	23.25
Foreign			23.3333	24.8889	26.3333	14

```
. drop if rep78>=.
(2 observations deleted)
. label define repair 1 Poor 2 Fair 3 Average 4 Good 5 Excellent
. label values rep78 repair
. tabdisp foreign rep78, cell(mpg) format(%9.2f) center
```

Car type	Poor	Fair	Repair Record 1978 Average	Good	Excellent
Domestic	21.00	19.12	19.00	18.44	32.00
Foreign			23.33	24.89	26.33

Treatment of string variables

The variables specifying the rows, columns, supercolumns, and superrows may be numeric or string. Also, the variables specified for inclusion in the table may be numeric or string. In the example below, all variables are strings, including `reaction`:

```
. use http://www.stata-press.com/data/r11/tabxmpl3, clear
. tabdisp agecat sex party, c(reaction) center
```

Age category	—— Democrat —— Female	Male	Party Affiliation and Sex —— Republican —— Female	Male
Old	Disfavor	Indifferent	Favor	Strongly Favor
Young	Disfavor	Disfavor	Indifferent	Favor

Treatment of missing values

The `cellvar()` variables specified for inclusion in the table may contain missing values, and whether the variable contains a missing value or the observation is missing altogether makes no difference:

```
. use http://www.stata-press.com/data/r11/tabdxmpl4
. list
```

```
      sex   response   pop

 1.     0          0    12
 2.     0          1    20
 3.     0          2    .a
 4.     1          0    15
 5.     1          1    11
```

```
. tabdisp sex response, cell(pop)
```

```
           Response
   Sex     0     1     2

     0    12    20
     1    15    11
```

In the above output, the $(1, 3)$ cell is empty because the observation for `sex` = 0 and `response` = 2 has a missing value for `pop`. The $(2, 3)$ cell is empty because there is no observation for `sex` = 1 and `response` = 2.

If you specify the `missing` option, rather than cells being left blank, the missing value will be displayed:

```
. tabdisp sex response, cell(pop) missing
```

```
           Response
   Sex     0     1     2

     0    12    20    .a
     1    15    11     .
```

Missing values of the row, column, superrow, and supercolumn variables are allowed, and, by default, missing values are given no special meaning. The output below is from a different dataset.

(Continued on next page)

```
. use http://www.stata-press.com/data/r11/tabdxmpl5
. list
```

	sex	response	pop
1.	0	0	15
2.	0	1	11
3.	0	.	26
4.	1	0	20
5.	1	1	24
6.	1	.	44
7.	.	.	70
8.	.	0	35
9.	.	1	35

```
. tabdisp sex response, cell(pop)
```

	response		
sex	0	1	.
0	15	11	26
1	20	24	44
.	35	35	70

If you specify the `total` option, however, the system missing values are labeled as reflecting totals:

```
. tabdisp sex response, cell(pop) total
```

	response		
sex	0	1	Total
0	15	11	26
1	20	24	44
Total	35	35	70

`tabdisp` did not calculate the totals; it merely labeled the results as being totals. The number 70 appears in the lower right because there happens to be an observation in the dataset where both `sex` and `response` contain a system missing value and `pop = 70`.

Here the row and column variables were numeric. If they had been strings, the `total` option would have given the special interpretation to `sex = ""` and `response = ""`.

Also see

[R] **table** — Tables of summary statistics

[R] **tabstat** — Display table of summary statistics

[R] **tabulate oneway** — One-way tables of frequencies

[R] **tabulate twoway** — Two-way tables of frequencies

Title

timer — Time sections of code by recording and reporting time spent

Syntax

Reset timers to zero

```
timer clear [#]
```

Turn a timer on

```
timer on #
```

Turn a timer off

```
timer off #
```

List the timings

```
timer list [#]
```

where # is an integer, 1–100.

Description

timer starts, stops, and reports up to 100 interval timers. Results are reported in seconds.

timer clear resets timers to zero.

timer on begins a timing. timer off stops a timing. A timing may be turned on and off repeatedly without clearing, which causes the timer to accumulate.

timer list lists the timings. If # is not specified, timers that contain zero are not listed.

Remarks

timer can be used to time sections of code. For instance,

```
program tester
        version ...
        timer clear 1
        forvalues repeat=1(1)100 {
                timer on 1
                mycmd ...
                timer off 1
        }
        timer list 1
end
```

449

Saved results

timer list saves the following in r():

Scalars

r(t1)	value of first timer
r(nt1)	# of times turned on and off
r(t2)	value of second timer
r(nt2)	# of times turned on and off
.	
.	
.	
r(t100)	value of 100th timer
r(nt100)	# of times turned on and off

Only values for which $r(nt\#) \neq 0$ are saved.

r() results produced by other commands are not cleared.

Also see

[P] **rmsg** — Return messages

Title

> **tokenize** — Divide strings into tokens

Syntax

<u>token</u>ize $\left[\left[\text{'}\right]\text{"}\right]\left[\textit{string}\right]\left[\text{"}\left[\text{'}\right]\right]$ $\left[\text{ , }\underline{p}\text{arse("}\textit{pchars}\text{")}\right]$

Description

tokenize divides *string* into tokens, storing the result in '1', '2', ... (the positional local macros). Tokens are determined based on the parsing characters *pchars*, which default to a space if not specified.

Option

parse(*"pchars"*) specifies the parsing characters. If parse() is not specified, parse(" ") is assumed, and *string* is split into words.

Remarks

tokenize may be used as an alternative or supplement to the syntax command for parsing command-line arguments. Generally, it is used to further process the local macros created by syntax, as shown below.

```
program myprog
        version 11
        syntax [varlist] [if] [in]
        marksample touse

        tokenize 'varlist'
        local first '1'
        macro shift
        local rest '*'

        ...

end
```

> ## Example 1

We interactively apply tokenize and then display several of the numbered macros to illustrate how the command works.

```
. tokenize some words
. di "1=|'1'|, 2=|'2'|, 3=|'3'|"
1=|some|, 2=|words|, 3=||

. tokenize "some more words"
. di "1=|'1'|, 2=|'2'|, 3=|'3'|, 4=|'4'|"
1=|some|, 2=|more|, 3=|words|, 4=||
```

```
. tokenize '""Marcello Pagano""Rino Bellocco""'
. di "1=|'1'|, 2=|'2'|, 3=|'3'|"
1=|Marcello Pagano|, 2=|Rino Bellocco|, 3=||
. local str "A strange++string"
. tokenize 'str'
. di "1=|'1'|, 2=|'2'|, 3=|'3'|"
1=|A|, 2=|strange++string|, 3=||
. tokenize 'str', parse(" +")
. di "1=|'1'|, 2=|'2'|, 3=|'3'|, 4=|'4'|, 5=|'5'|, 6=|'6'|"
1=|A|, 2=|strange|, 3=|+|, 4=|+|, 5=|string|, 6=||
. tokenize 'str', parse("+")
. di "1=|'1'|, 2=|'2'|, 3=|'3'|, 4=|'4'|, 5=|'5'|, 6=|'6'|"
1=|A strange|, 2=|+|, 3=|+|, 4=|string|, 5=||, 6=||
. tokenize
. di "1=|'1'|, 2=|'2'|, 3=|'3'|"
1=||, 2=||, 3=||
```

These examples illustrate that the quotes surrounding the string are optional; the space parsing character is not saved in the numbered macros; nonspace parsing characters are saved in the numbered macros together with the tokens being parsed; and more than one parsing character may be specified. Also, when called with no string argument, tokenize resets the local numbered macros to empty.

◁

Also see

[P] **syntax** — Parse Stata syntax

[P] **foreach** — Loop over items

[P] **gettoken** — Low-level parsing

[P] **macro** — Macro definition and manipulation

[U] **18 Programming Stata**

Title

> **trace** — Debug Stata programs

Syntax

Whether to trace execution of programs

> <u>set</u> <u>trace</u> { on | off }

Show # levels in tracing nested programs

> <u>set</u> <u>tracedepth</u> #

Whether to show the lines after macro expansion

> <u>set</u> <u>trace</u>expand { on | off } [, <u>perm</u>anently]

Whether to display horizontal separator lines

> <u>set</u> <u>trace</u>sep { on | off } [, <u>perm</u>anently]

Whether to indent lines according to nesting level

> <u>set</u> <u>trace</u>indent { on | off } [, <u>perm</u>anently]

Whether to display nesting level

> <u>set</u> <u>trace</u>number { on | off } [, <u>perm</u>anently]

Highlight pattern in trace output

> <u>set</u> <u>trace</u>hilite "*pattern*" [, word]

Description

set trace on traces the execution of programs for debugging. set trace off turns off tracing after it has been set on.

set tracedepth specifies how many levels to descend in tracing nested programs. The default is 32000, which is equivalent to ∞.

set traceexpand indicates whether the lines before and after macro expansion are to be shown. The default is on.

set tracesep indicates whether to display a horizontal separator line that displays the name of the subroutine whenever a subroutine is entered or exited. The default is on.

set traceindent indicates whether displayed lines of code should be indented according to the nesting level. The default is on.

set tracenumber indicates whether the nesting level should be displayed at the beginning of the line. Lines in the main program are preceded with 01; lines in subroutines called by the main program, with 02; etc. The default is off.

set tracehilite causes the specified *pattern* to be highlighted in the trace output.

Options

permanently specifies that, in addition to making the change right now, the traceexpand, tracesep, traceindent, and tracenumber settings be remembered and become the default settings when you invoke Stata.

word highlights only tokens that are delimited by nonalphanumeric characters. These would include tokens at the beginning or end of each line that are delimited by nonalphanumeric characters.

Remarks

The set trace commands are extremely useful for debugging your programs.

▷ Example 1

Stata does not normally display the lines of your program as it executes them. With set trace on, however, it does:

```
. program list simple
simple:
  1. args msg
  2. if '""'msg'"'"'=="hello" {
  3.         display "you said hello"
  4. }
  5. else display "you did not say hello"
  6. display "good-bye"
. set trace on
. simple
```
```
                                                      ── begin simple ──
  - args msg
  - if '""'msg'"'"'=="hello" {
  = if '""'"'=="hello" {
    display "you said hello"
    }
  - else display "you did not say hello"
you did not say hello
  - display "good-bye"
good-bye
                                                      ── end simple ──
. set trace off
```

Lines that are executed are preceded by a dash. The line is shown before macro expansion, just as it was coded. If the line has any macros, it is shown again, this time preceded by an equal sign and with the macro expanded, showing the line exactly as Stata sees it.

In our simple example, Stata substituted nothing for 'msg', as we can see by looking at the macro-expanded line. Because nothing is not equal to "hello", Stata skipped the display of "you said hello", so a dash did not precede this line.

Stata then executed lines 5 and 6. (They are not reshown preceded by an equal sign because they contained no macros.)

To suppress the printing of the macro-expanded lines, type set traceexpand off.

To suppress the printing of the trace separator lines,

```
──────────────────────────────────────────────── begin simple ──
──────────────────────────────────────────────── end simple ──
```

type set tracesep off.

The output from our program is interspersed with the lines that caused the output. This can be greatly useful when our program has an error. For instance, we have written a more useful program called myprog. Here is what happens when we run it:

```
. myprog mpg, prefix("new")
invalid syntax
r(198);
```

We did not expect this, and, look as we will at our program code, we cannot spot the error. Our program contains many lines of code, however, so we have no idea even where to look. By setting trace on, we can quickly find the error:

```
. set trace on

. myprog mpg, prefix("new")
                                                ── begin myprog ──
  - version 11
  - syntax varname , [Prefix(string)]
  - local newname "'prefix''varname'
  = local newname "new
invalid syntax
                                                ── end myprog ──
  r(198);
```

The error was close to the top—we omitted the closing quote in the definition of the local newname macro.

◁

❏ Technical note

If you are looking for a command similar to set trace for use in Mata, see mata set matalnum in [M-3] **mata set**.

❏

▷ Example 2

set tracedepth, set tracesep, set traceindent, and set tracenumber are useful when debugging nested programs. Imagine that we have a program called myprog1, which calls myprog2, which then calls a modified version of our simple program from example 1.

With the default settings, we get:

```
. program list _all
simple2:
    1.          args msg
    2.          if '"'msg'"'=="hello" {
    3.                  display "you said hello"
    4.          }
    5.          else {
    6.                  display "you did not say hello"
    7.          }
```

```
myprog2:
  1.          args msg
  2.          simple2 '"`msg'"'
  3.          display "good"
myprog1:
  1.          args msg
  2.          myprog2 '"`msg'"'
  3.          display "bye"
. set trace on
. myprog1 hello
  ────────────────────────────────────────────── begin myprog1 ──
  - args msg
  - myprog2 '"`msg'"'
  = myprog2 '"hello"'
  ────────────────────────────────────────────── begin myprog2 ──
    - args msg
    - simple2 '"`msg'"'
    = simple2 '"hello"'
    ──────────────────────────────────────────── begin simple2 ──
      - args msg
      - if '"`msg'"'=="hello" {
      = if '"hello"'=="hello" {
      - display "you said hello"
you said hello
      - }
      - else {
        display "you did not say hello"
        }
    ──────────────────────────────────────────── end simple2 ──
  - display "good"
good
  ────────────────────────────────────────────── end myprog2 ──
  - display "bye"
bye
  ────────────────────────────────────────────── end myprog1 ──
. set trace off
```

To see the nesting level for each line, you could use set tracenumber on.

```
. set trace on
. set tracenumber on
. myprog1 hello
  ────────────────────────────────────────────── begin myprog1 ──
01  - args msg
01  - myprog2 '"`msg'"'
    = myprog2 '"hello"'
  ────────────────────────────────────────────── begin myprog2 ──
02    - args msg
02    - simple2 '"`msg'"'
      = simple2 '"hello"'
    ──────────────────────────────────────────── begin simple2 ──
03      - args msg
03      - if '"`msg'"'=="hello" {
        = if '"hello"'=="hello" {
03      - display "you said hello"
you said hello
03      - }
03      - else {
03        display "you did not say hello"
03        }
      ──────────────────────────────────────────── end simple2 ──
```

```
02      - display "good"
good
                                                        ─────── end myprog2 ───
01   - display "bye"
bye
                                                        ─────── end myprog1 ───
. set tracenumber off

. set trace off
```

If you are interested only in seeing a trace of the first two nesting levels, you could set
`tracedepth 2`.

```
. set trace on

. set tracedepth 2

. myprog1 hello
                                                        ─────── begin myprog1 ───
  - args msg
  - myprog2 '"'msg'"'
  = myprog2 '"hello"'
                                                        ─────── begin myprog2 ───
    - args msg
    - simple2 '"'msg'"'
    = simple2 '"hello"'
you said hello
    - display "good"
good
                                                        ─────── end myprog2 ───
  - display "bye"
bye
                                                        ─────── end myprog1 ───
. set tracedepth 32000

. set trace off
```

By setting `tracedepth` to 2, the trace of `simple2` is not shown.

Finally, if you did not want each nested level to be indented in the trace output, you could set
`traceindent off`.

```
. set trace on

. set traceindent off

. myprog1 hello
                                                        ─────── begin myprog1 ───
- args msg
- myprog2 '"'msg'"'
= myprog2 '"hello"'
                                                        ─────── begin myprog2 ───
- args msg
- simple2 '"'msg'"'
= simple2 '"hello"'
                                                        ─────── begin simple2 ───
- args msg
- if '"'msg'"'"=="hello" {
= if '"hello"'=="hello" {
- display "you said hello"
you said hello
- }
- else {
  display "you did not say hello"
  }
                                                        ─────── end simple2 ───
```

```
- display "good"
good
```
── end myprog2 ──
```
- display "bye"
bye
```
── end myprog1 ──
```
. set traceindent on
```
```
. set trace off
```

◁

Also see

[P] **program** — Define and manipulate programs

[R] **query** — Display system parameters

[R] **set** — Overview of system parameters

[U] **18 Programming Stata**

Title

unab — Unabbreviate variable list

Syntax

Expand and unabbreviate standard variable lists

unab *lmacname* : [*varlist*] [, min(*#*) max(*#*) name(*string*)]

Expand and unabbreviate variable lists that may contain time-series operators

tsunab *lmacname* : [*varlist*] [, min(*#*) max(*#*) name(*string*)]

Expand and unabbreviate variable lists that may contain time-series operators or factor variables

fvunab *lmacname* : [*varlist*] [, min(*#*) max(*#*) name(*string*)]

Description

unab expands and unabbreviates a varlist (see [U] **11.4 varlists**) of existing variables, placing the result in the local macro *lmacname*. unab is a low-level parsing command. The syntax command is a high-level parsing command that, among other things, also unabbreviates variable lists; see [P] **syntax**.

The difference between unab and tsunab is that tsunab allows time-series operators in *varlist*; see [U] **11.4.4 Time-series varlists**.

The difference between tsunab and fvunab is that fvunab allows factor variables in *varlist*; see [U] **11.4.3 Factor variables**.

Options

min(*#*) specifies the minimum number of variables allowed. The default is min(1).

max(*#*) specifies the maximum number of variables allowed. The default is max(32000).

name(*string*) provides a label that is used when printing error messages.

Remarks

Usually, the syntax command will automatically unabbreviate variable lists; see [P] **syntax**. In a few cases, unab will be needed to obtain unabbreviated variable lists.

If the user has previously set varabbrev off, then variable abbreviations are not allowed. Then typing in a variable abbreviation results in a syntax error. See [R] **set**.

459

▷ Example 1

The `separate` command (see [D] **separate**) provides an example of the use of unab. Required option by (*byvar* | *exp*) takes either a variable name or an expression. This is not handled automatically by the `syntax` command.

Here the `syntax` command for `separate` takes the form

```
syntax varname [if] [in], BY(string) [ other options]
```

After `syntax` performs the command-line parsing, the local variable by contains what the user entered for the option. We now need to determine if it is an existing variable name or an expression. If it is a variable name, we may need to expand it.

```
capture confirm var 'by'
if _rc == 0 {
        unab by: 'by', max(1) name(by())
}
else {
        ( parse 'by' as an expression)
}
```

◁

▷ Example 2

We interactively demonstrate the unab command with the auto dataset.

```
. use http://www.stata-press.com/data/r11/auto
(1978 Automobile Data)
. unab x : mpg wei for, name(myopt())
. display "'x'"
mpg weight foreign
. unab x : junk
variable junk not found
r(111);
. unab x : mpg wei, max(1) name(myopt())
myopt():  too many variables specified
          1 variable required
r(103);
. unab x : mpg wei, max(1) name(myopt()) min(0)
myopt():  too many variables specified
          0 or 1 variables required
r(103);
. unab x : mpg wei, min(3) name(myopt())
myopt():  too few variables specified
          3 or more variables required
r(102);
. unab x : mpg wei, min(3) name(myopt()) max(10)
myopt():  too few variables specified
          3 - 10 variables required
r(102);
. unab x : mpg wei, min(3) max(10)
mpg weight:
too few variables specified
r(102);
```

◁

> Example 3

If we created a time variable and used `tsset` to declare the dataset as a time series, we can also expand time-series variable lists.

```
. gen time = _n
. tsset time
. tsunab mylist : l(1/3).mpg
. display "`mylist'"
L.mpg L2.mpg L3.mpg
. tsunab mylist : l(1/3).(price turn displ)
. di "`mylist'"
L.price L2.price L3.price L.turn L2.turn L3.turn L.displacement L2.displacement
> L3.displacement
```

◁

> Example 4

If `set varabbrev off` has been issued, variable abbreviations are not allowed:

```
. unab varn : mp
. display "`varn'"
mpg
. set varabbrev off
. unab varn : mp
variable mp not found
r(111);
. set varabbrev on
. unab varn : mp
. display "`varn'"
mpg
```

◁

Methods and formulas

unab, tsunab, and fvunab are implemented as ado-files.

Also see

[P] **varabbrev** — Control variable abbreviation

[P] **syntax** — Parse Stata syntax

[U] **11 Language syntax**

[U] **18 Programming Stata**

Title

> **unabcmd** — Unabbreviate command name

Syntax

unabcmd *commandname_or_abbreviation*

Description

unabcmd verifies that *commandname_or_abbreviation* is a Stata command name or an abbreviation of a Stata command name. unabcmd makes this determination by looking at both built-in commands and ado-files. If *commandname_or_abbreviation* is a valid command, unabcmd returns in local r(cmd) the unabbreviated name. If it is not a valid command, unabcmd displays an appropriate error message.

Remarks

Stata's built-in commands can be abbreviated. For instance, the user can type gen for generate or an for anova. Commands implemented as ado-files cannot be abbreviated.

Given a command name *c*, unabcmd applies the same lookup rules that Stata applies internally. If it is found, the full command name is returned in r(cmd).

▷ Example 1

```
. unabcmd gen
. return list
macros:
              r(cmd) : "generate"

. unabcmd kappa        // kappa is an ado-file
. return list
macros:
              r(cmd) : "kappa"

. unabcmd ka
command ka not found as either built-in or ado-file
r(111);
```

◁

unabcmd is included just in case you, as a programmer, want the command name spelled out. There is no reason why you should.

Also see

[P] **findfile** — Find file in path

[R] **which** — Display location and version for an ado-file

Title

varabbrev — Control variable abbreviation

Syntax

novarabbrev *stata_command*

varabbrev *stata_command*

Typical usage is

```
novarabbrev {
        ...
}
```

Description

novarabbrev temporarily turns off variable abbreviation if it is on. varabbrev temporarily turns on variable abbreviation if it is off. Also see set varabbrev in [R] **set**.

Remarks

▷ Example 1

```
program ...
        ... /* parse input */ ...
        novarabbrev {
                ... /* perform task */ ...
        }
        ...
end
```

◁

Also see

[P] **unab** — Unabbreviate variable list

[P] **break** — Suppress Break key

[R] **set** — Overview of system parameters

Title

> **version** — Version control

Syntax

Show version number to which command interpreter is set

> version

Set command interpreter to version #

> version # [, born(*ddMONyyyy*)]

Execute command under version #

> version # [, born(*ddMONyyyy*)] : *command*

Description

In the first syntax, version shows the current internal version number to which the command interpreter is set. When appropriate, a message is also presented indicating that the modern treatment of missing values is in force, even though the version number is less than 8.

In the second syntax, version sets the command interpreter to internal version number #. version # is used to allow old programs to run correctly under more recent versions of Stata and to ensure that new programs run correctly under future versions of Stata.

In the third syntax, version executes *command* under version # and then resets the version to what it was before the version #:... command was given.

For information about external version control, see [R] **which**.

Option

born(*ddMONyyyy*) is rarely specified and indicates that the Stata executable must be dated *ddMONyyyy* (e.g., 13Jul2009) or later. StataCorp and users sometimes write programs in ado-files that require the Stata executable to be of a certain date. The born() option allows us or the author of an ado-file to ensure that ado-code that requires a certain updated executable is not run with an older executable.

Generally all that matters is the version number, so you would not use the born() option. You use born() in the rare case that you are exploiting a feature added to the executable after the initial release of that version of Stata. See help whatsnew to browse the features added to the current version of Stata since its original release.

Remarks

version ensures that programs written under an older release of Stata will continue to work under newer releases of Stata. If you do not write programs and if you use only the programs distributed by StataCorp, you can ignore version. If you do write programs, see [U] **18.11.1 Version** for guidelines to follow to ensure compatibility of your programs with future releases of Stata.

❑ Technical note

When Stata is invoked, it sets its internal version number to the current version of Stata, which is 11.0 as of this writing. Typing version without arguments shows the current value of the internal version number:

```
. version
version 11.0
```

One way to make old programs work is to set the internal version number interactively to that of a previous release:

```
. version 9.0
. version
version 9.0
```

Now Stata's default interpretation of a program is the same as it was for Stata 9.0.

You cannot set the version to a number higher than the current version. For instance, because we are using Stata 11.0, we cannot set the version number to 11.7.

```
. version 11.7
this is version 11.0 of Stata; it cannot run version 11.7 programs
  (output omitted )
r(9);
```

❑

❑ Technical note

We strongly recommend that all ado-files and do-files begin with a version command. For programs (ado-files), the version command should appear immediately following the program command:

```
program myprog
        version 11.0
        (etc.)
end
```

❑

For an up-to-date summary of version changes, see help version.

Also see

[P] **display** — Display strings and values of scalar expressions

[R] **which** — Display location and version for an ado-file

[U] **18.11.1 Version**

Title

> **viewsource** — View source code

Syntax

> *viewsource* *filename*

Description

viewsource searches for *filename* along the ado-path and displays the file in the Viewer. No default file extension is provided; if you want to see, for example, kappa.ado, type viewsource kappa.ado.

Remarks

Say that you wish to look at the source for ml (documented in [R] **ml**). You know that ml is an ado-file, and therefore the filename is ml.ado. You type

```
. viewsource ml.ado
```

program (documented in [P] **program**) is not implemented as an ado-file:

```
. viewsource program.ado
file "program.ado" not found
r(601);
```

By the way, you can find out where the file is stored by typing

```
. findfile ml.ado
C:\Program Files\Stata11\ado\updates/m/ml.ado
```

See [P] **findfile**.

viewsource is not limited to displaying ado-files. If you wish to see, for example, panelsetup.mata, type

```
. viewsource panelsetup.mata
```

Methods and formulas

viewsource is implemented as an ado-file.

Also see

[P] **findfile** — Find file in path

[R] **which** — Display location and version for an ado-file

[R] **view** — View files and logs

Title

> **while** — Looping

Syntax

```
while exp {
        stata_commands
}
```

Braces must be specified with `while`, and

1. the open brace must appear on the same line as `while`;

2. nothing may follow the open brace, except, of course, comments; the first command to be executed must appear on a new line;

3. the close brace must appear on a line by itself.

Description

`while` evaluates *exp* and, if it is true (nonzero), executes the *stata_commands* enclosed in the braces. It then repeats the process until *exp* evaluates to false (zero). `while`s may be nested within `while`s. If the *exp* refers to any variables, their values in the first observation are used unless explicit subscripts are specified; see [U] **13.7 Explicit subscripting**.

Also see [P] **foreach** and [P] **forvalues** for alternatives to `while`.

Remarks

`while` may be used interactively, but it is most often used in programs. See [U] **18 Programming Stata** for a description of programs.

The *stata_commands* enclosed in the braces may be executed once, many times, or not at all. For instance,

```
program demo
        local i = '1'
        while 'i'>0 {
                display "i is now 'i'"
                local i = 'i' - 1
        }
        display "done"
end

. demo 2
i is now 2
i is now 1
done

. demo 0
done
```

The above example is a bit contrived in that the best way to count down to one would be

```
program demo
        forvalues i = '1'(-1)1 {
                display "i is now 'i'"
        }
        display "done"
end
```

`while` is used mostly in parsing contexts

```
program ...
        ...
        gettoken tok 0 : 0
        while "'tok'" != "" {
                ...
                gettoken tok 0 : 0
        }
        ...
end
```

or in mathematical contexts where we are iterating

```
program ...
        ...
        scalar 'curval'  = .
        scalar 'lastval' = .
        while abs('lastval' - 'curval') > 'epsilon' {
                scalar 'lastval' = 'curval'
                scalar 'curval'  = ...
        }
        ...
end
```

or in any context in which loop termination is based on calculation (whether it be numeric or string).

You can also create endless loops by using `while`,

```
program ...
        ...
        while 1 {
                ...
        }
end
```

which is not really an endless loop if the code reads

```
program ...
        ...
        while 1 {
                if (...) exit
                ...
        }
        // this line is never reached
end
```

Should you make a mistake and really create an endless loop, you can stop program execution by pressing the *Break* key.

Also see

[P] **continue** — Break out of loops

[P] **foreach** — Loop over items

[P] **forvalues** — Loop over consecutive values

[P] **if** — if programming command

[U] **13 Functions and expressions**

[U] **18 Programming Stata**

Title

> **window programming** — Programming menus and windows

Syntax

```
window fopen ...

window fsave ...

window manage subcmd ...

window menu subcmd ...

window push command_line

window stopbox subcmd ...
```

Description

The `window` command lets you open, close, and manage the windows in Stata's interface. Using the subcommands of `window menu`, you can also add and delete menu items from the **User** menu from Stata's main menu bar. `window push` adds "*command_line*" to the Review window.

Remarks

To see the complete documentation for programming windows and menus, type

```
. help window programming
```

For documentation on creating dialog boxes, type

```
. help dialog programming
```

Also see

[P] **dialog programming** — Dialog programming

[U] **18 Programming Stata**

Subject and author index

This is the subject and author index for the *Programming Reference Manual*. Readers interested in topics other than programming should see the combined subject index (and the combined author index) in the *Quick Reference and Index*. The combined index indexes the *Getting Started* manuals, the *User's Guide*, and all the reference manuals except the *Mata Reference Manual*.

Semicolons set off the most important entries from the rest. Sometimes no entry will be set off with semicolons, meaning that all entries are equally important.

* comment indicator, [P] **comments**
., class, [P] **class**
/* */ comment delimiter, [P] **comments**
// comment indicator, [P] **comments**
/// comment indicator, [P] **comments**
; delimiter, [P] **#delimit**

A

abbreviations,
    unabbreviating command names, [P] **unabcmd**
    unabbreviating variable list, [P] **unab**; [P] **syntax**
accum, matrix subcommand, [P] **matrix accum**
add, return subcommand, [P] **return**
ado-files, [P] **sysdir**, [P] **version**
    adding comments to, [P] **comments**
    debugging, [P] **trace**
    long lines, [P] **#delimit**
adopath command, [P] **sysdir**
adosize set command, [P] **sysdir**
adosubdir macro extended function, [P] **macro**
algebraic expressions, functions, and operators, [P] **matrix define**
all macro extended function, [P] **macro**
alphanumeric variables, *see* string variables, parsing
Anderson, E., [P] **matrix eigenvalues**
appending rows and columns to matrix, [P] **matrix define**
args command, [P] **syntax**
arithmetic operators, [P] **matrix define**
arrays, class, [P] **class**
.Arrdropall built-in class modifier, [P] **class**
.Arrdropel built-in class modifier, [P] **class**
.arrindexof built-in class function, [P] **class**
.arrnels built-in class function, [P] **class**
.Arrpop built-in class modifier, [P] **class**
.Arrpush built-in class modifier, [P] **class**
as error, display directive, [P] **display**
as input, display directive, [P] **display**
as result, display directive, [P] **display**
as text, display directive, [P] **display**
as txt, display directive, [P] **display**
ASCII text files, writing and reading, [P] **file**

_asis, display directive, [P] **display**
assignment, class, [P] **class**
Automation, [P] **automation**

B

Bai, Z., [P] **matrix eigenvalues**
BASE directory, [P] **sysdir**
basis, orthonormal, [P] **matrix svd**
Baum, C. F., [P] **intro**, [P] **levelsof**
Becketti, S., [P] **pause**
Bibby, J. M., [P] **matrix dissimilarity**
binary files, writing and reading, [P] **file**
Binder, D. A., [P] **_robust**
Bischof, C., [P] **matrix eigenvalues**
Blackford, S., [P] **matrix eigenvalues**
bootstrap sampling and estimation, [P] **postfile**
Boyle, J. M., [P] **matrix symeigen**
break command, [P] **break**
Break key, interception, [P] **break**, [P] **capture**
built-in, class, [P] **class**
_by() function, [P] **byable**
by *varlist*: prefix, [P] **byable**
byable, [P] **byable**
by-groups, [P] **byable**
_byindex() function, [P] **byable**
_bylastcall() function, [P] **byable**
_byn1() function, [P] **byable**
_byn2() function, [P] **byable**

C

c(adopath) c-class value, [P] **creturn**, [P] **sysdir**
c(adosize) c-class value, [P] **creturn**, [P] **sysdir**
c(ALPHA) c-class value, [P] **creturn**
c(alpha) c-class value, [P] **creturn**
c(autotabgraphs) c-class value, [P] **creturn**
c(born_date) c-class value, [P] **creturn**
c(byteorder) c-class value, [P] **creturn**
c(changed) c-class value, [P] **creturn**
c(checksum) c-class value, [P] **creturn**
c(cmdlen) c-class value, [P] **creturn**
c(console) c-class value, [P] **creturn**
c(copycolor) c-class value, [P] **creturn**
c(current_date) c-class value, [P] **creturn**
c(current_time) c-class value, [P] **creturn**
c(dirsep) c-class value, [P] **creturn**
c(dockable) c-class value, [P] **creturn**
c(dockingguides) c-class value, [P] **creturn**
c(doublebuffer) c-class value, [P] **creturn**
c(dp) c-class value, [P] **creturn**
c(eolchar) c-class value, [P] **creturn**
c(epsdouble) c-class value, [P] **creturn**
c(epsfloat) c-class value, [P] **creturn**
c(eqlen) c-class value, [P] **creturn**
c(fastscroll) c-class value, [P] **creturn**
c(filedate) c-class value, [P] **creturn**

c(filename) c-class value, [P] **creturn**
c(flavor) c-class value, [P] **creturn**
c(graphics) c-class value, [P] **creturn**
c(httpproxy) c-class value, [P] **creturn**
c(httpproxyauth) c-class value, [P] **creturn**
c(httpproxyhost) c-class value, [P] **creturn**
c(httpproxyport) c-class value, [P] **creturn**
c(httpproxypw) c-class value, [P] **creturn**
c(httpproxyuser) c-class value, [P] **creturn**
c(k) c-class value, [P] **creturn**
c(level) c-class value, [P] **creturn**
c(linegap) c-class value, [P] **creturn**
c(linesize) c-class value, [P] **creturn**
c(locksplitters) c-class value, [P] **creturn**
c(logtype) c-class value, [P] **creturn**
c(macgphengine) c-class value, [P] **creturn**
c(machine_type) c-class value, [P] **creturn**
c(macrolen) c-class value, [P] **creturn**
c(matacache) c-class value, [P] **creturn**
c(matafavor) c-class value, [P] **creturn**
c(matalibs) c-class value, [P] **creturn**
c(matalnum) c-class value, [P] **creturn**
c(matamofirst) c-class value, [P] **creturn**
c(mataoptimize) c-class value, [P] **creturn**
c(matastrict) c-class value, [P] **creturn**
c(matsize) c-class value, [P] **creturn**
c(maxbyte) c-class value, [P] **creturn**
c(max_cmdlen) c-class value, [P] **creturn**
c(maxdb) c-class value, [P] **creturn**
c(maxdouble) c-class value, [P] **creturn**
c(maxfloat) c-class value, [P] **creturn**
c(maxint) c-class value, [P] **creturn**
c(maxiter) c-class value, [P] **creturn**
c(max_k_current) c-class value, [P] **creturn**
c(max_k_theory) c-class value, [P] **creturn**
c(maxlong) c-class value, [P] **creturn**
c(max_macrolen) c-class value, [P] **creturn**
c(max_matsize) c-class value, [P] **creturn**
c(max_N_current) c-class value, [P] **creturn**
c(max_N_theory) c-class value, [P] **creturn**
c(maxstrvarlen) c-class value, [P] **creturn**
c(maxvar) c-class value, [P] **creturn**
c(max_width_current) c-class value, [P] **creturn**
c(max_width_theory) c-class value, [P] **creturn**
c(memory) c-class value, [P] **creturn**
c(minbyte) c-class value, [P] **creturn**
c(mindouble) c-class value, [P] **creturn**
c(minfloat) c-class value, [P] **creturn**
c(minint) c-class value, [P] **creturn**
c(minlong) c-class value, [P] **creturn**
c(min_matsize) c-class value, [P] **creturn**
c(mode) c-class value, [P] **creturn**
c(Mons) c-class value, [P] **creturn**
c(Months) c-class value, [P] **creturn**
c(more) c-class value, [P] **creturn**, [P] **more**
c(MP) c-class value, [P] **creturn**
c(N) c-class value, [P] **creturn**

c(namelen) c-class value, [P] **creturn**
c(noisily) c-class value, [P] **creturn**
c(notifyuser) c-class value, [P] **creturn**
c(odbcmgr) c-class value, [P] **creturn**
c(os) c-class value, [P] **creturn**
c(osdtl) c-class value, [P] **creturn**
c(pagesize) c-class value, [P] **creturn**
c(persistfv) c-class value, [P] **creturn**
c(persistvtopic) c-class value, [P] **creturn**
c(pi) c-class value, [P] **creturn**
c(pinnable) c-class value, [P] **creturn**
c(playsnd) c-class value, [P] **creturn**
c(printcolor) c-class value, [P] **creturn**
c(processors) c-class value, [P] **creturn**
c(processors_lic) c-class value, [P] **creturn**
c(processors_mach) c-class value, [P] **creturn**
c(processors_max) c-class value, [P] **creturn**
c(pwd) c-class value, [P] **creturn**
c(rc) c-class value, [P] **capture**, [P] **creturn**
c(reventries) c-class value, [P] **creturn**
c(revkeyboard) c-class value, [P] **creturn**
c(revwindow) c-class value, [P] **creturn**
c(rmsg) c-class value, [P] **creturn**, [P] **rmsg**
c(rmsg_time) c-class value, [P] **creturn**
c(scheme) c-class value, [P] **creturn**
c(scrollbufsize) c-class value, [P] **creturn**
c(SE) c-class value, [P] **creturn**
c(searchdefault) c-class value, [P] **creturn**
c(seed) c-class value, [P] **creturn**
c(smallestdouble) c-class value, [P] **creturn**
c(smoothfonts) c-class value, [P] **creturn**
c(smoothsize) c-class value, [P] **creturn**
c(stata_version) c-class value, [P] **creturn**
c(sysdir_base) c-class value, [P] **creturn**, [P] **sysdir**
c(sysdir_oldplace) c-class value, [P] **creturn**, [P] **sysdir**
c(sysdir_personal) c-class value, [P] **creturn**, [P] **sysdir**
c(sysdir_plus) c-class value, [P] **creturn**, [P] **sysdir**
c(sysdir_site) c-class value, [P] **creturn**, [P] **sysdir**
c(sysdir_stata) c-class value, [P] **creturn**, [P] **sysdir**
c(sysdir_updates) c-class value, [P] **creturn**, [P] **sysdir**
c(timeout1) c-class value, [P] **creturn**
c(timeout2) c-class value, [P] **creturn**
c(tmpdir) c-class value, [P] **creturn**
c(trace) c-class value, [P] **creturn**, [P] **trace**
c(tracedepth) c-class value, [P] **creturn**, [P] **trace**
c(traceexpand) c-class value, [P] **creturn**, [P] **trace**
c(tracehilite) c-class value, [P] **creturn**, [P] **trace**
c(traceindent) c-class value, [P] **creturn**, [P] **trace**
c(tracenumber) c-class value, [P] **creturn**, [P] **trace**
c(tracesep) c-class value, [P] **creturn**, [P] **trace**
c(type) c-class value, [P] **creturn**
c(update_interval) c-class value, [P] **creturn**
c(update_prompt) c-class value, [P] **creturn**

c(update_query) c-class value, [P] **creturn**
c(use_atsui_graph) c-class value, [P] **creturn**
c(use_qd_text) c-class value, [P] **creturn**
c(username) c-class value, [P] **creturn**
c(varabbrev) c-class value, [P] **creturn**
c(varkeyboard) c-class value, [P] **creturn**
c(varlabelpos) c-class value, [P] **creturn**
c(varwindow) c-class value, [P] **creturn**
c(version) c-class value, [P] **creturn**, [P] **version**
c(virtual) c-class value, [P] **creturn**
c(Wdays) c-class value, [P] **creturn**
c(Weekdays) c-class value, [P] **creturn**
c(width) c-class value, [P] **creturn**
capture command, [P] **capture**
casewise deletion, [P] **mark**
c-class command, [P] **creturn**
cdir, classutil subcommand, [P] **classutil**
certifying data, [P] **_datasignature**, [P]
    signestimationsample
_char(#), display directive, [P] **display**
char
    define command, [P] **char**
    list command, [P] **char**
    rename command, [P] **char**
char macro extended function, [P] **macro**
characteristics, [P] **char**
charset, set subcommand, [P] **smcl**
checkestimationsample command, [P]
    signestimationsample
checksums of data, [P] **_datasignature**
Cholesky decomposition, [P] **matrix define**
cholesky() matrix function, [P] **matrix define**
class
    definition, [P] **class**
    programming, [P] **class**
    programming utilities, [P] **classutil**
class exit command, [P] **class exit**
.classmv built-in class function, [P] **class**
.classname built-in class function, [P] **class**
classutil
    cdir command, [P] **classutil**
    describe command, [P] **classutil**
    dir command, [P] **classutil**
    drop command, [P] **classutil**
    which command, [P] **classutil**
classwide variable, [P] **class**
clear,
    ereturn subcommand, [P] **ereturn**; [P] **return**
    _estimates subcommand, [P] **_estimates**
    postutil subcommand, [P] **postfile**
    return subcommand, [P] **return**
    serset subcommand, [P] **serset**
    sreturn subcommand, [P] **return**; [P] **program**
    timer subcommand, [P] **timer**
clearing estimation results, [P] **ereturn**, [P] **_estimates**
close, file subcommand, [P] **file**
cluster estimator of variance, [P] **_robust**

cluster sampling, [P] **_robust**
Cochran, W. G., [P] **levelsof**
code, timing, [P] **timer**
coefficients (from estimation), accessing, [P] **ereturn**,
    [P] **matrix get**
coleq macro extended function, [P] **macro**
coleq, matrix subcommand, [P] **matrix rownames**
colfullnames macro extended function, [P] **macro**
collinear variables, removing, [P] **_rmcoll**
colnames macro extended function, [P] **macro**
colnames, matrix subcommand, [P] **matrix**
    rownames
colnumb() matrix function, [P] **matrix define**
colors, specifying in programs, [P] **display**
colsof() matrix function, [P] **matrix define**
_column(#), display directive, [P] **display**
columns of matrix,
    appending to, [P] **matrix define**
    names of, [P] **ereturn**, [P] **matrix define**, [P] **matrix**
    rownames
    operators on, [P] **matrix define**
command
    arguments, [P] **gettoken**, [P] **syntax**, [P] **tokenize**
    parsing, [P] **gettoken**, [P] **syntax**, [P] **tokenize**
commands,
    aborting, [P] **continue**
    repeating automatically, [P] **byable**, [P] **continue**,
    [P] **foreach**, [P] **forvalues**, [P] **while**
    unabbreviating names of, [P] **unabcmd**
comments, adding to programs, [P] **comments**
compatibility of Stata programs across releases, [P]
    version
compound double quotes, [P] **macro**
condition statement, [P] **if**
confirm
    existence command, [P] **confirm**
    file command, [P] **confirm**
    format command, [P] **confirm**
    matrix command, [P] **confirm**
    names command, [P] **confirm**
    number command, [P] **confirm**
    scalar command, [P] **confirm**
    variable command, [P] **confirm**
console,
    controlling scrolling of output, [P] **more**
    obtaining input from, [P] **display**
constrained estimation, programming, [P] **makecns**
constraint macro extended function, [P] **macro**
constraint matrix, creating and displaying, [P] **makecns**
context, class, [P] **class**
_continue, display directive, [P] **display**
continue command, [P] **continue**
Cook, R. D., [P] **_predict**
.copy built-in class function, [P] **class**
copy macro extended function, [P] **macro**
corr() matrix function, [P] **matrix define**
correlation, matrices, [P] **matrix define**

covariance matrix of estimators, [P] **ereturn**, [P] **matrix
    get**
Cox, G. M., [P] **levelsof**
Cox, N. J., [P] **levelsof**, [P] **matrix define**
create, serset subcommand, [P] **serset**
create_cspline, serset subcommand, [P] **serset**
create_xmedians, serset subcommand, [P] **serset**
creturn list command, [P] **creturn**
cross-product matrices, [P] **matrix accum**
cutil, *see* classutil

D

data,
    characteristics of, *see* characteristics
    checksums of, [P] **signestimationsample**
    current, [P] **creturn**
    preserving, [P] **preserve**
data label macro extended function, [P] **macro**
data signature, [P] **_datasignature**, [P]
    signestimationsample
_datasignature command, [P] **_datasignature**
date and time, [P] **creturn**
debugging, [P] **trace**; [P] **discard**, [P] **pause**
.Declare built-in class modifier, [P] **class**
declare, class, [P] **class**
define,
    char subcommand, [P] **char**
    matrix subcommand, [P] **matrix define**
    program subcommand, [P] **program**, [P] **program
    properties**
#delimit command, [P] **#delimit**
delimiter
    for comments, [P] **comments**
    for lines, [P] **#delimit**
Demmel, J., [P] **matrix eigenvalues**
describe, classutil subcommand, [P] **classutil**
destructors, class, [P] **class**
det() matrix function, [P] **matrix define**
determinant of matrix, [P] **matrix define**
diag() matrix function, [P] **matrix define**
diag0cnt() matrix function, [P] **matrix define**
diagonals of matrices, [P] **matrix define**
dialog
    box, [P] **dialog programming**, [P] **window
    programming**
    programming, [P] **dialog programming**, [P] **window
    programming**
dir,
    classutil subcommand, [P] **classutil**
    _estimates subcommand, [P] **_estimates**
    macro subcommand, [P] **macro**
    matrix subcommand, [P] **matrix utility**
    postutil subcommand, [P] **postfile**
    program subcommand, [P] **program**
    _return subcommand, [P] **_return**
    serset subcommand, [P] **serset**
dir macro extended function, [P] **macro**

directories and paths, [P] **creturn**
directory, class, [P] **classutil**
discard command, [P] **discard**
display command, [P] **display**; [P] **macro**
display, ereturn subcommand, [P] **ereturn**
display formats, [P] **macro**
display macro extended function, [P] **display**
displaying
    macros, [P] **macro**
    matrix, [P] **matrix utility**
    output, [P] **display**, [P] **quietly**, [P] **smcl**, [P]
    tabdisp
    scalar expressions, [P] **display**, [P] **scalar**
dissimilarity
    matrices, [P] **matrix dissimilarity**
    measures, [P] **matrix dissimilarity**
dissimilarity, matrix subcommand, [P] **matrix
    dissimilarity**
distance matrices, [P] **matrix dissimilarity**
DLL, [P] **plugin**
do-files, [P] **break**, [P] **include**, [P] **version**
    adding comments to, [P] **comments**
    long lines, [P] **#delimit**
Dongarra, J. J., [P] **matrix eigenvalues**, [P] **matrix
    symeigen**
double quotes, [P] **macro**
drop,
    classutil subcommand, [P] **classutil**
    _estimates subcommand, [P] **_estimates**
    macro subcommand, [P] **macro**
    matrix subcommand, [P] **matrix utility**
    program subcommand, [P] **program**
    _return subcommand, [P] **_return**
    serset subcommand, [P] **serset**
dropping programs, [P] **discard**
.dta file suffix, technical description, [P] **file formats
    .dta**
Du Croz, J., [P] **matrix eigenvalues**
_dup(#), display directive, [P] **display**
.dynamicmv built-in class function, [P] **class**

E

e() scalars, macros, matrices, functions, [P] **ereturn**,
    [P] **_estimates**, [P] **return**
e(functions) macro extended function, [P] **macro**
e(macros) macro extended function, [P] **macro**
e(matrices) macro extended function, [P] **macro**
e(sample) function, [P] **ereturn**, [P] **return**
e(scalars) macro extended function, [P] **macro**
e-class command, [P] **program**, [P] **return**
eigenvalues, [P] **matrix eigenvalues**, [P] **matrix
    symeigen**
eigenvalues and eigenvectors, [P] **matrix svd**, [P]
    matrix symeigen
eigenvalues, matrix subcommand, [P] **matrix
    eigenvalues**
el() matrix function, [P] **matrix define**

else command, [P] **if**
ending a Stata session, [P] **exit**
environment macro extended function, [P] **macro**
environment variables (Unix), [P] **macro**
equation names of matrix, [P] **matrix rownames**; [P]
     ereturn, [P] **matrix define**
ereturn
   clear command, [P] **ereturn**; [P] **return**
   display command, [P] **ereturn**
   list command, [P] **ereturn**
   local command, [P] **ereturn**; [P] **return**
   matrix command, [P] **ereturn**; [P] **return**
   post command, [P] **ereturn**, [P] **makecns**; [P]
     return
   repost command, [P] **ereturn**; [P] **return**
   scalar command, [P] **ereturn**; [P] **return**
error
   handling, [P] **capture**, [P] **confirm**, [P] **error**
   messages and return codes, [P] **error**, [P] **rmsg**, *also*
     see error handling
error command, [P] **error**
estat, [P] **estat programming**
_estimates
   clear command, [P] **_estimates**
   dir command, [P] **_estimates**
   drop command, [P] **_estimates**
   hold command, [P] **_estimates**
   unhold command, [P] **_estimates**
estimation
   commands, [P] **ereturn**, [P] **_estimates**
     accessing stored information from, [P] **matrix get**
     allowing constraints in, [P] **makecns**
     eliminating stored information from, [P] **discard**
     obtaining predictions after, [P] **_predict**
     obtaining robust estimates, [P] **_robust**
     saving results from, [P] **_estimates**
   results,
     clearing, [P] **ereturn**, [P] **_estimates**
     listing, [P] **ereturn**, [P] **_estimates**
     saving, [P] **ereturn**, [P] **_estimates**
estimators, covariance matrix of, [P] **ereturn**, [P]
     matrix get
existence, confirm subcommand, [P] **confirm**
exit class program, [P] **class exit**
exit, class subcommand, [P] **class exit**
exit command, [P] **capture**, [P] **exit**
exiting Stata, *see* exit command
expand factor varlists, [P] **fvexpand**
expressions, [P] **matrix define**
extended macro functions, [P] **char**, [P] **display**, [P]
     macro, [P] **macro lists**, [P] **serset**

F

factor variables, [P] **fvexpand**, [P] **intro**, [P] **matrix**
     rownames, [P] **_rmcoll**, [P] **syntax**, [P] **unab**
file
   close command, [P] **file**

file, *continued*
   open command, [P] **file**
   query command, [P] **file**
   read command, [P] **file**
   seek command, [P] **file**
   sersetread command, [P] **serset**
   sersetwrite command, [P] **serset**
   set command, [P] **file**
   write command, [P] **file**
file, confirm subcommand, [P] **confirm**
file, find in path, [P] **findfile**
file format, Stata, [P] **file formats .dta**
files,
   opening, [P] **window programming**
   reading ASCII text or binary, [P] **file**
   saving, [P] **window programming**
   temporary, [P] **macro**, [P] **preserve**, [P] **scalar**
   writing ASCII text or binary, [P] **file**
findfile command, [P] **findfile**
finding file in path, [P] **findfile**
Fisher, R. A., [P] **levelsof**
Flannery, B. P., [P] **matrix symeigen**
fopen, window subcommand, [P] **window**
     programming
foreach command, [P] **foreach**
format, confirm subcommand, [P] **confirm**
format macro extended function, [P] **macro**
formatting contents of macros, [P] **macro**
forvalues command, [P] **forvalues**
Frankel, M. R., [P] **_robust**
fsave, window subcommand, [P] **window**
     programming
Fuller, W. A., [P] **_robust**
functions
   extended macro, [P] **char**, [P] **display**, [P] **macro**,
     [P] **macro lists**, [P] **serset**
   matrix, [P] **matrix define**
fvexpand command, [P] **fvexpand**
fvunab command, [P] **unab**

G

g2 inverse of matrix, [P] **matrix define**, [P] **matrix svd**
Gail, M. H., [P] **_robust**
Garbow, B. S., [P] **matrix symeigen**
generalized
   inverse of matrix, [P] **matrix define**, [P] **matrix svd**
   method of moments (GMM), [P] **matrix accum**
get() matrix function, [P] **matrix define**, [P] **matrix**
     get
gettoken command, [P] **gettoken**
Global, class prefix operator, [P] **class**
global command, [P] **macro**
glsaccum, matrix subcommand, [P] **matrix accum**
Gould, W. W., [P] **_datasignature**, [P] **_robust**, [P]
     intro, [P] **matrix mkmat**, [P] **postfile**
graphical user interface, [P] **dialog programming**
Greenbaum, A., [P] **matrix eigenvalues**

Greene, W. H., [P] **matrix accum**
GUI programming, [P] **dialog programming**

H

hadamard() matrix function, [P] **matrix define**
Hamilton, J. D., [P] **matrix eigenvalues**
Hammarling, S., [P] **matrix eigenvalues**
Heinecke, K., [P] **matrix mkmat**
heteroskedasticity, robust variances, *see* robust
hold,
    _estimates subcommand, [P] **_estimates**
    _return subcommand, [P] **_return**
Huber, P. J., [P] **_robust**
Huber/White/sandwich estimator of variance, *see* robust,
        Huber/White/sandwich estimator of variance

I

I() matrix function, [P] **matrix define**
identifier, class, [P] **class**
identity matrix, [P] **matrix define**
if *exp*, [P] **syntax**
if programming command, [P] **if**
Ikebe, Y., [P] **matrix symeigen**
immediate commands, [P] **display**
implied context, class, [P] **class**
in *range* modifier, [P] **syntax**
in smcl, display directive, [P] **display**
include command, [P] **include**
information matrix, [P] **matrix get**
inheritance, [P] **class**
initialization, class, [P] **class**
input, matrix subcommand, [P] **matrix define**
input, obtaining from console in programs, *see* console,
        obtaining input from
instance, class, [P] **class**
.instancemv built-in class function, [P] **class**
instance-specific variable, [P] **class**
inv() matrix function, [P] **matrix define**
inverse of matrix, [P] **matrix define**, [P] **matrix svd**
invsym() matrix function, [P] **matrix define**
.isa built-in class function, [P] **class**
.isofclass built-in class function, [P] **class**
issymmetric() matrix function, [P] **matrix define**

J

J() matrix function, [P] **matrix define**
Jann, B., [P] **mark**

K

Kaufman, L., [P] **matrix dissimilarity**
Kennedy Jr., W., [P] **_robust**
Kent, J. T., [P] **_robust**, [P] **matrix dissimilarity**
Kish, L., [P] **_robust**

Klema, V. C., [P] **matrix symeigen**
Kolev, G. I., [P] **scalar**
Kronecker product, [P] **matrix define**

L

label macro extended function, [P] **macro**
label values, [P] **macro**
language syntax, [P] **syntax**
length macro extended function, [P] **macro**
level command and value, [P] **macro**
levelsof command, [P] **levelsof**
limits,
    numerical and string, [P] **creturn**
    system, [P] **creturn**
Lin, D. Y., [P] **_robust**
linear combinations, forming, [P] **matrix score**
lines, long, in do-files and ado-files, [P] **#delimit**
list,
    char subcommand, [P] **char**
    creturn subcommand, [P] **creturn**
    ereturn subcommand, [P] **ereturn**
    macro subcommand, [P] **macro**
    matrix subcommand, [P] **matrix utility**
    program subcommand, [P] **program**
    sysdir subcommand, [P] **sysdir**
    timer subcommand, [P] **timer**
list macro extended function, [P] **macro lists**
list manipulation, [P] **macro lists**
listing
    estimation results, [P] **ereturn**, [P] **_estimates**
    macro expanded functions, [P] **macro lists**
    values of a variable, [P] **levelsof**
local
    ++ command, [P] **macro**
    – command, [P] **macro**
    command, [P] **macro**
local,
    ereturn subcommand, [P] **ereturn**
    return subcommand, [P] **return**
    sreturn subcommand, [P] **return**
Local, class prefix operator, [P] **class**
long lines in ado-files and do-files, [P] **#delimit**
looping, [P] **continue**, [P] **foreach**, [P] **forvalues**, [P]
        while
lvalue, class, [P] **class**

M

Mac, pause, [P] **sleep**
MacKinnon, J. G., [P] **_robust**
macro
    dir command, [P] **macro**
    drop command, [P] **macro**
    list command, [P] **macro**
    shift command, [P] **macro**

macro substitution, [P] **macro**
    class, [P] **class**
macros, [P] **macro**; [P] **creturn**, [P] **scalar**, [P] **syntax**,
    also see e()
macval() macro expansion function, [P] **macro**
makecns command, [P] **makecns**
manage, window subcommand, [P] **window**
    programming
Mardia, K. V., [P] **matrix dissimilarity**
mark command, [P] **mark**
markin command, [P] **mark**
marking observations, [P] **mark**
markout command, [P] **mark**
marksample command, [P] **mark**
matcproc command, [P] **makecns**
mathematical functions and expressions, [P] **matrix**
    define
matlist command, [P] **matlist**
matmissing() matrix function, [P] **matrix define**
matname command, [P] **matrix mkmat**
mat_put_rr command, [P] **matrix get**
matrices, [P] **matrix**
    accessing internal, [P] **matrix get**
    accumulating, [P] **matrix accum**
    appending rows and columns, [P] **matrix define**
    Cholesky decomposition, [P] **matrix define**
    coefficient matrices, [P] **ereturn**
    column names, *see* matrices, row and column names
    constrained estimation, [P] **makecns**
    copying, [P] **matrix define**, [P] **matrix get**, [P]
        matrix mkmat
    correlation, [P] **matrix define**
    covariance matrix of estimators, [P] **ereturn**, [P]
        matrix get
    cross-product, [P] **matrix accum**
    determinant, [P] **matrix define**
    diagonals, [P] **matrix define**
    displaying, [P] **matlist**, [P] **matrix utility**
    dissimilarity, [P] **matrix dissimilarity**
    distances, [P] **matrix dissimilarity**
    dropping, [P] **matrix utility**
    eigenvalues, [P] **matrix eigenvalues**, [P] **matrix**
        symeigen
    eigenvectors, [P] **matrix symeigen**
    elements, [P] **matrix define**
    equation names, *see* matrices, row and column
        names
    estimation results, [P] **ereturn**, [P] **_estimates**
    functions, [P] **matrix define**
    identity, [P] **matrix define**
    input, [P] **matrix define**
    inversion, [P] **matrix define**, [P] **matrix svd**
    Kronecker product, [P] **matrix define**
    labeling rows and columns, *see* matrices, row and
        column names
    linear combinations with data, [P] **matrix score**
    listing, [P] **matlist**, [P] **matrix utility**

matrices, *continued*
    namespace and conflicts, [P] **matrix**, [P] **matrix**
        define
    number of rows and columns, [P] **matrix define**
    operators such as addition, [P] **matrix define**
    orthonormal basis, [P] **matrix svd**
    partitioned, [P] **matrix define**
    performing constrained estimation, [P] **makecns**
    posting estimation results, [P] **ereturn**, [P]
        _estimates
    renaming, [P] **matrix utility**
    row and column names, [P] **ereturn**, [P] **matrix**
        define, [P] **matrix mkmat**, [P] **matrix rownames**
    rows and columns, [P] **matrix define**
    saving matrix, [P] **matrix mkmat**
    scoring, [P] **matrix score**
    similarity, [P] **matrix dissimilarity**
    store variables as matrix, [P] **matrix mkmat**
    submatrix extraction, [P] **matrix define**
    submatrix substitution, [P] **matrix define**
    subscripting, [P] **matrix define**
    sweep operator, [P] **matrix define**
    temporary names, [P] **matrix**
    trace, [P] **matrix define**
    transposing, [P] **matrix define**
    variables, make into matrix, [P] **matrix mkmat**
    zero, [P] **matrix define**
matrix() pseudofunction, [P] **matrix define**
matrix,
    confirm subcommand, [P] **confirm**
    ereturn subcommand, [P] **ereturn**
    return subcommand, [P] **return**
matrix
    accum command, [P] **matrix accum**
    coleq command, [P] **matrix rownames**
    colnames command, [P] **matrix rownames**
    commands, introduction, [P] **matrix**
    define command, [P] **matrix define**
    dir command, [P] **matrix utility**
    dissimilarity command, [P] **matrix dissimilarity**
    drop command, [P] **matrix utility**
    eigenvalues command, [P] **matrix eigenvalues**
    glsaccum command, [P] **matrix accum**
    input command, [P] **matrix define**
    list command, [P] **matrix utility**
    opaccum command, [P] **matrix accum**
    rename command, [P] **matrix utility**
    roweq command, [P] **matrix rownames**
    rownames command, [P] **matrix rownames**
    score command, [P] **matrix score**
    svd command, [P] **matrix svd**
    symeigen command, [P] **matrix symeigen**
    vecaccum command, [P] **matrix accum**
matsize, [P] **creturn**, [P] **macro**
matuniform() matrix function, [P] **matrix define**
McKenney, A., [P] **matrix eigenvalues**

member
    programs, [P] **class**
    variables, [P] **class**
memory, reducing utilization, [P] **discard**
memory settings, [P] **creturn**
menu, window subcommand, [P] **window programming**
menus, programming, [P] **dialog programming**, [P]
    window programming
messages and return codes, *see* error messages and
    return codes
mkmat command, [P] **matrix mkmat**
Moler, C. B., [P] **matrix symeigen**
Monte Carlo simulations, [P] **postfile**
more command and parameter, [P] **macro**, [P] **more**
mreldif() matrix function, [P] **matrix define**

N

names
    conflicts, [P] **matrix**, [P] **matrix define**, [P] **scalar**
    matrix row and columns, [P] **ereturn**, [P] **matrix**
      define, [P] **matrix rownames**
names, confirm subcommand, [P] **confirm**
namespace and conflicts, matrices and scalars, [P]
    matrix, [P] **matrix define**
n-class command, [P] **program**, [P] **return**
.new built-in class function, [P] **class**
Newey–West standard errors, [P] **matrix accum**
_newline(#), display directive, [P] **display**
nobreak command, [P] **break**
noisily prefix, [P] **quietly**
nopreserve option, [P] **nopreserve option**
novarabbrev command, [P] **varabbrev**
nullmat() matrix function, [P] **matrix define**
number, confirm subcommand, [P] **confirm**
numeric list, [P] **numlist**, [P] **syntax**
numlist command, [P] **numlist**

O

object, [P] **class**
object-oriented programming, [P] **class**
.objkey built-in class function, [P] **class**
.objtype built-in class function, [P] **class**
observations, marking, [P] **mark**
off, timer subcommand, [P] **timer**
OLDPLACE directory, [P] **sysdir**
OLE Automation, [P] **automation**
on, timer subcommand, [P] **timer**
opaccum, matrix subcommand, [P] **matrix accum**
open, file subcommand, [P] **file**
operators, [P] **matrix define**
options, in a programming context, [P] **syntax**, [P]
    unab
orthonormal basis, [P] **matrix svd**

output,
    displaying, [P] **display**, [P] **smcl**
    suppressing, [P] **quietly**
output, set subcommand, [P] **quietly**
output settings, [P] **creturn**
overloading, class program names, [P] **class**

P

paging of screen output, controlling, [P] **more**
Park, H. J., [P] **_robust**
parsing, [P] **syntax**; [P] **gettoken**, [P] **numlist**, [P]
    tokenize
partitioned matrices, [P] **matrix define**
paths and directories, [P] **creturn**
pause command, [P] **pause**
pausing until key is pressed, [P] **more**
permname macro extended function, [P] **macro**
personal command, [P] **sysdir**
PERSONAL directory, [P] **sysdir**
Piantadosi, S., [P] **_robust**
piece macro extended function, [P] **macro**
Pitblado, J., [P] **_robust**, [P] **intro**
plugin, loading, [P] **plugin**
plugin option, [P] **plugin**, [P] **program**
PLUS directory, [P] **sysdir**
polymorphism, [P] **class**
post command, [P] **postfile**
post, ereturn subcommand, [P] **ereturn**, [P] **makecns**
postclose command, [P] **postfile**
postestimation command, [P] **estat programming**
postfile command, [P] **postfile**
postutil
    clear command, [P] **postfile**
    dir command, [P] **postfile**
_predict command, [P] **_predict**
predict command, [P] **ereturn**, [P] **_estimates**
predictions, obtaining after estimation, [P] **_predict**
preserve command, [P] **preserve**
preserving user's data, [P] **preserve**
Press, W. H., [P] **matrix symeigen**
program
    define command, [P] **plugin**, [P] **program**, [P]
      program properties
    dir command, [P] **program**
    drop command, [P] **program**
    list command, [P] **program**
program properties, [P] **program properties**
programming, [P] **syntax**
    dialog, [P] **dialog programming**
    estat, [P] **estat programming**
    Mac, [P] **window programming**
    menus, [P] **window programming**
    Windows, [P] **window programming**
programs,
    adding comments to, [P] **comments**
    debugging, [P] **trace**

programs, *continued*
    dropping, [P] **discard**
    looping, [P] **continue**
properties, [P] **program properties**
properties macro extended function, [P] **macro**
push, window subcommand, [P] **window programming**

Q

query, file subcommand, [P] **file**
quietly prefix, [P] **quietly**
quitting Stata, *see* exit command
quotes to expand macros, [P] **macro**

R

r() scalars, macros, matrices, functions, [P] **discard**,
    [P] **return**
r(functions) macro extended function, [P] **macro**
r(macros) macro extended function, [P] **macro**
r(matrices) macro extended function, [P] **macro**
r(scalars) macro extended function, [P] **macro**
rc (return codes), *see* error messages and return codes
_rc built-in variable, [P] **capture**
r-class command, [P] **program**, [P] **return**
read, file subcommand, [P] **file**
reading console input in programs, *see* console,
    obtaining input from
.ref built-in class function, [P] **class**
references, class, [P] **class**
.ref_n built-in class function, [P] **class**
regression (in generic sense), *see* estimation commands
    accessing coefficients and std. errors, [P] **matrix get**
Reinsch, C., [P] **matrix symeigen**
release marker, [P] **version**
releases, compatibility of Stata programs across, [P]
    version
rename,
    char subcommand, [P] **char**
    matrix subcommand, [P] **matrix utility**
repeating commands, [P] **continue**, [P] **foreach**, [P]
    forvalues
replay() function, [P] **ereturn**, [P] **_estimates**
repost, ereturn subcommand, [P] **return**
_request(*macname*), display directive, [P] **display**
reset_id, serset subcommand, [P] **serset**
restore command, [P] **preserve**
restore, _return subcommand, [P] **_return**
results,
    clearing, [P] **ereturn**, [P] **_estimates**, [P] **_return**
    listing, [P] **ereturn**, [P] **_estimates**, [P] **_return**
    returning, [P] **_return**, [P] **return**
    saving, [P] **ereturn**, [P] **_estimates**, [P] **postfile**, [P]
        _return, [P] **return**
_return
    dir command, [P] **_return**
    drop command, [P] **_return**

_return, *continued*
    hold command, [P] **_return**
    restore command, [P] **_return**
return
    add command, [P] **return**
    clear command, [P] **return**
    local command, [P] **return**
    matrix command, [P] **return**
    scalar command, [P] **return**
return codes, [P] **rmsg**, *see* error messages and return
    codes
returning results, [P] **return**
    class programs, [P] **class**
_rmcoll command, [P] **_rmcoll**
_rmdcoll command, [P] **_rmcoll**
rmsg, [P] **creturn**, [P] **error**
    set subcommand, [P] **rmsg**
_robust command, [P] **_robust**
robust, Huber/White/sandwich estimator of variance, [P]
    _robust
Rogers, W. H., [P] **_robust**
Rousseeuw, P. J., [P] **matrix dissimilarity**
roweq macro extended function, [P] **macro**
roweq, matrix subcommand, [P] **matrix rownames**
rowfullnames macro extended function, [P] **macro**
rownames macro extended function, [P] **macro**
rownames, matrix subcommand, [P] **matrix**
    rownames
rownumb() matrix function, [P] **matrix define**
rows of matrix
    appending to, [P] **matrix define**
    names, [P] **ereturn**, [P] **matrix define**, [P] **matrix**
        rownames
    operators, [P] **matrix define**
rowsof() matrix function, [P] **matrix define**
Royall, R. M., [P] **_robust**
rvalue, class, [P] **class**

S

s() saved results, [P] **return**
s(macros) macro extended function, [P] **macro**
sandwich/Huber/White estimator of variance, *see* robust,
    Huber/White/sandwich estimator of variance
save estimation results, [P] **ereturn**, [P] **_estimates**
saved results, [P] **_return**, [P] **return**
saving results, [P] **ereturn**, [P] **_estimates**, [P] **postfile**,
    [P] **_return**, [P] **return**
scalar,
    confirm subcommand, [P] **confirm**
    ereturn subcommand, [P] **ereturn**
    return subcommand, [P] **return**
scalar command and scalar() pseudofunction, [P]
    scalar
scalars, [P] **scalar**
    namespace and conflicts, [P] **matrix**, [P] **matrix**
        define
Schnell, D., [P] **_robust**

s-class command, [P] **program**, [P] **return**
scope, class, [P] **class**
score, matrix subcommand, [P] **matrix score**
scoring, [P] **matrix score**
scrolling of output, controlling, [P] **more**
seek, file subcommand, [P] **file**
serset
    clear command, [P] **serset**
    create command, [P] **serset**
    create_cspline command, [P] **serset**
    create_xmedians command, [P] **serset**
    dir command, [P] **serset**
    drop command, [P] **serset**
    reset_id command, [P] **serset**
    set command, [P] **serset**
    sort command, [P] **serset**
    summarize command, [P] **serset**
    use command, [P] **serset**
sersetread, file subcommand, [P] **serset**
sersetwrite, file subcommand, [P] **serset**
set,
    file subcommand, [P] **file**
    serset subcommand, [P] **serset**
    sysdir subcommand, [P] **sysdir**
set
    adosize command, [P] **sysdir**
    charset command, [P] **smcl**
    more command, [P] **more**
    output command, [P] **quietly**
    rmsg command, [P] **rmsg**
    trace command, [P] **trace**
    tracedepth command, [P] **trace**
    traceexpand command, [P] **trace**
    tracehilite command, [P] **trace**
    traceindent command, [P] **trace**
    tracenumber command, [P] **trace**
    tracesep command, [P] **trace**
settings,
    efficiency, [P] **creturn**
    graphics, [P] **creturn**
    memory, [P] **creturn**
    network, [P] **creturn**
    output, [P] **creturn**
    program debugging, [P] **creturn**
    trace, [P] **creturn**
shared object, [P] **class**, [P] **plugin**
shift, macro subcommand, [P] **macro**
signature of data, [P] **_datasignature**, [P]
    signestimationsample
signestimationsample command, [P]
    signestimationsample
similarity
    matrices, [P] **matrix dissimilarity**
    measures, [P] **matrix dissimilarity**
simulations, Monte Carlo, [P] **postfile**
singular value decomposition, [P] **matrix svd**
SITE directory, [P] **sysdir**

_skip(#), display directive, [P] **display**
Slaymaker, E., [P] **file**
sleep command, [P] **sleep**
S_ macros, [P] **creturn**, [P] **macro**
SMCL, [P] **smcl**
Smith, B. T., [P] **matrix symeigen**
Sorensen, D., [P] **matrix eigenvalues**
sort order, [P] **byable**, [P] **macro**, [P] **sortpreserve**
sort, serset subcommand, [P] **serset**
sortedby macro extended function, [P] **macro**
sortpreserve option, [P] **sortpreserve**
source code, view, [P] **viewsource**
sreturn
    clear command, [P] **return**
    local command, [P] **return**
Sribney, W. M., [P] **_robust**, [P] **intro**, [P] **matrix**
    mkmat
standard errors,
    accessing, [P] **matrix get**
    robust, _see_ robust
Stata,
    data file format, technical description, [P] **file**
        formats .dta
    exiting, _see_ exit command
    pause, [P] **sleep**
STATA directory, [P] **sysdir**
Stata Markup and Control Language, [P] **smcl**
Stewart, G. W., [P] **matrix svd**
stopbox, window subcommand, [P] **window**
    programming
string variables, parsing, [P] **gettoken**, [P] **tokenize**
subinstr macro extended function, [P] **macro**
subscripting matrices, [P] **matrix define**
Sullivan, G., [P] **_robust**
summarize, serset subcommand, [P] **serset**
Super, class prefix operator, [P] **class**
.superclass built-in class function, [P] **class**
suppressing terminal output, [P] **quietly**
svd, matrix subcommand, [P] **matrix svd**
svmat command, [P] **matrix mkmat**
svymarkout command, [P] **mark**
sweep() matrix function, [P] **matrix define**
symeigen, matrix subcommand, [P] **matrix symeigen**
syntax command, [P] **syntax**
syntax of Stata's language, [P] **syntax**
sysdir
    list command, [P] **sysdir**
    macro extended function, [P] **macro**
    set command, [P] **sysdir**
system
    limits, [P] **creturn**
    parameters, [P] **creturn**
    values, [P] **creturn**

T

tabdisp command, [P] **tabdisp**

tables
   N-way, [P] **tabdisp**
   of statistics, [P] **tabdisp**
Tan, W. Y., [P] **_robust**
tempfile command, [P] **macro**
tempfile macro extended function, [P] **macro**
tempname, class, [P] **class**
tempname command, [P] **macro**, [P] **matrix**, [P] **scalar**
tempname macro extended function, [P] **macro**
temporary
   files, [P] **macro**, [P] **preserve**, [P] **scalar**
   names, [P] **macro**, [P] **matrix**, [P] **scalar**
   variables, [P] **macro**
tempvar command, [P] **macro**
tempvar macro extended function, [P] **macro**
terminal
   obtaining input from, [P] **display**
   suppressing output, [P] **quietly**
Teukolsky, S. A., [P] **matrix symeigen**
time of day, [P] **creturn**
timer
   clear command, [P] **timer**
   list command, [P] **timer**
   off command, [P] **timer**
   on command, [P] **timer**
time-series
   analysis, [P] **matrix accum**
   unabbreviating varlists, [P] **unab**
timing code, [P] **timer**
TMPDIR Unix environment variable, [P] **macro**
tokenize command, [P] **tokenize**
trace() matrix function, [P] **matrix define**
trace of matrix, [P] **matrix define**
trace, set subcommand, [P] **creturn**, [P] **trace**
tracedepth, set subcommand, [P] **creturn**, [P] **trace**
traceexpand, set subcommand, [P] **creturn**, [P] **trace**
tracehilite, set subcommand, [P] **creturn**, [P] **trace**
traceindent, set subcommand, [P] **creturn**, [P] **trace**
tracenumber, set subcommand, [P] **creturn**, [P] **trace**
tracesep, set subcommand, [P] **creturn**, [P] **trace**
transposing matrices, [P] **matrix define**
tsnorm macro extended function, [P] **macro**
tsunab command, [P] **unab**
Tukey, J. W., [P] **if**
type macro extended function, [P] **macro**

U

unab command, [P] **unab**
unabbreviate
   command names, [P] **unabcmd**
   variable list, [P] **syntax**, [P] **unab**
unabcmd command, [P] **unabcmd**
.uname built-in class function, [P] **class**
unhold, _estimates subcommand, [P] **_estimates**
Unix, pause, [P] **sleep**
UPDATES directory, [P] **sysdir**

use, serset subcommand, [P] **serset**
user interface, [P] **dialog programming**
using data, [P] **syntax**

V

value label macro extended function, [P] **macro**
value labels, [P] **macro**
Van Kerm, P., [P] **postfile**
varabbrev command, [P] **varabbrev**
variable
   labels, [P] **macro**
   types, [P] **macro**
      class, [P] **class**
variable abbreviation, [P] **varabbrev**
variable, confirm subcommand, [P] **confirm**
variable label macro extended function, [P] **macro**
variables,
   characteristics of, [P] **char**, [P] **macro**
   list values of, [P] **levelsof**
   temporary, [P] **macro**
   unabbreviating, [P] **syntax**, [P] **unab**
variance
   Huber/White/sandwich estimator, *see* robust
   nonconstant, *see* robust
variance–covariance matrix of estimators, [P] **ereturn**,
      [P] **matrix get**
varlist, [P] **syntax**
vec() matrix function, [P] **matrix define**
vecaccum, matrix subcommand, [P] **matrix accum**
vecdiag() matrix function, [P] **matrix define**
vectors, *see* matrices
version command, [P] **version**
   class programming, [P] **class**
version control, *see* version command
Vetterling, W. T., [P] **matrix symeigen**
view source code, [P] **viewsource**
viewsource command, [P] **viewsource**

W

Weesie, J., [P] **matrix define**
Wei, L. J., [P] **_robust**
weight, [P] **syntax**
which, class, [P] **classutil**
which, classutil subcommand, [P] **classutil**
while command, [P] **while**
White, H., [P] **_robust**
White/Huber/sandwich estimator of variance, *see* robust
Wilkinson, J. H., [P] **matrix symeigen**
window
   fopen command, [P] **window programming**
   fsave command, [P] **window programming**
   manage command, [P] **window programming**
   menu command, [P] **window programming**
   push command, [P] **window programming**
   stopbox command, [P] **window programming**

Windows metafiles programming, [P] **automation**
Windows, pause, [P] **sleep**
Windows programming, [P] **automation**
Winter, N. J. G., [P] **levelsof**
`word` macro extended function, [P] **macro**
`write, file` subcommand, [P] **file**
writing and reading ASCII text and binary files, [P] **file**

Y

Yates, F., [P] **levelsof**

Z

zero matrix, [P] **matrix define**